A New Weave of Power, People and Politics

The Action Guide for Advocacy and Citizen Participation

Praise for *A New Weave of Power, People & Politics*

"Excellent material for activists everywhere. The Guide combines very practical tools with conceptual discussions that encourage people to contextualize and reflect critically on their own experience. Its advocacy approach is integrated – not merely a technical exercise of lobbying but a broader process that includes and draws on lessons of social and political struggle."

> PATRICIA ARDON, Regional Representative for
> Central America, CEDPA

"A very comprehensive guide book for activists. It helps people who work at different levels understand advocacy in a broader context – dealing with different kinds of power – rather than only policy advocacy. A solid blend of theory, frameworks and field experiences make for easy adaptation to the local context of users."

> NANI ZULMINARNI, Asia South Pacific Bureau of
> Adult Education (ASPBAE) and PPSW, Indonesia

A New Weave of Power, People and Politics

The Action Guide for Advocacy and Citizen Participation

Lisa VeneKlasen with Valerie Miller

Co-editors: Debbie Budlender and Cindy Clark

PRACTICAL ACTION
Publishing

Practical Action Publishing Ltd
Schumacher Centre for Technology and Development
Bourton on Dunsmore, Rugby,
Warwickshire CV23 9QZ, UK
www.practicalactionpublishing.org

First edition published in 2002 by World Neighbors
Reprinted 2008, 2011

ISBN 978 1 85339 644 1

Since 1974, Practical Action Publishing (formerly Intermediate Technology Publications and
ITDG Publishing) has published and disseminated books and information in support of
international development work throughout the world. Practical Action Publishing Ltd
(Company Reg. No. 1159018) is the wholly owned publishing company of Practical Action.
Practical Action Publishing trades only in support of its parent charity objectives and any
profits are covenanted back to Practical Action (Charity Reg. No. 247257, Group VAT
Registration No. 880 9924 76).

Special thanks to the Ford Foundation, Shale Adams, and the U.S. Agency for International
Development for their generous support for this project. This publication does not necessarily
reflect the views of The Asia Foundation, World Neighbors, of any of the other financial
supporters of this project.

Design and layout by Catheryn Koss
Illustrations by Marcelo Espinoza Inostroza (KCat)
Printed in India

Contents

Acknowledgements

This book builds on our fifty years of combined experience in advocacy, gender, human rights, popular education, and social change. Since 1982 we have had the great fortune of working together as activists, trainers, and organizers in the US and around the world with colleagues who share our commitments. Our hope is that the collective experience and knowledge found in this book will help build bridges and alliances between peoples for justice, equity, and peace.

We would like to thank some of the organizations where we have worked that have encouraged us to question and to pursue visions and innovation. In particular, The Asia Foundation and its Global Women in Politics Program, the Unitarian Universalist Service Committee, Women Law and Development International, Institute for Development Research, InterAction, Oxfam America, Centre for Development and Population Activities, Women in Law and Development in Africa, Washington Office on Latin America, and countless other groups that are no longer active.

Over these years, friends and colleagues around the world have challenged us with their courage, their creativity, and their searching questions about power, politics, and justice. They have enriched our learning and expanded our understanding. We thank them for their wisdom, their laughter, their candor, and their example. Their voices and inspiration are reflected throughout these pages. Thank you all: Malena de Montis, John Gaventa, Everjoice Win, Hope Chigudu, Srilatha Batliwala, Jethro Pettit, Deborah Barndt, Maria Suarez, Peggy Antrobus, dian marino, Fernando Cardenal, John Samuel, Nani Zulminarni, Dina Lumbantobing, Darcy Ashman, Florence Butegwa, Jody Williams, Margaret Schuler, Trish Ahern, Heather Robinson, Keboitse Machananga, Nader Tadros, Zie Gariyo, Peggy Healy, Dina Abad, Dinky Soliman, Mayela Garcia, Mariela Arce, Socorro Reyes, Winnie Byanyima, Cecilia Olea, Marlene Libardoni, Kay Stubbs, Roxana Vasquez, Rehana Hashmi, Sohail Warraich, Eva Maria Cayanan, Paty Ardon, Sue Thrasher, Kathy Bond-Stewart, Talent Nyathi, David Cohen, Peter Van Tuijl, Maureen Burke, Richard Healy, Ken Sharpe, Carmen Diana Deere, Jonathan Fox, Irungu Houghton, Larry and Sheila Wilson, Myles Horton, Lori Heise, Holly Bartling, Clare Moberly, Thomas Carothers, Asma Abdel Halim, Elizabeth Dasso, Molly Reilly, Rashida Dohad, Ruengrawee (Jieb) Ketphol, Madalene O'Donnell, Suzanne Kindervatter, Susan Carpenter, Chad Dobson, Carolyn Long, Peter Kornbluh, John Cavanagh, Jane Covey, and the supportive World Neighbors field staff who encouraged their organization to invest in and publish the book.

We would like to thank all of the participants in the Global Women in Politics Training of Trainers in Asia, Africa and Latin America, and in the Santa Fe Workshop for helping to create, adapt, and evaluate the tools and exercises in the book; and thanks to the participants of the workshops carried out under the auspices of the Women's Advocacy Initiative leading up to Beijing (through InterAction's Commission on the Advancement of Women) and the participants of the many workshops carried out under Women, Law and Development in Asia, Africa and Latin America for their collaboration and pioneering work in rights and advocacy.

We give special thanks to Carol Yost of The Asia Foundation for her faith in us and for her courage, persistence, and patience in making this book a reality. Also to Gordon Hein, Nilan Fernando, Steven Rood, and others in the Foundation for their continued support and encouragement. This book would never have happened without the generosity of the Ford Foundation, Shaler Adams, and Just Associates.

Heartfelt thanks to Cindy Clark; without her sharp eye for editing and design, her commitment and insights beyond her years, as well as her efficiency and endurance, this book would still not be finished. Thanks to Debbie Budlender for her remarkable ability to make sense of twisted sentences, for her steady support, and for her knowledge about gender and budgets; thanks to

Catheryn Koss who managed the daunting task of design, layout, and editing with agility and patience; and to Marcelo Espinoza whose creative drawings enlivened these pages.

Finally, we want to thank our families and loved ones who sacrificed and survived this prolonged birthing with us: to Ralph Fine for never doubting the value of this book or its authors, for giving of his generous counsel, questions, and spirit, and for fixing delicious meals for Valerie when her writing prevailed over her cooking; to Emery Bright, who reminded us to believe in dreams and whose day-to-day support and persistent pride and enthusiasm for this book and its author came through when it was needed most. To Lisa's brother Gordon, whose generosity and love made the major juggling act necessary to produce this book both possible and less painful; and to Julian Bright, whose own birth and early childhood paralleled the book's slow evolution, and who may never know what he missed of his mother's time and energy. Hopefully he will benefit from the people, ideas, and commitment contained in its pages.

Lisa VeneKlasen and Valerie Miller
Just Associates
2040 S. Street N.W.
Washington, DC 20009
www.justassociates.org

To our parents – Margaret and Gordon VeneKlasen and Verginia and George Miller – who taught us the values of community service, accountability, and civic responsibility, exemplified principles of fairness, and opened up their homes with enthusiasm and warmth to our friends and colleagues from around the world. We dedicate this book to you.

Foreword

In November 2001, some forty advocates, educators, and researchers from 18 countries in Africa, Asia, Europe, and the Americas gathered for a workshop in Washington, D.C. to reflect together on our work on advocacy and citizen participation.[1] In particular, we wanted to re-examine how these concepts are being used to achieve the broader goals of equity, social justice, and the global fight against poverty and discrimination. While the conversation was rich, and the grassroots commitments and innovations inspiring, for many of the veteran organisers and popular educators who were present there was a bitter-sweet assessment about the state of our work.

On the one hand, words like citizen participation and advocacy – which are at the heart of our values and concerns – have gained increased prominence over recent years in the mainstream lexicons of governments, donors, and civil society organisations. Groups working on these issues have enjoyed greater attention. New spaces for public involvement are emerging at local, national, and even global levels. On the other hand, as the words themselves gain currency the concepts on which they are based are at risk of losing their credibility and meaning. As they move from the margins to the mainstream, approaches to advocacy and citizen participation become somewhat sterile and technical, failing to take into account underlying realities of power and politics whlch exclude people from meaningful engagement in the policies and decisions which affect their lives.

At this workshop there was a sense of the need to return to fundamentals. There was a search for a more comprehensive approach that would link policy advocacy with broader concerns of building critical awareness for action, mobilizing and strengthening coalitions, dealing with conflicts across differences, and embedding participatory practices in broader movements for human rights and social justice.

There also was an awareness of the need for new understandings of how to assess power – especially as the simultaneous moves towards globalization and localization are changing the terrain of power relations. There were debates on how to decide whether and when to engage in new political spaces that the changing terrain is creating, and how to avoid tokenistic forms of participation. In general, there was a renewed recognition of the need to strengthen capacities of civil society groups – as well as of ordinary citizens – to engage in advocacy work as a fundamental right and skill of citizenship.

There also was a sense of urgency. Coming together as we did just a few weeks after September 11 and its ensuing events, we were concerned with how quickly issues of global security, shaped by notions of military might, were supplanting concerns with basic economic needs and human rights, shaped by peoples' participation. We heard stories from a number of countries, including the United States, of how spaces for citizens' voice and dissent were closing, while in other settings changing international forces were potentially creating ncw openings and alliances. Whatever the circumstances, we felt the very principles which we were discussing of how to use citizen participation and advocacy to insure greater equity, justice, and inclusion were at the heart of how to achieve more long-lasting concepts of peace and security.

Against this somewhat sombre mood, the opportunity at the workshop to review and discuss *A New Weave of Power, People & Politics: The Action Guide for Advocacy and Citizen Participation* offered new energy and positive relief. As we explored, the need to re-inject notions of power, citizenship, and human rights into the increasingly sterile debates on participation and advocacy, this guide provided us some vital concepts and approaches for beginning to do so. As we discussed the changing political terrain and began to envision new strategies for our work, this guide offered valuable tools that could help us build our own capacities for our work.

Of course, many of us who have worked in the arena of popular education and citizen action over the years may have a healthy scepticism of manuals. The American adult educator, Myles Horton at Highlander Centre (a good friend of both of the authors), was always concerned that manuals would become "recipes" or "cookbooks" for social change. Others in the development field warn against what they see as "blueprint" or "off the shelf" approaches. We have all seen our methods become reduced to techniques, devoid of their original meaning and purpose in rote applications in differing contexts.

That is why this book is important. It offers neither a recipe nor a blueprint. Rather it provides a guide for learning, exploration, and adaptation in a number of contexts. Unlike many guides, it is not written on the basis of abstract theory or "drive by" consultancies. Rather it is based on critical reflection by the authors over decades of experience in their collaborative work in actually doing popular education for democracy, human rights, and social justice in many continents of the globe. It is intended as a living tool to which others may add and contribute based on their own knowledge and experience.

The guide gives "a new weave" to a number of important issues, and in so doing makes a significant contribution to the growing international literature on citizen participation and advocacy.

First, while it offers concrete strategies and tools for citizen participation and advocacy, it locates them in the broader debates on the meanings of citizenship and democracy. At a time when many political institutions around the world are facing a crisis of legitimacy, as models of democracy and representation are re-examined, this approach challenges us to continue to construct new forms of citizenship, based on popular knowledge and respect for differences, in diverse contexts.

Second, at a time when there is increased talk of concepts such as a "rights-based approach" to development, "participation" and "good governance," this manual illustrates how better to understand what these concepts might mean in practice, based on peoples' own knowledge and experiences, as well as by showing how in real life they must be integrated with one another.

Third, the guide grows specifically out of the authors' particular concerns and experiences in the areas of gender and women's political participation. On the basis of this work, it speaks strongly to concerns for issues of inclusion, respect for differences and identities, and the need to address underlying attitudes and values – concerns which often get short-shrift in the focus on organizing campaigns, winning issues and changing policies.

A New Weave has been needed for a long time. Some thirty years ago, following her experiences in attempting to promote the concept of citizen participation in the American War on Poverty, Sherry Arnstein wrote, "the idea of citizen participation is a little like eating spinach: No one is against it in principle because it is good for you." However, she went on, "when the have-nots define participation as the redistribution of power, the American consensus on the fundamental principle explodes into many shades *of outright radical, ethnic, ideological, and political opposition.*"[2] This no doubt is a conundrum that many activists have experienced, and speaks as well to a number of current crises around the world. Often work on citizen participation and advocacy becomes stymied in the face of such confrontations. However, *A New Weave* insists that rather than ignoring power and conflict, citizen participation and advocacy work must *begin* with learning how to address these realities if real change is to occur.

For those us who have seen this action guide actually being woven and re-woven over the years – including many of us at the Washington workshop – its release is in itself a cause for celebration. Like many good popular

educators and activists, the authors have been so busy doing the work on the ground, and so willing personally to share their experiences with others, that getting the time to document and extend their learning more broadly has always been difficult. And throughout, they have steadfastly refused pressures to give quick fixes and simple answers to complex issues. That in itself is the greatest strength of *A New Weave* – it grows not only from the head but from the heart, not only from intellectual and methodological curiosity but from long-term personal commitment and engagement with the struggles of others in both south and north. It may have taken a long time and a lot of effort to weave, but will be a stronger and more enduring resource as a result. Thanks.

John Gaventa
Institute of Development Studies
March 8, 2002

NOTES

[1] 'Making Change Happen: Advocacy and Citizen Participation', co-sponsored by the Asia Foundation, ActionAid, and the Participation Group at the Institute of Development Studies, November 28 – 30, 2001.

[2] Sherry Arnstein, 'The Journal of the American Institute of Planners,' Vol 35, No 4, July 1969. Quoted further in this Guide, page 30.

Introduction

Who is the Action Guide for?

This Action Guide is designed for people and organizations grappling with issues of power, politics, and exclusion. It goes beyond the first generation of advocacy manuals to delve more deeply into questions of citizenship, constituency-building, social change, gender, and accountability. The Guide is designed for:

- **non-governmental organizations (NGOs) and grassroots groups** interested in a rights-based approach to advocacy that combines policy influence activities with strategies to strengthen citizen participation, awareness, and organization;

- **donor institutions** interested in supporting comprehensive advocacy programs that focus on overcoming exclusion and subordination, as well as on building more democratic forms of public decisionmaking;

- **development agencies** interested in engaging their own service delivery structures and beneficiaries in the pursuit of development solutions through the political process;

- **trainers, activists, organizers, and researchers** interested in building bridges between civil society, government, business, and other influential people and institutions to promote more accountable political processes and responsive development policies.

What Is the Guide's Approach to Advocacy?

The Guide's approach to advocacy is geared to improving the lives and participation of marginalized people and forging broad alliances for reform across society. We define this as *citizen-centered advocacy*, sometimes referred to as transformative, people-centered, participatory, or social justice advocacy.

We understand advocacy as a political process that involves the coordinated efforts of people in changing existing practices, ideas, and distributions of power and resources that exclude women and other disadvantaged groups. From this perspective, advocacy deals with specific aspects of policymaking, as well as the values and behavior that perpetuate exclusion and subordination. Thus, advocacy is both about changing specific decisions affecting people's lives and changing the way decisionmaking happens into a more inclusive and democratic process.

Inevitably, advocacy will involve tensions. This book does not have a technical formula for influencing governments or other structures of power. Instead, it aims to help activists analyze, plan, and manage strategies with a clear understanding of potential risks. Advocacy strategies will vary widely in response to particular circumstances, issues, opportunities, and constraints.

The Guide is like a quilt-making kit. Rather than preset designs, it contains a rich selection of patterns, pieces, and fabrics. From this colorful mix, the user can stitch together an advocacy strategy to fit particular contexts, needs, and visions.

Key Features of the Guide's Approach to Advocacy

- Focuses on building the capacity of marginalized groups to express their voices and use their vote to make change.
- Ties issue-based strategies to accountability and strengthening citizenship.
- Applies rights-based approach to policy change and concrete problem-solving.
- Is grounded in an analysis of the dynamics of power and exclusion, using gender frameworks and other tools.
- Promotes strategies aimed at both influencing specific policy decisions and making the culture and practice of decisionmaking more democratic.
- Extends advocacy to many arenas of political and policy influence. It does not presume that the locus of decisionmaking is solely the legislative process.
- Helps organizations combine development and service provision activities with political organizing and policy influence.
- Seeks to balance the tensions between the need to acknowledge difference and diversity and the need to build collective solutions, agendas, and alliances.
- Forges connections between global, national, and local advocacy efforts.
- Draws attention to the unique risks and opportunities for doing advocacy in different contexts and political moments.
- Incorporates a long-term vision of change with commitment to social justice and equity.
- Combines constituency- and organization-building with leadership development, awareness building, policy research, and political analysis.

Conceptual and Experiential Sources for the Action Guide

The Guide draws on the training, research, and organizing experiences of the authors and many colleagues over the last 30 years. These collective experiences were gathered in Asia, Africa, Latin America, the Middle East, Europe, the former Soviet Union, and North America. They range from participatory research and community development, to neighborhood organizing and legal rights education, to large-scale campaign advocacy. The frameworks, tools, and ideas were initially drawn together for a draft Guide in 1997 for a series of "training of trainers" workshops conducted in Africa, Asia, and Latin America by the Global Women in Politics Program of The Asia Foundation, with Women in Law and Development in Africa, Zimbabwe, Center for Legislative Development, Philippines, and Cenzontle, Nicaragua.

For nearly four years prior to its final revision, the Guide was used and adapted by groups around the world.

Building on the work of countless activists, practitioners and theorists, the Guide's primary sources of inspiration have included:

Citizen action organizing

Based on the Saul Alinsky community organizing model, the citizen action approach has been shaped by the Midwest Academy, a US training institute for neighborhood and labor organizing. It has been further adapted by groups in the Philippines doing grassroots organizing. Citizen action advocacy generally relies on an organizer to mobilize a community around common concerns. Through that process, community members develop their leadership capacity and make decisionmakers more accountable to poor and other disadvantaged people.

Popular adult education

Inspired originally by Brazilian educator Paulo Freire, this approach critiques traditional education in which learners are treated as passive recipients of knowledge. In contrast, popular education uses an adult's experience as the core of the learning process. It validates and expands each person's knowledge, thus empowering him or her to take action. It promotes critical consciousness which enables people to understand how their situations are molded by systemic inequalities and helps to motivate collective action for change.

Gender analysis, theory, and practice

These perspectives help to understand the visible and invisible natures of discrimination and subordination. They focus on ways to transform unequal power relations between men and women in the social, economic, and political arenas, and in both public and private realms.

Participatory development techniques

These techniques have offered insights particularly on community-centered initiatives for development, including participatory appraisal, evaluation, research, and project design.

Women's rights as human rights

These strategies seek to expand women's rights and often use law as an organizing tool to enable women to gain the confidence and skills necessary to seek public solutions to personal and social problems. Advocacy uses and attempts to reform the international human rights system so that it serves women and other marginalized groups better.

Theoretical discussions about power, agency, and democracy

We have drawn from the work of scholars concerned with the problems of poverty, participation, and subordination who have examined how excluded groups can better engage in public life. Among these scholars are John Gaventa, Sonia Alvarez, John Samuel, Tom Carothers, Srilatha Batliwala, Steven Lukes, Maxine Molyneux, Malena de Montis, Amartya Sen, Virginia Vargas, Chantal Mouffe, and Jonathan Fox.

Approaches to conflict and negotiation

The work of Adam Curle, Larry Susskind, Susan Carpenter, John Paul Lederach, Guy and Heidi Burgess, and Deborah Kolb have provided us with holistic approaches to conflict that address power imbalances and intractable social problems. They weave together strategies of consciousness-raising, education, and organizing as the foundation for negotiating and dealing with social conflict.

Navigating the Action Guide

This book covers many topics. There is a variety of exercises, tools, resources, tips, and stories. In some cases, we present several

---

"Frequently, despite improved policies and laws, public institutions and society continue to operate with the values and behavior that lead to the exclusion of large numbers of people from resources and options to solve common problems. Building democracy takes more than changing policy, it takes changing the political system itself. It demands an intensive, holistic process of political change that requires developing individual consciousness about how the political system contributes both to community and social problems and to problem-solving. It involves skills in analysis, planning, negotiation, and communication, as well as strong civil society organizations with alternative, flexible models of leadership and decisionmaking."

Global Women in Politics Advocacy Initiative, The Asia Foundation, 1999

---

exercises or frameworks designed for similar purposes so that you can select which best meet your particular circumstances. You may find some sections slightly repetitive. Since we realize people will photocopy particular pages, we chose to repeat some of the major themes for clarity.

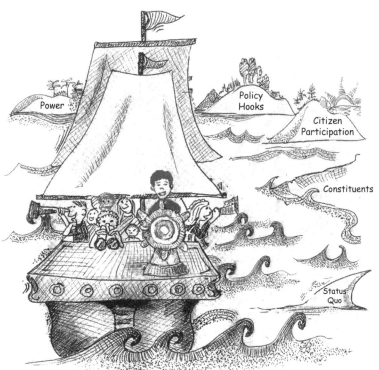

Most activists and trainers have very little time for lengthy reading. It is hard to know where to begin and where to look in the limited time available unless you have a specific training or planning need. To make the book more manageable, on the next page we provide a detailed description of each chapter. We also offer a special training and capacity-building Annex at the end of the Guide that provides workshop and planning ideas for different users and needs. This section is intended to help planners and trainers take full advantage of the book efficiently. The Guide is structured in three parts:

Part 1: Understanding Politics

Effective citizen politics requires conceptual clarity. Advocacy is not a value-neutral technology. Certain concepts define our vision of social and political change. They also help us to interpret reality and make strategic choices. Concepts such as power, gender, equity, and participation shape our methodology and strategies, while concepts such as democracy and citizenship direct our vision. That is why we begin the manual with an exploration of concepts, assumptions, and values.

Part 2: Planning Advocacy

Good planning provides the basis for effective citizen advocacy work. Most users will find this section immediately relevant to their needs. It includes planning tools and helps to guide processes. Participatory planning builds

constituencies for change while educating and empowering individual citizens.

Part 3: Doing Advocacy

The last section provides ideas and stories about doing advocacy. There are fewer exercises in this section. Instead, there are tips and examples to inspire activists to be both creative and careful when designing actions that fit their unique context.

Your Advice on Using the Guide

Above all, we would like to hear your feedback and stories about how you have used and adapted the Guide, what you have found useful, and what has not been useful to you. We encourage you to send us your training workshop designs, materials, and advocacy experiences to inform our own understanding and practice and to help us refine the Guide for future editions. Enjoy the book.

Part One: Understanding Politics

Core Concepts, Assumptions, and Values

This first part of the Guide focuses on the basic conceptual building blocks for advocacy planning and action.

Chapter 1: Politics and Advocacy

Being political takes more than understanding how the "system" operates. For disadvantaged communities, political participation demands a new way of thinking in order to understand and challenge unequal relationships of power as they are perpetuated by culture, social norms, politics, and decisionmaking. This chapter introduces some basic concepts and definitions, including "what is politics?" and "what is advocacy?" as well as some exercises for understanding and getting involved in political change.

Chapter 2: Democracy and Citizenship

Our understanding and vision of democracy and citizenship help us define the kind of political system for which we are striving, as well as the roles, rights, and responsibilities of all the people and institutions involved. This chapter examines different perspectives on these concepts which inform our approach to advocacy. It also offers exercises to guide discussions on democracy and citizenship.

Chapter 3: Power and Empowerment

Power is probably the most decisive ingredient in politics, advocacy, and citizenship. When advocates challenge the social order, their understanding of power dynamics is crucial for success and for survival. This chapter explores different concepts and tools for demystifying and sharpening our analysis of power and for understanding citizen empowerment.

Chapter 4: Constructing Empowering Strategies

Advocacy is a process of building citizenship and political education. If advocacy strategies are meant to engage and empower citizens, then people's participation in the choices and construction of strategies is the first step in fighting exclusion and developing power, critical consciousness, and political skills. This chapter offers concepts and tools to equip citizens, leaders, and organizations to better promote inclusive politics and empowered citizens. It concludes with the framework that defines this Guide's approach to advocacy.

Part Two: Planning Advocacy

Tools, Process, and Politics for Citizenship and Action

Planning for advocacy is vital for effective strategies and impact. But planning, if done in a participatory manner, can also be a political education, organizing, and consciousness-raising activity. Part Two of the Action Guide covers the tools, steps, and processes of advocacy planning that build citizen empowerment.

Chapter 5: The Basics of Planning for Citizen-Centered Advocacy

Advocacy planning involves certain basics, including the development of an overall strategy (long-term), a campaign (medium-term), and tactics, actions, or activities (short-term) as well as a way to monitor and measure the success of your efforts. However, participatory approaches to advocacy planning are more than a set of tools and steps for improving impact. They are constituency-building and citizen education strategies that attempt to put equity and inclusion into practice.

Chapter 6: Planning Moment #1—Looking Inward
Engaging in advocacy is a strategic choice that will have a major impact on an organization. This chapter aims to help you gain a clearer sense of who you are and where you stand before you attempt to change the world around you.

Chapter 7: Planning Moment #2—Understanding the Big Picture
Every context has its own distinct characteristics that lead to ever-changing political opportunities and challenges. Contextual mapping involves identifying how a political system is organized and how different forces, people, organizations, and ideas shape the political space. This chapter offers tools to better understand the "big picture" in which your advocacy takes place.

Chapter 8: Planning Moment #3—Identifying and Defining Problems
Citizen-centered advocacy is about seeking solutions to problems in the political and policy arena. The starting point is a clear understanding of a problem that is widely and deeply felt by a large community or constituency. This chapter offers tips on how to make sure you have a clearly defined problem as well as how-tos for participatory problem definition with constituency groups. These approaches can be adapted both for groups that have already chosen their issue and groups that are beginning the process of defining their issue.

Chapter 9: Planning Moment #4—Analyzing Problems and Selecting Priority Issues
Effective advocacy requires breaking down a large problem into separate issues in order to identify the policy connections and determine which issues are most compelling for further action. This chapter offers a number of tools and exercises to prioritize and select issues.

Chapter 10: Planning Moment #5—Mapping Advocacy Strategies
Problems and issues have many causes and many possible solutions. Advocacy strategies need to be multidimensional to get at the systemic causes of an issue. It is unlikely that a single organization can carry out a complete strategy addressing all of the causes. Limited resources mean a group must choose which aspect to tackle. This chapter presents a series of tools that help to construct and compare strategies.

Chapter 11: Planning Moment #6—Finding Policy Hooks and Political Angles
Policy hooks connect the solution of your issue to the formal political and policymaking arena. To identify a policy hook, you need information about policies, laws, budgets, and the institutions and procedures that determine their content. There are basics about different political systems and ways that policy is developed and decided that help to guide the identification of entry points for influence. This chapter offers an overview of various policymaking arenas to help guide you in determining the policy hook for your advocacy.

Chapter 12: Planning Moment #7—Forces, Friends, and Foes
Advocacy targets specific decisionmakers and institutions, which generates both friends and enemies. It is important to know who they are and what their power is relative to your solution. This chapter contains various tools for identifying, classifying, and weighing who is at the table and who is under it.

Part Three: Doing Advocacy

While Part Two concentrates on the planning of advocacy, Part Three looks at ways of doing advocacy. The planning and doing are part of a cyclical process in which planning informs action and this action, in turn, informs further planning. The cycle builds a deeper understanding of politics and an improved ability to influence policy. This part of the Guide contains fewer exercises and more stories and tips to inspire activists to be creative in their own contexts.

Chapter 13: Messages and Media—Educating and Persuading

A vital piece of advocacy is a compelling message tailored and disseminated specifically for a defined audience. This chapter covers a variety of approaches for reaching, educating, and persuading audiences by using the mass media and alternative media.

Chapter 14: Outreach and Mobilization

While advocacy should build citizen participation, success also depends on the power that organized numbers of people can wield in the political arena. In this chapter we look at how outreach and mobilization serve to achieve both a policy objective and build citizen power.

Chapter 15: Maneuvering on the Inside—Lobbying and Negotiating

This chapter is about getting to the decisionmaking table and advancing your issue once you get there. Engaging directly in discussions to persuade and convince decisionmakers is an important part of successful advocacy and provides useful lessons about politics and power for citizens.

Chapter 16: Advocacy Leadership

Advocacy requires strong leaders and groups who understand power, people, and process. Advocacy leaders face a perpetual juggling act of promoting collaboration and encouraging new leadership on the one hand, while giving direction and vision on the other. These require different skills and styles. This chapter focuses on the aspects of leadership that facilitate broader participation and organizational collaboration.

Chapter 17: Alliances and Coalitions

Coalitions and alliances can greatly enhance social justice advocacy by bringing together the strength and resources of diverse groups to create a more powerful force for change. But they are difficult to form and sustain. This chapter focuses on their dynamics and ways to strengthen them. We examine how to improve communication, decisionmaking, conflict management, and political accountability.

PART ONE
UNDERSTANDING POLITICS
CORE CONCEPTS, ASSUMPTIONS, AND VALUES

In many countries and communities, people feel apprehensive about getting involved in politics. Some feel that politics is a distant, inaccessible land where only the powerful tread. While these views of politics are based on reality, an important first step for getting involved in advocacy is to discuss and unravel such fears and assumptions. Thus, we begin the Guide with a brief discussion of key concepts that shape our understanding of politics, citizenship, power, government, and change.

Chapter 1: Politics and Advocacy

To be political takes more than understanding how the system operates. Promoting inclusive politics and policymaking through advocacy involves understanding and addressing power dynamics that perpetuate disadvantage and privilege. In this way, advocacy is not just about policy change; it is about changing the culture and process of politics. This chapter discusses "what is politics?" and "what is advocacy?" and includes some exercises for warming up to politics.

Key concepts:

- Formal, informal, and transformative politics
- Different views of advocacy
- The Guide's definition of advocacy
- Rights-based advocacy

Chapter 2: Democracy and Citizenship

Our understanding and vision of democracy and citizenship help us define the kind of political system we are striving for and the roles, rights, and responsibilities of all the actors. This chapter examines different perspectives on these concepts that inform our approach to advocacy and offers exercises to guide discussions on democracy and citizenship.

Key concepts:

- Democracy in a changing world
- Citizenship as "makers and shapers"
- Citizen rights and responsibilities
- Power and political change strategies

Chapter 3: Power and Empowerment

Power is probably the most decisive ingredient in politics, advocacy, and citizenship. When advocates challenge the established order, their understanding of power dynamics is crucial for success and for survival. This chapter explores different concepts and tools for demystifying and sharpening our analysis of power, and for empowering people through advocacy.

Key concepts:

- Sources and uses of power
- Alternative expressions of power
- Visible, hidden, and invisible power
- Public and private power
- Empowerment and its conflicts and risks
- CHAZ! empowerment framework
- Measuring empowerment

Chapter 4: Constructing Empowering Strategies

Advocacy *is* citizen education. When advocacy strategies are meant to engage and empower people, their participation in the choices and construction of strategies is the first step in developing citizen consciousness and political skills. This chapter offers concepts and tools to equip citizens, leaders, and organizations to construct empowering strategies. It concludes with the framework that defines this Guide's approach to advocacy.

Key concepts:

- Constituency-building
- Political consciousness
- Popular education theory
- Participatory learning

- Key gender concepts for people, power, and politics
- Conceptual framework for citizen-centered advocacy

1 Politics and Advocacy

"Let us teach both ourselves and others that politics does not have to be the art of the possible...but that it also can be the *art of the impossible*, that is, the art of making both ourselves and the world better."

Vaclav Havel, President of Czechoslovakia, 1990

"I have come to the conclusion that politics are too serious a matter to be left to politicians."

Charles de Gaulle, French Statesman

"Politics is for upliftment . . . not for personal gain . . . ."

A group of Garifuna women in Belize[1]

In many countries, engaging in advocacy first requires overcoming an aversion to politics (see box below). People who have survived repressive regimes, violent conflict, and other kinds of political instability often fear politics. In older democracies, apathy can be an equally stubborn barrier to getting involved in advocacy. The first part of this chapter helps you bring to the surface some of the misgivings about what is "political" in order to establish a level of comfort with the subject. This lays the foundation for further learning and action. The exercises in this chapter are also useful for more experienced activists who may think of politics only in terms of formal public decisionmaking such as political parties,

---

Reflections on Politics from Uganda

Why do many people say NGOs are not part of politics?
People's perception of politics is generally negative, and development is viewed as an apolitical activity.

- Many people equate politics with being affiliated to a party. So, apolitical is the same as non-partisan. Claiming to be apolitical has been a survival strategy for many NGOs operating under restrictive regimes. The strategy provides women and poor people with a safe working space where they can be critical of the government and demand changes without being perceived automatically as subversive.
- Donors have contributed to NGOs' avoidance tactics because of their own concerns about a government backlash. The donors make clear to potential grantees that they do not support political activities. But they also use the prevalence of NGOs as indicators of stability and democracy, hence politics!
- Politics is associated with those who govern, whilst the governed are assumed not be involved in politics.

What are some of the key features we want to see in a new politics?

- transparent decisionmaking
- willingness to negotiate
- broad-based participation
- openness to change
- equitable distribution of resources
- power sharing
- productive economy

Ugandan workshop of women activists, 1994

Formal Politics
Refers to legislatures, national assemblies, political parties, governments, international agencies, and public policy and resources.

Informal Politics
Refers to what happens in civil society, families, communities, neighborhoods, and organizations.

legislatures, and government. The exercises can help to extend their political thinking to the informal realms of decisionmaking in organizations, communities, and families.

Some Reflections on Politics

This Guide is based on an understanding of politics that bridges formal and informal institutions, processes, values, and expressions of political life. *All* social relationships and dynamics are political, from the home to the corridors of government. The perception that politics is only the privilege of those in formal political power serves to reinforce exclusion. It can perpetuate people's sense of powerlessness about their ability to create change.

In many countries, despite important political openings in recent years, formal politics continues to be controlled by a handful of interests. Civil society groups organize to inject diverse voices into the process, but political parties and elites retain most public power and resources. Even the newer parties often forsake some of their broader reform agenda in order to "play the political game."

Outside the formal realm, decisionmaking reflects similar forms of discrimination and control. For example, inequalities in the family often restrict women's public involvement. In the face of these challenges, some contemporary social movements not only want to partici-

pate in the formal political process—they want to change the very boundaries, practice, and culture of politics.[2]

Some feminists and gender activists describe their alternative approach to politics as transformative politics. **Transformative politics** refers to political activities within and outside the formal political realm that seek not only to influence public decisions, but to reshape the rules and structures of public decisionmaking to be more inclusive and equitable.

We envision politics as the dynamic and often, unequal process of negotiations and decisionmaking, in both the formal and informal spheres, that determines access to resources and opportunities. The tendency of politics in many countries has been to concentrate decisionmaking and resources while excluding many voices and interests—such as those of

A Redefinition of Politics from Ugandan Women

What is politics? It is decisionmaking, and managing and planning the use of resources. The inputs necessary to make politics happen are ideas, skills, technology, money, and people.

Where does politics happen? At all levels and in all institutions, including the family, local councils, within the workplace, in churches, and in Parliament.

How does politics happen? Politics is a continuous process of negotiation between different interests and interest groups.

What do you need to be political? Skills and knowledge about decisionmaking procedures and a sense of your own power and how to use it.

What do women need in order to participate effectively in politics?
- a change in the culture of politics to make it more accessible and inclusive
- self-confidence, information, and skills for political influence
- political consciousness to be able to understand issues and solutions with a political mind
- an understanding of power and an ability to identify sources and ways of using power
- resources—human, material, financial
- accountability to constituencies they claim to represent
- negotiating skills
- a vision of a better future

Ugandan workshop of women activists and parliamentarians, 1994

ethnic minorities, women, small businesses, trade unions, and peasants. When disadvantaged groups become engaged in politics and advocacy, they seek public recognition for their problems, as well as a more equitable distribution of resources and opportunities to solve those problems. They also often demand that the state legitimize and protect their rights in both the public and private realms.

How to begin the discussion of politics?
Before doing the following exercises, start off with a trust-building and personal reflection activity that allows people to say something about themselves and what they care about. See Chapter 7 and the Annex for possible exercises.

Purpose

To demystify politics and develop a broad definition that envisions politics as a process of negotiation and decisionmaking occuring in all aspects of life.

Process

(Time: 1 hour)

This exercise has two parts. In the first part, a plenary brainstorming exercise is used in which participants call out words that they associate with the word "politics." In the second part, participants form small groups to analyze four illustrations. The questions for the analysis can be handed out or written on a piece of flipchart paper for everyone to read.

Facilitator's Tips

Common Responses to the First Question: corruption, lies, abuse, repression, control, dictatorship, censorship, rules, power, fear, prejudice, thugs, etc. *Note:* The words usually have negative associations.

Common Responses to the Second Question:
- We judge politics from the perspective of the players in formal politics.
- Our image of politics is negative.
- Politics is too difficult to comprehend.
- Politics is about the power of control, abuse, and money. Since we have no money and no power, it's useless to think about politics.

From workshops in Africa and the former Soviet Union

1. The facilitator describes the purpose and process of the exercise.

2. Brainstorming: The facilitator asks the following questions and jots down participants' responses on a flipchart. At this stage the facilitator does not introduce any new information.
   - What words would you use to describe politics?
   - What do these words tells us about how we think about politics?

3. Small Group Work: Divide participants into small groups and distribute a copy of the illustrations to each group. Ask the groups:
   - What do they see in each illustration?
   - How does the picture relate to politics?
   - In each picture, who are the key people that might be involved in decisionmaking?
   - What does it tell us about who has more power and who has less power in politics and decisionmaking?

4. Plenary: Ask participants to share their reflections from the small groups. To avoid repetition, after the first group has presented, ask the other groups only to add any new thoughts not covered by previous groups.

5. Conclusions and Input: Summarize the main points from the presentations. You might want to highlight that power expresses itself in all kinds of decisionmaking in our lives. For this reason, politics can be seen as a negotiation process between people with different interests and perspectives in all areas of life.

A.

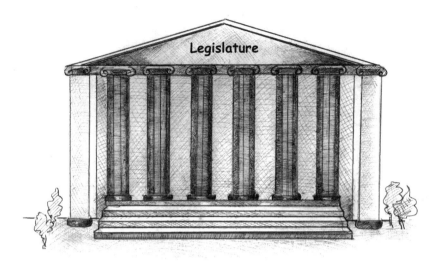

B.

C.

Facilitator's Tips

Throughout the Guide we provide a series of drawings to help promote discussions. However, since Images do not always translate easily across cultures, we encourage you to find drawings or photos that best reflect your own setting.

D.

E.

F.

What Is Advocacy?

The rapid growth of advocacy training in the last decade has generated a wide variety of definitions, approaches, and strategies. Diverse advocacy approaches are not just different ways of reaching a similar end. They embody different values, political views, and goals, and thus seek different ends. The distinctions have important implications for excluded groups such as women, indigenous communities, and ethnic minorities. Advocacy initiatives concerned with empowerment, citizenship, and participation appear different from those that focus only on policy reform.

Some definitions of advocacy refer to policy change or the technical aspects of advocacy while others explicitly refer to power. Some focus on *who* does advocacy and *who* is meant to benefit from advocacy. Advocacy is not just about getting to the table with a new set of interests, it is about changing the size and configuration of the table to accommodate a whole new set of actors. Effective advocacy challenges imbalances of power and changes thinking. We discuss these differences in more detail later on in this chapter.

UNDERSTANDING POLITICS

> *"We're not certain whether we have a translation for 'advocacy' or whether we should just use the word 'advocacy' in English. Part of the confusion has to do with the way the concept was imported from the outside as if it were a new technology—as if we didn't already know advocacy. Latin America's history is full of examples of people facing power. How can we think that advocacy is new?"*
>
> Peruvian activist, 2001

Purpose

To explore how different definitions of advocacy reflect different values, aspirations, and political views.

Process

(Time: 1–1½ hours)

1. Divide participants into small groups and give each a copy of the drawings on the next page. There are two sets of drawings showing different ways of doing advocacy. Provide the following instructions in a handout or write on flipchart paper.

Facilitator's Note

For a training or planning effort, it is helpful to begin with participants' definitions in order to learn more about their political views and questions. If participants are unfamiliar with advocacy, you may need to take a step back. Before doing this exercise, you can describe examples of advocacy or ask them to read a few brief case examples, and then discuss some of the distinguishing features. (See Chapter 15 for examples.)

Discussion Steps and Questions

- Describe what is happening in each box.
- Compare the roles and actions of the organizers and the citizens in each scenario. Describe the power relationships in each. Who has more and who has less control over the process?
- In which case will the citizens gain more knowledge and skills? Which will be more empowering to the citizens? In which case will the organizer gain more knowledge and skills?
- What are the primary differences between the two kinds of advocacy in the drawing?
- What would you guess to be the final impact in each case?

2. After each group has discussed the questions, ask them to share their analysis with each other in plenary.

3. Conclusion and Input: Provide only a short summary wrap-up because participants will develop their own definitions of advocacy in the next exercise.

1

Parliament

"Experts" bring people's issues (the water problem) to policymakers

2

Health

People organize to bring their own issues to policymakers

Purpose

Advocacy involves activities directed at different audiences, goals, and strategies. Developing a common definition can improve communication in the advocacy planning process. The purpose of this exercise is to deepen people's thinking about what advocacy is, and to reach a common definition to guide the planning.

Process

(Time: 1–2 hours)

1. Divide participants into small groups and ask them to discuss the following questions. Their thoughts should be noted on flipchart paper to share with the group in plenary.
   - What is advocacy?
   - Name three outcomes of effective advocacy.
   - What kinds of activities does advocacy involve?

2. In the plenary, ask participants to identify three to five similarities among the groups' responses to the first question and three to five differences. Write the similarities and differences on two different sheets of newsprint and discuss.

3. Ask participants to debate and agree on the four or five most important outcomes and activities and circle these.

4. If you have extra time, discuss the definitions on the next page. Highlight the key characteristics of the different definitions.

5 Conclude with a brief reflection about whether and how the discussion changed participants' understanding of advocacy.

Examples for Facilitators

Here are some advocacy definitions from the Asia-Pacific Advocacy Training of Trainers, co-hosted by GWIP and the Center for Legislative Development in 1997.

- One definition focused on outcomes. *"Advocacy is strategic action that influences decision making (for and against) in order to improve the social, economic, political environment toward the improvement of the community."*
- Another focused on action and process. *"Advocacy is about bringing positive changes to all levels of society through the identification of issues, taking of a position, mobilization of resources, organization of structures and mechanisms, and implementation of strategies."*
- The third group focused on both outcomes and on process. *"Advocacy is a continuous process which leads to positive change in attitudes, behavior, and relationships within the family, workplace, and community, and state and society (i.e., all social institutions)."*
- Some groups use the word "for" rather than "with" when referring to the relationship between the organizers and the communities that will benefit from advocacy. One group defined advocacy as *"to advocate on behalf of the voiceless."* Another group said that advocacy was *"working with the voiceless, organizing people to speak for themselves."*

There is no pure form of advocacy. Most advocacy strategies include aspects of several of the following definitions. At the same time, different definitions reflect different assumptions about how politics and power operate, and how change happens. We discuss this in more detail in the next two chapters. For now, we list some of the influential advocacy definitions. We conclude with the definition of advocacy that informs this Guide.

Public interest advocacy: This is typically large-scale campaign-style advocacy often involving professional lobbyists, media experts, pollsters, and fundraisers. These actors mobilize resources and influence in pursuit of policy reforms on social and political issues with the goal of serving the broad public interest.

Policy advocacy: Policy advocacy initiatives focus exclusively on the policy agenda and a specific policy goal. These advocates usually assume that policy change will produce real change on the ground.

Social justice advocacy: A number of organizations worldwide describe their advocacy this way. Strategies involve political and policy influence around issues that directly affect people's lives, especially the lives of the poor and marginalized. Oxfam and the Advocacy Institute (USA) describe it like this: "Advocacy consists of organized efforts and actions based on the reality of 'what is.' These organized actions seek to highlight critical issues that have been ignored and submerged, to influence public attitudes and to enact and implement laws and public policies so that visions of 'what should be' in a just, decent society become a reality." They stress the need "to embrace power relationships and people's participation . . ."[3]

People-centered advocacy: (See the definition on the next page.) These strategies aim to empower poor people to advocate for their rights and interests themselves. This approach challenges the notion that policy is the terrain of "experts." For ActionAid (UK), people-centered advocacy "supports and enables *people to better negotiate on their own behalf*, for basic needs and basic rights."[4]

Participatory advocacy: Participatory advocacy extends the boundaries of public decisionmaking by engaging civil society groups in policy debates. It is founded on the belief that democratic governance is the task of citizens as well as governments. This type of advocacy aims to expand public space and citizenship. (Also see the discussion on deliberative democracy in the next chapter.)

Feminist advocacy: Feminist advocacy refers to strategies, skills, and tools used to influence decisionmaking processes in the public and social arenas in order to eliminate inequalities between women and men. It often challenges other forms of oppression and exclusion. Feminist advocacy seeks to achieve respect for diversity and difference, and to contribute to cultural, social, and political change for women's full and active citizenship.[5]

The Action Guide's Working Definition of Advocacy

Citizen-centered advocacy shares many of the principles of the previous definitions. Like them, ours is explicitly value-based and em-phasizes changing unequal relationships of power. We are concerned with how imbalances are perpetuated by social and economic relationships and values in both the public and private arenas. We also share the aspiration of other approaches for equity, justice, and rights.

The approach of this Guide emphasizes how advocacy planning and action can promote more inclusive decisionmaking and citizenship.

The Guide's Definition of Advocacy

Citizen-centered advocacy is an organized political process that involves the coordinated efforts of people to change policies, practices, ideas, and values that perpetuate inequality, prejudice, and exclusion. It strengthens citizens' capacity as decisionmakers and builds more accountable and equitable institutions of power.

We think that the process of articulating priorities, interests, and rights through planning advocacy is as important as the act of claiming them through political organizing.

People-centered Advocacy

John Samuel, the Executive Director of the National Centre of Advocacy Studies in India, defines people-centered advocacy as follows:

"To be effective and efficient, people-centered advocacy needs to:

- **Empower those who have less conventional economic, social, or political power**, using grassroots organizing and mobilization as a means of awareness and assertion of the rights and social responsibilities of citizens.
- **Resist unequal power relations (like patriarchy) at every level:** from personal to public, and from family to governance. The challenge for public advocacy groups is to accomplish this using our meager financial, institutional, and human resources. To effectively influence government or corporate power structures, public advocacy can draw on five major sources that cost nothing:
  - The power of people or citizens
  - The power of direct grassroots experience or linkages
  - The power of information and knowledge
  - The power of constitutional guarantees
  - The power of moral convictions
- **Bridge micro-level activism and macro-level policy initiatives.** Public advocacy initiatives that are practiced only at the macro-level run the risk that a set of urban elites, equipped with information and skills, will take over the voice of the marginalized. Public advocacy groups must make sure they are continually sensitive to the grassroots situation and organically bridge the gap between citizens and policy change.

Grassroots organizing and mobilization lends credibility, legitimacy, and crucial bargaining power to public advocacy. In the Indian context, grassroots support and constituency are the most important factors that determine the credibility of the lobbyist—not his or her professional background or expertise. Activists with an adequate level of expertise and mass support have proven to be better lobbyists than professional experts. Grassroots mobilization and advocacy must work together if we are to achieve real progress at the macro-level."

Citizen-centered approaches have four consistent features:

1. The advocacy planning process engages marginalized people in analyzing, strategizing, and making decisions to improve their lives and claim their rights as citizens;

2. A political hook links citizen organizing and education to specific changes in social, economic, and political decisionmaking and policy;

3. A continuous analysis and negotiation of power relationships helps ensure actions are consistent with a long-term vision of equitable change;

4. The pursuit of alliances and bridges among diverse sectors and groups builds common ground, strength, and legitimacy for change.

Citizen-based advocacy strategies vary widely and may target decisionmaking at global, regional, national, or local levels. Strategies combine:

*   using the media to shape public opinion,
*   lobbying decisionmakers,
*   educating the public,
*   organizing constituency groups,
*   developing leadership among citizens,
*   raising political awareness,
*   conducting research,
*   building coalitions, and other activities.

Advocacy relies on a variety of leaders, activists, and organizations with different skills and talents, as well as committed citizens who are willing to take some risk to change their lives. When held together by a set of common prin-

Advocacy's Political/Policy Hooks Focus on:

Who decides: legislators, heads of state, appointed officials, policy-makers, judges, ministers, boards of advisors, managing directors, administrators, etc.

What is decided: laws, policies, priorities, regulations, services, programs, institutions, budgets, statements, party platforms, appointments, etc.

How decisions are made: accessibility of citizens to information and the decisionmaking process, extent of consultation with and direct say of citizens; accountability and responsiveness of decisionmakers to citizens and other stakeholders, etc.

How decisions are enforced, implemented, and evaluated: ensuring accountability so that decisions are put into action, laws enforced equitably, etc.

ciples and commitments, they learn to respect their distinct roles and responsibilities and develop accountable structures of decisionmaking within their organizations.

The Guide's approach is grounded in the notion that citizens have a right to be involved in decisions affecting their lives. Advocacy success is measured by changes in:

*   the quality and strength of citizen engagement and organization;
*   the presence of excluded voices and interests on the policy agenda and in decionmaking processes;
*   the level of public accountability to all sectors of society; and
*   values, ideas, and behavior shaping social roles and responsibilities, and assumptions about political and economic choices and models.

UNDERSTANDING POLITICS

What Do We Mean by Rights-Based Advocacy?

Rights-based advocacy builds on the legitimacy of economic, social, cultural, and political rights gained through UN conventions and procedures. It works both to implement these rights and expand them to respond to new forms of discrimination and indignity.

Rights are a basic ethical foundation for citizen-centered advocacy. They anchor our work in universal aspirations for freedom and fairness and in certain principles:

- People have a right to have a voice in the decisions shaping the quality of their lives;

- Basic economic and social resources and protections—from health care to freedom from violence in the home—are not special privileges. Rather, they are basic rights.

Political and economic structures that systematically exclude social groups from resources and decisions are important targets of rights-based advocacy efforts.

When rights are enshrined in laws and international conventions—such as freedom of speech, of association, and other political and civil rights—they provide a legal framework for action. In such cases, advocacy is about compliance, enforcement, and equal protection.

When rights are not enshrined in law—as is the case with most economic, social, and cultural rights related to housing, healthcare, wages, or the environment—then advocacy focuses on legislation and policy change. As advocates identify new areas of potential rights, they work to gain acceptance for them. Rights are part of an evolving framework that gives meaning to people's aspirations and dreams of human dignity. (See pages 32-34 for more discussion of rights.)

NOTES

[1] From *Citizens and Governance: Civil Society in the New Millenium*, a report prepared by the Commonwealth Foundation in partnership with Civicus, 1999, London.
[2] Alvarez, Sonia E., Evelina Dagnino, and Arturo Escobar, eds. *Cultures of Politics, Politics of Cultures: Re-Visioning Latin American Social Movements*. (Boulder: Westview Press, 1998).
[3] Advocacy Institute and Oxfam America, *Advocacy Learning Initiative* (draft version), 1999.
[4] Chapmen, Jennifer and Amboka Wameyo, *Monitoring and Evaluation Advocacy: A Scoping Study*, ActionAid, London, 2001.
[5] Definition developed by participants during the *Course on Feminist Advocacy*, held in Brazil in March 2001 as part of the project, "Strengthening Advocacy Skills of Latin American NGOs that work on Reproductive and Sexual Rights," organized by AGENDE (Brazil), Centro de la Mujer Peruana Flora Tristan (Peru), and Equidad de Genero (Mexico), 2001.

2 Democracy and Citizenship

"Citizens are the owners of society. The government is made by the people. People are you and me simply."

Zimbabwean[1]

"As citizens, we are responsible for how we are governed. The main issue is . . . to broaden citizens' participation. . . especially in decisionmaking on crucial issues of security, peace, and military."

Marina Liborakina, Russian activist[2]

It is difficult to talk about people, power, and politics without discussing citizenship and democracy. These are highly debated concepts, much like advocacy. But some reflection on what they mean is vital for planning and doing effective advocacy. These concepts help us define what kind of political system we are striving for, and the roles, rights, and responsibilities of all the participants. In this chapter, we look at different perspectives on these concepts that have informed the Guide's approach to advocacy. We also include exercises to guide your own discussions about citizenship and democracy. (In Chapter 7, there are additional exercises.)

The Meaning of Democracy in a Changing World

The many changes occurring around the globe are stretching and reshaping forms of social organization and decisionmaking processes. To meet the challenges of the times, advocates and organizers may find it helpful to revisit the meaning of democracy and citizenship in their work.

Throughout the world, many countries have undergone exciting reforms that have opened up political processes to people. In countries such as the Philippines and South Africa, authoritarian governments have been brought down. In others, governments have taken significant measures to include women and other marginalized groups in public life. Countries such as Brazil, Bolivia, and Thailand have institutionalized laws about people's participation in policymaking. Fairer elections have occurred without violence in dozens of countries where people have voted for the first time.

But there is a long road between successful elections and accountable governments. Along this road civil society continues to struggle for a legitimate voice and for honest, committed leaders to help guide the process. As economic globalization changes the terrain of economic development and the power of national governments, the challenges for improving political structures and relationships grow.

> "The transition to democracy is a narrative of the exclusion of women. What is needed is a new geography to give women space. This new space which women seek is one where there is negotiation between those with power and those without."
>
> Aminata Diaw[3]

Challenges for Democracratic Governance

In *Citizens and Governance: Civil Society in the New Millennium*, the Commonwealth Foundation and Civicus spell out some of the challenges for democratic governance.

"After the end of the Second World War, newly independent countries attempted to consolidate national development efforts. During the second half of the twentieth century, the powers and responsibilities of the nation-states rose to commanding heights. Yet . . . these nation-states are under siege. Forces of globalization are taking control of economic development beyond their reach. Transnational corporations and global capital markets increasingly determine the economic agenda. International financial institutions are playing a major role in shaping decisions about trade, economy, and development.

"The revolution in telecommunications and information technology has brought another dimension to globalization . . . . What some have—or have not—is . . . more visible and known to others. . . . But the web is not world wide: those people, countries, and regions with no access to it become marginalized and fall behind. . . .

"Universal expectations for better standards of living are putting more pressure on governments to deliver. Yet, at the same time, governments find themselves with fewer resources and reduced capacities to respond meaningfully to those expectations.

"In addition, new problems face humanity that cut across the borders of nation-states. Terrorism, drugs, HIV/AIDS, degradation of natural resources, migration, ethnic and nationalist 'identity politics', and religious extremism are widespread. They require trans-border solutions. Yet existing institutions at national and international levels designed fifty years ago are proving inadequate to respond to these emerging problems.

". . . a wide array of new development actors in civil society has emerged. These are NGOs, women's organizations, cooperatives, self-help groups, and a myriad of other forms of civil society organizations, both secular and religious. More resources, human and financial, are going to these organizations. Their experiences and capacities are being increasingly used by governments and intergovernmental bodies. Greater attention, visibility and influence are being gained by them. At the same time, citizens themselves are being expected and exhorted to play their part in development."

Commonwealth Foundation and Civicus, *The Way Forward: Citizens, Civil Society and Governance in the New Millennium*. London: Commonwealth Foundation, 1999.

Discussing Democracy

Although democratic political reforms have been welcomed, the devastating side effects of other changes have been hard on some people, especially the marginalized. These economic and political negatives have stimulated analysis and reflection by a wide range of international organizations.

The following quote from the International Institute for Environment and Development (IIED-UK)[4] summarizes this thinking:

> "In many countries, representative democracy has been heavily criticized for its inability to protect citizens' interests. Marginalized groups in both the North and the South often do not participate effectively in such representative democracy. The poor are often badly organized and ill served by the organizations that mobilize their votes and claim to represent their interests. The crisis of legitimacy faced by institutions in the eyes of poor people (and a growing number of middle-income citizens) is now widely documented. Drawing from participatory research in 23 countries the recent 'Consultations with the poor' report, prepared [by the World Bank] for the World Development Report 2001, concludes: 'not surprisingly, poor men and women lack confidence in the state institutions even though they still express their willingness to partner with them under fairer rules.'"[4]

The meaning of democracy is often controversial among activists. In many workshops, people have resisted a full discussion of democracy because it often provokes heated, even angry, debate. This is partly because some people seem to equate democracy with the external imposition of models that do not seem to fit the reality of their context. This is especially true where the promise of democracy has not materialized. This resistance also sometimes arises out of confusion about the relationship between political democracy and economic liberalization. In some places, democracy means "free market," and people's experience with the free market has been mixed and the subject of considerable debate.

It is precisely these sensitivities that make the subject worth discussing. The following exercise, *What is Democracy*, helps people begin to grapple with the meaning and practice of democracy in more depth.

Exercise: What is Democracy?

Purpose

To explore diverse understandings of the concept of democracy, and to identify how our views of democracy shape advocacy strategies.

Process

(Time: 1 hour)

1. Explain the purpose of the activity. You may want to introduce the topic with a discussion about how the world and a specific country have changed, or as a follow-up to the *Historical Analysis of the Political Landscape* exercise in Chapter 7.

2. Divide participants into small groups to discuss three questions:
   - What is democracy?
   - What are some of the most difficult barriers to building democracy?
   - What can be done to address these barriers?

Common Responses to "What is Democracy?"	Common Responses to "Difficult Barriers to Democracy?"	Common Responses to "What Can Be Done?"
• Leaders are accountable • The will of the majority • Competition for political power • Right to voice your opinions • Freedom to be part of any organization • Governments change and can be rejected • Equality • Rights • Representation • Free market • Citizen action • Elections	• Poverty • Apathy • Corruption • Abuse of power • Traditional ways of doing things • International forces like globalization and the IMF • Political parties don't change • Discrimination • Inequality: in reality, people are not equal • Intolerance • Violence, hatred • Conflict • Resistance to change • Lack of information	• Systems that force leaders and officials to talk directly to citizens • More citizens involved in decisions • Respect for difference and rights • Less fear and violence • Less destabilizing external forces • More ethical leaders • More organized citizens • More economic resources and opportunities • More information • Respect for sovereignty

Responses from workshops in Asia and Africa

3. After 30–45 minutes, ask the groups to share their responses in plenary. The second and third groups should only add to what the first group presents. Encourage participants to identify differences, disagreements, and common points.

4. Synthesis: Note that there are many different models and definitions of democracy. This is a topic that is being shaped by new leaders and citizens every day. You may want to clarify the differences between economic liberalization and democracy. You can also hand out and discuss the different definitions of democracy found on the following page.

UNDERSTANDING POLITICS

Democracy in Theory

Different concepts of democracy implicitly inform our approach to advocacy and participation. The following definitions, taken from a dictionary on political theories, show some of the basic conceptual differences.

"**Democracy:** Form of government in which supreme power is held by the people and exercised directly or through elected representatives. The word comes from the Greek for 'people's rule.' Although democracy comes in many forms, nowadays the concept generally implies majority rule, minority and individual rights, equality of opportunity, equality under the law, and civil rights and liberties.

- **Liberal democracy** is government characterized by the twin pillars of democratic institutions, on the one hand (e.g., elections, representative legislatures, checks and balances), and democratic protections on the other (e.g., the personal freedoms guaranteed by the U.S. Bill of Rights). Liberal democracies typically occur in capitalist economies and stress private property rights. The approach emphasizes individual rights over the popular will.

- **Popular democracy** stresses self-rule by a free and equal people, sees government as an expression of the 'people's will,' and thus seeks to maximize citizen participation. It does this both electorally and in other ways, as it recognizes that the outcomes of elections do not always reflect the popular will.

- **Representative (or indirect) democracy** is the form of government in which legislation is enacted by representatives who are elected by the citizenry. In contrast to direct democracy, the majority delegates power to a minority nominated to act in their interest. The minority is mandated to do this either in response to the majority's express wishes or according to the representatives' own judgment.

- **Direct (or participatory) democracy** is a form of government in which the citizenry itself makes legislative decisions instead of delegating the power to elected representatives. This is often considered the 'purest form of democracy.' Referendums and petitions, in which all voters can participate, are examples of direct democracy.

- **Social democracy** is based on the belief that . . . economic equity and social equality—can be achieved through democratic institutions via redistribution of wealth within a mixed-market economy in a welfare state."

A World of Ideas: A Dictionary of Important Theories, Concepts, Beliefs, and Thinkers by Chris Rohmann, New York: The Ballantine Publishing Group, 1999.

Citizens as "Makers and Shapers"[5]

A discussion of democracy inevitably reaches the subject of citizenship. And like democracy, the meaning of citizenship is also open to debate. For example, some political theorists argue that a good citizen is one who displays trust and obedience. Some believe that ordinary people lack sufficient judgment and knowledge and should therefore rely on their leaders to solve problems. Other theorists argue that the individual as active citizen is rapidly disappearing, and is being replaced by the individual as consumer.

> "Citizenship is very tied to the idea of democracy. Democracy is the first name and citizenship is the last name."
>
> Latin American activist, 2001

> "New approaches to social citizenship seek to move beyond seeing the state as bestowing rights and demanding responsibilities of its subjects. In doing so, they aim to bridge the gap between citizen and the state by recasting citizenship as practiced rather than given . . . This recognizes the agency of citizens as 'makers and shapers' rather than as 'users and choosers'. . . ."[6]

In contrast, people concerned about participation and advocacy say that the problem is not that people are politically incompetent or distracted by the consumer economy. Rather, the problem is the continued concentration of power in the hands of a few. They believe that more involvement by people in decisions affecting them would improve both government and people's quality of life. Some believe that people's participation is a basic right (regardless of whether one is a "legal citizen"), and that constructive engagement with government, if possible, is the best way to address social and economic problems and conflict. Above, scholars from the Institute of Development Studies in the U.K. describe active visions of citizenship.

Citizenship is learned through education, socialization, exposure to politics, public life, and day-to-day experiences. Promoting active citizenship among people who have been marginalized from politics is not a straightforward task. Citizenship does not just happen naturally in response to increased public space or political opportunity. Citizenship is more than voting or fulfilling public obligations. It is not only choosing officials and using the system; citizenship involves making and shaping the system's structures and rules.

A common vision of citizenship is helpful for advocacy. It is also important to recognize that the values of citizenship vary from context to context. For example, in South Africa, people might define a good citizen as someone who actively fights racism. In Russia, being a good citizen might be associated with economic liberalism, and individual self-reliance might be valued over collective action. In countries that have emerged from years of conflict, often a good citizen is seen as one who seeks peaceful resolutions and reconciliation. In older democracies, where a significant portion of citizens are not exercising their right to vote, citizenship is often expressed through participation in activities such as volunteer neighborhood crime watch and clean-up efforts.

In all contexts, the changing views of citizenship are marked by battles that determine whose concerns get incorporated as legitimate and whose get excluded. The outcomes decide who is considered a full citizen and who is not.

So, what kind of citizenship do we want to promote? What skills, aptitudes, and values will this citizenship demand? What are the responsibilities of the state? How can advocates build constructive alliances between government, the private sector, and citizens? How can we integrate learning of this kind into the advocacy process? What does all this mean for organizers and advocates?

> "The idea of citizen participation is a little like eating spinach: No one is against it in principle because it is good for you. Participation of the governed in their government is, in theory, the cornerstone of democracy—a revered idea that is vigorously applauded by virtually everyone. But when the have-nots define participation as the redistribution of power, the American consensus on the fundamental principle explodes into many shades of *outright radical, ethnic, ideological, and political opposition.*"
>
> Sherry R. Arnstein[7]

Purpose

To enable participants to explore their understanding of what it means to be a good citizen and what responsibilities governments have in promoting citizenship and citizen rights.

Process

(Time: 1 hour)

1. Introduce the topic, explaining that there are many debates about the meaning of citizenship.

2. Organize participants into small groups to discuss the following questions.
   - What makes a "good" citizen?
   - What can governments do to encourage "good" citizenship?
   - What can citizens do to encourage "good" citizenship?

3. After 20–30 minutes of discussion, ask groups to share their responses in plenary. As before, ask the subsequent groups only to add to what has already been said.

4. Synthesis: Summarize the responses of the participants. Highlight similarities and explore some of the differences. This exercise can be complemented by the exercise on page 33, which looks more closely at rights and responsibilities. Alternatively, you can introduce some of the thinking about citizenship described on the next page.

Many people live in countries or communities where they have never witnessed active, critical citizenship. Some cultures value obedience to authority more than independent thought and action. Activists from these countries may feel conflicted about what being a citizen means. Debates on the meaning of citizenship can be empowering for people who are trying to understand and shape their role as citizens.

UNDERSTANDING POLITICS

Common Responses to "What Makes a Good Citizen?"	Common Responses to "What Can Governments Do?"	Common Responses to "What Can Citizens Do?"
• Is concerned about others, particularly disadvantaged • Promotes collective action and a collective spirit • Respects others, encourages respect for human rights • Mediates conflict • Encourages tolerance • Is hopeful about change • Is well-informed • Participates in community and national affairs • Monitors powerful interests • Knows how to make demands • Promotes participatory democracy in politics, at home	• Protect and promote rights • Make clear information available so people understand what's going on • Encourage sensitivity to differences based on gender, age, race, etc. • Provide easily understood information about policy choices and final outcomes • Involve citizens directly in policymaking • Provide citizenship education • Implement affirmative action to include women and poor people in the political process	• Be well informed about their community and the world • Encourage people to work together to solve problems • Encourage people to respect differences • Help to negotiate conflicts • Educate others • Inspire others • Organize others

Responses from workshops in Asia, Africa, and the former Soviet Union

History of Citizenship Concepts

Civil citizenship took shape in the 18th century western world. It refers to the rights that are necessary for individual freedom, such as the rights to free speech and assembly, property rights, and equal rights before the law. Over the years, excluded groups have fought to have these rights extended.

Political citizenship emerged from struggles in the 19th century. It emphasizes rights to participate in the exercise of political power—whether as a voter, a candidate, or public official. Women, minorities, and poor people waged battles well into the 20th century to gain universal suffrage, which was previously granted only to male property owners. In some countries those struggles continue into the 21st century.

Social citizenship emerged against the background of the growing inequities of the 20th century. It focuses on minimum rights and standards of economic, cultural, and social well-being. Disadvantaged groups and their allies are currently still working to gain legitimacy for this view of citizenship and rights.

Adapted from T.H. Marshall, *Class, Citizenship, and Social Development*, Westport: Greenwood Press 1973 and Virginia Vargas, *Procesos de Formacion de las Ciudadanias Globales en el Marco de Sociedades Civiles Globales*, Lima Peru, 1999.

Citizen Rights and Responsibilities

Debates about citizenship are shaped by our understanding of the rights and responsibilities of citizens and the roles and responsibilities of government. People's struggles for dignity have produced various definitions of citizenship emphasizing different dimensions of rights (see box above), likewise, with responsibilities. The range covers a wide political stretch and provokes vastly different responses. Some people believe that mayhem will result if all citizens jump into the decisionmaking process with their diverse interests. Others feel that accommodating diversity is the only way to avoid the conflict that would result if the process were not responsive to differences.

We have found that it is important for people to explore government roles and responsibilities and identify areas where government and citizens have joint responsibilities.

The following exercise has been used to help participants explore their own beliefs about citizen rights and responsibilities. This exercise will probably elicit more concrete responses than the previous exercise. The previous exercise encourages participants to look at general questions of good citizenship and government responsibility. The next exercise builds on that discussion and draws out ideas about obedience and respect for authority, and explores whether rights come from governments, citizens, or both.

Purpose

To enable participants to define citizen rights and responsibilities and to examine their evolution.

Process

(Time: 1 hour)

1. Divide participants into small groups. Ask them to brainstorm two lists, one of rights and one of responsibilities. You may want to introduce the exercise highlighting the changing meaning of citizens. For example, traditionally citizen duties were conceptualized within the notions of the "common good"—voting, obedience to laws, and military service in wartime. Today, citizenship involves expanding duties.

Common Responses to "Rights"

- civil and political rights: freedom of association, speech, movement, religion
- the right to vote
- property rights
- right to advocate and demand government accountability
- equal rights before the law
- right to organize and protest
- right to information
- right to protection and freedom from sexual or domestic violence

Some participants may also include social and economic rights, such as

- right to adequate schooling
- right to healthcare
- right to sexual preference
- right to a job with a decent wage
- right to decent housing
- right to clean environment
- right to food security
- rights related to reproductive health
- right to development

Common Responses to "Responsibilities"

- being aware of social issues
- engaging in public debate and political life, voting
- being concerned about and taking steps to combat disadvantage and injustice
- promoting collective action
- treating others equally
- fostering tolerance and respect for human rights in all relationships and institutions
- joining others to demand that rights be enforced

Responses from workshops in Africa, Asia, and the former Soviet Union

2. After about 30–45 minutes, bring groups together in plenary to share their definitions. To avoid repetition, have the groups following the first only add to the common list.

3. Discuss the list. The following questions may be used to deepen understanding:

- Who decides who has which rights?
- Are rights changing? If so, who is changing rights and how are they changing?

Synthesis

One of the important lessons of this discussion is that the meaning of citizenship and the rights and responsibilities of citizens are changing. Citizens themselves are playing a big role in that change. Governments also play a role in shaping the rights of citizens, but that role also seems to be changing. The important political and civil rights that shape basic freedoms may not be sufficient to ensure that everyone has equal rights because people are not all equal in reality.

UNDERSTANDING POLITICS

Citizenship and Rights: Some Tensions

Centuries of human struggle and scholarship led to the adoption of the Universal Declaration of Human Rights in 1948 by the countries of the United Nations. But beyond just *defending* and *protecting* these rights, many people argue that we need to *expand* human rights so that the disadvantaged, who have less access to resources and protections, get a fairer deal. As a result, new rights, such as the right to a clean environment or reproductive health, have been introduced through national and international initiatives.

Although modern-day conceptions of citizenship are grounded in the notions of equality and universality, there are tensions about the gap between theory and reality. Some activists reject the concepts of universality and equality altogether, even the validity of a rights approach. They emphasize that differences, such as race and gender, can never be reconciled. Other activists point out the advantage of using these universal rights as aspirations for change. Despite the problems, they argue that the concept of universal rights gives legitimacy to struggles for justice.

It is in these tensions over difference and inequality that the struggle for rights and citizenship unfolds. Rights are not simply bestowed on people from a larger authority. They are a product of a long history of political activism. Through such struggles, excluded populations can gain a strong sense of their role as protagonists and citizens.

Perceptions of Power and Political Change Strategies

What prevents and what enables citizens to engage actively in democratic processes? What kinds of skills and values do citizens need and how can these be communicated through our advocacy activities?

Scholar-practitioner John Gaventa argues that understanding citizenship and citizen compe-

---

Identity Politics and Beyond

The current struggle over rights, responsibilities, and citizenship has emerged in part from the efforts by some groups to fight discrimination through what some academics call "identity politics." Identity can be both individual and collective. Each person has multiple identities—defined by race, gender, religion, class, age, ethnicity, sexual preference, among others. People of certain "identities," such as ethnic and racial minorities, have been consistently excluded from many societies. By becoming aware of their own particular identity and the forces that discriminate, these groups become engaged politically. They express their citizenship by exercising and working to expand and enforce their rights.

Identity politics can, on the one hand, help to build political bonds of solidarity among people of shared identities. On the other hand, such an approach can also lead to discriminatory forms of politics that focus narrowly on individual group interests.

By forming alliances with others on issues of common concern, excluded groups can more effectively advance their rights and build more inclusive societies. In the process, their efforts hold the potential for generating new ideas about the practice of politics and citizenship which, in turn, can encourage the creation of new rights.

See Outhwaite, William and Tom Bottomore, eds. *The Blackwell Dictionary of Twentieth-Century Social Thought.* Oxford: Blackwell Publishers, 1993.

Gender and Citizenship

Recent contributions from women's groups and gender scholars have expanded the citizenship debate. The concept of *engendered citizenship* takes the rights and responsibilities of individuals in the formal political arena and applies them across all social relationships and institutions. Feminist activists and scholars argue that the concepts of democracy, equality, and rights are as important in the home as they are in the legislature. They extend the boundaries of the "common good" beyond the public arena to include the family. They say that it is as important for a "good" citizen to share the responsibilities for the caring of children and older family members as it is to be involved in public activities. They argue that if men took more responsibility for domestic duties, women would be more active in public and economic life. Further, men's contribution at home would help reduce social problems that are linked to parental neglect. They argue that this could also reduce male-related problems, such as violent crime, because men's lives would be more balanced. At present, society treats what happens in the private world of the family as unrelated to citizenship. For women, however, the chance to be a citizen is often determined by what goes on in that private world.

See Maxine Molyneux's *Gender, Citizenship and Democracy: Reflections on Contemporary Debates,* 1997

UNDERSTANDING POLITICS

tencies demands a clear analysis of power. Different views of political power embody different ideas about *why* citizens do not engage in public life, and *what* is needed to build citizen activism. He draws on contributions by others to help us decipher how our assumptions about the political process shape our strategies. In the chart on the following page, Gaventa compares three alternative and overlapping theories about political power. He explains:

". . . democracy . . . is not played on a level field. Vast inequalities of power and re-sources separate the haves and the have-nots, the powerful and the powerless. The answer to the question 'what are citizen competencies . . . critical for democracy building?' depends in part on one's answer to the questions of 'What is power? How does it affect citizens' capacities to act and partici-pate for themselves?'

"If we approach the question of citizenship with the first view of power in mind, our emphasis will be on building political efficacy and advocacy to participate in and influence decisionmaking on key issues. If we use the second dimension of power . . . then our

focus will be on organizing to build broad-based citizen organizations to overcome. . . barriers. Who participates will be as important as how to participate effectively. But if we are empowering citizens to deal with the third dimension of power, then the questions of knowledge and values, of what people are participating about, become the critical variables, and the development of critical consciousness the crucial strategy.

". . . to be effective, citizenship requires the capacity to empower oneself in each of these areas. It requires the ability to advocate, the capacity to organize and to build lasting citizens'-based organizations, the capacity to develop one's own critical capacities, strengthened by popular knowledge, informa-tion and culture.

"In practice, this becomes very difficult to do, and tensions develop within and across grassroots organizations around which goals are most important. Those who are 'at the table' and working on strategies of coopera-tion and collaboration with the powerholders may shy away from groups who are perceived as taking a conflict approach because they are questioning 'who sits at the table.' Groups that are working to organize to win a local campaign on a specific issue, may not want to focus on education and leadership development, or to debate what the table ought to look like. Groups focusing on leadership development and education may be not very good at creating sustaining organizations, or on understanding the intricacies of the political process, once they find that they have gotten to the table. Funders upon whom many of the groups are dependent may encourage the support of one approach over another.

". . . The critical challenge . . . is . . . to develop a unified approach that educates for consciousness, mobilizes for action and advocates on the issues simultaneously. . . Such an approach requires developing new networks and constellations of organizations in differing sectors who can work together for common goals." [9]

Transforming Strategies

As Gaventa points out, a combination of all three approaches is necessary to open the

Citizenship & Political Power[9]				
	HOW DOES POLITICAL POWER WORK?	**WHY DON'T CITIZENS PARTICIPATE?**	**HOW TO BUILD CITIZENSHIP**	**LIMITATIONS OF HOW-TO**
1st view	Pluralist; power is the result of open competition; fair winners and losers; public arena is free and equal.	Individual choice; satisfied; apathetic or lack of information and skills.	Advocacy training; public interest (see Chapter 1 definition) and lobbying with professional media and lobbyists.	No direct citizen participation; ignores power dynamics, privilege and disadvantage; no consultation or accountability to grassroots.
2nd view	Bias against the have-nots where power maintained through systemic discrimination and privilege; need clout, bargaining skills, and resources to compete and win; power conflictual; public arena only.	Systemic barriers demand that citizens develop citizenship skills and organization to make voices heard and place issues on agenda.	Build broad-based citizen organizations and alliances around common grievances; use power of numbers to get to the bargaining table and win issues; organizers to train citizen leaders and organizations.	Dependence on outside organizer; emphasis on skill-based organizing neglects questions of consciousness and values; accepts politics as usual; ignores power abuses among grassroots; assumes homogeneous needs of poor and marginalized.
3rd view	Power maintained through ideology, values and institutional barriers in both public and private; hegemony prevents conflicts from arising.	Institutional bias combined with internalized oppression; have-nots have no resources and are paralyzed by self-blame, lack of self-esteem; hierarchy and privilege are justified by ideology and socialization.	Foster people's knowledge and critical consciousness to resist dominant values; promote alternative relationships and structures; education and analysis as basis of citizenship; indigenous leadership and organizing.	Emphasis on consciousness and local reality gives too little attention to skills and organization needed for political action; need to match local understanding with information on global issues.

political process to diverse voices. For example, we may need the highly skilled lobbyists and media expertise emphasized in the first approach to influence an increasingly diffuse global policy process. On the other hand, lobbying may change policy, but it will not change the structures and culture that perpetuate exclusion. Lobbying without citizen organizing will not address the roots of exclusion and discrimination that shape power.

The problem with the second approach is that organizing, too, is unlikely to address the deeper structural and social causes of inequality. In fact, many citizen organizations imitate the same patterns of discrimination that they were formed to combat. A new practice of citizen leadership requires an integrated strategy involving participatory education processes to build people's ability to analyze their reality and internalize their rights as citizens. It also takes new alliances and broad-based democratic organizations that tap the power of working together as well as respecting and using people's difference.

Advocacy that is geared to building citizenship and reshaping political culture draws heavily on the theory and practice of participation and popular education. The Guide's approach to advocacy focuses more explicitly on addressing power relations as they express themselves through social conflicts and problems,

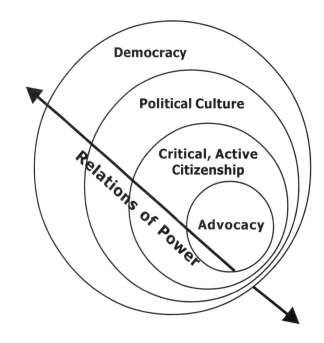

ranging from reproductive health to land rights.

So, at the heart of our approach to advocacy are the ever-changing dynamics of power. The following graphic describes the Guide's vision of advocacy where citizenship, political culture, and democracy are connected like layers of an onion and are all shaped by relations of power.

In the next chapter, we look more closely at power and empowerment, and discuss linking learning and action for citizen empowerment. This discussion provides the methodological base for the rest of the Guide.

NOTES

[1] *Democratic Governance in Zimbabwe: Citizen Power*, Africa Community Publishing and Development Trust and the Commonwealth Foundation, Harare, 1999.
[2] *Public Policy Advocacy: Women for Social Change in the Yugoslav Successor States*, The Star Project, Zagreb, 1998.
[3] In Taylor, Viviene *Marketisation of Governance: Critical Feminist Perspectives from the South*, SADEP/DAWN, 2000.
[4] Pimbert, Michel and Tom Wakeford, "Overview—Deliberative Democracy and Citizen Empowerment" in *PLA Notes* (Notes on Participatory Learning and Action), International Institute for Environment and Development, February 2001.
[5] Cornwall, A and Gaventa, J, "Bridging the Gap: Citizenship, Participation and Accountability" in *PLA Notes* (Notes on Participatory Learning and Action), International Institute for Environment and Development, February 2001.
[6] Ibid.
[7] Sherry R. Arnstein, The Journal of the American Institute of Planners, vol 35, no 4, July 1969.
[8] Gaventa, John. "Citizen knowledge, citizen competence and democracy building", in Stephen L Elkin, (ed.), *Democracy and Citizen Competence*, Penn State Press, 1998. Previously published in *The Good Society*, 5 (3): 28-35, Fall, 1995.
[9] Adapted from Gaventa, John. "Citizen knowledge, citizen competence and democracy building", in Stephen L Elkin, (ed.), *Democracy and Citizen Competence*, Penn State Press, 1998.

3 Power and Empowerment

"...many leaders understand power negatively, as being control and domination; something that cannot be shared without shaking its centre, rather than seeing it in a positive light as something that enables ..."

Zimbabwean 1999[1]

"Martin Luther King, Jr. defined power as the ability to achieve a purpose. Whether or not it is good or bad depends on the purpose."

Grassroots Policy Project, 2001[2]

Power is an integral dynamic of politics. Defining, analyzing, and building power is a vital and continual part of citizen-centered advocacy. Yet, power turns out to be one of the more uncomfortable and difficult topics to address in our work.

Power can seem especially monolithic and impenetrable for people who have lived under regimes that deny or repress citizen participation. Our experience has shown that people engaging in politics for the first time, and even more seasoned activists, often see power as sinister and unchanging. Such a one dimensional perspective can paralyze effective analysis and action. In reality, power is both dynamic and multidimensional, changing according to context, circumstance and interest. Its expressions and forms can range from domination and resistance to collaboration and transformation. This is good news for advocates whose strategies depend upon new opportunities and openings in the practice and structures of power.

However, programs promoting advocacy and democracy too rarely incorporate an understanding of underlying power relationships and interests despite the importance that analysts place on these dynamics. The failure to deal with the complexities of power can lead to missed opportunities and poor strategic choices. Worse, it can be risky and counterproductive not only for advocates, but also for donors and others promoting development and democracy. (See box on next page.) Experts and practitioners in the fields of conflict resolution and democracy-building increasingly stress the importance of incorporating power into their analysis and actions. (See *Power, Advocacy, and Conflict* on page 46.)

In this chapter, we attempt to demystify and reveal the many faces of power. We look at power as an individual, collective, and political force that can either undermine or empower citizens and their organizations. It is a force that alternatively can facilitate, hasten, or halt the process of change promoted through advocacy. For this discussion we draw on practical experience and theory, particularly related to poverty and women's rights where power has been analyzed from the vantage point of subordination and discrimination.

While this chapter focuses on defining power, in Part Two we offer a variety of tools and frameworks for mapping and analyzing power and interests.

Facilitator's Note

Understanding power involves both personal and political analysis of institutions and values. Since values reflect strongly held beliefs, analyzing them requires sensitivity. For this reason, exercises that deal with these issues are best conducted in an environment where participants feel comfortable and secure with each other.

The Missing Link of Power

In examining US democracy initiatives abroad, Thomas Carothers of the Carnegie Endowment for International Peace emphasizes what he calls "the missing link of power" as one key factor undermining change efforts. Giving short shrift to structures of power and interests, he points out, has led to program failures in many cases, from efforts of judicial reform to campaigns for legislative change.

"... aid providers responding to the lack of formal justice in a country assess the judicial system, for example, and conclude that it falls short because cases move too slowly, judges are poorly trained and lack up-to-date legal materials, the infrastructure is woefully inadequate, and so on. The aid providers then prescribe remedies on this basis: reform of court administration, training and legal materials for judges, equipment for courtrooms, and the like. What they tend not to ask is why the judiciary is in a lamentable state, whose interests its weakness serves, and whose interests would be threatened or bolstered by reforms. The assistance may temporarily alleviate some of the symptoms, but the underlying systemic pathologies remain."

To address this problem, Carothers poses one of the major challenges we attempt to address in this Guide -- how to incorporate an analysis of interests and power relationships into our strategies.

"Some democracy promoters cling to what one critic calls the 'Walt Disney view of democratization' in which the endings are always happy and no one ever gets hurt. They have trouble moving toward a grittier world view, one that does not assume entrenched concentration of political power will melt away. . .

". . . many projects reflect little hard thinking on these points, and rely on simplistic ideas about institutional modeling – teaching judges and politicians that corruption is bad will substantially cut bribe taking, teaching citizens about the importance of voting will overcome their political apathy, and on and on.

"As democracy aid providers pay more heed to the interests and power relationships . . . they should not expect to find cut-and-dried answers. . . Factoring in the relevant interests and power relationships requires, above all, close, thoughtful analysis of the local scene . . . A focus on interests and power inevitably pushes aid providers to think more about process than endpoint, about how to stimulate and help along processes of sociopolitical change rather than merely to reproduce [institutional] forms . . . Truly grappling with the local context shows providers that aid efforts are likely to be much slower, difficult, and risky."

Thomas Carothers, *Aiding Democracy Abroad: The Learning Curve*. Washington, DC: Carnegie Endowment for International Peace, 1999.

Looking at Power

Getting to understand power may begin as a personal process where the simple act of talking about it openly can help people grapple with the controversy and discomfort surrounding the topic. The following two exercises help to initiate reflection about power by focusing on personal assumptions and encounters with power. They encourage people to identify their own sources of power as a way to challenge narrow views of power and powerlessness. These exercises can be followed by the *Power Flower* exercise in Chapter 6 which looks at identity and public power more deeply.

Basic Concepts of Power

"Power can be defined as the degree of control over material, human, intellectual and financial resources exercised by different sections of society. The control of these resources becomes a source of individual and social power. Power is dynamic and relational, rather than absolute — it is exercised in the social, economic and political relations between individuals and groups. It is also unequally distributed – some individuals and groups having greater control over the sources of power and others having little or no control. The extent of power of an individual or group is correlated to how many different kinds of resources they can access and control.

Different degrees of power are sustained and perpetuated through social divisions such as gender, age, caste, class, ethnicity, race, north-south; and through institutions such as the family, religion, education, media, the law, etc. Our understanding of power would be incomplete, unless we recognise its partner, ideology. Ideology is a complex structure of beliefs, values, attitudes, and ways of perceiving and analyzing social reality. Ideologies are widely disseminated and enforced through social, economic, political and religious institutions and structures such as the family, education system, religion, the media, the economy, and the state, with its administrative, legislative and military wings. The economic, political, legal and judicial institutions and structures set up and mediated by the state tend to reinforce the dominant ideology and the power of the dominant groups within it, even though their stated objectives and policies may be superficially egalitarian. While ideology does a far more effective job of sustaining an unequal power structure than crude, overt coercion and domination, we should not forget that it is always being reinforced by the threat of force, should anyone seek to rebel against the dominant system.

But neither power, ideology, nor the state are static or monolithic. There is a continuous process of resistance and challenge by the less powerful and marginalised sections of society, resulting in various degrees of change in the structure of power. When these challenges become strong and extensive enough, they can result in the total transformation of a power structure."

From the Asia Pacific Bureau of Adult Education's (ASPBAE) 1993 study undertaken with FAO's Freedom from Hunger campaign as quoted in *Women's Empowerment in South Asia – Concepts and Practices*, Srilatha Batliwala, ASPBAE/FAO (Draft), 1993.

Purpose

To introduce the concept of power and to encourage people to recognize their own power and potential. This is a quick way to begin to explore participants' views of power. If you have more time, the next exercise allows for more in-depth analysis.

Process

(Time: 30 minutes to 1½ hours)

1. Hand out copies of the illustrations on the next page with the following questions:
   - Identify and describe the kind of power depicted in each of the four drawings.
   - Explain the impact of this kind of power on citizen participation.

2. A brainstorming discussion is guided by two questions. Responses are recorded on flipchart paper.
   - What are the main sources of power?
   - What are your potential sources of power as a citizen?

> "To effectively influence the power structures of government or corporate interest, one needs other sources of power. In the context of public advocacy, six major sources are:
> - The power of people and citizens' mobilization
> - The power of information and knowledge
> - The power of constitutional guarantees
> - The power of direct grassroots experience and networking
> - The power of solidarity
> - The power of moral convictions"
>
> *John Samuel, National Centre for Advocacy Studies, India*

Follow-up

This exercise focuses on the visible aspects of power. The next exercise, *Feeling Power and Powerlessness*, looks at the more invisible psychological, emotional, and social aspects of power.

Common Responses for "Sources of Power"
- control
- money and wealth
- position
- knowledge and information
- might and force
- abuse
- capacity to inspire fear

Common Responses for "Alternative Sources"
- persistence
- information
- being just
- organization and planning
- our own knowledge
- our own experience
- commitment
- righteousness
- numbers*
- solidarity
- humor

This list combines the responses of activists from 10 different countries.

* The *power of numbers* is, potentially, a huge source of power, but it is often not used effectively. For example, in most countries, women are the majority of voters, but are under-represented in decisionmaking and have less access to public resources. Mobilizing alternative sources of power requires ways of challenging an ingrained sense of powerlessness.

Exercise: Feeling Power and Powerlessness

Purpose

To explore personal experiences with power and powerlessness and what they tell us about alternative sources of political power.

Process

(Time: 2 hours)

1. Give each participant a large sheet of paper and markers.

2. Ask them to draw a line down the middle. On one side they draw a situation that has made them feel powerful. On the other side they draw a situation that has made them feel powerless.

3. Ask each person to explain their drawing.

> Many people do not feel confident about drawing. They may ask if they can just write the answer using words. Explain that drawing is often a more effective way of reflecting about and expressing emotions. Having to think creatively about how to express yourself often makes you think about experiences vividly with fresh eyes. Encourage the most resistant people to use symbols and stick figures. The quality of the artwork is not important.

4. After all of the drawings have been explained, copy your notes onto newsprint. Point out that the words people use to describe experiences with power illustrate their discomfort. For example, associations with control, violence, abuse, force, and money often make people feel ashamed. Highlight the individual stories that demonstrate that people are not completely powerless. For example, they have power through organizing, working together, problem-solving, getting information, or doing what is ethical.

Personal experiences of feeling powerful or powerless can encourage participants to use empowering methodologies. Advocates often believe that they must speak for the communities with whom they work and solve their problems. Through this exercise, they can see that it is more helpful to offer skills and information, and so enable communities to solve their own problems.

Listen for the feelings and actions that embody the emotional, spiritual, and psychological elements of power or powerlessness. Jot these down on a piece of paper. Here are examples from workshops.

Common Responses for "Situations that make you feel Powerful"

- overcoming fear or a feeling of ignorance by pushing myself to take action
- recognition by others of what I did
- finding a creative way to solve a problem that seemed unsolvable
- being able to handle a difficult assignment
- succeeding as a leader
- caring for and helping others
- joining a group with other people who have the same problem
- capacity to inspire fear

Common Responses for "Situations that make you feel Powerless"

- disrespect and putdowns
- being ignored
- being stereotyped and denied opportunities to prove oneself
- lack of control
- loss
- ignorance
- shame
- isolation

The list combines responses from several countries.

Expressions of Power

To get a handle on the diverse sources and expressions of power – both positive and negative – the following distinctions about power can be useful.

Power Over

The most commonly recognized form of power, *power over,* has many negative associations for people, such as repression, force, coercion, discrimination, corruption, and abuse.[3] Power is seen as a win-lose kind of relationship. Having power involves taking it from someone else, and then using it to dominate and prevent others from gaining it. In politics, those who control resources and decisionmaking have *power over* those without. When people are denied access to important resources like land, healthcare, and jobs *power over* perpetuates inequality, injustice, and poverty.

In the absence of alternative models and relationships, people repeat the *power over* pattern in their personal relationships, communities, and institutions. This is also true of people who come from a marginalized or "powerless" group. When they gain power in leadership positions, they sometimes "imitate the oppressor." For this reason, advocates cannot expect that the experience of being excluded prepares people to become democratic leaders. New forms of leadership and decisionmaking must be explicitly defined, taught, and rewarded in order to promote more democratic forms of power.

Practitioners and academics have searched for more collaborative ways of exercising and using power. Three alternatives – *power with, power to,* and *power within* – offer positive ways of expressing power that create the possibility of forming more equitable relationships. By affirming people's capacity to act creatively, they provide some basic principles for constructing empowering strategies.

Power With

Power with has to do with finding common ground among different interests and building collective strength. Based on mutual support, solidarity, and collaboration, *power with* multiplies individual talents and knowledge. *Power with* can help build bridges across different interests to transform or reduce social conflict and promote equitable relations. Advocacy groups seek allies and build coalitions drawing on the notion of *power with.*

Power To

Power to refers to the unique potential of every person to shape his or her life and world. When based on mutual support, it opens up the possibilities of joint action, or *power with.* Citizen education and leadership development for advocacy are based on the belief that each individual has the *power to* make a difference.

Power Within

Power within has to do with a person's sense of self-worth and self-knowledge; it includes an ability to recognize individual differences while respecting others. *Power within* is the capacity to imagine and have hope; it affirms the common human search for dignity and fulfillment. Many grassroots efforts use individual story telling and reflection to help people affirm personal worth and recognize their *power to* and *power with.* Both these forms of power are referred to as *agency* – the ability to act and change the world – by scholars writing about development and social change.

"Power is integral to all conflict . . . practitioners must become aware of their own power, their assumptions about power and the values and goals they bring to conflict situations. They must also explicitly assess how power is operating in the conflictive relationships, evaluate their own role, and seek the appropriate process in conflicts of significant power imbalance.

"In each conflict situation, it is important to ask questions such as: What are the sources of power for those in conflict? Is there a significant power imbalance? Is power being misused or abused? How can the less powerful become more empowered? What intervention is most appropriate?"

Carolyn Shronk-Shenk[4]

Adam Curle, one of the pioneers in conflict resolution, highlights the problems of power in peace-making and emphasizes consciousness-raising, advocacy, and negotiation as critical moments in the process. The following matrix provides a synopsis of his ideas (see also John Paul Lederach). He traces the movement from unpeaceful to peaceful relationships by comparing levels of power with levels of awareness and moments in the process. When a conflict is hidden or latent, education and consciousness-raising help make people aware of the problem and the power imbalances inherent in the situation. (See Chapter 4.)

As people become conscious of a conflict and their own interests, many move to action and confront the problem through advocacy and activism. If successful, the process increases the balance of power and legitimizes their efforts for change. Once inequities have been addressed, and only then, do negotiation and sustainable peace become possible.

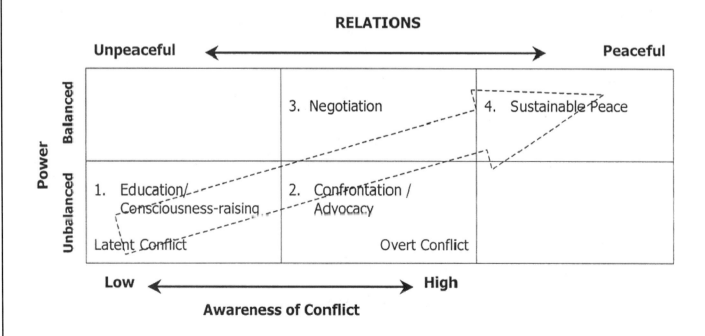

Adam Curle's *Framework for Moving to Peaceful Relations in Making Peace,* Tavistock, 1972.
John Paul Lederach, *Preparing for Peace: Conflict Transformation Across Cultures,* Syracuse UP, 1995.

Many Levels of Political Power

What makes political power even more difficult to analyze and confront is the fact that it does not always operate in visible ways. To help activists and advocates navigate power more effectively, we describe three interactive dimensions of *power over* that shape the parameters of political participation and advocacy. These range from the more obvious and visible to those that operate largely unnoticed behind the scenes. We also discuss some of the strategies used to influence and engage these different expressions of power. The less visible dimensions are, of course, more difficult to engage since power tends to be concealed and diffuse, embedded in cultural and social norms and practices.[5]

"Social norms and institutions are the key obstacles faced by poor women and men as they attempt to eke out a livelihood against the odds. Poor people's experience demonstrates again and again that the informal rules or social norms are deeply embedded in society, and that 'rules in use' override formal rules . . . It is precisely because of the embeddedness of social norms that change in one part of a bureaucratic social system cannot bring about systemic changes . . ."

Deepa Narayan, *Can Anyone Hear Us?*[6]

---

1. Visible Power: Observable Decision-making[7]

This level includes the visible and definable aspects of political power – the formal rules, structures, authorities, institutions, and procedures of decisionmaking. Examples include elections, political parties, laws, legislatures, budgets, corporate policy, by-laws, etc. There are two main ways that visible power discriminates against certain interests and people:

- biased laws and policies that may seem "neutral" but clearly serve one group of people at the expense of others, such as health policies that do not adequately address women's specific needs, or the more obvious form of exclusion, like age and gender requirements for employment;

- closed, corrupt, or unrepresentative decision-making structures that do not adequately involve the voices or interests of the people they are intended to serve.

Citizens and donors naturally place considerable importance on influencing and responding to visible expressions of power, such as electing more women and minorities to office, or reforming discriminatory laws. These are important strategies but are not sufficient to overcome society's unwritten rules and power dynamics that often override the system's formal rules.

Despite the existence of fair laws and decisionmaking structures, politics never occurs on an even playing field. Behind-the-scenes, political, economic, social, and cultural forces operate to shape who gets to sit at the decisionmaking table and whose issues get addressed. The example in the box on the next page, *Visible and Invisible Agendas in Action* illustrates these hidden and invisible dimensions of power.

2. Hidden Power: Setting the Political Agenda

This level of *power over* is less obvious and, hence, more difficult to engage. Certain powerful people and institutions maintain their influence by controlling who gets to the decisionmaking table and what gets on the agenda. These dynamics exclude and devalue the concerns and representation of other less powerful groups, such as women and the poor. Excluded groups often point out that they and their issues, such as toxics, land rights, and domestic violence, are both invisible to the society at large and absent from the political agenda. Difficulties in gaining media coverage can further inhibit visibility and legitimacy since media outlets often do not see these groups' issues as "mainstream" or newsworthy.

Visible and Invisible Agendas in Action

The advocacy experience of Zimbabwean women's groups demonstrates the complexities of visible and invisible power dynamics. The groups were concerned about women's inheritence and property rights, as growing numbers of women and children were left destitute when their husbands died due to a social phenomenon commonly called "property grabbing." Immediately after a death, the wife's in-laws would quickly take over and remove the property of the couple, leaving the widow with nothing. In the early 1990s, groups launched an advocacy campaign to reform property laws to give widows basic legal protection against such injustices. They believed that broad public support coupled with the facts about the problem would compel legislators to reform the laws. Unfortunately, the advocates did not fully account for the power of tradition, custom, or society's unwritten laws. They underestimated both the opposition by vested interests and the political sensitivity around the cultural dimensions of the issue.

The traditional authorities were firmly against the reform. They felt that, by challenging customary law, the new law would further erode their control over their communities. These authorities were also the President's main source of political support in rural areas and had considerable influence. Many other politicians opposed the reforms as a western feminist import that would destroy the African family. The reform never had a chance.

The advocates took their battle to the High Court. They hoped they could win the case on the grounds that customary practice contradicted the constitution. But they lost there too. While the activists navigated the formal procedures of public politics with skill, the invisible power of culture and vested interests defeated them.

In some contexts, powerful political and economic interests attempt to discredit disadvantaged groups, making it impossible for citizens without resources or affiliation to get their voices heard, even if they represent a substantial population. In some cases, leaders are vilified or even killed. By preventing important voices and issues from getting a fair public hearing, policymaking can be skewed to benefit a few at the expense of the majority.

This second level of *power over* also works to hide problems and influence the agenda by controlling access to information. If people are unaware of a problem, they are unable to make informed choices or participate in public decisions that can contribute to its solution. For example, numerous communities around the world have suffered serious illness or death due to toxic waste. When confronted, those responsible for the pollution have often denied that the substances are dangerous. Yet lawsuits have later revealed that they knew about the potential health impacts but chose to keep them a secret.

For marginalized communities, being denied information can reinforce feelings of powerlessness, ignorance, and self-blame, but it also can spur people to action. In many countries, issue-focused advocacy efforts have sometimes evolved into Right to Know campaigns when governments and other bodies have refused to provide information. To address this dimension of power, NGOs and community groups frequently join with academic institutions or investigative journalists to uncover the nature and scope of a problem.

Advocacy groups challenge this level of *power over* by creating broad-based constituencies for policy and institutional reform that reduce systemic discrimination. In building strong and accountable organizations they tap their *power with* others to get to the table. They produce and disseminate analysis and alternative perspectives about their issues and politics.

They also attempt to develop ties with powerful allies to increase their political voice and presence. These strategies have been pursued effectively by environmental, AIDS, women's and rights groups, among others.

3. Invisible Power: Shaping Meaning

Probably the most insidious of the three dimensions of power, this third level operates in ways that render competing interests and problems invisible. Significant problems and issues are not only kept from the decision-making table, but also from the minds and consciousness of the different players involved, even those directly affected by the problem. By influencing how individuals think about their place in the world, this level of power shapes people's beliefs, sense of self, and acceptance of their own superiority or inferiority. In many societies, for example, men and women have been taught to accept their respective roles and relationships as natural. Socialized consent prevents people from questioning or envisioning any possibilities for changing these relationships or addressing injustices.

Processes of socialization, culture, and ideology perpetuate exclusion and inequality by defining what is normal, acceptable, and safe. Schools, the media, corporate interests, and religious and political leaders, among other influential forces, shape values and norms that prevent change. In many countries values and prejudices regarding women and racial minorities are evident in and reinforced by stories and images that appear in school books, ads, and the press. They perpetuate negative stereotypes that limit the roles and aspirations of these groups. In turn, women and minorities often internalize such views and blame themselves for their predicament.

Paradoxically this kind of *power over* can also foster resistance and action in people when they come together around common issues. People can gain a sense of the *power within* themselves and *with* others to change the

> In the Annex, more information and exercises on the dynamics of *power over* are provided for those who want to explore these issues in more detail. We include an analysis of dominant and subordinate behaviors and factors of exclusion and discrimination.

conditions that hurt and limit them. For example, women's consciousness-raising and education efforts have fueled advocacy to change school curriculum and sensitize the media (see Chapter 13, page 246). These collaborative strategies have engaged NGOs, governments and the private sector in reforms aimed at portraying girls and women more positively and ensuring more diverse ethnic representation.

This third level of power can be the most difficult and contentious to deal with. Social values and beliefs are extremely sensitive and personal. In politics, ideology, more than other arenas of conflict, seems to be a battleground with limited compromises. We discuss this in detail in Chapter 15.

The chart on the next page examines the mechanisms of visible, hidden, and invisible power and the kinds of advocacy strategies that can be used to counter them.

Facilitator's Note

Throughout the Guide we present a variety of frameworks. We offer them with certain reservations. Frameworks help condense and synthesize complex information and thus provide people with a quick overview of ideas and relationships. Yet, they also can lead to oversimplification and lose the dynamism and complexities they are trying to represent. In grappling with the questions they raise, you may want to restructure them so they better reflect your circumstances.

UNDERSTANDING POLITICS

Power, Political Participation, and Social Change			
MECHANISMS AND	**VISIBLE POWER**	**HIDDEN POWER**	**INVISIBLE POWER**
MECHANISMS: Different expressions and forms of power Participation in public decision making seems relatively straightforward on the surface. It appears to be determined by the political context, clout, resources, and expertise of different political actors. Yet invisible and hidden mechanisms of power shape the effectiveness of citizen participation. These mechanisms can lead to powerlessness, conflict, marginalization, and resistance. Different strategies are required to counter these mechanisms so that political participation can be more inclusive and so people can exercise their rights and responsibilities as citizens. (See below.)	*Formal institutions, officials and instruments:* Visible mechanisms of power shape the formal ground rules of society. *Formal institutions and officials:* President, Prime Minister, legislature, courts, ministries, police, military, etc. United Nations, IMF, World Bank; Private sector: industry, multinational corporations, chamber of commerce, businesses, etc. *Instruments:* Policies, laws, constitutions, budgets, regulations, conventions, implementing mechanisms etc. *Forms of discrimination:* biased laws/policies (for example health care policies that do not address women's reproductive needs); closed and unrepresentative decisionmaking structures (parliaments, courts, etc.)	*Exclusion and delegitimization:* Certain groups (and their issues) excluded from decisionmaking by society's and politic's unwritten rules, practices, and institutions. The media does not often consider these groups' issues to be mainstream or newsworthy. They and their grievances are made invisible by intimidation, misinformation, and co-optation. Leaders are labeled trouble-makers or unrepresentative; issues such as domestic violence are relegated to the private realm of the family and therefore not subject to public action. Crucial information is concealed or inaccessible.	*Socialization and control of information:* Processes, practices, cultural norms, and customs shape people's understanding of their needs, roles, possibilities, and actions in ways that deter effective action for change. Among marginal groups, socialization internalizes feelings of subordination, apathy, self-blame, powerlessness, unworthiness, hostility, anger, etc.
STRATEGIES: Principal advocacy strategies to counter powerlessness and exclusion Social justice advocacy requires comprehensive action strategies that address the different forms of visible, hidden, and invisible power by tapping alternative sources of power (power with, within, and to). (The arrows reflect the interactive relationships between the different forms of power and the different types of strategies.)	- Lobbying and monitoring - Negotiation and litigation - Public education and media - Policy research, proposals - Shadow reports - Marches and demonstrations - Voting and running for office - Modelling innovations - Collaboration - Etc.	- Building active constituencies around common concerns - Strengthening organizations, coalitions, movements, and accountable leaders - Mobilizing around shared agendas; demonstrating clout through direct action - Participatory research and dissemination of information that legitimizes the issues of excluded groups	- Education for confidence, citizenship, collaboration, political awareness, political analysis, and using alternative media - Sharing stories, speaking out and connecting with others, affirming resistance, linking concrete daily problems to rights - Investigation, action research, and dissemination of concealed information

More Thoughts on the Public and Private Angles of Political Power

Gender theory adds another perspective for understanding different levels and expressions of power which are applicable to women as well as men. It critiques the focus on *visible* power as the place where all politics takes shape. Practitioners and scholars familiar with the challenges of women's empowerment explain that political power takes shape in three interacting levels of a woman's life. Change will not occur, they argue, unless political strategies look at and address power in the public, private, and intimate realms.

The **public realm of power** refers to the *visible* face of power as it affects women and men in their jobs, employment, public life, legal rights, etc.

The **private realm of power** refers to relationships and roles in families, among friends, sexual partnerships, marriage, etc.

The **intimate realm of power** has to do with one's sense of self, personal confidence, psychology, and relationship to body and health.

For an individual woman, the experience of power and powerlessness will be different, based on race, class, or age, and may even be contradictory in different realms of her life. For example, a woman politician who appears confident in public may accept a subordinate role in her family; she may even survive abuse in her private relationships while keeping up

UNDERSTANDING POLITICS

When Women Exercise Power

"Experience shows that, generally, whenever and wherever women have entered politics and political institutions, one of two things happened:

- they either get co-opted and/or corrupted by the dominant political culture (which also often means distancing themselves from the needs and issues of the mass of women); or,

- if they are unwilling to play by the rules of the game, they are rendered ineffective and marginalized.

"Either way, neither was the cause of women advanced, nor was the nature of politics itself challenged or altered in any meaningful way. There are three main reasons for this, in my view.

- Lack of a critical mass of women in political institutions.

- Lack of linkages between women in politics and women's movements.

- Women's experience of power in the private and public sphere.

"Since women have been denied power in the public domain for millennia, their only experience in the exercise of power is, by and large, in the familial or private sphere. Even in the private domain, however, most women have had to exercise power indirectly, through their influence on the key men of the household. Thus women have been conditioned to uphold male power, and to seek power through their influence on men. They have little experience of joining together with men — much less with other women — in the pursuit of wider social projects, or of using power for a different end.

"Conversely, women's only model for the exercise of power in the public sphere is that created by the patriarchal dominant class and caste. The culture of power which they have witnessed has been that of power over, not power on behalf of or for a larger social good. The model of political power has come to mean amassing wealth and influence for self, community, and party, the dispensing of patronage, and the promotion of narrow interests."

Srilatha Batliwala, *Political Representation and the Women's Movement*, Lecture given in Hyderabad, India, May 1997, under the auspices of the Women and Society Forum of ASMITA.

---

with the demands and image of her public duties. Throughout the world, it is common for a woman to face the same work demands as her male partner, but be primarily or solely responsible for the maintenance of the home and children. The challenge of AIDS prevention further illustrates some of the contradictions that occur with regard to relations of power in the intimate realm. Many seemingly educated, empowered women and men around the world fail to take measures to protect themselves against the disease despite the knowledge and resources to do so.

Acknowledging these layers and contradictions can be helpful in understanding the tensions generated by empowerment for many women. Political change and advocacy strategies that focus solely on the public realm may overlook some critical challenges facing women who are leaders, active citizens, and public officials when they return to their homes and families. It is from this perspective that women activists argue that good citizenship for women and for men is not solely about public behavior.

The chart below[8] can be used to explore how the three different layers interact with factors of exclusion and discrimination (see the Annex, page 337) to determine the obstacles and opportunities for empowerment.

Analyzing and Navigating the Many Levels of Power

What does this way of classifying power mean for advocacy planning and action? Above all, it means that analysis has to explore many angles and strategies to incorporate activities that address all of the levels of power affecting change. A further challenge is that all levels or forms of power are usually operating simultaneously at any given moment. Frequently, advocacy efforts focus on the more visible aspects of power, but overlook others. This limits their long-term impact.

Most groups are not able to undertake all of the necessary activities to maneuver power dynamics. Different groups bring different strengths and resources to advocacy. Only by building their *power with* others can they create more holistic and effective strategies.

Parts Two and Three of this Guide focus in detail on strategies that deal with all levels of power. In Chapter 10, we discuss a framework for comprehensive advocacy planning that attempts to direct planning to all levels and realms of power. In the next chapter we discuss learning approaches geared to citizen empowerment that draw on the three views of

Relationship among the Three Arenas of Power						
	GENDER	**CLASS**	**RACE / ETHNICITY**	**SEXUAL ORIENTATION**	**RELIGION**	**ETC.**
Intimate - self esteem - self image						
Private - partner - family - children						
Public - local - regional - international						

power discussed earlier.

What Is Empowerment?

How can advocacy address the negative forms and results of *power over*? As the previous discussion emphasizes, policy change alone is insufficient for this many-leveled task.

Social justice advocates want their strategies to empower people to stand up for their rights, and help create just, healthy societies. In this way, empowerment is both a strategy and a goal of citizen-centered advocacy. However, like many concepts related to social change, empowerment is a debated topic. Despite the term's popularity, it has multiple and some-times misleading meanings.

Most of the definitions come from experiences of working with women and poor communities to promote participatory development. These definitions have some common features that are useful for advocacy work. They combine the goals of building confidence with those of eliminating barriers that underpin exclusion and powerlessness.

Save the Children defines (the end result of) empowerment as, "people can make choices and take actions on their own behalf with self-confidence, from a position of economic, political and social strength."[9]

Alternatively, Srilatha Batliwala describes the process:

> "The term empowerment refers to a range of activities from individual self-assertion to collective resistance, protest and mobilization that challenge basic power relations. For individuals and groups where class, caste, ethnicity and gender determine their access to resources and power, their empowerment begins when they not only recognize the systemic forces that oppress them, but act to change existing power relationships. Empow-erment, therefore, is a process aimed at changing the nature and direction of systemic forces that marginalize women and other disadvantaged sectors in a given context."[10]

Asian activists define women's empowerment as "the process and the result of the process" of:

- challenging the ideology of male domina-tion and women's subordination;

- enabling women to gain equal access to and control over resources (material, human, intellectual, financial);

- transforming the systems, institutions (family, education, religion, media, etc.), and structures (legal, political, economic, social) through which the ideology and practice of subordination is reinforced and reproduced.[11]

"Institutional change is often easier than at the personal level . . . most people resist changes to their personal space even when it involves extending their horizons. It is not easy for people to reach . . . critical consciousness in their personal lives due to an intrinsic need to belong. In Africa or less developed countries, insurance from a sense of belonging takes over social welfare functions of the state, therefore imposing major barriers on people's consistency in political consciousness. Particularly for marginalised groups such as women, what one does within an institutional setting is often different from the compromises made in private lives in order to belong. This should not be labelled as inconsistency because the ability to recognise power and its uses and to act within one's context for self-preservation is actually 'strength'."

Hope Chigudu, Chair, Global Fund for Women, personal correspondence, 2001

On the following page, we present two empowerment frameworks that illustrate graphically the different stages and elements of the process. The *Political Empowerment Process* on the top of the page was developed for human rights activists. It looks at some of the dimensions and ingredients of empowerment that contribute to new forms of political power built through citizen action. Following the arrows upward, that chart shows that individuals develop a political and collective awareness by analyzing and reflecting on their own lives and working on problems with others.

Below it, the *Women's Empowerment Framework* was designed to assist development practitioners to understand and address the overlapping problems of poverty and gender inequality. In this framework, the upward movement goes from addressing basic needs to rights under the categories of participation and control. Both frameworks can be used to stimulate discussion about the meaning, process, and challenges of empowerment for citizen-centered advocacy.

The Conflicts and Risks of Empowerment

Empowerment is a process that involves individual discovery and change. Most discussions of empowerment speak about it as a gradual forward-moving process. However, it is far from linear, predictable, or easy. Empowerment is really more like a dance that takes two steps forward and three steps back before moving slowly in a spiral around the floor.

For both men and women, it involves questioning their roles and the world around them. This questioning can cause friends, family, and the larger community discomfort and even anger. It is these tensions that make women appear to have contradictory levels of empowerment in public and at home (see quote on previous page), and may cause some people to withdraw from the process, even if it promises to benefit them in the long-term. This is a central challenge in developing new leadership, especially at the grassroots level. At another level, political change efforts, especially involving group rights and social beliefs, like women's organizing, can generate backlash and be dangerous to those involved. Sometimes a way to prevent backlash when working with women is to include men in the process so they do not feel threatened. We discuss other ways of dealing with conflicts caused by change in other chapters throughout the Guide and in more detail in Chapter 16.

The Political Empowerment Process

Dimensions	Ingredients

Political Power
- ← Ethical, accountable political leaders
- ← Government and public recognition of citizens' rights and knowledge
- ← Citizen involvement in monitoring change
- ← Strong citizen organizations consulted regularly by government
- ← Legal, policy, and state institutional reform

↑

Empowerment
- ← Reflection on actions
- ← Developing new leaders
- ← Building citizens' groups
- ← Lobbying
- ← Planning and implementing strategies
- ← Organizing and communicating information about rights, laws, and problems
- ← Gaining skills

↑
↑
↑

Collective Consciousness
- ← Analysis of common problems
- ← Questioning why things are the way they are
- ← Self-reflection
- ← Dialogue with others

↑

Individual Consciousness

Adapted from Margaret Schuler, Empowerment and the Law: Strategies of Third World Women, OEF International, 1986.

The Women's Empowerment Framework

Levels of Empowerment	Description
Control	Women and men have equal control over production and the distribution of benefits
↑	
Participation	Women and men participate equally in decision-making in all programs and policies
↑	
Conscientization	Women and men believe that gender roles can be changed and equity is possible
↑	
Access	Women gain access to resources such as land, labor, credit, training, public services, legal rights on an equal basis with men
↑	
Welfare	Women's and men's material needs, such as food, income, and health care, are met

Developed by Sarah Hlupekile Longwe, Gender Specialist, Zambia.

The Chaz! *(Aha!)* Framework

The Chaz! framework below illustrates the spiraling, contradictory process of empowerment. This Framework for Women's Empowerment and Political Consciousness was created by women leaders in a Central American workshop on advocacy. [12] While developed from the experience of women's organizing, it offers important insights for advocacy with any marginalized group. The chart was generated in response to the question: *What is political consciousness and how do you promote it?*

The framework begins in the upper left with the **Unending Process** of change and empowerment. The two circles represent the **self** (I) and **the collective** (we). As the two circles con-nect, both gain power. This is represented by the outward moving edges of the circle. The **male symbols** around the edges of the circles represent the boundaries of patriarchy that women's empowerment comes up against.

Moving clockwise, the next area of the framework describes the process of "conscientization." It begins with **information** that stimulates **questions** and anger as a woman recognizes injustice and powerlessness. As she interacts with others, she discovers common predicaments, and begins to doubt that she is to blame for her situation. Her questioning is deepened by exploring ideas like **discrimination, equality, equity,** and **rights.** These ideas help her label her constraints and legitimize her desire for change.

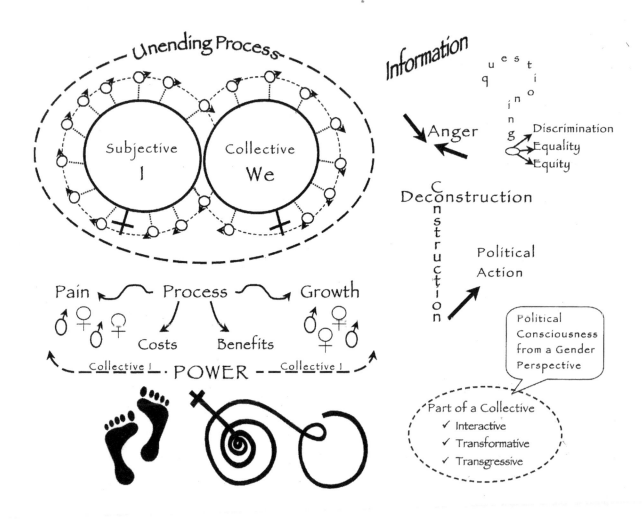

Moving to the bottom right, a woman **deconstructs** (breaks apart) and reconstructs her worldview and sense of self by questioning, labeling, and feeling anger. This is the starting point for **political action** to change the aspects of her life that limit her. Political consciousness is **interactive** (developed in relation with others), **transformative,** and **transgressive** (it pushes boundaries).

Finally, at the bottom left we see the conflicts of **empowerment**. The process involves **growth** and **pain**, **costs** and **benefits**. The **spiraling circle** with the **footprints** at the side illustrates the entire empowerment process. The questioning, analysis, and anger lead in a circling inward path until difficult decisions cause a woman to awaken to a new awareness (aha!) and **leap** forward to land on her feet ready to begin the process again. In some cases, the loss and pain can be soothed by links and solidarity with others. However, sometimes the conflict is so extreme as to cause a woman to retreat, and fear or oppose change.

Measuring Empowerment

Measuring empowerment is an important, if extremely difficult, element of monitoring and evaluating citizen-centered advocacy. It is one of those qualitative things that is hard to put your finger on, but you usually know it when you see it. Gender and development practitioners suggest the following indicators as possible measures:

- freedom of mobility

- involvement in major household decisions

- relative freedom from family control

- political and legal awareness

- involvement in community and political activities

- economic security

- awareness of choices

- awareness of own health

- participation in groups

- desire for information and new experiences

The meaning of empowerment varies according to context and who is doing the measuring. However, there is agreement that monitoring and evaluation processes that contribute to (rather than detract from) empowerment must be participatory. In a participatory research project on health, rural Mexican women, with the assistance of an outside facilitator, developed a set of empowerment indicators to assess their own personal change over time. The participatory process was, in itself, a learning and empowering activity for the women involved.[13]

The following chart includes a selection and summary of the indicators they developed. The numbers indicate a progression from least empowered (#1) to most empowered (highest number on the list).

In the next chapter, we deepen the discussion of empowerment in advocacy with a focus on political consciousness.

Sample Empowerment Indicators for Women's Health Issues

Level of Schooling	Other Education	Social Participation	Salaried Work	Domestic Work
1. Did not go to school 2. Illiterate 3. Incomplete elementary education 4. Elementary 5. High school 6. Preparatory school 7. Bachelor's 8. Master's 9. Doctorate	1. No workshop 2. A few workshops or courses 3. Several workshops 4. "Multiplier" or facilitator of workshops 5. Advisor, defines program strategies	1. None 2. Beneficiary 3. Active participation 4. Has a formal position 5. Position and recognition 6. Management 7. Leadership	1. Does not work 2. Works, economically dependent 3. Works, spends money on herself, still doesn't earn enough to be economically independent 4. Works, values her contribution for the family 5. Works, values her contribution for herself 6. Entrepreneur, owns property	1. Takes care of more than five people, they do not help 2. Three or more dependents, they do not help 3. Does the domestic work alone 4. Only women help her 5. "Others help" 6. Her partner shares the family responsibilities

Availability of Services	Living Space	Contraception	Physical / Emotional Violence	Sexual Violence
1. Without water 2. With water, light 3. And with pavement 4. With sufficient food 5. With public security 6. With public transportation 7. With health and educational services	1. Lives with other relatives 2. Lives with more than five people 3. Lives with more than two people per room 4. Lives with two or one person per room 5. Has her own home	1. Lets others make decisions 2. Disagree, couple doesn't use anything 3. Disagreement, they use natural methods 4. Disagreement, she uses but not openly 5. They use, others disapprove (mother-in-law, priest, etc.) 6. Use condoms, agree	1. She is abused, cries, holds it in 2. She takes it out on the children 3. Occasional violence, she doesn't do anything 4. She is abused (hits, silence, anger) 5. She was abused, separated, turned in 6. She is not abused, discusses things to reach agreement 7. Good relationship, emotional support	1. He violently forces her if she refuses to have sexual relations 2. There is frequent sexual violence 3. Sometimes there is sexual violence 4. There is not sexual violence 5. She does not allow forced sexual relations 6. There is no sexual violence, there is pleasure

NOTES

[1] Quoted from "Harnessing the Creative Energies of Citizens", by Ezra Mbogori and Hope Chigudu, in the African Regional Synthesis for the Civil Society in the New Millenium Project of the Commonwealth Foundation, London.

[2] The Grassroots Policy Project has developed a set of excellent materials that help groups understand and analyze power. See their website at www.grassrootspolicy.org.

[3] Common responses to the question "What is power?" from dozens of workshops with development workers, rights activists, professors and local government in Africa, Asia, Latin America, Eastern Europe, and Russia.

[4] Carolyn Shronk-Shenk, *Mediation and Facilitation Training Manual.* Akron, PA: Mennonite Conciliation Service, 2000.

[5] See John Gaventa (1980), Grassroots Policy Project (2001), Steven Lukes (1974), Naila Kabeer (1994).

[6] Deepa Narayan, *Can Anyone Hear Us?*, (Voices of the Poor series) World Bank, 2000

[7] Also see Grassroots Policy Project, ibid.

[8] Malona de Montis, Santa Fe Workshop, 1999

[9] From *Empowerment Through People, Programs and Institutions: A Report of the Facets Phase III Workshop.* Save the Children, 1998.

[10] Srilatha Batliwala, "The Meaning of Women's Empowerment: New Concepts from Action" in *Population Policies Revisited,* Sen, Chen, Germain, Harvard University Press, 1994.

[11] Srilatha Batliwala, 1994, op.cit., Chapter 1.

[12] GWIP/Cenzontle Advocacy TOT workshop held in Nicaragua in June 1998.

[13] The chart was developed by Gloria Sayavedra and Mayela Garcia, Red de Mujeres Pro Derechos de Educación y Salud. It is the product of research funded by the MacArthur Foundation and was constructed based on the life stories of 40 women from 10 states of Mexico.

4 Constructing Empowering Strategies

> "Justice and power must be brought together, so that whatever is just may be powerful, and whatever is powerful may be just."
>
> Pascal

Citizen education and empowerment is a central element of advocacy. If advocacy strategies aim to empower people to be "makers and shapers," then their participation in choosing issues and planning strategies is an important first step for advocacy. *How* education is carried out determines *what* is learned. For this reason, participatory methodologies are among the main building blocks for the approach proposed in the Guide.

Building people's participation is also good politics in the sense that it lends the power of numbers to a cause. It is sometimes also referred to as **constituency-building**.

This chapter is designed to help you construct empowering learning and organizing processes for your advocacy. It begins with a discussion of constituency-building and political consciousness. We then look at how participatory learning methods strengthen citizen and rights education programs. We discuss gender as a useful way of recognizing and integrating differences in learning and organizing.

Citizen empowerment—a process of learning and action that strengthens people's self-esteem, analytical and organizing skills, and critical consciousness so they can gain a sense of their rights and join together to develop more democratic societies.

Constituency—a group of people or a community who have a common concern and whose interests are advanced by organizing and engaging in advocacy to solve that problem.

Why Is Constituency-Building Critical for Advocacy?

Constituency-building refers to the activities aimed at strengthening the involvement of those most affected by an issue in the design and leadership of advocacy. Effective constituency-building enhances the organization and political voice of people, and lends legitimacy and leverage to change efforts.

In recent years, there has been growing interest among donors and international NGOs in building constituencies for advocacy. However, by focusing on constituencies solely for the purpose of legitimizing and bolstering policy claims without concern for the longer-term questions of power and citizenship, some of these efforts have been criticized as "instrumentalist" and worse, have alienated communities otherwise interested in supporting change. These negative cases have shown that people may distrust anyone, not just political parties or politicians, who presumes to speak on their behalf.

A lot of advocacy support has concentrated on helping NGOs maneuver in the policymaking arena. But there has been less effort aimed at building the active involvement of the people who are meant to benefit from policy change. Not enough NGOs can say they represent anyone but themselves (although the principles they stand for may be universal). Usually the communities that NGOs serve are not involved in setting their advocacy agenda. Although the

NGOs may have policy successes, without grassroots participation, short-term policy gains are easily lost.

What Do We Mean by "Constituent"?

The word "constituent" comes from the electoral and legislative process. It usually refers to the people in a given geographic area who are represented by an elected official regardless of whether or not they voted for that person or party. Ideally, what their constituents want and need should be high on the agenda of legislators. This rarely occurs so neatly in practice. Public office is usually subject to competing demands that are more powerful than constituents. But constituents retain the ultimate power of voting their representatives out of office if fair elections are held regularly.

For example, in advocacy efforts to protect Brazilian rainforests, the constituents are, first, the Indian communities whose survival is threatened by cattle ranching, industry, and population growth. Second, they are the people around the world who understand the ecological importance of rainforests and do not want

In advocacy, the concept of "constituent" includes:

- people who have a direct stake in an advocacy solution because they are directly affected by the problem, and will benefit from the strategy (*primary constituents*);
- people who care deeply about the problem although they may not experience it personally, and are willing to make their voices heard (*secondary constituents*).

to endanger the rich variety of species nor the lives of the indigenous communities. The Indians and the organizations that work with them are the frontline of advocacy. But the advocacy depends on people around the world who express their support through votes, letters to the media and legislators, and funding.

How Constituency-Building Changes Strategies

The rationale for top-down, as opposed to constituency-building approaches, comes partly from the belief that quick results justify the means and partly from the belief that

The Constituency-Building Challenges of Environmental Advocacy in Chad

Environmental advocacy groups operating in Washington, D.C. and Europe found themselves in conflict with communities in Chad who were meant to benefit from their efforts. The international advocates were trying to halt construction of a pipeline that would have caused serious environmental destruction. "When we came in, we came in too forcefully, too directly," said a European activist. "We were saying, 'Stop the pipeline in the name of the people.' The people were saying, 'Maybe we can have a better life. We want the pipeline.' So we had to step back and rethink our approach." In the end, activists and the local constituents had to find a compromise between environmental protection and the potential economic development that the pipeline might generate. As one local human rights advocate explained, "We had to look for ways to make the project better, not kill it." The demands that the NGOs came up with included a 2-year moratorium on any decision by the World Bank, an end to corruption, an environmental impact study, better compensation for peasants who would lose land or trees, and the creation of monitoring mechanisms.

Based on the Washington Post story, "Watchdog Groups Rein in Government in Chap Oil Deal", Douglas Farah and David B. Ottaway, January 4, 2001.

"experts" should solve problems and deal with the policy world. Beyond being consulted about their grievances or mobilized in support of a policy, ordinary citizens are not seen as having much of a role to play.

In contrast, a citizen-centered or constituency approach transforms the role of "beneficiary" from a passive recipient to an active agent of change. Organizations around the globe that are more citizen-centered are changing the way they operate and enabling "beneficiaries" to co-direct their own development. Some programs combine service delivery with community organizing in an effort to meet community needs while empowering people to get at the root causes of problems. For example, the Young Women's Christian Association (YWCA) in many countries has become involved in legal rights organizing while also conducting self-help courses and other support services to provide poor women with better opportunities.

We're all concerned about how land is being used and who owns it. How can we work together to address the root causes of this problem?

The chart on the next page illustrates some of the ways that citizen-focused advocacy differs from the traditional development approach.

Constituency-building strategies vary depending on how constituents are affected by the advocacy issue and their relationship with the lead organization. Identifying your constituencies may not be simple. Many advocacy organizations are intermediaries whose direct clients may not be the constituents. We discuss these different relationships in Chapters 6 and 8.

Rescuing vs. Organizing

Shifting the traditional relationship of NGOs as rescuers to organizers and partners of marginalized groups is not easy. Rescuing is simpler because the rescuer controls the process. Organizing, in contrast, means letting go of some of that power, letting the people we want to rescue decide what to do, and helping them do it. Some NGO staff say that the poor communities they work with do not seem interested in change.

Why is it that people just don't seem to care?...they wait for us to come and help them but never initiate on their own.

Too often, NGOs mistake resistance or a lack of power for apathy.

What Is Political Consciousness?

Engaging marginalized communities in advocacy is not easy. Poverty, discrimination, and adversity can breed paralysis and resignation. It can also generate frustration and anger that can foster hostility and hopelessness. This is reinforced by the tendency of society to "blame the victim" and the "victim" to internalize social prejudices. For example, many landless peasants believe they are to blame for being poor because they are ignorant. Other people see them as undisciplined and lazy. In reality, peasants often work long hours for extremely

Contrasting Views of Development and Social Change

Traditional development sees . . .		Citizen-centered advocacy sees . . .
Problems	➝	**Issues**
Basic needs	➝	Basic rights
Symptoms	➝	Systemic causes
Poverty and welfare	➝	Unequal distribution of power and resources
Projects	➝	Strategies and actions
Static plans, definable results	➝	Continuous planning and analysis
Mission	➝	Vision for political change
Beneficiaries and clients	➝	Citizens, constituents, and allies
Education and information	➝	Consciousness raising and organizing
Consultation and partnership	➝	Joint decisionmaking, local leadership, complementary roles, alliances
Outputs	➝	Political and social change to benefit marginalized
Satisfaction of needs	➝	Transformation of power relations

low wages. Similarly, in many countries, women do not seek legal redress when raped because they are ashamed. Society and the legal system reinforce this shame by insisting, "She must have asked for it." What appears to be acquiescence may be the only option that people have to resist the psychological consequences of subordination. What does it take to help people recognize, understand, and act to address the injustice in their own lives? As Chapter 2 emphasizes, many different competencies are needed. But a core competency has to do with political consciousness.

Effective organizers think politically. They try to be informed about the world around them,

> **Political consciousness**—a way of seeing, caring about, and acting in the world that is guided by an understanding of fairness and justice and an awareness of power and inequity in social, political, and economic systems, relations, and values.

and continually question why things happen. Political thinking begins with political consciousness. These are some of the many basic elements of political consciousness:

1. knowledge about how the political and economic systems function;

2. a sense of history and current events;

3. a lens for analyzing why and how imbalances of power operate;

4. concern about how these things destroy human potential and dignity;

5. a sense of rights, responsibilities, and solidarity with excluded groups.

Political consciousness is both a *tool* and an *objective* of social justice advocacy. As a tool, political consciousness motivates critical analysis of political dynamics on many levels. As an objective, developing political consciousness provides the basis for the sustained and informed citizen participation necessary to hold powerful interests accountable.

UNDERSTANDING POLITICS

Becoming politically aware can help unravel the self-doubt fostered by subordination and discrimination, and enable people to recognize their individual power and link with others to address common problems.

Building Political Consciousness: Drawing on the Theory and Practice of Popular Education

Many people have contributed to the notion of political consciousness. The Brazilian educator Paulo Freire has had an enormous influence on our understanding of how the learning process can build consciousness for social change. Freire taught literacy to Brazilian peasants and workers at a time of political repression. Out of this experience, he developed methods for nurturing critical awareness as a first step in enabling the poor to fight for their rights. His approach became known as popular education.

Freire's influence is seen in many participatory methodologies for learning, evaluation, and planning. Educators and organizers have revised popular education theory and practice to include other axes of disadvantage besides poverty and class. They have also made adjustments for historical and contextual differences.

Levels of Consciousness

Freire talked about four different stages of awareness. The description on the next page of his analysis is borrowed from *Helping Health Workers Learn*, which applied popular education methodologies to the problems of healthcare. While the categories are simple, the analysis acknowledges that the human psyche never fits neatly into boxes. The description helps us look at the different dimensions of consciousness that shape people's view of what is possible in their lives.

Freire and Legal Rights Education

"The basic premise of Freire is that the ignorance and powerlessness of the poor and by implication, women, are rooted in social structures that determine the unequal exercise of power in society. The remedy is social transformation, for which education is a prerequisite — an education that enables people to reflect on themselves and their roles in both the old and new societies and to develop the capacity to participate rationally, critically, and democratically in public life. . . . Since human beings are essentially creative beings, significant change will come from their own transforming action. The role of educator in this process is to engage in a 'dialogical praxis' with the participants, recognizing that they are equally knowledgeable, if not more so, about their own situation. Implicit in this method is a critique of traditional educational approaches, particularly extension training, which assume that the educator possesses the knowledge needed by the 'learners' and that this knowledge can be imparted to them.

". . .Empowering strategies assume that the grassroots have the capacity to understand the issues, develop the skills to articulate alternatives, and mobilize its resources to press for effective change. . . . Whether they begin with legislative change or advocacy, or another focus, they always include an educational component which progressively moves [people] from learning about rights and injustice toward an understanding of the causes of their inferior status, to the articulation of alternatives, and the development of organizing and political skills . . ."

Schuler, Margaret. "An Approach to Women, Law, and Development: Conceptualizing and Exploring Issues and Strategies" in *Empowerment and the Law: Strategies of Third World Women*, OEF International, 1986, p.33–34.

1. Magic Awareness

At this stage, people explain the events and forces that shape their lives in terms of myths, magic, or powers beyond their understanding and control. They tend to be fatalistic, passively accepting whatever happens to them as fate or "God's will." Usually they blame no one for the hardships and abuses they suffer. They endure these as facts of life about which they cannot (and should not) do anything. Although their problems are great — poor health, poverty, lack of work, etc. — they commonly deny them. They are exploited, but are at the same time dependent upon those with authority or power, whom they fear and try to please. They conform to the image of themselves given to them by those on top. They consider themselves inferior, unable to master the skills and ideas of persons they believe are 'better' than themselves.

2. Naive Awareness

A person who is naive has incomplete understanding. Persons at the naive stage of awareness no longer passively accept the hardships of being "on the bottom." Rather, they try to adapt so as to make the best of the situation in which they find themselves. However, they continue to accept the values, rules, and social order defined by those on top (authorities, big landholders, etc.). In fact, they try to imitate those on top as much as possible. For example, they may adopt the clothing, hair styles, and language of outsiders, or choose to bottle feed rather than breast feed their babies. At the same time, they tend to reject or look down upon their own people's customs and beliefs. Like those on top, they blame the hardships of the poor on their ignorance and "lack of ambition." They make no attempt to critically examine or change the social order.

3. Critical Awareness

As persons begin to develop critical awareness, they look more carefully at the causes of poverty and other human problems. They try to explain things more through observation and reason than through myth or magic. They start to question the values, rules, and expectations passed down by those in control. They discover that not individuals, but the social system itself, is responsible for inequality, injustice, and suffering. They find that it is set up to favor the few at the expense of the many, yet they see that those in power are in some ways also weak, and are also 'dehumanized' by the system. Critically aware persons come to realize that only by changing the norms and procedures of organized society can the most serious ills of both the rich and the poor be corrected.

As their awareness deepens, these persons also begin to feel better about themselves. They take new pride in their origins and traditions. Yet they are self-critical and flexible. They do not reject either the old or the new, but try to preserve from each what is of value. As their self-confidence grows, they begin to work with others to change what is unhealthy in the social system. Their observations and critical reasoning lead them to positive action.

In addition to the three stages just discussed, Freire describes another stage, which he calls "fanatic awareness." This is a step beyond naive awareness, but off the main track toward the development of critical awareness.

4. Fanatic Awareness

Fanatic means extreme beyond reason. A fanatically aware person (or group of persons) rejects completely those in power and everything they represent, without trying to separate the good from the bad. At the same time, he (sic) often returns to the traditional customs, dress, and beliefs, but in an exaggerated form. Whereas the outlook of persons with critical awareness is mostly positive, that of fanatics is often destructive. Their opinions tend to be rigid, not flexible. Their actions seem to result more from hatred than from understanding. Rather than learning and communicating with others as equals, they tend to repeat the standard radical doctrines of their popular, yet powerful, leaders.

Persons at a fanatic level of awareness are not self-critical, independent thinkers as are those with critical awareness. They are captive to the ideas of their power-hungry leaders. In some ways, they are still servants and products of the social system against which they rebel. If and when they succeed in overthrowing the social order, the new system they set up may in some ways be as rigid and unjust as the old system it replaces.

In reality, of course, no one is wholly at one stage or another. Many of us are fatalistic about some things, naive about others, critically aware about others, and at times a bit fanatic.

But naming the stages helps us understand how power shapes our vision about our place in the world, the causes of our problems, and our ability to change them.

Text and illustrations from Werner, David and Bill Bower, *Helping Health Workers Learn*, The Hesperian Foundation, California, 1982.

Fostering Political Consciousness

A group of Latin American women's rights activists described political consciousness and how to stimulate it through the process framework they developed below.

"A politically conscious woman has an internalized commitment that inspires her to pursue change in all aspects of her life from her day-to-day existence to her political engagement; her consciousness compels her to try to be consistent in her values and beliefs in all areas of life."

"The steps in the process are not linear, but rather a recurring, interactive, and iterative process filled with conflict and difficulty as well as growth and change."

The framework includes four overlapping expressions of consciousness—passive, questioning, analytical, and critical. The chart below describes how a person moves to the different levels of consciousness.

Levels of Consciousness		
From Passive to Questioning Consciousness	**From Questioning to Analytical Consciousness**	**From Analytical to Active Critical Consciousness**
- You assume gender roles and duties are "natural" - You are not familiar with other perspectives or ways to live your life. If you are, you find them threatening and you criticize them - You begin to have access to information and experiences different from what is familiar - You begin to question aspects of your life and to search for self-esteem and answers to your problems	- You begin to name and analyze situations that you have lived - You begin to confront and place blame; you feel angry - You begin to discover how a woman's identity is a social, cultural, economic and political construction; not a predetermined role incapable of change - You reaffirm your self-worth and potential for change	- You begin to develop your critical analysis - You take political action - You face the interpersonal and social conflict that your changes generate - You create spaces to negotiate fundamental areas of life, like work (home and job), family, your sexuality and related changes

From the GWIP/CENZONTLE-Central America Advocacy Training of Trainers Workshop, held in June 1998.

Features of Participatory Learning

There are different empowering learning approaches that help people to ask questions, discover new truths, and practice solving real life problems. Freire spoke about popular education as a participatory process of action-reflection-action. While popular education has spawned a myriad of participatory learning methods, the basic process always involves problem identification, analysis, and the pursuit of solutions through dialogue, self-awareness, and organizing.

Some of the features and assumptions of participatory learning methodologies are described below.

The Political Nature of Education

No education is neutral. *How* one learns is linked to *what* is learned. Education can teach people how to conform or it can encourage independent thinking and creative change. A learning process that validates what learners know and challenges them to examine their ideas more deeply, can empower them to think independently, seek information, and act on their knowledge.

Relevance

People absorb and act on information that is directly related to their daily lives. Relevance is vital to motivation.

Linked to Problem-Solving

Adults often learn faster when the information they gain addresses the problems they face directly.

Dialogue and Mutual Learning

Dialogue can ensure that the learner's concerns are the focus of the educational process. By promoting a more equal educator/learner relationship, dialogue involves joint discovery and helps learners to gain confidence in their own ability.

Recognizes Differences among People While Seeking Common Ground

The same power imbalances that generate conflict in society are present in groups brought together to learn, plan, and act. Naming these differences and adjusting for power dynamics is a vital starting point for empowerment. The approach contrasts with the tendency to see marginalized groups as homogenous, and to ignore the power differences

---

Studies show that adults remember:
- 20% of what they hear
- 40% of what they hear and see
- 80% of what they discover for themselves

In any education process, there are four important ingredients:
1. the learner
2. the facilitator
3. the content (the topic)
4. the process (how the content is learned)

---

between educators/organizers and "people from the community."

Problem-posing and Open-ended Learning

One of the facilitator's roles is to ask questions that assist learners to examine their own situation and deepen their understanding of the problems they face. The facilitator also introduces new ideas and information to supplement and broaden the analysis.

An Iterative Process without Predictable Steps and Outcomes

Although participatory learning methods use a certain set of techniques, the process is not linear. Because the facilitator cannot anticipate how learners will think and interact, he or she must listen and engage in the process. There are no mechanical formulas for developing an empowering learning process.

Moves from the Concrete to the Abstract and Back

Traditional education, especially at higher levels, usually begins with theory and then tests the theory against reality. This is why some highly educated NGO leaders may be uncomfortable beginning analysis with a concrete description of a problem (e.g., women's health is poor due to too many children and inadequate nutrition) rather than an abstract explanation (e.g., reproductive health needs). When trainers start with a theoretical explanation, they can derail the empowering effect of analyzing and discovering things for oneself.

The Dialogue Process

Some educators refer to problem-posing in participatory learning as the "but why?" method. The facilitator's questions encourage learners to ask why problems exist and so probe their social, economic, cultural, and political roots.

Stimulating discussion with adults who are not used to speaking up in public can be difficult. Even people who are more comfortable speaking publicly may not have much experience with critical questioning. The problems people face may be so threatening that they find it impossible to talk about them. For this reason, it may be helpful to begin discussion with relevant examples rather than asking directly about problems. Some distance allows people to get comfortable with a topic, and after discussion, they may be able to relate the analysis to their own lives more readily. For this purpose, participatory learning approaches often use "codes" to start the reflection process.

Problem-posing for analysis

Tips for Outside Facilitators

- Know the group you are working with. Prior research and observation will give you a sense of the problems facing this particular group. Use examples familiar to them to stimulate discussion.
- Remember that political analysis involves making connections between the past and the present as well as examining how privilege, power, and disadvantage mold real-life problems. (See Chapter 7 for ways of analyzing the context and moment.)
- Give people ample time to discuss a thorny topic with each other. A participant, rather than the facilitator, can sometimes more easily challenge misinformation or stereotypes.

Codes: Opening Discussion on Difficult Problems

A code can be a drawing, role play, game, skit, song, or story that presents a familiar problem in a concrete way. Usually, it does not provide answers, solutions, or morals. It simply depicts a situation that then becomes the focus of dialogue. The development of a suitable code requires observation and consultation. A code is especially helpful for dealing with personally sensitive problems such as rape, domestic violence, and AIDS.

Discussing Codes

The steps listed on the next page can help facilitators to guide dialogue around codes. They do not always follow a predictable sequence. Rather, the facilitator is responsible for guiding the spiraling process that takes people from the personal to the concrete to the abstract and back again.

Introductory Step: Self-Analysis and Affirmation

Dialogue requires confidence and trust-building. If participants have not developed a sense of group solidarity, encourage them to introduce themselves and get to know others. Questions like "What inspires me?" or "What are my hopes and fears for myself, my family, my community?" can help build trust and affirm the importance of everyone's contribution. The idea of beginning the dialogue process with personal analysis and affirmation was added to Freire's original process by activists working with women. This is an important step because values and self-esteem are central to the way we learn and interact with the world.

Step 1: Description of what you see happening in this picture (skit, code, etc.)

Using the code, encourage participants to carefully describe what is happening—something that may be a daily occurrence for them. Often more schooled people use shorthand terminology to describe situations, such as "gender violence" or "conflict." This step tries to avoid such abstraction by talking about concrete details.

Step 2: First Analysis—Why is this happening?

Begin to ask why people are doing what they are doing in the picture or skit. Keep asking why so that participants question as well as describe. Take advantage of the comfort people may feel in probing a situation that is not directly related to their own lives. It is useful for the facilitator to know enough about the issue to be able to formulate questions that help people analyze and that challenge myths, stereotypes, or misinformation.

Step 3: Real Life Comparison—Does this happen in your community? In your life?

Encourage people to give examples of how the situation in the code happens in their lives.

Step 4: Related Problems—What problems does this lead to?

This step looks at the consequences of the problem. Again in this step, the facilitator can provide additional information to supplement what participants contribute.

Step 5: Deeper Analysis—What are the root causes of these problems?

This step encourages learners to probe deeper into problems. Why does this happen? Once learners have had sufficient time, the facilitator can expand with additional information. The facilitator should also challenge simplistic explanations. In Chapters 7 and 8 we present some frameworks that may be useful for this step.

Step 6: Alternatives and Action—What can we do about it?

Linking education to action is essential for empowerment and effective advocacy. How will people use their new knowledge to change their situation? In this step, information about policies, law reform, budgets, and basic rights can assist people in defining what they can do. (See Chapters 10 and 11.) Step 6 can start by asking "What can we do to address this problem here in our community?" and "How can we bring about policy change to obtain more resources or better protection?". Local solutions, such as setting up community committees to monitor water use, are as important as solutions at the national or international levels. This step can serve as an initial brainstorming for a group that then can lead to further analysis and organizing. (See Chapters 13–15.)

Rights and Citizen Education Programs: Lessons Learned

A wide variety of rights and civic education programs exist worldwide with mixed impact. The low success rate of many of these programs often has to do with the programs' emphasis on information alone as the key to empowerment. Such programs typically provide pamphlets, flyers, and brief talks that simplify legal information or describe how the political process works. While information is essential for people to exercise their rights and participate effectively, it is *not only lack of information* that keeps women, poor people, and other marginalized groups from exercising their rights. Information alone will not make people engage and feel they have rights.

Some of the reasons that information-centered education programs fail to reach the people who need them most are:

- There is no clear link between the information about laws, rights, and government procedures and the concrete problems people face daily.
- Delivery of information that treats citizens as passive recipients can reinforce the perception that the law, rights, and government are too complicated and not intended for people like them.
- In places with low literacy levels, written materials reach very few people.

Making expert information simple is not enough. The more important task is making knowledge relevant to people's needs and experience so it can help them solve problems and improve their lives. Most people do not see the world through a legal or human rights lens. Making rights and citizenship real means starting with everyday problems and then making the connection to rights through analysis, confidence-building, and organizing.

Tips for developing effective citizenship and legal rights education programs include:

- **Know your audience.** Assess their needs, talents, knowledge, and interests before designing materials and workshops. Gain their "buy-in" by clarifying and negotiating goals and activities.
- **Be problem-centered, not information-centered.** For example, instead of starting by explaining laws and rights, begin by having people analyze common problems. Then introduce discussion of the laws and rights linked to those problems. Instead of producing a pamphlet on "Family Law," focus the pamphlet on "Family Problems" or "Who's Responsible for Taking Care of Children" (maintenance and custody) and describe common situations people face.
- **Let learners define concepts in their own terms.** In a local government support project in India, PRIA (Society for Participatory Research in Asia) conducted an educational campaign with citizens and local government officials in dozens of *panchayat* (local government bodies). The curriculum centered on three questions: "What is democratic governance?", "What are our roles in the *panchayat?*", and "How can these roles be performed well?". These questions enabled officials and citizens to define how they can work together to achieve their aims, and the type of information and expertise they need to do this.[1]
- **Link new information to problem-solving and daily experience**. Discussions can begin with analysis of problems, and continue with the introduction of new information prior to deciding on action.
- **Incorporate action planning as a final step of legal and civic education.** "What are we as a group going to do with this information?", "What are we as individuals going to do next?", "How can we use this information to address this problem and exercise our basic rights?".
- **Distribute written materials at discussions, street theater, or other media programs to give people something to help them remember.**

Combining Legal Rights and Citizenship: Peru-Mujer

One program that effectively combined legal rights information and strategies to promote people's participation was Peru-Mujer's legal literacy program with poor urban women in Peru. The program trained women leaders who had been elected by their grassroots association to be legal promoters. The promoters were trained in popular education techniques and the basics of the law. They used drawings as codes to generate discussions about real life problems. The discussions then went on to explore legal solutions. Mutual support groups were formed among women who decided to seek a legal solution despite social pressures, for example in domestic disputes. Eventually, the legal promoters were officially recognized by the Ministry of Justice. They were given credentials which allowed them to defend women in the lower courts on matters such as birth certificates, voting rights, marriage, divorce, custody of children, and other domestic disputes.

Other Participatory Learning Methods

Over the last 25 years, activists have built on Freire's approaches and developed methods that assist people in analyzing their own problems through participatory research. They have designed participatory tools such as maps, matrices, and frameworks that assist in gathering information about a problem, analyzing it and developing strategies to solve it. For example, communities concerned about

poverty begin by mapping the individual and collective resources in their surroundings. They then construct matrices that help analyze the data and use it in decisions about expanding community economic projects or creating new ones.

The World Bank and other international donor agencies have adapted some of the methods such as Rapid Rural Appraisal. These draw on community knowledge about problems so that agencies can design more effective

Facilitator-as-Organizer, Organizer-as-Educator: Changing Roles

Popular education originally saw the role of the facilitator as creating a process where learners could affirm their own knowledge, analyze problems, and discover answers for themselves. The facilitator was discouraged from intervening and directing in any way.

In political advocacy, this role changes. A better term would be facilitator-as-organizer or organizer-as-educator. The facilitator is part of the process, not an objective outsider. In this central role, he or she has to recognize and deal with power imbalances between him or herself and the participants. For example, the facilitator has information that can help the people in their change efforts and has the obligation to question perspectives that are based on poor information or negative stereotypes. The challenge is *how and when* to deliver additional information so as not to derail the empowering process of analysis. Facilitators need to use their information in a way that promotes critical thinking in the learning/action process.

Another responsibility involves recognizing differences among the participants so that facilitators can promote mutual respect and negotiate tensions. Acknowledging differences among people involved in advocacy helps build strong organization and quality leadership. If we understand difference, we can better divide tasks according to talents, skills, and experience. We discuss this challenge in more detail in Chapter 16.

development interventions. Large-scale initiatives of this kind include the Participatory Poverty Assessments (PPAs) promoted by the World Bank. These approaches can help planners gain an understanding of problems from a grassroots perspective, but do not necessarily lead to a critical consciousness or local control over development. This only happens if the empowerment approach is explicitly built in and people are directly involved in decisionmaking. (See Chapter 5 for more discussion about types of participation.)

Empowerment and Difference: Thinking about Gender

Understanding differences is as critical to empowerment and education as defining common experiences and interests. A gender lens gives social justice activists a way of sharpening their understanding of difference, exclusion, and discrimination. The box *Key Gender Concepts* on the following page offers some basics for creating a gender lens.

Gender analysis can strengthen advocacy interventions and education because it enables us to:

- understand how social problems affect men and women differently and so find solutions that are comprehensive and fair;

- identify and address different kinds of barriers to participation;

> "Not so long ago, the tasks [women's] movements faced primarily involved working to achieve better treatment for women—a squarer deal. The concentration was mainly on women's well-being—a much needed corrective. The objectives have, however, gradually evolved and broadened to incorporate—and emphasize—the active role of women's agency. No longer the passive recipients of welfare-enhancing help, women are increasingly seen as active agents of change: the dynamic promoters of social transformations."
>
> Amartya Sen , Nobel Prize Winner for Economics

- involve both women and men by adjusting the timing and structure of advocacy activities to fit into their different schedules;

- minimize power struggles between men and women, in the private and public sphere, that are provoked by change efforts;

- understand how poverty, gender, age, location, race, ethnicity, religion, and other factors interact to shape disadvantage;

- understand the visible and invisible expressions and impact of power;

- understand the meaning of justice, equity, and respect for human rights in different ways.

Key Gender Concepts for People, Power, and Politics

In this Guide we draw directly from gender theory and practice. The following key concepts help sharpen our understanding of subordination and empowerment.

Equality vs. Equity: Many people see social change as aiming at equality of opportunity. But systemic discrimination puts some people in a better place than others to take advantage of opportunities. So, if we want to address disadvantage effectively, it is important to address the underlying barriers and measure success by equity of impact, not just equality of opportunity. (See discussion of equality in Chapter 2.)

Gender as a social construct: Sex is biologically determined, and is the same across cultures and across time. But the attributes and roles prescribed for men and women, boys and girls are culturally specific. Gender is learned through a process of socialization in a particular society. From birth, boys and girls are encouraged to behave a certain way and to aspire to different life goals and perform particular roles. Parents, teachers, peers, and many aspects of culture and society reinforce these patterns. There is considerable variation in gender roles from culture to culture.

The question of power: As discussed in Chapter 3, power is a critical ingredient in social change. A gender lens provides insights into collaborative and controlling forms of power. It stresses the importance of changing patterns of *power over*. We also need to be aware when our actions may increase divisions and conflict, and be sure that those who will bear the consequences understand and accept the risks.

The gender division of labor: Both men and women work, but they tend to do different work. Men's work is usually valued more than women's. Work can be divided into three categories: productive, reproductive, and community work. Productive work is the production of goods and services for consumption and trade. It normally earns money for the person who does it. Men tend to do more *productive* work than women. *Reproductive* work involves the care and maintenance of the household. It includes childcare, cooking, water and fuel collection, shopping, and family health care. Although it is crucial for human survival and often involves many hours of labor, it is usually not considered "real" work. It thus is given little formal or monetary value. It is done mainly by women. *Community* work is the collective organization of social events and services, community projects, ceremonies, and similar events. It is done by both women and men, although they usually perform different tasks. Lack of recognition of certain categories of work distorts policy planning because much of women's labor is not counted.

Adapted from *Two Halves Make a Whole: Balancing Gender Relations in Development*, Canadian Council for International Cooperation, MATCH, Ottawa, 1991; and *Gender Frameworks* by Maitryee Mukhopadhayay, et.al. Oxford: Oxfam UK, 1997.

UNDERSTANDING POLITICS

NOTES

[1] Dass, Purvi. *Capacity Building of Newly Elected Gram Panchayat Members in Haryana, Madya Pradesh and Rajasthan*. PRIA, 2000.

Framework for the Action Guide
Putting Together the Pieces of Citizen-Centered Advocacy

This framework explains the Action Guide's logic and conceptual approach to advocacy. We first present the framework's elements separately, explaining each as we go. Then we present the entire framework so you can see how the pieces relate to one another. All the arrows and shapes in the framework may look overwhelming. But if you take a moment to read through this section, it may help you understand the content and structure of the Guide better.

The Center Spiral

At the heart of the framework are citizenship, rights, and empowerment. This is both an individual and collective process where consciousness is shaped by reflection, new information, new experiences, participation in groups and connection with others who share the same concerns. The *Chaz!* framework in Chapter 3 and the empowerment process in Chapter 4 give more detail about this aspect. Learning and planning methodologies are also described in Chapter 4 and 5. In treating advocacy as citizen education, we seek to build new forms of citizen organization and leadership, and thereby strengthen civil society and democratic governance.

Citizenship, rights, and empowerment are both the subject and object of advocacy. The rest of the framework describes the planning and action process for achieving these core objectives, beginning with an overall Vision of Change.

Vision of Change

Effective advocacy strategies are guided by a clear vision of long-term political change (Chapter 6). This vision needs to articulate what politics and decisionmaking should look like in the public and private spheres (Chapter 3). It goes beyond the policy and institutional reforms of policy advocacy to include the ethical demands of advocacy that affirm inclusion, respect, and democratic process. Articulating this vision creates a bond between the people and organizations involved in advocacy (Chapter 16). The shared vision can guide the necessary strategic choices a group needs to make, for example during lobbying and negotiation activities (Chapter 15).

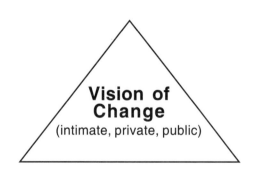

An initial version of the framework was refined and further developed in a workshop with Latin American activists in 1998.

Political Context and Moment

After defining your vision of change, your choice of advocacy issues and strategies depends on your analysis of the political situation. Historical, demographic, economic, cultural, and other factors make each situation unique (Chapter 7). This macro-analysis helps you identify the political opportunities, obstacles, and risks facing your advocacy strategy. Your map of the political landscape will be refined once you choose the focus of your advocacy (Chapters 7, 10, 11).

> **Analysis of context and power relations**

How to Follow the Two-Way Arrows that Connect the Outer Circle with the Central Spiral

These arrows describe the diverse processes and activities that take activists and constituents from one phase of advocacy to the next. They serve as a reminder that the way each step is achieved has everything to do with whether the advocacy effort actually strengthens participation. Constituents must be involved in advocacy planning for them to learn from and own the advocacy and to gain skills, consciousness, and organization.

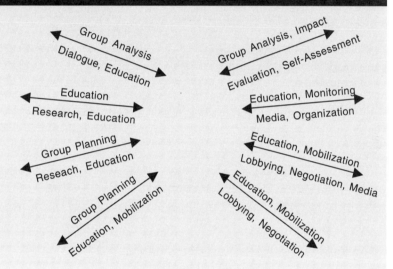

Phases of Advocacy Planning and Action (the outer circle)

The key phases in the advocacy process are arranged counterclockwise around the central spiral. Although the steps imply a linear sequence, the reality is not linear. As Chapter 5 describes in detail, strategies evolve in an iterative way—the consequences of each action provide insights that help refine the next action. This is why the arrows are two-directional. This means that the original plan may change considerably as the advocacy progresses.

We have tried to make the notion of different phases of advocacy easier to understand by dividing them into three parts. But in practice, each step and phase are not so neatly divided. The three parts are:

- planning (steps on the left side of the circle);
- citizen organizing and influence strategies (the bottom, center box);
- policy action and impact (at the bottom center and on the right side).

Throughout Part Two we break down advocacy planning and action into more specific "moments" that do not directly correspond to the broader phases described in the framework.

Planning

Defining Problems

Advocacy involves finding policy solutions to concrete problems. Engaging constituents in defining the problem begins the process (Chapter 8).

Analysis of Opportunities, Priorities, and Issues

After an initial analysis, the problem can be broken down into a manageable issue—one slice of the overall problem (Chapter 9). For example, rape is one slice of the larger problem of violence against women. Analysis of opportunities and priorities will guide your choice of issue. What issues have the best chance of being addressed and which are the most important for constituents? Describing the issue in a way that convinces both the general public and the political players is important because it sets the stage for mobilizing and negotiation. Identification of the "policy hook"—the aspect of the policy arena that needs to be changed—is vital. (Chapter 11).

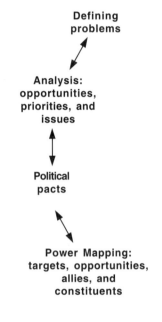

Defining problems

Analysis: opportunities, priorities, and issues

Political pacts

Power Mapping: targets, opportunities, allies, and constituents

Political Pacts — Agreeing on Roles and Goals

Early on in advocacy, the roles of organizers, lobbyists, planners, etc. begin to take shape. The organizations and individuals involved need to reach an agreement with each other and with constituents on goals, strategies, and roles. This agreement expresses the trust that allows advocates to represent constituents and must be reaffirmed at various times throughout the advocacy process. (Chapter 16). Communication among the different advocacy actors is the basis of trust and representation in sustainable citizen organization.

Power Mapping — Who Are the Players?

The players include targets, opponents, allies, and constituents of your advocacy. Who is the primary decisionmaker with the power to solve the problem? Who will support and resist you? What is the power of the different players relative to one another? What are their interests with respect to the issue?

Citizen Organizing and Influence Strategies

"Doing Politics"

The box at the bottom of the framework shows different advocacy activities. These actions move your issue on to the political and public agenda. Most of the strategies are discussed in Part Three. The exception is research and education, which is used throughout advocacy, and dealt with in many chapters of the *Guide.*

Action Strategies and Activities "Doing Politics"

- Research
- Development of policy proposals
- Lobbying
- Protest - cooperation
- Alliances, coalitions
- Outreach, education
- Media
- Awareness-raising and appropriation of rights
- Litigation
- Negotiation
- Modelling innovations
- Etc.

Policy Action and Impact

Political Pact for Negotiation

As the advocacy advances and you engage in lobbying and negotiation, it is important to find common ground among supporters about what is being proposed. A pact or agreement on what is negotiable and non-negotiable gives negotiators both the mandate and the flexibility to maneuver when there is no time for consultation.

Lobbying and Negotiating Change

On the strength of your earlier steps, eventually the advocacy reaches the negotiation stage when you discuss and bargain over solutions face to face with politicians, bureaucrats, or other decisionmakers.

Follow-up and Monitoring

Policymakers and politicians do not always keep their promises. Mechanisms for accountability are needed. In some cases, citizens act as independent watchdogs. In others they work side-by-side with government. In some places, there are laws that mandate citizen monitoring of government decisionmaking.

Ideally, you measure the success and failures of your advocacy all along the way. But at this stage, groups should formally measure how far things have gone and what needs to be done to take things forward. The *Advocacy Action and Impact Chart* in Chapter 10 is a useful tool for measuring progress, as well as for setting objectives.

Internal Organizational Assessment

In addition to measuring the success of the advocacy, for sustained organizational commitment and cohesion it helps to do an internal assessment of how far you have come, what has or has not gone well, whether you have effective organizational decisionmaking mechanisms, and whether there are sufficient opportunities for new leadership, representation, etc.

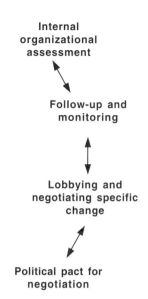

Internal organizational assessment

Follow-up and monitoring

Lobbying and negotiating specific change

Political pact for negotiation

Framework: Citizen-Centered Advocacy

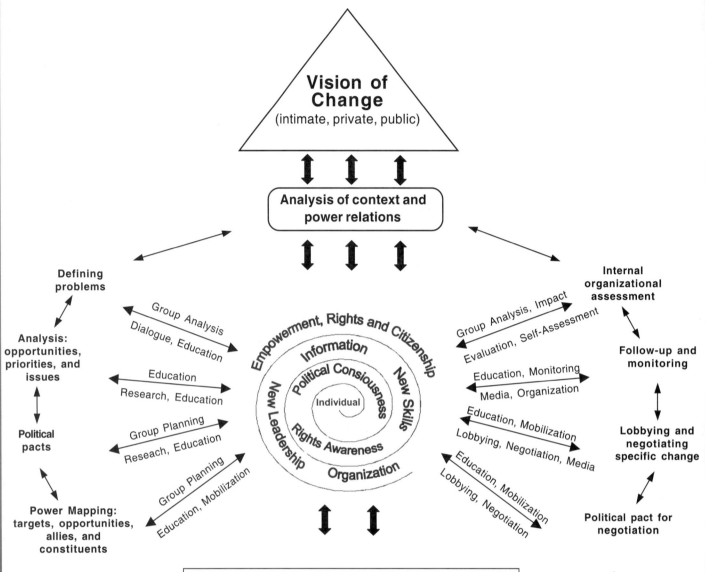

PLANNING ADVOCACY

Planning for advocacy is a citizen education, organizing, and consciousness raising activity.

Advocacy planning involves analysis, debate, priority setting, research, and decisionmaking, and can thus strengthen citizen participation just as political action does. Planning for advocacy has three important functions:

- *as a tool*, planning clarifies strategic directions and opportunities within particular political and organizational contexts.

- *as an organizational strengthening process*, planning builds organizational and leadership capacity and commitment as people share new ideas and information, and engage in dialogue, negotiation, and analysis.

- *as a citizen empowerment strategy,* participatory planning creates new knowledge, awareness, skills, and confidence.

Part Two of this guide looks at the following elements of advocacy planning:

Chapter 5: The Basics of Planning for Citizen-Centered Advocacy

Participatory approaches to advocacy planning are more than a set of tools and steps for improving impact. They are constituency-building and citizen education strategies that attempt to put the ideas of equity and inclusion into practice. Rather than a linear, predictable sequence of steps, advocacy planning is iterative. The ever-changing nature of politics demands constant adjustments in the plan. Thus, we call the "steps" moments.

Key concepts:

- Key moments of advocacy planning
- Participation in advocacy planning
- Levels of advocacy participation: local to global

Chapter 6: Planning Moment #1 – Looking Inward

Engaging in advocacy is a strategic choice that will have a major impact on an organization. For that reason, it is important to have clarity regarding 1) the individuals that will influence planning and action and 2) the organization's vision, mission, and key strategies. It is also important to assess how the organization is perceived by others. This chapter aims to help you gain a clearer sense of who you are and where you stand before you attempt to change the world around you.

Key concepts:

- Who am I? Identifying ourselves and our interests
- Who are we as an organization? Vision, mission, credibility
- strategy
- Where are we going?
- How do we look to others? Gauging visibility and

Chapter 7: Planning Moment #2 – Understanding the Big Picture

Every context has its own distinct characteristics that lead to ever-changing political opportunities and challenges. This chapter offers tools for contextual analysis to better understand the "big picture" in which your advocacy takes place. Analysis involves identifying how a political system is organized and how different people, organizations, and ideas shape the political space.

Key concepts:

- Mapping the political landscape
- Understanding political transitions for advocacy
- Mapping civil society

Chapter 8: Planning Moment #3 – Identifying and Defining Problems

Advocacy is about seeking solutions to problems in the political and policy arena. The starting point is a clear understanding of a problem that is widely and deeply felt by diverse communities or constituencies. This chapter offers tips on how to make sure you have a clearly defined problem, as well as how-tos for participatory problem definition with constituency groups. These approaches can be adapted both for groups that have already chosen their issue and groups that are beginning the process of defining their issue.

Key concepts:

- Problems and issues
- Problem statements
- Participatory approaches for defining problems
- Participatory assessments
- Focus groups

Chapter 9: Planning Moment #4 – Analyzing Problems and Selecting Priority Issues

Effective advocacy requires breaking down a large problem into many issues to identify the policy connections and determine which issues are most compelling for further action. This chapter offers a number of tools and exercises to prioritize and select issues.

Key concepts:

- Analyzing priority issues
- Analyzing root causes
- From problems to issues: comparing impacts and solutions

Chapter 10: Planning Moment #5 – Mapping Advocacy Strategies

Problems and issues have many causes and many possible solutions. Advocacy strategies will always be multidimensional to get at the systemic causes of an issue. It is unlikely that a single organization can carry out a strategy that addresses all of the causes. With limited resources, groups must choose which aspect to tackle. This chapter presents a series of tools that help to construct and compare strategies.

Key concepts:

- Different advocacy strategies
- Factors shaping an advocacy strategy
- Mapping alternative strategies
- Drafting advocacy goals and objectives
- Advocacy action and impact chart

Chapter 11: Planning Moment #6 – Finding Policy Hooks and Political Angles

Policy hooks connect the solution of your issue to the formal political and policymaking arena. To identify a policy hook, advocates draw on information about policies, laws, budgets, and the institutions and procedures that determine their content. This chapter offers an overview of various policymaking arenas to help guide you in determining the policy hook or entry point for your advocacy.

Key concepts:

- National policymaking and different entry points
- Phases of policymaking
- Budget analysis and advocacy
- International policy advocacy opportunities

Chapter 12: Planning Moment #7 – Forces, Friends and Foes

Political change entails targeting specific decisionmakers and institutions, which can generate both friends and enemies. This chapter contains various tools for identifying and classifying who is at the table and under the table and what their relative power is in relation to your solution.

Key concepts:

- SWOT analysis: internal and external forces
- Identifying political, economic, cultural, and ideological forces
- Power map: identifying players and positions
- Choosing targets for advocacy action
- Choosing and involving allies
- Ranking and dealing with opponents

Planning is necessary because we:

- have limited resources;
- have a limited timeframe in which we want to accomplish certain objectives;
- want to be increasingly accountable to our constituents and partners;
- must achieve some concrete results as well as a systematic process;
- operate in changing and sometimes unpredictable environments;
- need to have a clearly articulated common aim to minimize conflicts and differences.

What Is Advocacy Planning?

Advocacy planning is the development of:

An Overall Change Strategy
This is usually a long-term plan that embodies your vision and reflects where you are, where you want to go, and how you can get there.

A Campaign
This is a medium-term plan with activities aimed at influencing the policy environment and public opinion. The activities are intended to achieve some of your advocacy strategy objectives.

Tactics, Actions, or Activities
These are usually short-term activities within a larger change strategy, designed for a specific moment and opportunity. They could include research and media work to shape the campaign and capture the attention of people in power in relation to your issue. These activities are often referred to as strategies.

Impact Assessment
This involves monitoring your impact so you can change your strategy, campaign, and activities as necessary.

However, planning for advocacy is more than just a set of tools and steps for improving impact. Participatory approaches to planning further advocacy goals by putting into practice more equitable power relations and more inclusive forms of citizenship. Participatory planning for citizen-centered advocacy:

- *Builds organization and networks.* Participatory analysis and decisionmaking help

PLANNING ADVOCACY

Immeasurable Goals

Maruja Barrig, a strategic planning expert from Latin America, points out that planning for social and political change is very different from planning for development projects such as building wells or providing health services. In development projects, the goals are measurable. But political change goals like empowerment are difficult to measure because real examples are scarce. Therefore we are hard pressed to describe what they look like. Advocacy strategies often try to "operationalize values" that do not have clear models in the real world. This makes them more difficult to envision and quantify. That is why it is important to find creative ways to measure these processes. Barrig says that measuring shorter-term results that are steps on the way to larger change may be more practical than trying to measure long-term results.

Barrig, Maruja, "Planificacion Estrategica" in *Mujeres Al Timon*, a book produced as part of a women's advocacy and political participation project coordinated by Agende (Brazil), Equidad de Genero (Mexico), Flora Tristan (Peru), and other Latin American women's NGOs.

strengthen leadership and communication within and among organizations.

- *Promotes political education.* It involves new knowledge about power and politics and experiences that develop citizenship.

- *Strengthens planning for negotiation.* The process delineates a clear map of interests and levels of power among the key actors.

- *Builds constituencies.* When we involve many stakeholders—and particularly the people most affected by the advocacy issue—more people will be informed and motivated, and the campaign will have more legitimacy and clout.

Advocacy planning is a continual process. If some groups have not been involved in the initial stages of planning, they can be included later when plans are being reviewed and modified.

How Advocacy Planning Differs from Other Types of Planning

The temptation to follow donor trends and be project-oriented has made many organizations reactive rather than proactive. Advocacy planning, on the other hand, needs to be strategic. Being strategic means making careful choices about how to use and leverage scarce resources. It is about achieving both our short-term aims (such as educating citizens about their legal rights) and our long-term vision for social change (for example, respect for human rights and more consultative public decisionmaking). Being strategic demands a careful analysis of external opportunities and constraints as well as internal organizational resources for addressing a problem. However, since advocacy involves maneuvering in a complex political system where power dynamics generate conflict, planning for advocacy

differs from traditional strategic planning tools in key ways.

Unlike many approaches to strategic planning where goals, objectives, activities, and evaluation are presented as a seamless and logical pattern, advocacy planning acknowledges that there are hidden agendas, different values and ideologies, incomplete information, and conflict. Further, planning and doing advocacy happen side by side. After every action it is often necessary to adjust goals in planning our next step. So assessment is a continual task in advocacy, rather than a step at the end of the planning sequence. Strategic planning for advocacy is always a work in progress.

Citizen-centered planning includes a variety of other features:

- It is not seen as value-neutral. Values and commitment are just as important as "facts."

- It is not a linear set of steps with predictable outcomes. It is an iterative process of examination and adjustment.

- It gives direction to action, yet is also geared to responding to unforeseen opportunities.

- It should, if possible, involve the people most affected by a particular problem in planning and action—from setting the agenda to leading the campaign.

- It draws upon and strengthens the analysis, awareness, and organization of marginalized sectors.

- It involves conflicts and negotiation.

- It places equal value on academic and NGO expertise and grassroots experiences. It seeks to integrate knowledge from different disciplines into a holistic strategy.

Key Steps or "Moments" of Advocacy Planning

Many approaches to planning call the phases of planning "steps," and present them sequentially. However, advocacy planning involves a lot of "two steps forward, one step backward." For example, you may begin with a macro-analysis of the context in which you are operating, but as you learn more about your issues and policymaking, you will also learn more about the context and will then go back to refine your analysis. Because of this, we call the planning phases "moments" rather than steps.

Though they are not linear, there is a certain sequence to the moments of planning. For example, it helps to begin by looking inward (organizational self-assessment) and then move to looking outward (contextual analysis).

PLANNING ADVOCACY

The iterative process of advocacy planning

With participatory planning, it is not just the continual analysis that makes the process spiral rather than linear. It is also the fact that planning involves different people with different and sometimes conflicting interests.

The following moments are covered in Parts Two and Three of this Guide:

Personal and Organizational Assessment

We start with a self-analysis by the organizers and advocates. We then move to organizational assessment by looking at a group's vision, mission, and strategies, and developing a long-term political vision to guide advocacy planning. (Chapter 6)

Contextual Analysis

This involves understanding the political context at the local, country, regional, and global levels. It includes discussion of visible and invisible power dynamics that marginalize some groups from the political process. (Chapter 7)

Problem Identification and Analysis

In this planning moment, groups define and prioritize their problems for potential advocacy. It involves important decisions for citizens and is key for building the constituency. (Chapters 8 and 9)

Choosing and Framing the Advocacy Issue

The analysis of problems and exploration of possible solutions helps groups to slice a big problem into manageable advocacy issues. Framing the issue is about describing your cause in order to have wider public appeal. (Chapters 9 and 13)

Long-term and Short-term Advocacy Goals

The long-term goals specify the political, economic, and social changes the advocacy efforts seek to accomplish. These goals establish the basis for setting maximum and minimum positions for negotiations with decisionmakers. The short-term goals describe the desired outcomes for the specific advocacy solution. (Chapter 10)

Power Mapping

This moment of analysis helps planners identify the targets, allies, opponents, and constituents for their advocacy. It examines stakeholder interests, positions, and conflicts. It reveals hidden mechanisms of power that affect marginalized groups' participation as well as important allies within decisionmaking structures. Power mapping is essential for planning, negotiating, and calculating risks. (Chapters 10 and 12)

Policy and Situational Research

This moment involves gathering information about the policies, laws, programs, and budgets shaping your issue, and about its causes and the people it affects. This information will make your advocacy clearer and provide material for your media, outreach, lobbying, and negotiations. (Chapters 8 and 11)

Advocacy Objectives

With the power maps and policy information, you can draft a set of advocacy objectives. These will spell out the desired changes in policy and decisionmaking structures, as well as how you will use political space and strengthen citizen engagement. Finally, they indicate how the advocacy will ultimately improve people's lives. These objectives are continuously refined. (Chapters 10 and 11)

Activities, Actions, Tactics, and Implementation

Advocacy objectives help you define action strategies. The nature of the political environment, opponents, and targets will inform your

---

Tips for Effective Advocacy Planning

Use Simple Tools
Analytical frameworks and role play exercises presented in the Guide enable groups of people to think creatively and systematically about complex issues. (See especially *What Is Your Political Vision?* on page 99, the *SWOT Analysis* on page 214, *Mapping Power* on page 219, the *Forcefied Analysis* on page 216 and *Triangle Analysis* on page 171.

Clarify Jargon
Terms such as gender equity, democracy, empowerment, women's rights, and mobilization are complex ideas that different people understand in different ways. It helps to discuss them in detail to identify differences and similarities in interpretation before beginning to plan. Defining key concepts enables people to interpret and give their own meaning to citizenship and politics. Part One offers suggestions about how to do this.

Involve Facilitators
You may want to have a facilitator assist the planning process within your organization or coalition. An external and skilled person is often helpful when planning brings together different organizations with different interests and contributions.

Keep It Dynamic
Good planning is made of equal parts of information, excitement, commitment, and participation. Find ways to involve everyone in different tasks.

Bring Values and Assumptions to the Surface
Differences, power imbalances, and hidden stereotypes cause misunderstanding and conflict that will slow down planning and action. Begin your planning with the introductory exercises from Chapter 6 or the Annex. Deal with these matters openly when they arise. Also see the discussion of conflict management in Chapter 16.

---

media, outreach, lobbying, and negotiation tactics. (Chapters 10,11, and Part Three.)

Measuring Progress and Adjusting Action

Ongoing evaluation helps to ensure that advocacy responds to political opportunities and follows organizational priorities. Evaluation allows groups to adjust their actions to changing situations. (Chapter 10)

The Importance of Participation in Advocacy Planning

How planning is done is just as important as how well a plan is defined. There are many reasons why participation is critical for effective advocacy. When we focus on building

citizenship, two reasons stand out. First, planning *is* learning and decisionmaking. Many initiatives that claim to be participatory actually consult people, but the real decisions about plans and directions are made elsewhere. Being involved in making decisions is key to empowerment and creates ownership, motivation, trust, and impact. Participation by staff, board, and constituents in all aspects of planning helps to:

- generate commitment;
- create shared ideals and directions;
- speed up action (but may slow progress initially);
- surface and cope with conflicts and differences;

These people have given us some great information.
Let's go back to the office and analyze it.

- assess political risks;
- improve organizational accountability;
- increase self-confidence and critical consciousness.

Secondly, participation in advocacy planning provides new citizenship experiences and skills in such areas as:

- analyzing problems, power, and context;
- setting objectives;
- locating resources;
- preparing budgets;
- leading meetings;
- organizing campaigns;
- identifying and negotiating diverse interests;
- collective problem-solving;
- speaking in public;
- evaluating accomplishments.

Citizen-centered advocacy is based on the premise that participation in public decisionmaking is a right. Participation in

advocacy planning begins to give shape and meaning to this right for citizens.

The kind of participation may differ at different stages in the planning process. In the early stages of choosing issues and defining solutions, constituents and allies can be fully involved. As you move into the fast-moving policy arena, the pressure for quick responses to opportunities may make full participation more difficult.

> Participation is empowering only when those who participate make decisions and choices.

Making Participation Work

There is general agreement that active participation by intended beneficiaries—such as poor people, women, and workers—in planning is necessary for lasting success, both in terms of empowerment and social change. Everyone from water-user groups and women's rights activists to the World Bank is calling for more participation. Participation is a buzzword that has many meanings depending on who is using the term. The typology on the following page explains how the word "participation" is used to describe very different processes with very different results with regard to power, empowerment, and learning.

Although there are no perfect models, some people see ideal participation as one where everyone participates equally. But people's contributions are not equal—people participate in different ways and make different kinds of contributions. In order to enable different perspectives to be heard, it is essential to acknowledge how differences can translate into unequal power dynamics, and then adjust the dynamics to facilitate more equal communication and decisionmaking.

Here are some points to consider in making participation work:

Look At Who Is Involved

Participatory planning will involve the following people in different moments:

- staff and volunteers, directors, and board
- members and affiliates
- constituencies, including excluded groups that will benefit from advocacy
- partner organizations involved in the advocacy effort or related issues
- individual and organizational allies

Value Diverse Perspectives

Ideally everyone should have a voice in deciding the broad direction of the organization and strategy. The selection of the issue and more specific aspects of planning may require a smaller group who can represent the concerns of others at some stages in the planning process. Differences also bring debate and disagreement into the planning process. See Chapters 8, 15, 16, and the Annex for tips on conflict, prioritizing, and consensus-building.

Involve Constituents

It is particularly important for constituents— those most affected by the problem—to be involved in choosing and analyzing the issue, exploring strategies, leading meetings, speaking in public, organizing events, and other roles. (See Chapters 8 and 14.)

PLANNING ADVOCACY

Engagement and Participation

"Engagement in social and community participation has inevitably brought citizens in closer contact with the institutions and processes of governance. Conversely, leaders of projects, programs and policy research initiatives have increasingly sought the voices and versions of poor people themselves. Where citizens have been able to take up and use the spaces that participatory processes can open up, they have been able to use their agency to demand accountability, transparency, and responsiveness from government institutions. . . . These moves offer new spaces in which the concept of participation can be expanded to one of 'citizenship participation', linking participation in the political, community and social spheres."

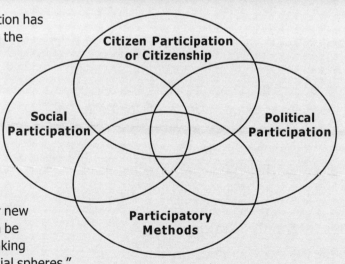

Cornwall, Andrea and John Gaventa "Bridging the gap: citizenship, partnership and accountability" in *PLA Notes: Deliberative democracy and citizen empowerment*. International Institute for Environment and Development, February 2001.

Different Types of Participation	
Typology	**Characteristics of Each Type**
Token Participation or Manipulation	People sit on official committees, but they are not elected and have no real power.
Passive Participation	People participate as recipients of information. They are told what has been decided or what has already happened. The administration or project management passes on this information, but does not listen to people's responses.
Participation by Consultation	People participate by being consulted or by answering questions. External agents define problems and information gathering processes, and control the analysis. The professionals are under no obligation to include people's views.
Participation for Material Incentives	People participate by contributing resources, for example labor, in return for food, cash, or other material incentives. People provide these resources but are not involved in decisions as to what is done. They have no stake in carrying on with things when the incentives end.
Functional Participation	People participate at the request of external agencies to meet predetermined objectives. There may be some shared decision-making, but this usually happens only after the big decisions have already been made by external agents.
Interactive Participation	People participate in joint analysis and development of action plans. Participation is seen as a right, not just the means to achieve project goals. The process involves methodologies that seek all the different perspectives and use structured learning processes. Because groups are involved in decision-making, they have a stake in maintaining the project. Local institutions are strengthened.
Self Mobilization	People participate by initiating actions independently of external institutions. They develop contacts with external institutions for the resources and technical advice they need, but control how the resources are used. The mobilization may or may not challenge existing distribution of wealth and power. Government and NGOs sometimes provide support for self mobilization.

This was initially designed to assess participation in development projects, but has been adapted and revised for different purposes. See Biggs (1989), Hart (1992), Pretty (1995), and Cornwall (1995).

Build Trust

Trust emerges through open communication and respect for different talents and perspectives. Some groups outline participants' responsibilities in a pact or agreement. In this pact, constituencies mandate leaders to act on their behalf during fast-paced moments of advocacy when full consultation is impossible.

Use Interactive Dialogue

Often the most constructive learning and planning will use a series of open questions or a simple framework for structured discussion.

Listening is as important as speaking, and often, encouragement to speak involves waiting in silence for a voice.

Work in Small Groups

Wherever possible, work in small groups where each individual can speak more easily. Be conscious that gender, age, and other factors may make it difficult for some people to voice their opinions. Follow up with larger meetings to pull together the contributions of the small groups.

Use Participatory Needs Assessments

Participatory community needs assessments and surveys enable grassroots groups to be involved in assessing their situation and choosing the issues and solutions to the problems that affect them. Because they live with the issues, they have important insights about why a problem exists and what would solve it. They also have the anger and motivation to push hard for change. (See chapter 8, 15, and 16.)

Integrate Experience and Expertise

Generating decent solutions requires a combination of practical know-how and theoretical expertise where both kinds of knowledge are valued and examined. Marginalized communities have the knowledge of firsthand experience, yet they often need more information to make good choices and formulate arguments.

On the other hand, college-educated advocates may have theoretical and factual knowledge, but they will not usually have the perspective or understanding of local problems that community people have. Sometimes experts are stuck in boxes (a single discipline) that do not provide coherent explanations or analysis. When different groups work together in advocacy, they need to respect each other's perspectives, interests, and contributions, and find ways to make decisions together that integrate their knowledge.

Schedule Time for Planning As Part of the Strategy

Allocate adequate time for participation and include planning as a regular activity in your advocacy timeline. Use these planning moments for education, consciousness-raising, and building organization.

Balancing Perspectives

Different individuals and organizations play different roles and have different responsibilities in advocacy. Some are grassroots organizers, others are lobbyists or policy researchers while some play still different roles. Each of these perspectives makes a vital contribution to advocacy. However, there is often a tendency to value some more than others. It is critical that advocacy leaders not allow these differences to evolve into a hierarchy in which one role is considered more important than another. For example, many advocacy campaigns have failed when the lobbyists and others close to decisionmaking begin to dominate the planning agenda.

Levels of Advocacy Planning: Local to Global

Many of today's advocacy strategies require planning and action on more than one level of policymaking. For planning on a global level, for example, face-to-face discussion and decisionmaking are more difficult. While information technology has made global and regional planning easier, it has also reinforced inequalities. The further an advocacy planning process extends beyond the local level, the more it is necessary to have multilayered systems of communication, decisionmaking, and feedback.

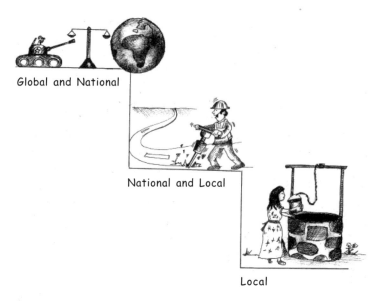

Global and National

National and Local

Local

Local

Participatory planning is sometimes easiest at the community, neighborhood, or city level where face-to-face interaction is not complicated by distance.

National

Often, planning for national level advocacy involves coordination of different organizations that serve as intermediaries for a variety of community-based and local groups. National advocates rely on their allies to be in touch with local groups and involve them in analysis, planning, and decisionmaking. National advocates need to remember that participatory planning takes time and should be careful to take this into consideration in their timelines.

Regional

Regional planning efforts entail communication among the participants at different levels. Again, timelines need to accommodate discussion and decisions across borders. The Internet is often useful for regional advocacy planning. However, regional organizers need to make sure that groups without Internet access are fully informed and can offer input.

Global

Like regional planning, global processes need to coordinate and provide information and feedback to the different players so that the final planning decisions include input from all levels. This input is crucial since some partners will be taking on greater risks than others. Their opinions need to be included to avoid unnecessary danger. Internet access is usually crucial for this level of work.

Multilevel participation in planning and carrying out global advocacy helps to:

- build new forms of citizenship that increase the voice of excluded groups;
- give legitimacy to people's voices in the eyes of global policymakers;
- create a network to monitor and enforce so that global policy promises become real at the national and local levels.

6 Planning Moment #1: Looking Inward

For many organizations, getting involved in advocacy requires a shift from short-term project planning to long-term strategic thinking. It also requires that the organization engage directly with politics and power. These are big changes. Becoming a policy player is a strategic choice that will mean changes in the organization's mission, staffing, priorities, relationships, and strategies. Before you decide to do this, it is important to be clear about who and where you are now.

This process of "looking inward" is equally important for the individuals doing and planning advocacy: staff, organizers, activists, lobbyists, and constituents. The analysis of power that shapes the advocacy plan should start with the people doing the advocacy. Organizations are made up of different people with different identities shaped by class, race, gender, age, country of birth, and other factors. These differences influence our perspectives and shape the power dynamics within our organizations, with our partners and in the larger political environment. Diversity enriches planning, but it also generates conflicts. If we do not explore these differences, they may cause problems rather than serve as a source of richness and creative energy.

This chapter will help you begin the planning process with a clearer sense of who you are and where you stand before you attempt to change the world around you. It can be especially useful to those who are moving from traditional development work to programs that integrate advocacy and citizen participation.

Four Steps to Looking Inward

This planning moment has four steps:

STEP 1: Who Am I?

Clarify individual perspectives, values, and assumptions that influence planning and action choices. This step can also help people feel less inhibited about speaking up in a group and working as a member of a team.

STEP 2: Who Are We?

Assess the vision, mission, and key strategies of our organizations, and define a new long-term vision for political change that will inform the advocacy work. This can create a sense of solidarity and shared commitment.

STEP 3: Where Are We Going?

Discuss the pros and cons of engaging in or expanding advocacy work for our organizations. This helps get buy-in for new directions and allows groups to analyze the implications of their choices.

STEP 4: How Do We Look To Others?

Evaluate the organization's image, reputation, relationships, and credibility with key stakeholders—especially with constituencies and policymakers. This diagnosis will later feed into a more in-depth analysis of opportunities and threats when you focus on a specific advocacy issue.

PLANNING ADVOCACY

For more guidance on coping with major organizational change, we recommend *From the Roots Up: Strengthening Organizational Capacity through Guided Self-Assessment,* Peter Gubbels and Catheryn Koss, World Neighbors, Oklahoma, USA, 2000.

Step One: Who Am I? Identifying Ourselves and Our Interests

We get involved in advocacy because we want to improve society and influence the course of history. But we are also part of society and history. Who we are and how we think affects what we care about and how we relate to others. Self-analysis helps to identify our strengths and weaknesses and clarify the power dynamics in a group. What we learn from self-analysis can then be used in improving our participation and in changing the wider power relations affecting our advocacy. There are many creative ways of approaching self-understanding. (The exercises in *Annex 2* complement the following ones for this purpose.)

Looking inward

Purpose

- To clarify characteristics that shape who we are such as class, race, gender, religion, and age.
- To identify how we think our organization can contribute to positive change.
- To strengthen our ability to communicate as a team.

Process

(Time: 1 hour)

The facilitator can use the categories in the box or others to divide the group into sub-categories, called "lifeboats." For example, under decade of birth, the facilitator calls out "1950s," "1960s," and so on.

1. The facilitator calls out specific sub-categories. Participants scramble to find others in the same lifeboat. Informally take note of how many participants are in each sub-category.

2. After all participants have grouped themselves by sub-category, they have 10 minutes to talk with each other about what distinguishes them from people in other sub-categories. Then each lifeboat grouping has a chance to tell the full group how they are different.

3. Repeat this process with as many other categories as you would like.

Categories

- Country or region
- Decade of birth
- Cultural background
- Ethnic group
- Gender
- Race
- Occupation/work
- Opinions on a particular issue
- Religion
- Other

PLANNING ADVOCACY

Discussion

This exercise can help people get to know one another and loosen up, but its usefulness depends on how it is processed. Discussion about personal differences can raise sensitivities. On the other hand, people usually enjoy talking about themselves and, in a comfortable environment, will be open.

Once participants have returned to plenary discussion, the facilitator can ask some of the following questions:

- Were there some lifeboats that were fuller than others? Why?
- What are the unique things that each lifeboat brings to the table?
- What are the implications of the imbalances in numbers and characteristics for planning?

From *Naming the Moment: Political Analysis for Action* by Deborah Barndt, The Jesuit Centre for Social Faith and Justice, Toronto, 1989.

Purpose

This exercise complements the *Lifeboat* exercise, but is also a useful introduction to a broader analysis of power. It helps to:

- identify who we are individually and as a group in relation to those with power in our societies;

- deepen our understanding of how identity, power, subordination, and exclusion affect our organizations, ourselves as individuals, and advocacy planning.

- illustrate how power is dynamic and relational.

Process

(Time: 45 minutes–1 hour)

This exercise has three steps which look at our social, organizational, and political identities. These three identities together make up what is called the identity triangle.

Social Identity

We look at social identity using the power flower. This tool looks at who we are in relation to those who have power in society. We use the outer circle of petals to describe the dominant social identity. The group usually fills in the outer circle of petals together. We use the inner petals to describe the social identity of individuals. Participants usually fill in the inner petals by themselves (see next page).

1. Before the exercise, draw the power flower on a large piece of paper and place it on the wall. Each petal represents one category, which can include: sex, race, ethnic group, language, religion, family type of arrangements (single, extended, etc.), social class, age group, education, ability/disability, geographic region (origin), geographic region (current), etc.

2. As a group, discuss each category and the characteristics of those who have most power in the society. In the outside circle of the petal, fill in these dominant characteristics. (For example, which sex or which ethnic group has the most power.)

3. Hand out pieces of paper with pre-drawn flowers on them to each person. Ask people to work individually and write in the outer circles of their flowers the dominant characteristics that were agreed on by the group.

4. Ask each person to write their own identities for each petal/category on the flower's inner circle.

The other sides of the triangle—organizational identity and political identity—can be discussed after doing the "social flower." The elements for organizational and political identity usually differ more than for social identity between cultures and contexts. Some possible dimensions are:

Organizational Identity

- *Category of the organization:* e.g., government, NGO or type of NGO, private sector, community-based or peoples' organization, social movement, coalition, labor union, women's organization

- *Structure:* e.g., collective, hierarchical, voluntary, paid, professional, business

- *Position within the organization:* e.g., director, head of specific program, member, trainer, technical specialist, lobbyist, volunteer

Political Identity

- It is difficult to prescribe a process for analyzing political identity. The categories – left, right, and center – are common in most contexts, but the shades of difference in political identity in different contexts cannot be universalized. This analysis can be broken down in terms of political tendency or political party affiliation.

Discussion

Once each person has completed their social identity flower, the facilitator can lead a discussion around questions such as:

- How many of your individual characteristics are different from the dominant identity? Which characteristics cannot be changed? What does this say about your own power or potential for power?

- What does the exercise reveal about us as a group? What are the differences and similarities in relation to the dominant power? How can that influence our work?

- What does this exercise tell us about identity and power more broadly?

The Complexity of Individual Identity

This analysis helps reveal the relationships between people involved in advocacy and the processes of subordination that affect their lives. Because each individual has many identities, individuals can be dominant in one relationship and subordinate in another. For example, being a woman or man is only one part of an individual's identity. Other aspects such as age, class, race, and ethnicity also affect that person's social relations and power. While each situation presents a unique configuration of power imbalances and dynamics, in most hierarchies of power wealthy males are dominant. To be effective in advocacy, we need to take these things into consideration within organizations and in every activity.

PLANNING ADVOCACY

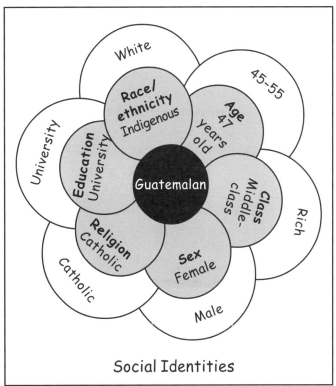

Social Identities

Adapted from Barbara Thomas, *Educating for a Change: Between the Lines*, The Dorothy Marshall Institute. Toronto 1991. See also Chantal Mouffe.

Exercise: Naming Political Assumptions

Purpose

Analysis and planning is improved by being aware of the lens through which we view the world. Our lens is influenced by our assumptions and values. Because these differ among people, different people can look at the same situation and see entirely different things. The purpose of this exercise is to identify the political assumptions that shape our opinions and analysis.

Process

(Time: 45 minutes–1 hour)

1. In plenary, ask the group to brainstorm the assumptions that shape their views of politics, power, and social change. If the group is large, divide into small groups to brainstorm. To help them develop a list of assumptions, participants may want to consider the following questions:

   - What do we assume to be true about processes of social change?
   - What do we assume to be true about power and conflict?
   - What do we assume to be true about the political process?

2. After 10–15 minutes, ask the group(s) in plenary to make up a common list of assumptions they bring to the task of advocacy planning.

   - What are some of the assumptions we share?
   - Where are there differences?
   - How do these assumptions affect our choices about what we do?

The following assumptions were listed in the manual *Naming the Moment*.

> **"When we do this analysis, we assume that . . .**
> . . . our social situation is filled with tensions between social groups and within them.
> . . . history is made as these groups come into conflict and resolve conflicts.
> . . . some groups have power and privilege at the expense of other groups.
> . . . this oppression is unjust, and we must stop it.
> . . . if we want to participate actively in history, we must understand the present as well as the past.
> . . . we can learn to interpret history, evaluate past actions, judge present situations and project the future.
> . . . because things are always changing, we must continually clarify what we are working for.
> . . . to be effective, we must assess the strengths and weaknesses of our own group and those working with and against us.
> . . . at any moment there is a particular interrelationship of economic, political, and ideological forces.
> . . . these power relationships shift from one moment to another.
> . . . when we plan actions, our strategy and tactic must take into account these forces and relationships.
> . . . we can find the free space that this particular moment offers.
> . . . we can identify and seize the moment for change!"

From Deborah Barndt, *Naming the Moment: Political Analysis for Action, A Manual for Community Groups.* Toronto: The Jesuit Centre for Social Faith and Justice, 1989.

Step Two: Who Are We as an Organization?

Most strategic planning begins with a review of an organization's vision, mission, and overall strategy or objectives. These elements set the parameters for choosing a new strategy or expanding an existing one. However, many organizations do not have a written vision or mission or, if they do, the staff or members do not know it. Advocacy involves long-term action that will create many choices. You will need the vision, mission, and strategy to help direct decisionmaking along the way.

Different people define these elements in different ways. We have found the following definitions[1] useful:

A **Vision** is how an organization would like the world to be in the future. Visions express ideals and may not be easily attainable in a given period of time. A shared vision can provide momentum for individuals working together, and can be a statement of social commitment.

A **Mission** is an organization's purpose given its vision for the future and translates the vision into practical action. A mission:

- *guides* policy decisions about alternative actions;
- *prioritizes* activities, demands, and the use of resources;
- *channels* collective action in one direction; and
- *provides meaning* and motivation for hard work.

Overall Strategy refers to the set of activities that the organization carries out to accomplish its mission. Strategy is broader than programs.

Our focus on strategy instead of objectives may be confusing for those who have participated in strategic planning exercises that follow the Vision-Mission-Objectives (V-M-O) framework. Defining objectives is important. However, at this stage in planning, organizational assessment is intended to define the parameters for engaging in advocacy. Redefining the organization's vision, mission, strategies, and objectives will require a more intensive strategic planning process.

The real life examples and comments on the following page can be used to better understand vision, mission, and strategy.

Why Political Visions?

The project orientation of most donors and development programs has encouraged the habit of thinking only in two to three year funding cycles. Political instability, repression, and persistent poverty also discourage many people from having faith in the future or believing they have a role in running their society. In many countries, thinking beyond day-to-day survival seems a waste of time.

Some activists and educators feel that people, especially the poor and disadvantaged, can be discouraged by a vision with an ideal that they will not be able to achieve in their own lifetimes. Others believe the process can unify and motivate groups in important ways. For example, the vision of social justice articulated by the American civil rights leader, Martin Luther King, in the *I Have a Dream* speech mobilized people in the United States during the sixties and still inspires people today. The challenge for activists and trainers is how to balance the vision with the need to set achievable goals.

But a long-term political vision is important for effective advocacy. First, a vision helps us to imagine how we want people and institutions to behave so that values like justice and equality are realized. A vision inspires. Second, advo-

PLANNING ADVOCACY

Example Vision, Mission & Strategy Statements			
	VISION	**MISSION**	**STRATEGIES**
Example #1 From a women's legal research and action network	The existence of gender equity in [specific region] where women and men are co-partners and co-decisionmakers at all levels, and governments are committed to the removal of barriers that prohibit this.	To promote understanding of and practical strategies to further gender equity through: - socio-legal research demonstrating the negative impact of inequality, and - education and advocacy to achieve informed policy and attitudinal change.	Research, analysis, education, and advocacy on crucial legal problems affecting women. The dissemination of information in different forms aimed at: -policymakers, and -women with a basic educational level
Comments on #1	*The vision, mission, and strategy provide a clear sense of the organization's ideal future, their key purpose and their primary actions. The use of the term 'gender equity' may be confusing for people who are not aware of gender issues. However, its meaning for this particular group has been spelled out in the vision. The mission includes strategies.*		
Example #2 From a Women and AIDS network	A society where women enjoy reproductive rights.	To increase women's knowledge and their attainment of reproductive rights for all women.	-Mobilization -Access to information and services -Programs geared towards enabling women to control resources
Comments on #2	*Terms such as 'reproductive rights' and 'mobilization' do not clearly describe what the organization hopes to achieve. For example, in the vision, we don't know what "enjoy reproductive rights" means. In certain cases, this may be intentional for public acceptance and to avoid backlash. But it is even more confusing because the organization's name suggests that it focuses on AIDS. The vision and mission do not explain how AIDS prevention or support fit into the reproductive rights mission. The strategies are too general. Access to what kind of information and services? For whom? To what end? Control over what kinds of resources?*		
Example #3 From a women's wing of a trade union federation	To defend the rights of women.	-To increase women's participation in decision-making in the trade unions. -To create gender awareness in all trade union structures. -To empower women workers to know and exercise their rights in the workplace and at home.	-To form women workers' committees. -To mobilize women workers to join and become active in trade unions.
Comments on #3	*This vision is more suitable as a mission statement because it states the purpose of the organization. The vision as an ideal future could be restated as: "A democratic trade union movement where women and men workers are equally represented in the leadership and the rank and file, and where the policies and benefits are equitable and adequate." The mission statement is really a list of strategies. The strategies could be activities under each of the strategies.*		

cacy is a never-ending series of shifting situations involving difficult choices and unexpected outcomes. A clear political vision serves as a guide for making strategic decisions. If you do not know where you are headed, it is difficult to decide which direction to go today.

The following vision exercise reinforces a core tenet of transformative politics—that politics is both a public and private matter. When we focus only on public politics, we overlook the other social institutions that perpetuate discrimination and subordination.

Purpose

To define the characteristics of political life in the ideal future as expressed in roles, relationships, and values in decisionmaking at all levels.

Process (Steps 1–2)

(Time: 1½–2 hours)

1. Divide participants into four small groups of five to six people.

2. Ask each group to choose a facilitator who will guide the visioning with the following questions:
   - What would you like politics or decisionmaking to look like in ten years in:
     - the family?
     - a community or neighborhood?
     - an NGO or association?
     - the national legislature?
     - international policymaking institutions (e.g., World Bank, IMF, WTO)?

> You can also include the *couple* (those involved in an intimate relationship, in marriage or some other form of union) as a category. Understanding this relationship of power is key for advocacy on AIDS and reproductive and sexual rights and health.

3. Ask each group to describe their vision and write it on a large piece of paper.

4. Ask groups to hang their visions around the room. Let participants walk around, read, and discuss the visions with each other. This is called a gallery walk because participants view and discuss each other's work independently and informally.

5. Ask participants to return to their groups and choose one of the six areas—the couple, family, community, NGO, legislature, or international policymaking institution. Make sure that groups do not all choose the same arena. Then ask each group to develop two short plays—no more than seven minutes each—comparing how the arena operates today with their vision of the future.

Discussion

After all the skits are presented, discuss each vision separately. Then compare the differences and similarities between the scenarios. An important point to draw out is:

- Change requires more than policy reform. There need to be changes in the underlying values and social habits that perpetuate inequality. Advocacy planning needs to take into account the structural and ideological roots of discrimination and subordination.

Facilitator's Tip

The exercise uses skits and theater to help participants look at how power works. Often people relate easily to the real-life situations presented and can learn at the same time as they enjoy the drama. Skits are a quick and easy method for people to understand vision and decisionmaking. They avoid the rhetoric that often happens in long discussions. To make skits entertaining and useful, there should be a set of guidelines—including a time limit and discussion questions. (See Augusto Boal, *Legislative Theatre*, for more suggestions)

PLANNING ADVOCACY

Example: Visions of Decisionmaking

In the ideal family:

- decisionmaking and responsibility are shared among all family members, including children and adult women;
- no domination; everyone has the right to say "no," argue, or negotiate;
- no discrimination within the family;
- all members know their rights;
- women are not economically dependent; women's household work is valued.
- both husband and wife are involved in deciding the number of children and when to have them, and share responsibility for the children and the household.

In the ideal community:

- decisionmaking is shared among representatives from all groups of the community irrespective of their social and cultural status, religious and political beliefs, or gender; fifty percent of the representatives are women;
- gender-sensitive leaders are selected by the groups in a democratic and participatory process;
- people are informed about rights and care about the "common good;"
- people have the skills to analyze problems and take initiative to solve them;
- people understand and are committed to democratic process.

In the ideal NGO:

- decisionmaking is carried out in consultation with representatives from grassroots and all levels of the organization; fifty percent of the representatives are women;
- NGOs and associations are political and see themselves as important catalysts for change with a strategic long-term commitment;
- There is no stereotyping of women's roles in NGOs;
- there is less paternalism and more respect for grassroots communities and beneficiaries.

In the ideal national legislature:

- the diversity of the population is accurately reflected, with differences, concerns, and issues emerging; fifty percent of the representatives are women;
- women's issues are raised as important, addressed, and solved by both women and men.

From an Asian regional advocacy training workshop. This group was not asked to think about the global policymaking arena or the couple.

The following illustrations show what people in different parts of the world have presented in the *What Is Your Political Vision?* exercise. The values and behavior illustrated in the skits are similar across cultures, although the specifics are different. These drawings can also be used as an exercise to analyze the dynamics of decisionmaking in different arenas in the present and compare them with the possible future. Such an exercise can also help find common characteristics in the different arenas of the family, organization, and Parliament.

DECISIONMAKING RELATIONSHIPS TODAY

DECISIONMAKING RELATIONSHIPS IN THE IDEAL FUTURE

The Family

NGOs

PLANNING ADVOCACY

DECISIONMAKING TODAY | DECISIONMAKING IN THE IDEAL FUTURE

National Legislature

People demonstrate to make their voices heard

People discuss their proposal with policymakers

Facilitator's Tips about Visions and Vision Statements

There are lots of different ways to do visioning. Some facilitators prefer open-ended questions and asking people to dream. Others prefer to be concrete about the timeframe. We have found that visioning for advocacy can be facilitated by a question specifically about politics and decisionmaking, such as, "How would you like decisions to be made?". By focusing on decisionmaking, the vision makes power relations a focus for the planning process. The political vision exercise also helps groups look at the values that guide their advocacy work. Sometimes capacity-building for advocacy is reduced to a mechanistic series of universal techniques for policy change. Looking at power and values helps the vision to be grounded in the political and cultural context as well as define a social commitment.

In essence, the vision exercise asks, "What kinds of political, social, and economic systems do we want to live in?". That question often leads to another question, "What is democracy?" . Sometimes a discussion about democracy is useful and at other times, not. (See Chapter 2, page 25.)

The visioning exercise provides the basis for writing a vision statement. When we assess a vision statement, we usually ask, "Does this reflect the overall dream of this organization, or does it sound more like an activity?". Other ways to help people formulate a vision statement might be:

- Imagine a world that does not need this project or this organization—what would that world look like?
- Explain that a vision is a description of society and ask them to complete the phrase beginning "a society where . . ."

Step Three: Where Are We Going?

Reviewing who you are as an organization lays the foundation for knowing what you can do in the short-term. Before an intensive planning process, it is helpful to discuss informally where you want the organization to go. Strategic questions can generate ideas for alternative approaches that can be explored later on in the planning process.

Strategic questions[2] may be asked about:

- problems the organization wants to solve;
- availability of the necessary resources;
- political space in which the organization operates;
- the organization's internal capacities;
- allies and competitors.

All organizations find themselves periodically at a crossroads when they need to reexamine their vision and mission, and figure out what strategies will allow them to take advantage of new opportunities. This is the case when an organization becomes involved in or expands its involvement in advocacy. Even an advocacy organization will need to decide where it is going when it considers new and different social problems, targets, campaigns, and arenas of policy.

The Pros and Cons of Getting Involved in Advocacy

The strategic questions that follow are formulated to help an organization weigh the pros and cons of engaging in advocacy.[3] Each organization will have different priority questions.

- What resources and strengths can your organization offer advocacy work? What added resources are needed?

- What skills does your organization currently have to do effective advocacy work? What additional skills are needed?
- What are the benefits to your organization?
- What are the risks to your organization?
- How will advocacy affect your organization's activities and mission?
- Will your organization need to alter its mission and programs?
- How will doing advocacy work affect your membership and your relationship to the communities you serve?
- Which other actors with whom you have a relationship—such as NGOs, labor unions, university, professional organizations, individuals—are your likely allies? (This question is difficult to answer unless you have decided on your issue.)
- With which other groups do you need to build relationships to succeed?
- How will advocacy work affect your organization's legal and financial situation?

Step Four: How Do We Look To Others? Gauging Visibility and Credibility

Assessing your organization's visibility and credibility with potential constituency groups and with official political players is another valuable part of organizational self-assessment in preparation for advocacy. This assessment will be revisited in more depth further along in the planning process once you have chosen your advocacy focus. The following two exercises, *Official Political Credibility Checklist* and *Constituent Credibility Checklist*, can help you assess your relationship, your reputation, and your general image.

PLANNING ADVOCACY

Purpose

To assess how your organization is perceived by powerful political players as a basis for planning advocacy activities. This checklist contains criteria presented from the perspective of opinion leaders in the formal policymaking and political arena. The list may not be the same as your own views of what is important about your organization. For example, many policy players may be interested in the size of an organization. They believe that the bigger you are, the more important you are. For people in the NGO community and groups working on social justice advocacy, bigger is not always better. But this checklist assesses external credibility.

Coalitions can undertake this exercise to determine the collective strength of their member organizations.

Process

(Time: 1 hour)

This activity can be done in two ways:

- If your organization is large, do the exercise as an individual survey given to all staff, board, and members. Tally all the responses and then discuss the findings with as many respondents as possible.

- If the number of people does not exceed 15–20, you can do the exercise collectively.

- Identify the primary political officials and players you are likely to encounter and deal with in your advocacy. You will have to be as specific as possible. For example, among political players you might include legislators, policymakers in different institutions and agencies, and opinion leaders (such as religious leaders or media figures) who influence relevant ideas about social justice, equality, etc.

- You may want to apply the checklist separately to different groups of players rather than more generally. For example, you can assess your credibility with legislators, and then with the bureaucracy or ministries.

- Some criteria may not be relevant to your organization. Select the criteria that are relevant and, if necessary, add your own criteria. Rate your organization from one (low or poor) to three (high or excellent) on each criterion.

Adapted from IDR's *Advocacy Sourcebook* by Miller and Covey, based on a framework from Mark Lattimer, ActionAid Advocacy Workshop, India, 1995.

Official Political Credibility Checklist

Size of membership	_____	Contacts with political parties	_____
Status of membership (e.g., professional status)	_____	Contacts with corporate or other powerful entities	_____
Provider of quality services	_____	Quality of information (research/publications/briefings)	_____
Links with client group or community	_____	Recognized theoretical or practical expertise in given field	_____
Size/status of client group	_____	Age of organization	_____
Mechanisms of internal accountability	_____	Size of organization	_____
Links with funding agencies	_____	Wealth of organization	_____
Links with supporter or affiliated bodies	_____	Efficiency of organization	_____
Status of board members, patrons	_____	Financial transparency of organization	_____
Perception of staff integrity and competence	_____	Legally incorporated organization	_____
Perception of leaders' or officers' integrity and competence	_____	Perceived independence of organization	_____
Links/contacts with government:		Level of positive media exposure	_____
Executive	_____	Level of public recognition of organization	_____
Legislative/Parliament	_____		
Agencies/Ministries	_____	Controversial Issues*	
Judiciary	_____	(3 for avoiding controversy;	
Policy/Military	_____	0 for being connected to	
Local officials/Municipal Councils	_____	controversy)	_____
		TOTAL	_____

Adapted from the *Advocacy Sourcebook* by Valerie Miller and Jane Covey, Institute for Development Research, Boston, 1997.

PLANNING ADVOCACY

*Controversial issues vary between cultures and contexts. They are issues that are sensitive politically and socially, and that can provoke heavy debate, political embarrassment, and even violent conflict. Advocacy with disadvantaged sectors such as farmers, workers, and women is often controversial. Issues that are seen as questioning power relationships and religious or cultural beliefs are almost always controversial. Usually powerful people do not like controversy because it can threaten the status quo. Organizations that have a history of engaging in controversial issues need to keep their public image as clean as possible to keep doors open. But there are times when conflict cannot be avoided and when controversy is the best way to bring attention to your issues and generate political debate.

Assessing Visibility and Credibility with Constituencies

Assessing your organization's presence and reputation with potential constituencies is as important as assessing your public image among powerbrokers. This diagnosis may need to begin with a discussion about who are potential or real constituency groups. As we discuss in Chapter 4, constituencies are the people who are most affected by the problems of poverty, social injustice, and inequality that you are addressing.

Many NGOs may not have a direct relationship with the people most affected by the problems that they are attempting to address. These intermediary organizations usually provide information, training, assistance, or coordination for advocacy while their partners or beneficiaries have a more direct relationship with the constituency.

Who are your constituents?

The following four questions will help to clarify who your constituencies are:

- Who does your organization serve directly?
- What role do these people and communities play in your organization and in your advocacy?
- Who benefits from your organization directly?
- Who does your organization hope will (eventually) benefit from successful advocacy?

The local constituency in advocacy is the people who will directly benefit from the changes you hope to achieve. However, your activities may also benefit other groups who are working with your constituency. For example, an agricultural education NGO helps rural extension workers to make their interventions more responsive to both women and men farmers. The constituency is the farmers, but there is also a direct benefit to the extension workers.

This analysis can be useful because partners, beneficiaries, and constituents are all stakeholders, but they may sometimes have different priorities. Donors, government, other NGOs, management, and staff are also stakeholders with their own priorities that may even conflict with your own. As an organization, you will want to be aware of all these stakeholders and be responsive to them when appropriate. However, often there are so many pressures that groups forget about their constituencies, particularly if their program does not include direct contact with them.

In Chapters 4, 9, 10, and 14, we discuss constituency-building in detail.

Purpose

To assess your organization's relationship and credibility with real and potential constituencies. The rating will give you a sense of how well you know your constituency, how well they know you, and how well you relate to each other. It may give you ideas about the strategies you need to build the trust and connection necessary to engage them in advocacy.

Process

(Time: 1 hour)

After identifying your potential and real constituencies, assess your credibility and visibility with them using this checklist. Add your own criteria that address the specific nature of your constituency. You may want to identify 2-3 major constituencies and assess your credibility with each one.

This activity can be done in two ways:

- If your organization is large, do it as an individual survey given to all staff, board, and members. Tally the responses and discuss the results with as many respondents as possible.

- If there are fewer than 15–20 people, do the survey collectively.

Constituency Credibility Checklist	
Frequency of direct contact with constituents	_____
Organizational recognition by constituents	_____
Equality and reciprocity of partnership	_____
Depth of knowledge of staff about the social hierarchies and problems faced by your constituents	_____
Trackrecord (e.g., delivery on promises)	_____
Two-way information flow	_____
Joint decisionmaking	_____
Level of trust and respect	_____
Personal connections	_____
TOTAL	_____

Adapted from *Organizing for Social Change: A Manual for Activists* by Bobo, Kendall, and Max. Midwest Academy, Seven Locks Press, 1991.

Rate your organization from one (low or poor) to three (high or excellent) under each criterion. Your constituents can be a geographic community or a social grouping. Key constituents can be asked their opinions, including what they value most about the relationship and what they would change.

Discussion

- How can we adapt our community-based activities to engage constituents more directly in the planning, decisionmaking and implementation of advocacy? How will this change the timeline and budget for our programs? Will we need new skills to do this?

- How can we mobilize and maintain grassroots support and involvement in our advocacy?

- How can we prevent putting the grassroots supporters at risk from political backlash?

- How can we reduce the potential resistance by men and gain their support for increasing women's involvement and leadership in advocacy?

- If we engage in global and regional advocacy, what kind of information technology will we need to keep ourselves, our partners, and our constituents involved? Is this feasible?

- How do we educate donors about the financial and time implications of constituency-building?

PLANNING ADVOCACY

NOTES

[1] Adapted from *Strategic Thinking: Formulating Organizational Strategy Workshop, Facilitator's Guide*, Institute for Development Research, Boston, 1997.

[2] Ibid.

[3] Adapted from *The Advocacy Sourcebook* by Valerie Miller and Jane Covey, Institute for Development Research, Boston, 1997.

Planning Moment #2: Understanding the Big Picture

Mapping the Political Landscape

One of the important first steps in planning is mapping the political landscape. Each context has its own characteristics that create changing political opportunities and challenges. Mapping involves identifying how a political system is organized and how different forces, people, organizations, and ideas shape the political space. When we refer to the political landscape, we usually mean the national level, but the global and local levels are also important.

There are many ways to do a contextual analysis. Some of the underlying questions in this analysis are:

- Who has what kind of power?
- Who has more power?
- Who has less power?
- How is this imbalance maintained?
- How can the imbalance be changed?

Analyzing the Larger Context:
Many forces, ideas, institutions, and people interact to shape the political context.

To look at these questions, we offer three exercises:

- *Structural Analysis* describes how the economic and social structure is organized. It defines who are the haves, who are the have-nots, and the common beliefs about why things are this way. This analysis helps us to understand power dynamics.

- *Naming the Powerful* identifies the decisionmakers and influential people in the economic, political, cultural, and ideological spheres.

- *Historical Analysis of the Political Landscape* looks at the relative power, autonomy, and strength of the state, market, and civil society and how these have changed over time.

This analysis will provide a better understanding of the larger context in which you are operating. You will be able to deepen this analysis once you have chosen your advocacy issue and set goals and objectives (see Chapter 9). Chapter 12 will help you refine your analysis at that stage of planning.

Facilitator's Note

Contextual analysis can be hard work and is best conducted in small groups. The analysis focuses mainly on a particular country, and only people who are familiar with that country's context can do it. In a regional workshop, people can be divided by country, even if some people work alone.

Sometimes people may not know the answers to the questions posed in the exercises. You may want to invite a resource person who is knowledgeable about politics, social movements, and history to provide additional input. You can also give participants copies of interesting articles, papers, and/or a list of references where they can get additional information.

Many activists use an implicit structural analysis in their work and planning. Discussing the analysis in an explicit way clarifies differences as well as commonalities. For people who have less experience with politics and analysis, examining the political landscape in this way can be enlightening.

Purpose

To analyze how the social, political, and economic structures in a country are organized in order to better understand the distribution of resources and the dynamics of power.

Process

(Time: 1½ hours)

1. Using the *Social Tree* in the illustration below, describe the meaning of each of the elements.

   - The *roots* are the base of the social structure—its **economic** system. Economics has to do with who owns what, the primary sources of income and economic productivity, how people survive, their conditions of life, and how economic resources are distributed.

   - The *trunk* is the **social and political** structure that makes the system run smoothly. It regulates the system through laws, policies, and institutions.

   - The *leaves* are the **ideological, cultural, and social** elements of society. This includes beliefs and institutions such as churches, schools, and the media that shape values, ideas, and norms.

2. Divide participants into three groups. Ask each group to analyze a different element of the social system. Give them 20–25 minutes to complete the task and then ask them to share their work in plenary.

3. Discuss each group's analysis. Then do a collective analysis of how the different aspects interrelate.

Questions for Group Discussion

Economic System

- What are the main industries (e.g., agricultural, mining, service, manufacture, trade)?
- What are the main goods produced and exported (e.g., timber, shoes)?
- What are the main imports?
- What services are produced (e.g., tourism, banking)?
- What are the dominant corporations? Who owns them?
- Identify between five and eight main sources of formal employment (e.g., tourism, mining, agriculture, electronics, service).

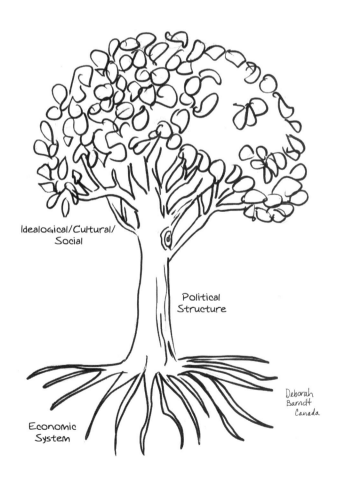

Idealogical/Cultural/Social

Political Structure

Economic System

Deborah Barndt Canada

PLANNING ADVOCACY

- What percentage of workers are employed in the informal economy?
- Where are women employed? Where are men employed? Where are young people employed? Do employment and income levels differ on the basis of ethnicity and gender?
- What roles do foreign corporations play in the economy? What role do multilateral organizations like the IMF and the World Bank play?

Political Structure

- Who/which institutions make the laws? How are laws enforced?
- Who/which institutions make the key budget decisions?
- What kinds of people are elected and appointed to government? Do they represent diverse economic, gender, racial, and ethnic interests?
- Do certain kinds of people benefit more from political processes than others? Who?

Ideological, Cultural, and Social Elements

- What are the main expressed values of government (e.g., freedom, unity)? Are these different from the values reflected in how government actually operates?
- How does society treat women? How does it treat ethnic groups?
- What are the main family-related values? How is "the family" defined? What roles are given to men, women, boys, girls?
- What values and lifestyle does the media promote?
- Which cultural institutions shape the values and ideas besides government structures?
- Does society tolerate difference from the "norm" in terms of social identity and political perspectives? Does society tolerate nonconformist behavior and thinking?
- What are some of the ideas and values where there is significant conflict or dissent? Agreement?

Overall Analysis

- How does the economic system influence the legal and political systems?
- How do the legal and political systems influence the economic system?
- How does the value system shape the legal and political systems and vice versa?
- How does ideology reinforce social and economic hierarchies?

Example

The following is a structural analysis from a group in Canada. The group analyzed their social structure in relation to the issue of free trade. Because their analysis focused on one issue, they were able to probe more deeply.

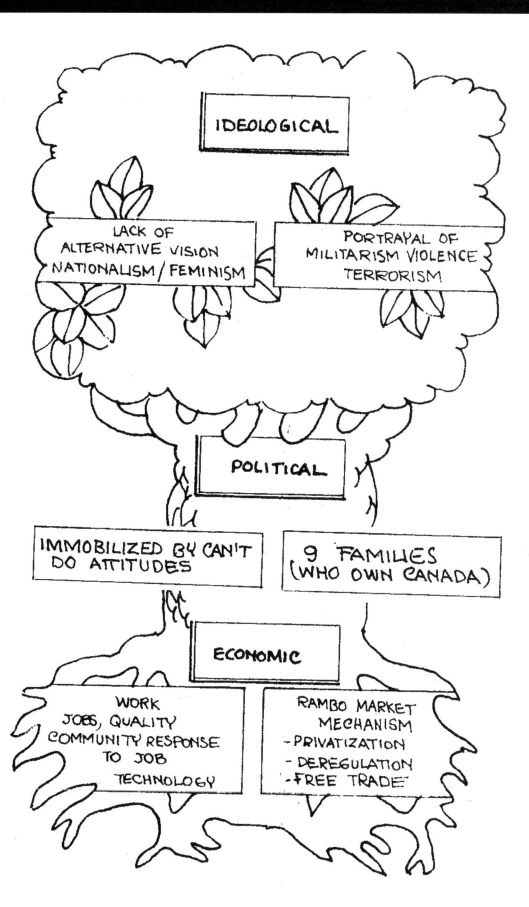

IDEOLOGICAL

LACK OF
ALTERNATIVE VISION
NATIONALISM / FEMINISM

PORTRAYAL OF
MILITARISM VIOLENCE
TERRORISM

POLITICAL

IMMOBILIZED BY CAN'T
DO ATTITUDES

9 FAMILIES
(WHO OWN CANADA)

ECONOMIC

WORK
JOBS, QUALITY
COMMUNITY RESPONSE
TO JOB
TECHNOLOGY

RAMBO MARKET
MECHANISM
- PRIVATIZATION
- DEREGULATION
- FREE TRADE

PLANNING ADVOCACY

Purpose

To identify the key economic and political decisionmakers in your community or context and to define their key interests. The analysis produced through this exercise can inform your selection of issues and advocacy solutions. It can also help to identify common interests and potential conflict.

Process

(Time: 1½–2 hours)

To ensure participation and to divide up this large task, small group work is best. If your group does not know the answers to some of the questions, you can suggest research to find out more. Gathering this kind of information can be very empowering for citizens and is an important part of *doing* advocacy. Alternatively, analysts sympathetic to your interests can help provide the information. But if a trained researcher assists, make sure that the researcher does not *do the analysis for* the participants. Inquiry and discovery are vital parts of citizen education.

1. Using the results from the *Structural Analysis*, make a chart that lists the main *economic* groups (or players). Identify who the decisionmakers are in each group. Put names in the "Who?" column. Then define what appear to be their main interests and note these in the last column. The following questions may help focus the analysis.

   - What issues have they been involved in recently? How do they affect the community or constituency?

   - What interests do these players promote?

   - Are the dominant interests nationally-based or international?

	Who? (Leaders)	Interests
Banks		
Major Industry		
Chamber of Commerce		
Trade Associations		
Major Property Owners		
International Agencies/ Donors		
Other Opinion Leaders		

2. Identify the *political* groups, decisionmakers (elected, appointed, or otherwise) in formal government, and define their critical interests. The following questions may facilitate the analysis:

   - Who are the national legislators in the area (MPs, Congressional Representatives, Senators, etc.)? List names.

   - Who are the regional, state, or district officials in your area?

   - What form of government exists at the local level? Does it operate under a single official? Who has the most authority and budgetary control?

   - Who are the chief officials at the level at which you are operating (national, local, regional)?

   - In what major issues and policies have they been involved?

- How do these issues and policies affect your constituencies?
- What local communities and groups (including civil society) are politically important?
- In what issues have they been involved recently? How do these affect your constituencies?

3. Identify the *media* groups and decisionmakers (owners, editors, and journalists) and how they make decisions. The following questions may facilitate your analysis:

- Who owns the main newspapers and television and radio networks?
- How much control do they exert over the content of the media?
- Whose interests do they promote? Whose interests are invisible?
- How does this affect your constituencies and issues?

4. Finally, repeat this process for religious and civil/social service leaders and use these questions if desirable:

- Who are the main religious leaders? On what political and social issues do they speak out?
- Whose interests do they represent? How does this affect the constituencies with whom you work?
- Who are the main civic leaders?
- Do the dominant NGOs and civic groups promote a specific agenda?
- How do these groups affect your constituencies?

Synthesis

Once you have completed this exercise, synthesize with an overall analysis that answers the more general questions about the political context and moment of your advocacy, such as:

- Where are the most serious changes needed?
- Where is there potential risk of danger?
- Where are there big opportunities?

Adapted from *Naming the Moment: Political Analysis for Action* by Deborah Barndt, The Jesuit Centre for Social Faith and Justice, Toronto, 1989.

PLANNING ADVOCACY

The State, the Market, Civil Society, and the Family

The next form of contextual analysis involves historical reflection about how the government, the market, civil society, and the family have changed over a period of years. Analysis of the impact of war, economic upheaval, natural disasters, and other important events tells us more about the opportunities and challenges for citizen organizing and advocacy today. This analysis can also be used more simply to examine forces that make up the current advocacy context.

As with most political terminology, there is some disagreement about what the following concepts mean. But most people agree that each refers to an arena that has written and unwritten rules that define the relationships and processes within that arena.

The **State** consists of the people, procedures, and institutions of government. The state's authority and duties, and people's access to public decisionmaking, resources, and opportunities are defined and regulated through laws and policies. Policies and laws are enforced and implemented through government ministries, the police, courts, schools, local government and ministries, and other institutions. Different states exert various levels of control on civil society and on the market, and regulate relationships in the family through family law. An authoritarian or centralized state can handicap a healthy civil society with too many restrictions. In contrast, a small state may not be able to ensure the basic welfare of the population. Different parts of the state do not always work together. Internal conflicts between institutions and individuals can create advocacy opportunities or constraints.

Debates on the Ideal Role of the State

Some people believe that the state should be smaller. They believe that the market and civil society should handle more economic and social matters without government interference. Others believe that the state plays an important role in regulating the excesses of the market and protecting basic rights. They feel that civil society is not able on its own to meet the social and welfare needs of all members of the population. We discuss a related debate on the extent of the state's responsibility for people's welfare under citizenship in Part One.

Civil Society refers to the arena of social interaction between the family, market, and the state[1] where the level of community cooperation, voluntary association, and networks of public communication determine its potential. Civil society includes non-profit institutions, NGOs, and grassroots groups that sometimes provide services or represent citizen interests (e.g., human rights organizations, labor unions, community development groups, private universities). In a vibrant civil society, people work together to solve problems and have a high degree of trust in one another and in public institutions. In a strong civil society, there are many different types of groups, communication is open, and there is a high level of public involvement. A repressive state controls social relationships and organizations and often breaks down the values that enable people to work together. In many countries emerging from years of authoritarian rule, there are few community groups. In this situation, it can be difficult to motivate people to work together for long-term collective solutions. Civil society is not homogenous, nor harmonious. As in the other arenas, there are patterns of privilege, exclusion, conflict, and ideological difference.

The **Market** refers to the arena where the exchange of goods and services occurs and where business, industry, trade, and consumption happen. Most political scientists believe that the state should set the basic rules of the market so as to protect the rights and responsibilities of the buyer, the seller, the worker, the investor, and others. They also assert that the state must not hinder competition. The market can have both a positive and negative effect on civil society. On the one hand, liberalization can encourage entrepreneurship and growth that may benefit many people. On the other hand, competition for scarce goods and services can undermine the cooperative spirit that is key to a strong civil society.[2] A completely unregulated market can generate extreme inequality which destroys civic values, such as fairness and reciprocity, and may generate social violence. The distribution of economic resources is a key factor in determining the opportunities and conflicts in the market and society at large.

The **Family** is defined by a set of relationships created by birth, lineage, marriage, common law partnership, or other social commitments. These relationships usually extend beyond a single household to other households and groups. The family can be an important source of individual well-being and stability. It can also be the source of abuse of basic rights and freedoms. The family promotes social attitudes and values that influence the nature of the state, civil society, and the market. It is a central force in shaping relationships between men and women. Although the family is considered a private realm, there are usually laws to regulate some aspects of family relationships.

The degree of overlap between the sectors tells us something about political opportunities. For example, when civil society is tightly controlled by the state, independent citizen action is difficult, or even impossible. When civil society and the state are very far apart, government may be completely unresponsive to civil society. This can happen, for example, when a state is so corrupt that it is incapable of ensuring basic justice and welfare.

PLANNING ADVOCACY

Relative Power of Different Sectors

The relative power of the state, the market, civil society, and the family vary from country to country. "Advocacy is located at the intersection of the sectors where civil society (NGOs, community-based organizations, and others) acts from the private domain for the public good. Advocacy efforts challenge the precept that the state and the market represent the dominant public domain. Citizens also legitimately claim the 'public space' when they give voice to values and goals important to a society. Demands for land tenure rights expressed by village women's associations, for example, are an expression of this reality. . . . Advocacy is also important when unrestrained freedoms of private market interests jeopardize the common good. Consumer unions are often the vanguard of protecting individuals against unscrupulous business practices. . . ."

Valerie Miller and Jane Covey. *The Advocacy Sourcebook: Frameworks for Planning, Action and Reflection*, Institute for Development Research, Boston, 1997, p. 10

Purpose

To apply the concepts of the state, the market, civil society, and the family to an historical analysis that examines the relative power and autonomy of each of these sectors over a 5–20 year period. The analysis reveals how the government, market, and civil society have changed over time and how these changes affect opportunities for advocacy.

Process

(Time: 2½ hours)

1. Review the concepts of the state, the market, civil society, and the family. One way to do this is to give four small groups one concept each to define. After 10 minutes, they can share their definitions in plenary. The concepts can then be refined with input from everyone. If the concept is completely unfamiliar, you can use the definitions on pages 116-117. You can give each participant a copy of these definitions or your own definitions. It is important that all participants have the same understanding of the concepts.

2. Trace the past 5–20 years in your country. Identify two or three milestones when an internal or international incident brought noticeable change in the political, economic, and social lives of people. Such moments include wars, natural disasters, changes in government, or severe economic crisis.

3. At each milestone along the timeline, assess the relative power of the state, the market, civil society, and the family. Did the state control the market? Or did the market have greater influence over political and social life? Was civil society well organized and relatively harmonious? And what was its relative power compared to government and to the market? Make a circle for each of the four sectors with the size of the circle showing its relative power and influence. Show the relative autonomy or connected-ness of each of the sectors through the degree of overlap among the circles.

Other Concepts and Categories

Some political scientists define an additional category called *political society* to cover political parties. Some groups want a category of *culture* to be included in the exercise to represent the overall values and social practices of the society. Other groups have drawn a larger circle around all the other categories to represent the power and influence of the *international realm*.

4. Once you have completed drawing the circles at different points on the timeline, analyze all of the diagrams. Discuss how historical changes create opportunities and constraints for advocacy today. Adapt the following discussion questions to suit your situation. If your country has recently undergone a major change, you may have specific issues to probe.

The original framework in *The Advocacy Sourcebook: Frameworks for Planning, Action and Reflection* had three circles representing the state, civil society, and the market. We have added a fourth circle to represent the family. Women's rights advocates in Africa said this circle was important because of the family's role in shaping women's status and choices in many countries of the world.

Discussion

- Does one of the sectors predominate in shaping people's lives, choices, and opportunities? For example, the family may be the predominant influence on the lives of girls and women, while the market may be the most important for peasant farmers.

- If the market is the largest circle, what kinds of challenges and opportunities does that pose for the state, civil society, and the family?

- If the state is the largest circle, what kinds of challenges and opportunities does that pose for the market, civil society, and the family?

- How does the family resist the influence of the other sectors? How does it reinforce the power and influence of the other sectors? How has this changed over time?

- How have historical changes restricted or expanded opportunities to promote people's participation in public life?

- What contradictions among the state, the market, civil society, and the family can open up or reduce opportunities for organizing?

Examples

The following timeline examples are from activists in the Asia Pacific.[3]

The Philippines: Raissa Jajurie, SALIGAN Alternative Legal Assistance Center

"In 1972, martial law was declared by the government. We had a very strong state and market. We even had crony capitalism within the state. Civil society was relatively small because of the repressive policies of the government. In 1983, an opposition leader was assassinated and this provided the stimulus for civil society to become bigger and to engage in more active mobilization and struggle.

"By 1986, we had a broad-based revolution which ousted the President from the Philippines. Now we have a more active (bigger) civil society that has gained enough influence to reach the formal power in the state.

"At present [1997], we have new liberal economic policies that have allowed the market to grow more influential than the state. Civil society also increased its influence with the emergence of more and more, and stronger organizations. In the face of the economic dislocation caused by neoliberalism, civil society will have to rise up to the challenge of how to influence economic policy and actors. The family remains a constant influence on the beliefs and values of people, as well as the church. The family and the church are very interconnected as a source of conservative social influence."

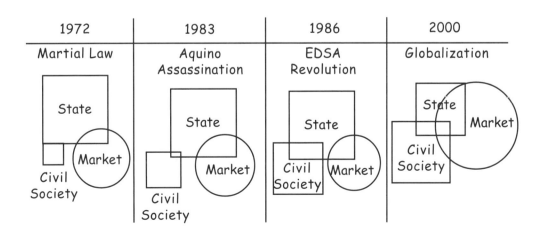

PLANNING ADVOCACY

Mongolia: Itgel Lonjid from the Liberal Women's Brainpool

"From 1921–1990, Mongolia was a socialist country with a centrally planned economy. In 1990, there was a democratic change that influenced everyone. From 1990 up to now, we still see the transition period to a market-oriented society. This transition generated many political changes. We have formed a multiparty parliament and have had a presidential election. Also, civil society is gaining strength. I can say that civil society was very weak in the past because, although there were some so-called NGOs, they were all initiated by the state. We can't say that there were really NGOs.

1921-1990	1990	1990-1997
Socialist	Democratic	Transition

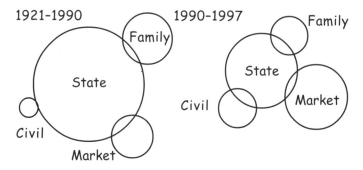

"NGOs and other associations began to emerge after the democratic change in 1990, and at the same time, freedom of speech began to stimulate people's minds. The democratic change demanded new skills and knowledge from people, and so they are having difficulty adjusting to the new environment.

"Before, the state dominated and there was no market economy nor civil society. But the family had the second most important role next to the state, because everyone respects and obeys the elder members of the family. Prior to democratic change in 1990, family rules were so strict that even young people obeyed them. Since 1990, the role of the family is changing. Young people stopped respecting their elders and crimes within the family increased. On the other hand, I can say that civil society is growing. Now there are around 770 NGOs in Mongolia. Lastly, the role of the state decreased and the market increased."

Analysis of the Circles

If the state is a much larger circle, the opportunities for political change and political space are usually limited. A powerful state often means a controlling, repressive state. In such cases, advocacy may be risky, or focus exclusively on local, community issues.

If the circle representing civil society is relatively small, why is this so? Does this mean that people seldom work together on community problems? Does it mean that people have little faith in the state and in each other? A small civil society circle means that advocacy will require intensive political consciousness raising and organization-building activities. Bringing people together around basic needs is often the first step toward building political skills and interest in collective action.

In many countries, the sizes of the circles are changing as the market grows and the state shrinks. If the market grows to be larger than the state, will it be difficult to protect people's interests and environmental, labor, and social rights? Will more availability of goods produce negative kinds of consumerism? On one hand, there may be increased and beneficial opportunities for economic productivity with a growing market. In some countries, however, economic growth has been accompanied by growing poverty and an increased concentration of wealth. Poverty consumes people's time and energy as they struggle for survival. This can make it difficult to motivate people to take collective action. Further, a shrinking state has less capacity to enforce laws that protect people and the environment.

A relatively large family circle can have negative implications. It can imply that traditional and cultural beliefs restrict women's ability to become involved in public life. In contrast, the family may be a stabilizing force in some countries where conflict and change have disrupted social harmony.

Ways to Understand Transitions in the Political Landscape

Which issues and strategies you choose depend on the possibilities for different types of political action in your country, and the risks attached to each. The chart on page 123 describes common characteristics of governments before and during a transition to a more open, democratic system. Academics describe these three phases as different "regime" types. The characteristics help highlight possibilities and risks. For example, in countries without effective legislative bodies, lobbying lawmakers is not very helpful. Where the government is repressive, some groups may choose confrontational strategies and enlist international support for protection. Other groups may choose quiet, behind-the-scenes negotiation using personal contacts.

Pre-transition: Protest and Repression

Looking for Advocacy Opportunities at Different Transition Moments

While every country is different, they often share similar problems and possibilities during different stages. Of course, transitions do not all move from a negative situation to a positive one, and even if they do, there are many conflicts and digressions along the way. The following characteristics assume negative to positive change. Some groups have found this analysis useful as a way to assess their context.

In the **pre-transition** or closed regime type:

- political organizing and education opportunities are often found at the community level on local issues, such as water, housing, and healthcare;

- often the strongest associations are user groups, church groups, and clubs. These offer good opportunities for education and organizing;

- direct challenges to government are risky;

- law reform initiatives are possible unless they deal with basic rights or resource distribution;

- organizing around the provision of basic services can be a useful way to engage communities, laying the groundwork for more significant change in the future;

- there may be less risk for policy initiatives in the international arena.

> "Important decisions affecting citizens' daily lives are becoming more and more globalized. These decisions range from trade and labor to food policies. To tackle globalization, civil society actors are linking across borders to work together on common concerns and demands. Often where governments have failed to work together, civil society associations have put aside differences to work for common agendas. The emerging global civil society is both promising and challenging."
>
> Commonwealth Foundation and Civicus.
> *The Way Forward: Citizens, Civil Society and Governance in the New Millennium*, 1999.

Transition: Peaceful Demonstrations of Citizens' Demands

Consolidating Democratic Process: Using and Participating in Law Reform

In the **transition** regime type:

- reform creates opportunities to build organization;

- broad public education programs can raise awareness about the political system and need for change;

- civic education can help people understand and work with government;

- some governments engage in reform because of donor pressure;

- issues and tactics must be chosen carefully so as to maintain the political space necessary for future organizing;

- activist groups may feel reluctant to shift from a confrontational posture to engage with government;

- organizing around basic needs can promote people-government interaction.

In the **consolidating democratic process** stage:

- legal reform and lobbying initiatives provide opportunities to build public involvement;

- there is increased space for political groups, such as human rights committees and lawyers associations who often focus on political change in cities;

- expanding and securing rights and democratic practices for excluded populations requires promotion of their organizations, leadership, and critical consciousness, and may provoke backlash;

- including women, workers, poor people, and other marginalized groups remains a constant challenge. Even in the oldest democracies, equity and equality can be controversial when they challenge established power dynamics.

In-depth Mapping of Civil Society

Civil society is both the engine and focus for advocacy. Understanding the characteristics of civil society is important for planning. The regime type gives an idea of the potential for civil society, but advocacy opportunities depend on the number and types of associations in civil society as well as their values. Often when a closed political system opens, initially there is conflict and deep divisions within civil society.

CIVICUS, a worldwide network promoting the effectiveness of civil society, has developed a Civil Society Index called the *CIVICUS Diamond Tool*. The index looks at four different dimensions of civil society: structure, values, space, and impact.

Structure
- How large is civil society in terms of institutions and organizations?

- What are its component parts and what resources does it have?

Values
- What are the values, norms, and attitudes of civil society?
- How inclusive are they?
- What are the areas of consensus and dissent?

Space
- What is the legal, political, and sociocultural space in which civil society operates?
- What laws, policies, and social norms affect its development?

Impact
- What is the contribution of civil society to solving specific social, economic, and political problems?
- What impact does civil society have on the public policy making process?

PLANNING ADVOCACY

Characteristics of Regime Types		
PRE-TRANSITION (less open)	**TRANSITION** (opening up)	**MORE OPEN SYSTEM**
- centralized power and sometimes personalistic rule - one party system - low tolerance for opposition - very little public dissent - very little respect for human rights - minimal freedom of association - control of the media - public appears to be apolitical	**Stage 1: Political Liberalization** - consideration of legal reform - relaxation of restrictions on individual and group rights and freedoms - controlled permission to citizens and opposition to engage in the public arena **State 2: Democratic Transition** - increased opportunities for political competition - increased public dissent and engagement with the state - more active opposition - negotiation between government and citizens and opposition - elections - re-writing the constitution	- relatively fair, free elections - increased public debate - increased tolerance for dissent - increased conflict among different social groups - creation of institutions for public participation - strengthening of the rule of law, the role of legislatures and independence of the judiciary - growing public expectation of government - growing citizen awareness of their rights and the political process

Mapping and analyzing civil society with this tool can help groups better identify potential allies and understand the context in which they are operating.

Sometimes the kind of overall analysis described in this chapter can paralyze people because so many factors seem to work against change. Yet opportunities open up in surprising ways when you engage in political change work. What appears impossible at one moment may lead to unexpected allies and sources of power at another. These can then produce a chain reaction of positive change. Taking risks to expand political space is one of advocacy's important functions. Careful analysis helps your organization to avoid pitfalls and choose the best options.

NOTES

[1] Bratton, Michael, *Civil Society and Political Transition in Africa,* Remarks presented at a Faculty NGO Seminar at Boston University, April 1994.

[2] See Birdsall, Nancy, *Why Inequality Matters: Some Economic Issues*; Carnegie Endowment for Peace, Discussion Paper #5, August 2001.

[3] From the Advocacy Training of Trainers cosponsored by TAF's Global Women in Politics program and by the Center for Legislative Development (CLD) in Manila, 1997.

8 Planning Moment #3: Identifying and Defining Problems

Advocacy strategies look for solutions to real problems. The success of advocacy depends on how the problem is selected, who cares about the problem, and how well it is understood.

But many advocacy strategies have difficulty in achieving their goals because the problem they seek to address:

- is not clearly defined or understood;
- is not perceived as a priority problem by a large number of people — especially by excluded groups whom the advocacy is intended to benefit;
- is not narrowed down sufficiently to a *specific issue* with a workable strategy.

Sometimes these mistakes occur because advocacy strategies respond more to donor trends than real needs and opportunities for change. Sometimes, NGO staff "cook up" a project or strategy based on well-intentioned assumptions about the problems that "poor women" or "rural farmers" face. Meanwhile poor women and farmers may have different priorities and desired solutions. In other cases, the way a problem is defined does not match the way it is experienced by those people. So those affected cannot relate to the proposed solution.

In this chapter, we offer tips for identifying advocacy problems, including participatory

> Being involved in defining problems pulls people into the political and advocacy process at a personal level. Looking at one's own reality and making choices about what really matters and what really needs to be solved is an important step in building critical awareness and active citizens.

ways of defining problems with constituency groups. These approaches are suitable both for advocacy groups starting out and for groups that have *already chosen* their issues. The tips and how-tos can help the latter refine their understanding of how the issue is experienced by people, and get buy-in from and broaden their constituencies.

Understanding Problems for Advocacy Planning

For advocates, a problem is a negative situation affecting a specific group of people. Examples of problems are poor healthcare, corruption, unemployment, gender violence, crime, or environmental degradation. These general problems are found in many places, but their characteristics vary widely depending on the context.

Each problem is made up of a variety of different *issues*. A "good" advocacy issue is focused enough so that it can be linked to a clear policy/political solution and can be easily communicated to many people.

For example, poor healthcare is a problem nearly everywhere in the world, but the specific *issues* differ widely from country to country. In the United States, one critical issue is the price of prescription drugs. In Malawi access to basic health services is a bigger issue. In advocacy, it is important to first understand the broad problem. But it is also important to define and prioritize issues because each issue will have its own hook that links it to specific policies, people, and institutions with power (see Chapter 11).

For social justice advocacy, priority problems are those that have a serious effect on

Problems ⟶ Issues ⟶ **Advocacy Strategies**

marginalized groups in society, like women, small-scale farmers, and migrant workers. Some advocacy problems concern both marginalized groups and other social sectors and thus provide good opportunities for building bridges and a broader support base.

Generally, there are two types of problems: **process** problems and **concrete** problems. Although they are often interconnected, each type presents different dilemmas and possibilities for organizing and political work.

Process Problems

Process problems relate to how decisions are made and implemented. They include transparency, accountability, corruption, discrimination, and repression.

It is sometimes difficult to mobilize around process problems because they seem too abstract. When people are struggling with basic survival issues, it is difficult to explain why these problems matter. In such cases, concrete problems are a better starting point for advocacy.

However, there are times when many different people feel strongly about process problems.

For example, during times of reform and political transition, process problems like corruption and repression can be the rallying cry that unifies many sectors of society. Similarly, international policymaking meetings, like the World Trade Organization meetings, the Social Summit, and the UN 4th World Conference on Women, are all moments when advocacy has effectively focused on process problems.

Like all problems, broad process concerns eventually need to be broken down into concrete issues in order to push for specific policies, budgets, practices, and programs.

Concrete Problems

These are problems with a concrete or physical impact. They often have to do with basic needs or violations of basic rights such as land use or ownership, healthcare, education, toxic wastes, and gender violence. To solve these problems, you often also need to address process problems. Nevertheless, the immediacy of the concrete problems usually makes them an easier starting point to mobilize people. Concrete problems are also sometimes called "fundamental" problems.

Commentary on Practical vs. Strategic Interests

Some gender analysts use a planning tool that looks at problems by distinguishing between *practical needs* and *strategic interests*. *Practical needs* are needs that, if met, will improve a woman's life but not change her subordinate status. Water and health care are examples. *Strategic interests* are interests that, if met, will challenge the inequality between men and women. Legal rights and domestic violence are examples. This distinction has helped to broaden the thinking of many development agencies. However, it is not so useful for advocacy. Often a practical problem is easier to mobilize around and, in the end, turns out to be just as strategic. Further, advocacy is itself a political, strategic way of challenging inequality, regardless of the issues.

Problem Statements: Getting Specific

A *problem statement* is a short description of the problem in a specific context. Producing a common problem statement helps avoid confusion and conflicting interpretations of the problem later on in planning.

For example, we often think "reproductive health," "constitutional reform," or "corruption" adequately describe a problem. But these shorthand terms do not give enough information if different people and organizations are to work together. For example, the problem of reproductive health may be understood by some people as lack of access to contraception and prenatal care. For others it includes feelings of shame regarding sexuality. Both views have to do with reproductive health, but each calls for a different strategy. Sometimes these shorthand descriptions describe a solution—reproductive health—not a problem.

The characteristics of problems will be different in different countries. The increasingly global scale of some advocacy initiatives makes it even more important to have a clear problem statement to facilitate clear communication between activists. But it is equally important for the staff of a single organization to produce a common problem description. See the problem statement examples in the box below.

The exercise on the following page can be helpful for groups that have already chosen their problem to better describe how the problem is experienced from the perspective of real people. It can also help reframe the shorthand description of a problem in a more effective way.

PLANNING ADVOCACY

Examples of Problem Statements	
SHORTHAND DESCRIPTIONS	**PROBLEM STATEMENTS**
Inadequate Girls' Education *(from Ghana)*	There is a higher school drop-out rate among girls because many parents believe that investing in girls' education is a waste of resources since they will get married. In addition, teachers and school materials do not reinforce the importance of girls' education. Some parents also need to put their kids to work to be able to survive.
Poor Healthcare *(from Zimbabwe)*	Basic health care is too expensive for low-income and poor people, and inaccessible to most rural residents. Drugs are unavailable and costly. Hospitals and clinics are understaffed or staffed by poorly qualified personnel. People are not educated about their health and are unable to demand better treatment or clarify what ails them and their families. This problem has a greater impact on women and children, who have specific healthcare needs, and who must look after other family members when they are ill.
Labor Rights Abuses *(from India)*	Workers work 12-hour days in poorly lit plants. Wages are less than 50 cents per hour. Frequently workers do not receive their wages for extended periods of time. They are unable to make demands because of threats that they will lose their job.

Purpose

- To understand that broad problems have many different dimensions and that the nature of the problem varies according to the context and the individual.

- To begin to see who might be the potential constituency groups for advocacy.

Process

(Time: 1 hour)

In this exercise, small groups of three to four participants identify the concrete characteristics of a problem from the perspective of two individuals in their country who experience the problem. This analysis is presented on newsprint in the form of a drawing. The presentations are followed by in-depth discussion.

1. Choose two different individuals in your country who are affected by the problem. Describe them in detail, including age, race/ethnicity, gender, family arrangements, employment or income source, class, and location. For example, in Peru you might choose the two distinct cases on the problem of poor reproductive health on the next page.

2. Draw a line down the middle of a piece of newsprint. On each side, draw a figure to represent each of the individuals. Write the person's characteristics at the bottom of the page under their feet.

3. Identify the specific concerns or symptoms that each person faces in relation to the broad problem. What would this woman or man say are her/his specific concerns? How does this person feel the problem? For example, a person is unlikely to say, "poor reproductive health services" but may say, "I don't want to have more children." Write these concerns and problems around each of the figures in random order as in the drawing.

4. Once you complete step 3, identify other problems that the individuals might not mention and write these in a different color. For example, these could include a lack of legal information or access to courts.

5. Present the drawings to the full group for discussion and deeper analysis.

Discussion

Comparing the two characters in each drawing:

- What would each person consider to be the priority concern?
- Are there common specific issues facing the two different figures?
- What are the most important differences in their experiences? Why do you think these differences exist?

Comparing all of the drawings:

- Of the different individuals in the drawings, who is the most affected by the problem? Why?
- Which aspects of the problem will require more research with the affected people to understand the issues and overall problem better?
- Are there commonalities that link the individuals that might offer possibilities for broad alliances?

Follow-up

You can complete this exercise by developing a problem statement. You can also draw up a list of questions to be answered through participatory research.

Her husband hits her

She doesn't have money for medicine

She doesn't trust the people at the medical clinic

She has many children

She has a lot of work

22 years old, born in a rural, indigenous community. She studied through 4th grade in elementary school. She had her first child when she was 14 years old. Now she has four children and works on a farm.

She is embarassed to ask for information on sexually transmitted diseases

Her children receive sex education in school

Her partner refuses to use condoms

She doesn't make time to go to a doctor regularly

37 years old, born in the city. She has some university education and had her first child when she was 25. She now has two children, is divorced, and works in an office.

PLANNING ADVOCACY

From a regional Latin American advocacy workshop held in Brazil in 2001.

Some Guiding Questions to Get Specific About Problems and Constituencies

An advocacy strategy often takes shape around a problem that is already the focus of ongoing work. But it still helps to describe what the problem looks like in the eyes of those who feel it. Since people are diverse, they often feel the problem differently. So it is important to know who is affected, and how, and who really cares about the problem.

Here are some questions to help with that analysis:

Who Defines This as a Problem?

Answering this question will tell you who some of your potential constituents, supporters, and opponents are. If the people who suffer most from the problem do not think it is a priority, then they are unlikely to get involved in the advocacy. Or — for example, in the case of people exposed to toxic chemicals — they need more information to get involved.

Consultation at the local level to define the problem and break it down into issues helps to build constituencies. However, some advo-cates believe that there is no time for this kind of grassroots consultation on a burning issue. They say that they already *know* what people care about and do not need to ask. But without the buy-in of local people, it will be difficult to engage them in the continuous efforts of support and monitoring change.

Who Is Directly Affected by This Problem?

The people who are most directly affected by a problem have the most to gain from a solution. These people are the local or primary constituency. In a global campaign, the local constituency may be spread across many different countries. Often, they are the most motivated to seek a solution. They also give your advocacy legitimacy in the eyes of policymakers who otherwise may dismiss advocates as troublemakers. The local constituency may be diverse with regard to gender, class, race, and other characteristics. Developing a detailed profile that includes some of these factors will help you focus your education, outreach, and other advocacy activities. In addition, if the problem affects particular communities, it can be helpful to know about local decisionmaking structures and local leaders.

Tips on Getting to Concrete Issues

NGOs and advocates often refer to problems in the abstract. They speak about problems of "globalization," "women's subordination," or "unemployment." These large problems are important, but they may be too broad and abstract to be clear advocacy issues. Advocacy issues link more easily to a clear policy or political solution when they are focused. A more concrete meaning will also help mobilize and engage people.

For example, during a budget advocacy workshop, the Uganda Debt Network narrowed the broad problems on the left hand side into the more focused advocacy issues on the right.

Rural Poverty ⟶	Inadequate access to extension services
Healthcare ⟶	Primary healthcare costs and quality
Education ⟶	Quality and fees for public elementary schools
Corruption ⟶	Demands for bribes by teachers and healthcare workers

Who Cares Deeply that this Problem Should Be Solved?

Experienced organizers know that frustration and anger can be good indicators that a person is motivated to work for change. These deep emotions are not always immediately visible. In particular, they are often slower to come out in communities where social structures, poverty, or other factors make people appear resigned or apathetic. Discussion, probing, and trust will help to surface people's concerns.

Who Is Not Affected but Cares Enough to Support Change?

People can also care deeply about issues that do not affect them directly. For example, many people are concerned about environmental degradation although they do not experience it in their own backyard. People also express solidarity because they believe in group rights related to gender, race, religion, and sexual orientation.

Constituency-Building Approaches for Defining Problems

Defining problems is an important step in constituency-building and citizenship. It also informs your problem statement and lays the basis for your choice of strategies. *Problem definition* is iterative like the rest of advocacy planning (see Chapter 6). Through ongoing analysis, people narrow their focus to a single common concern that is actionable. Generally,

> Regardless of whether you begin advocacy planning before or after a problem has been identified, participatory consultation and discussion with constituents and stakeholders helps to develop a common definition of the problem and begins to build ownership of the advocacy.

For Issue-Focused Groups:
Where constituencies and stakeholders have identified or share a common concern, the broad problem is already clear. The task then is to narrow it down to a concrete issue by finding out what people are most concerned about. Later you can narrow down further by considering what is actionable through advocacy.

For Groups Without an Issue Agenda:
Where there is no common focus, activities such as participatory surveys and public dialogue will surface problems. Further analysis and negotiation will help identify a priority problem and a specific issue. The process meanwhile builds local grassroots constituencies because it allows for face-to-face learning and confidence-building.

the analysis involves:

- asking, listening, discussing, debating, and negotiating;

- introducing facts and analysis to inform the discussion;

- narrowing the lens on the higher-priority aspects of the problem;

- using additional research and dialogue with groups living with the problem to further define the problem.

If the problem definition process utilizes broad consultation and face-to-face discussion, it can:

- broaden interest in advocacy;

- stimulate the emergence of potential local leaders—people who feel strongly enough to dedicate their time and energize others;

- produce a clearer understanding of the problem and priority issues;

- facilitate political awareness, where citizens recognize how the political process can both perpetuate injustices and offer ways to find solutions.

PLANNING ADVOCACY

Purpose

- To understand how different ways of asking questions elicit different responses and create different impressions;
- To clarify how these shape the quality of information you receive and either help or hinder your organizing efforts.

Process

(Time: 1 hour)

The illustrations on the next page show different ways of asking questions. Usually, organizations enter a community with a clear agenda. In the second picture, the organization is asking about the concerns of the people present, using open-ended questioning. In the first picture, technical experts are explaining a problem they have already identified rather than opening a discussion for people to describe how they experience it.

1. Ask participants to look carefully at the two pictures in the illustration and describe what is happening in each. Compare what is happening using the following questions:
   - What is the role of the outsider? How is she/he perceived by the community?
   - Does the community feel involved in the learning? Why or why not?
   - What do you think will be the product of each of these discussions with regard to problem identification and group motivation?
   - Which approach(es) will elicit the most accurate information about what people care about?
   - Have you seen either approach?

2. After the participants have discussed and compared the two pictures, summarize the differences between the approaches. Refer to Chapter 4 on participatory learning and Chapter 5 on types of participation.

Tips on Talking with Strangers in Public Spaces

Finding out what people really care about requires respect for others, ease in speaking with others, and active listening. Active listening means listening carefully, asking people to clarify what they have said, and interpreting nonverbal cues like facial expression and posture. It is also important to be aware of what you communicate to others by your own posture, eye contact, and general appearance. You do not need to look exactly like the people you speak with in order to make them feel at ease. What is important is your attitude, a sense of solidarity, and your skill in asking questions. (See *Annex 1* for more on the skills of active listening.)

#1

#2

Specific Participatory Approaches

Participatory approaches to problem definition combine dialogue, communication, and trust-building. If you are an outsider, there are several steps and approaches you need to consider in order to engage potential constituents effectively.

Step 1: Getting to Know Constituents

Getting to know your constituents involves two tasks. First, you have to get accurate information about their needs and options. Second, you need to build enough trust to be able to work together. The approaches you use depend on the scale and level of your advocacy. For example, global advocacy will utilize the Internet much more. When you are an outsider, here are some different ways to get to know your constituents and their backgrounds:

From existing documentation
Information about the problem and the community you are working with is probably available through development and donor agencies, UN organizations, the World Bank, government statistics bureaus, and universities.

From observation
Just by watching carefully, an external organizer can learn something about what people are like, what they care about, who their leaders are, and other important information.

By visiting gathering sites
Places like bars, grocery stores, sports fields, and wells are a good way to meet several people at once. Often specific kinds of people meet in particular locations. In some countries, many people gather and talk at shopping malls, especially young and older people. In contrast, you will usually meet only children and women at a pump or well in a rural village.

Public calls for action
Using media such as a radio or newspaper spot, a town meeting, a poster campaign, or an electronic mailing list can ask people who care to contact the organizers. These public calls begin a dialogue between organizers and people who are concerned about an issue. This method will mainly reach people who are already informed.

Step 2: Ways to Identify Problems

There are several ways to engage people in discussing problems and issues, including:

- a written survey using a questionnaire;
- one-on-one interviews and door-to-door canvassing;
- a participatory needs assessment;
- focus group discussions,
- informal conversation in public spaces

Choosing a suitable approach depends on:
- the audience you want to reach;
- the information you want to get and to communicate;
- the involvement you hope to generate;
- the relationship you want to establish;
- the resources you have at your disposal.

We discuss these approaches below:

Surveys
A survey uses a questionnaire to obtain facts, ideas, and opinions from individuals. It can provide information about what people care about and can be used to show the magnitude of a problem or demand. The findings can be persuasive for your advocacy message.

However, surveys are labor intensive and demand a lot of preparation. Drawing up a questionnaire requires skill. It is important to avoid bias and leading questions if you want the results to be taken seriously. A written survey which people fill in themselves saves time and costs in terms of interviewers. However, it often gets a poor or biased response because not everybody completes the questionnaire or is literate. And it does not allow people to meet and talk face-to-face. A survey conducted face-to-face provides an opportunity for the interviewer to talk to the interviewee. That conversation can be an important part of advocacy.

Timing is key for house-to-house surveys

Because people respond individually in a survey, it is not the best way to build collective spirit or enable people to find common ground. A questionnaire can be used together with focus group discussions, a workshop, or another type of group-building encounter.

One-on-one interviews and door-to-door canvassing

These methods are useful for probing sensitive issues. They avoid the discomfort people may feel about talking in public (see note on risk and safety on page 142). Face-to-face interviews enable you to discover things that may not arise from a questionnaire, such as anger and frustration. Citizen action organizations in the USA have often gone door to door to find out what people are concerned about. The strategy works best where people live close to one another. It also depends on having enough people to go door to door and on the willingness of people to talk to them.

Participatory needs assessment

A participatory needs assessment is a group-based survey of a community's perceptions of their problems and desired solutions. There are many approaches and techniques, and countless manuals that describe them. Some participatory assessments—such as rapid rural

appraisal—can involve many different groups within a community and facilitate the exchange of ideas. These are discussed in more detail on page 140.

Focus group discussions

These discussions bring together 5–25 people who live in a common situation to discuss their views and concerns. Focus groups can generate more information than one-on-one interviews because the dialogue produces more ideas and an exchange of views. Using focus groups for citizen education and advocacy is described on pages 142-146.

Informal conversation in public spaces

This can be the least costly and simplest way to talk with a range of people. Unfortunately, certain kinds of people have more time or ability to talk than others. For example, older and younger people tend to have more time. And often men have more time and opportunity than women. These differences may skew your results.

Nevertheless, public spaces can be a good way to gain information and reach people on issues they care about. For example, when UK-based Christian Aid organized a campaign to get supermarkets to purchase goods in a

PLANNING ADVOCACY

socially responsible manner, it organized in front of the supermarkets talking to shoppers. Similarly, a campaign around water use can be organized at wells in rural areas. The strategy works because it is easy to link the issue with what people are doing at the public place—gathering water, getting medical treatment, standing in lines for public services, buying food, picking up children from school. The location sparks discussion and helps you identify who is affected and who cares.

Most of the approaches above are ideal for local constituency-building because they involve face-to-face discussion. Some can also be more labor intensive and costly. For national, regional, and global advocacy, the

local processes will need to be adapted and can be complemented by electronic surveys. A drawback to using electronic tools is that many marginalized groups are not computer-literate and have no access to the technology.

Identifying problems involves a two-way dialogue in which concerns, opinions, and information are shared. The outside facilitator is not just there to ask questions. The facilitator must also probe and can introduce new ideas and information. In this way, the dialogue can be a moment for:

- education and information;
- group building;
- exploring community potential;
- building a relationship between organizers and constituents where each side recognizes the contribution of the other.

Some Thoughts on Power Differences within Groups

Development and government agencies sometimes treat communities or groups, such as poor people and women, as if they were homogeneous. In the end, these projects have failed because the most powerful members in the groups dominate while other people's needs and interests are not satisfied. Every community or social group has a hierarchy of power and control that may be constructed along gender, race, class, age, or other lines.

It is important to consider this hierarchy when organizing. For example, women's voices are usually heard less in mixed groups. Women often do not feel confident to speak in the company of men. In some cases, women may not be allowed to meet in public without their husband or father's permission. At the same time, men may feel threatened when they are excluded from women's meetings and not informed about what is happening. Organizers need to be sensitive to these possible dynamics and make adjustments to be inclusive.

Depending on the level of gender equality in a given context, it may be advisable to work with women and men separately during the problem identification and analysis and issue selection process. Because these moments are critical for investment in and ownership of the advocacy process, it is important that each individual be able to engage and contribute his or her ideas without hesitation. Once the analysis has been completed, women and men can come together to share their views and look for common ground. Even when these adjustments are made, conflict may arise. (See Chapters 15 and 17 for ideas on managing conflict.)

Remember that gender is only one determinant of power. There are also important differences among women and among men. Recognizing the different axes of power that are in play in different contexts is vital for effective advocacy and constituency-building. Treating people with common problems as the same only serves to reinforce inequalities and keep people from being active citizens.

Access and Control Profile

One way to identify inequalities in a community or group is with the *Access and Control Profile*. This gender analysis tool shows the power differences between women and men, but can also be applied to any disadvantaged subgroup. For example, you can add economic status, race, age, or religion. The profile asks questions about who has access to and who controls resources. *Access* refers to the opportunity to make use of something. *Control* has to do with decision making about the use of resources and benefits. Because it asks these important questions, development of a participatory profile can be motivating and politicizing for those involved. Analysis of difference and power dynamics in one's own community is important for political awareness.

RESOURCES	Access		Control	
Economic and productive	Men	Women	Men	Women
Land				
Equipment				
Education and training				
Labor				
Cash				
Other				
Political				
Leadership				
Education and training				
Information				
Citizenship skills				
Legal rights				
Other				
BENEFITS				
Income				
Property ownership				
Basic needs (food, clothing, shelter)				
Education				
Political power and prestige				
Other				

PLANNING ADVOCACY

Adapted from: March, Smyth, and Mukhopadhyay, *A Guide to Gender-Analysis Frameworks*, Oxfam Publishing, Oxford 1999, 34.

The chart below can be used by organizers to map out and prioritize the best places to identify problems.

- **Column 1** asks you to list the various places where the kind of data you need could be best gathered: door-to-door; gathering places (e.g., self-service laundries, wells, bars, parks/playgrounds, lines for services, stores and malls, etc.); places where people experience the problems (if consumers are angry about the high prices at the local market, talk to them outside the market); places where the problem is treated (human services agencies, hospitals, health clinics, counseling centers).

- **Column 2** asks you to think of the kind of data that you need to gather from interviews with individuals in each of the areas.

- **Column 3** asks you to generate kinds of questions that can be asked of each source in order to get the data you need.

- **Column 4**, because an organizer's time is precious, asks you to prioritize the locations which are most useful for discussing issues with a range of people.

Identifying Problems & Issues				
POSSIBLE DATA GATHERING PLACES	**NAMES OF PLACES / PEOPLE**	**WHAT INFORMATION DO WE NEED?**	**QUESTIONS TO ASK IN EACH SITUATION**	**RANKED ORDER OF IMPORTANCE**
Door-to-Door				
Gathering Places				
Public spaces				
Places Where People Experience the Problem				
Where Problem is Treated				
Places to Get Documentation of the Problem				
Where to Get Information on Root Cause				
People Who Cause the Problem				

Adapted from *How to Make Citizen Involvement Work*, Duane Dale, Citizen Involvement Training Project, University of Massachusetts, Amherst, 1978.

After talking to people about the problems and issues they face, the following chart can be used to help you map and start analyzing your findings. Both of these charts can be used by a number of organizers and constituents as joint tools of planning and analysis.

Comparisons of Perceptions of the Problem						
How the...	community	local power structure	general public	NGOs & social services	government (district / national)	regional / international agencies (World Bank)
perceive(s) the problem						
perceive(s) the solutions						
perceive(s) the community						

When you have filled in the chart, the following questions may help guide your analysis of the information:

- Where are the differences?
- Which differences do you need to clear up first?
- Where are the conflicts?
- What can be done to clear up the conflicts?
- Why do the conflicts exist?

Adapted from *How to Make Citizen Involvement Work*, Duane Dale, Citizen Involvement Training Project, University of Massachusetts, Amherst, 1978 and *From the Roots Up*, by Peter Gubbels and Catheryn Koss, World Neighbors, 2000.

PLANNING ADVOCACY

More on Participatory Assessments

Typically, participatory assessments have been used for development projects. When effectively done, they provide a comprehensive picture of a community's situation—its needs, resources, values, expectations, problems and their causes, as well as the community's internal dynamics and social hierarchies. Unfortunately, some assessments result in a "shopping list" of needs without any

real analysis. Often they do not move on to identifying solutions. Participants learn skills and gain confidence, but they often do not get the tools to influence political and economic decisionmaking.

Participatory assessments are known by a variety of names: community needs assessments, participatory or action research, organizational diagnosis, participatory rural or rapid rural appraisals, and social assessments. Many of the techniques and exercises used

Participatory Research in Nicaragua

In the 1980s, the Nicaraguan Ministry of Education sponsored a pilot participatory assessment in the rural village of El Regadio as a follow-up to the 1980 national literacy campaign. The Ministry wanted to use the assessment in designing a nationwide strategy to promote community-based education linked to development. With the help of external staff, community leaders conducted a questionnaire survey on the needs, problems, and possibilities for better education and organization in the village. The external staff members all had a background in community development and popular education, and one person lived in the community for several months during the assessment. The external staff assisted the community team responsible for coordinating the process by helping them set goals, develop appropriate survey questions, design and carry out a survey, use participatory methods, and analyze information once it was gathered. Based on this assessment, community members then made decisions about a variety of local development projects and used advocacy to gain support for their changes with local officials.

The community regarded the survey with a combination of surprise, suspicion, and pride. They remembered previous surveys run by local landowners interested in expanding their holdings, by corrupt government officials interested in getting cheap resources, and by urban-based professionals interested in gathering data. But they realized that a survey run by local people was different. Community residents came together to discuss the findings, which were drafted on large charts. Many residents spoke publicly for the first time. One man leaned on his friend to overcome his nervousness in expressing his opinion. Two women disagreed with the finding that only two women "worked." "We women live working," they pointed out.

Residents ranked their problems and prioritized solutions. Members of the two agricultural cooperatives proposed to diversify their production and use the land more efficiently. In order to present their information and conclusions to officials, residents produced a booklet which they printed themselves on a handmade silk screen. Convincing government agronomists who had not been part of the process to back their ideas was difficult. In some cases, officials felt their authority was being undermined. After much negotiation and intervention from higher authorities, the relevant ministry agreed to support the residents' proposal. As a result of the changes, the cooperative increased its dairy and grain production and was awarded a prize for being the most outstanding community enterprise in the region. Village women formed a vegetable production group, and several went on to take up leadership in regional organizations working on development.

From Lisa VeneKlasen, *El Regadio*, unpublished report, 1983.

are drawn from popular education and community development. They include power maps and stakeholder analyses, community surveys, problem ranking exercises, community resources mapping and inventories, and planning frameworks.

Participatory Assessments as Citizen Education and Organization Strategies

Participatory assessments vary in the level of community involvement and control over how the information is used. Approaches that involve the community in all stages—from deciding what kind of information to gather to planning follow-up action—tend to be the most effective for building citizen participation. These approaches build community capacity, leadership, and citizenship skills. They enable people to work with and hold government and other relevant agencies accountable.

In community-directed assessments, groups such as women's associations or water users initiate the assessment and decide if and when they need an outside NGO or academic group to help them with some steps in the process. In other instances, NGOs, international agencies, and outsiders initiate the assessment. Ideally, outsiders work closely with the community to make the process as participatory as possible. Support institutions can play an important role in helping groups acquire analytical tools and skills for advocacy.

Participatory assessments can be ideal for beginning an advocacy effort as they build local constituent involvement and surface critical issues. But participatory assessments are not always empowering. Sometimes, participants are seen only as information sources or implementers for activities that are decided elsewhere. In some cases, the community is not told the final results of the as-

sessment. The interventions raise expectations that leave people feeling disillusioned. As a result, people lose interest in participating in any surveys or advocacy efforts.

The Costs and Benefits of Participatory Assessments

The common argument against participatory assessments is that they are time consuming and resource intensive. Because of this, they tend to be small-scale or rushed. Smaller NGOs are often unable to afford the staff time. Many organizations end up arguing with their donors on whether such an assessment is necessary, despite the fact that they improve the efficiency and effectiveness of outside interventions. On the other hand, large development institutions and donors are themselves increasingly attempting participatory assessments. For example, The World Bank has carried out numerous Participatory Poverty Assessments around the globe. The methodology and level of real participation vary widely. In some cases the assessments have presented opportunities for local NGOs to engage with their constituents and with governments in a way that was previously impossible.

For More on Participatory Assessment

Also see the website for the Participation Group at the Institute of Development Studies, Sussex, UK: http//www.ids.ac.uk/ids/particip for a variety of cases and resources on participatory assessment; *The Myth of Community: Gender Issues in Participatory Development*, Irene Guijt and Meera Kaul Shah, Editors, Intermediate Technology Publications Ltd., London, 1998; and *Power, Process and Participation: Tools for Change*, Rachel Slocum, Lori Wichhart, et al., Editors, Intermediate Technology Publications Ltd., London, 1998.

PLANNING ADVOCACY

More on Focus Groups

Focus group approaches can be adapted for community organizing and problem definition. The idea of focus groups comes originally from the advertising world. There, small discussion circles are used to test people's tastes, interests, and responses to new products. Political advisors and researchers use focus groups to measure public opinion, test policy ideas, and political priorities. Development agencies use focus groups to gain information for program design. Women's and citizens' groups have used focus groups to develop alternative policy frameworks and legislative agendas.

Focus groups can be run in a variety of ways with different degrees of community participation and control. Standard politically-motivated focus groups tend to be led and controlled by an outside facilitator. The process tends to be extractive; participants from the local community generally do not gain any new information and serve mainly as information providers.

On the other hand, participatory focus groups are facilitated discussions that involve debate, analysis, and planning. They can serve as both a research tool and a learning dialogue for those involved, and can be linked to local action and organizing.

Focus groups are usually one to two hours in length. They can follow a structured format that involves 6–10 questions, each with follow-up questions that probe for more details. Alternatively, they can be based on only one or two broadly framed questions that open up a free interchange. Discussion is led by one or two facilitators who are assisted by a record keeper. The facilitator can either actively lead the conversation or remain silent and let the dynamics of the group take over.

In Botswana, South Africa, Benin (see page 144), and the Philippines, women's organizations have used focus groups to develop a national gender platform and strengthen their base. These initiatives integrated the voices of

Important Note on Risk

Asking questions and encouraging people to speak their mind is not always a good idea. At certain times it may be risky for local people. For example, sometimes when peasants meet with outsiders, local bosses follow-up with intimidation. Peasants' lives can then be in danger. Similarly, in many communities it is dangerous for women to speak with strangers, let alone voice their opinion on sensitive issues like rape or incest. If they do so, they may be threatened by male family members. If your consultation is going to take the lid off problems that are hidden, make sure that there are support services if people need help. For example, in Kenya in the late 1980s, a legal rights group launched a campaign against family violence. They placed posters throughout Nairobi asking people to denounce this "crime." They were overwhelmed by women calling for help and were not able to meet the demand. The campaign seemed to provoke more family conflict when women spoke out. In the end, the organizers decided to take down the posters and redirect their strategy.

Asking questions in a tightly controlled political context is especially risky. To minimize risk:
- work with local groups where possible;
- get to know the local area, its social and cultural taboos, and its political dynamics before organizing public discussion;
- if you hold focus groups or public meetings, prepare facilitators well beforehand.

grassroots women into documents that were then used in electoral and legislative advocacy. Over a two-year period, an alliance of citizens' groups in Panama carried out focus groups with different sectors throughout the country to define an alternative to the government's Five Year Development Plan. The alternative plan has been used in a range of advocacy activities.

PLANNING ADVOCACY

Focus groups were a core activity of a two-year women's political participation strategy in Benin carried out by four local NGOs and the Global Women in Politics (GWIP) program in the late 1990s. Emerging from decades of dictatorship, Benin held its first fair elections in 1991. The project took shape with the aim of getting women more involved as citizens in the political reform process and as an alternative to training women to run for elections. Despite elections, GWIP and its partners knew that citizenship was a relatively new concept for Beninese women. They felt that the few women who would stand for elections were unlikely to promote a women's rights agenda. Most citizens did not see the relevance of politics to their lives, so the key parties and legislators were free to set their own agendas. Progress toward government accountability seemed unlikely without more engagement by civil society.

The project created a process that brought women together to express their interests and concerns. Following focus group discussions, women elected representatives from each group to participate in the development of a Women's Issues Platform in the capital city, Cotonou. The Platform was to be used in advocacy with candidates, voters, and legislators. The project created a microcosm of democratic process for both the participating NGOs and the grassroots women with whom they worked.

Before the project, the four local partner organizations worked mainly in traditional development and education initiatives. They had not been exposed to advocacy or formal politics. It took some time before everyone recognized and had a common understanding about the linkages between development and democracy. At first the partners felt that gathering the opinions of their "beneficiaries" was a waste of resources. But eventually they agreed and carried out 70 focus groups, involving more than 1,000 women and every district of the country.

The project initiated a formal alliance between the partners. By the end of the project, the four partner groups saw themselves not only as providers of social and economic services, but also as catalysts for citizen organizing and influence. They had also established strong links with a vast network of grassroots women who were ready to speak up in their village and in the policymaking arena. Their alliance enabled them to allocate resources to implement the advocacy plan.

What Are the Lessons?

- Training and analysis with the NGO leaders and their community-based staff was an important component throughout the project. But it was only near the end that it became clear to everyone that the project was about democracy as a set of values, attitudes, and ways of relating rather than just about structures and procedures. In retrospect, it might have been better to begin with an intensive dialogue and reflection about the definition of politics, democracy, citizenship, gender, and women's rights.

- Beforehand, all of the community-based animators were trained in participatory discussion methodologies and were given a detailed guidebook to support them. Although the training and guidebook were insufficient to help them in the difficult task of facilitating focus groups, the process itself was valuable.

- While the partners recognized the importance of accurate documentation of the focus group discussions, there were not enough resources for rapporteurs or tape recorders, so rich information was lost, affecting accuracy.

- Organizational hierarchies, social attitudes, and traditional patterns of relating to the "beneficiaries" conflicted with the use of participatory methodologies. The NGO leaders did not feel it was worthwhile to train community-based staff, although this staff ran most of the focus groups. The value of listening to local people was not recognized until the end of the project.

- Synthesizing and analyzing the raw focus group material into a set of priorities involved intensive behind the scenes work by a research expert with the NGO leadership. It proved to be a challenge for the NGO leaders to remain true to the voices of the grassroots women and resist overanalyzing and reinterpreting women's statements. Conflicting approaches to handling the information tapped into deeply held values about the hierarchy of knowledge, reflecting the attitude that uneducated grassroots women know less than the educated urban NGO staff about their own environment.

- Democracy language became a stumbling block in communication between the partners, GWIP, and the donor. Because the project was concerned more about recreating the practice and values of democracy in the context of a focused project as a step toward dealing with elections and legislation, it was tough to agree on measurements of success. Importantly, this case demonstrates that the process itself can be a valid measurement.

PLANNING ADVOCACY

Excerpts From the Benin Focus Group Facilitator's Guide

The community-based animators were trained in participatory methodologies and focus group techniques. They were given a 4-page guide with suggestions on how best to organize the discussion time for a group of 15 women. It suggested:

- Introductions - 30 minutes
- Brainstorming Session - 45 minutes
- Small Group Discussion - 45 minutes
- Report back to the larger group and discussion - 45 minutes
- Conclusion - 15 minutes

The Guide also gave tips about schedule and logistics, for example, setting a time that accommodates women's demands at home and in the field, arranging chairs in a circle, and having flipchart paper and markers handy. It noted, "although not all of the women will be able to read, a visual record will validate what people are saying." The Guide lists some of the possible issues and problems women may mention, and encourages the facilitators to probe these areas:

- "Safety: Do you feel your community is safe? Do you feel that there is safety in your family? . . .
- Health: Do you have problems finding a doctor or clinic to help you when you or your family are sick?
- Environment: Is it difficult to find wood for cooking? Why? Is garbage and sewage a problem?
- Infrastructure: Are the roads within your community in good condition? Is there easy access to other towns, markets, water? Are the bridges in your area safe?
- Family Life (relations): Are there any problems in families that affect life for women in this community? How are these problems perceived by men? By women? Are you familiar with the laws about marriage, children, etc.?
- Property: Do women own land or other property in your area? Why/why not? Do women inherit property when their husbands or fathers pass away?
- Work: What do women do for money? For food? How much time do domestic chores take most women?"

The Guide also offers tips for building trust and confidence in a group, and tips on asking questions:

"Remember that the women with whom we are discussing are the experts on their lives and the issues that they face. It is the facilitator's job to make them feel comfortable enough to speak their mind. . . . Ask questions in concrete terms. It is difficult to get the kind of information needed to develop the platform by asking abstract or theoretical questions, like 'tell me about the status of women.' The facilitators may want to give information that will help participants reflect about their own situation."

Choosing priority issues from among many urgent problems is not an easy task. It is a multi-step process involving analysis and negotiation within a group. Analysis is central to advocacy planning from beginning to end. The poor choices that arise from inadequate analysis can be costly and, in politics, sometimes dangerous.

Analysis is about asking why. Probing for hidden truths is a habit and a skill. It is vital to political awareness and informed citizenship. But sometimes asking why- why- why is not acceptable, or may be politically risky.

Another challenge in analysis for advocacy planning is that there are many different causes of problems. The causes can be interconnected and even contradictory. A systematic approach to analysis helps to structure the probing.

It is also helpful to be aware of the lens through which you are looking. For example, if you look at the cultural factors that shape a problem, you will see something different than if you look at economic factors. And if you look at economic factors, your understanding of economics will shape what you see. One person may say that people are poor because wages are low and workers are unorganized. Another person may say that it is due to a lack of education and training.

Prioritization and analysis are connected. To make choices, a group needs clear criteria for ranking problems in order of importance. The group will probably debate both the criteria and the analysis since people see things differently and have diverse interests, even when they share a common problem. Choosing priorities involves looking at the causes and impact of problems as well as analyzing solutions. You need to decide which strategy is feasible for your group and which offers the most political gain. In social justice advocacy, problems related to exclusion and inequity are a priority.

This chapter provides six tools for problem analysis and prioritization. These tools can help people to:

- understand the interrelated root causes of a problem;
- adopt common criteria for choosing priority issues;
- define and prioritize aspects of the problem (*issues*) that will be the focus of advocacy;
- identify the additional information they need about the political and policy dimensions before finalizing the strategy.

For groups already engaged in advocacy on a specific issue, these tools can help refine strategies and get broader constituency involvement. The tools are divided into three groups as follows:

1. Analysis for Prioritizing Problems

- *Priority Group Analysis*
- *Problem Identification and Prioritization*

Both of these exercises are helpful for analysis with constituency groups, but can also be modified for priority-setting in organizations. These link priority-setting to criteria related to exclusion and need.

2. Many Causes, Many Solutions

- *Causes, Consequences, and Solutions*
- *The Problem Tree Analysis*
- *Simple Structural Analysis*

These tools help to define the specific causes and issues that make up a broad problem. Mapping the causes, consequences, and solutions of a problem can be a good way to begin analysis because it produces a comprehensive map of a problem. This is the first exercise in this group, while the other two look at root causes. The consequences part helps identify who is hurt by the problem and how. The analysis will remind advocates that policy change alone will not fully address the issue.

3. Comparing and Choosing an Issue

- *Checklist for Choosing an Issue*

This exercise compares different issues by using criteria related to the potential impact of advocacy.

Although all the exercises are complementary, you can choose which ones best suit your group's planning needs. At a minimum, we recommend you use the *Causes, Consequence, and Solutions* exercise and combine it with one of the priorities exercises.

Facilitator's Note

The more participatory the analysis can be, the greater the buy-in and motivation will be for doing and sustaining advocacy. Participatory problem analysis and priority setting:

- involves negotiation and debate;
- is an educational and consciousness raising experience;
- increases skills and information.

This kind of analysis is especially valuable for critical awareness because it helps people to challenge the official or common explanations for why things happen.

Problem analysis is not just looking at causes. Exploring all the possible solutions helps you choose your direction in a more informed way. Identifying consequences and solutions shows that comprehensive strategies are crucial for long-term success.

Purpose

To analyze the different needs and potential of a marginalized group within a community. This exercise can be applied to the problems currently being addressed by a program or organization.

Process

(Time: 1-2 hours)

1. Divide participants into groups of ten or less. Give each group newsprint and markers.

2. Ask participants to draw one large circle on the newsprint with a smaller circle inside it. The large circle represents the whole community. The small circle is the marginalized group that you choose to prioritize.

3. Ask participants to write in the larger circle all the problems being addressed by the program that affect the entire community. Use symbols to represent these problems if the participants are non-literate.

4. Next ask participants to write problems which affect the priority group in the inner circle. Some of these problems will be the same as in the larger circle and some may be different.

Discussion

Together, analyze the circles and problems. Here are some possible questions to help guide the discussion:

- How do the problems in the two circles differ? How are they the same?

- What solutions will give priority to the needs of the marginalized group and have potential to gain support from the larger community?

- What can the marginalized group contribute (e.g., knowledge, people, other resources)?

Example

SARTHI, an NGO based in Rajasthan India, has been helping Adivasi women organize themselves around rehabilitation and management of common lands. (Adivasi are an indigenous tribal community.) The largest circle represents the problems that affect the Adivasi community. Because the SARTHI program focuses on the rehabilitation of grazing lands, problems related to the lack of vegetative matter are listed. Some of the program-related problems affecting the women (the priority group) are the same as those facing the whole community. Others mainly affect the women.

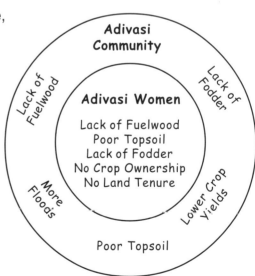

From *A Manual for Socio-Economic and Gender Analysis: Responding to the Development Challenge,* by Barbara Thomas-Slayter, Rachel Polestico, Andrea Lee Esser, Octavia Taylor and Elvina Mutua, SEGA, Clark University: Massachusetts,1995, p. 97.

PLANNING ADVOCACY

Purpose

This exercise helps to:

- identify and rank priority problems in a group using a simple set of criteria;
- gain historical perspective on the problems;
- assess the impact of each problem from the points of view of those involved.

Process

(Time: 1-2 hours)

This exercise can be used as part of a participatory assessment for a community program, within an organization or in a workshop with representatives of different groups. There are two ways to do the exercise; which you choose depends on where you are in the problem definition process.

1. Determine the major problems.

    1a. If you have not yet done a problem definition activity, begin by presenting a list of sectors or groups (e.g., women, peasant farmers, small businesses) on flipchart. Choose the sectors from those that are related to your organization's work. Go through the list, asking participants to name the main problems in each different sector or group. Help participants understand the difference between the core problems and the symptoms of these problems. For example, educational disadvantages faced by girls may be a symptom of economic hardships that force parents to choose which children to send to school.

    1b. Brainstorm a list of problems that are on the agenda of the groups involved or draw from problems already identified in a participatory way.

2. Write each problem on a separate card. If the problem is one that occurs in relation to several sectors, use a different colored card for each sector.

3. Develop criteria with the group for categorizing each of the problems as "Most Serious," "Serious," and "Less Serious." The criteria could include number of people affected, severity of consequences, frequency, etc. Write the list of criteria on flipchart paper.

4. Referring to these criteria, ask the participants to sort the problem cards into the three categories. If there are several sectors, keep the cards for each sector separate. Write codes (MS for Most Serious, S for Serious, LS for Less Serious) on the back of each card.

5. Decide together on the time period over which you will measure change – whether, for example, it is two years, five years or ten years. Ask participants to think about whether, during this time period, each problem has gotten *Worse,* stayed the *Same,* or gotten *Better.* Sort the cards into these three groups. Write codes on the back of each card according to the change category (W for Worse, S for Same, and B for Better).

6. Make a matrix. Label the rows: "Getting Worse," "Staying the Same," and "Getting Better." Label the columns: "Most Serious," "Serious," and "Less Serious." If you have organized the cards by sector, make a separate matrix for each sector. Then place each card into the correct cell of the matrix.

Discussion

- Why are certain problems getting worse?
- Why are some problems improving?
- What role does government play in this?
- What other powerful actors have influenced the changes?
- What role have citizens and organizations played in the changes?
- Are the most serious problems getting better or worse?
- What can citizens and government do to change this?

Follow-up

The problems in the Getting Worse/Most Serious box are often the best place to concentrate your advocacy. Following their identification, they need to be analyzed further in order to select the most compelling issue that will serve as the focus of your advocacy work.

	Most Serious	Serious	Less Serious
Getting Worse	Malnutrition Domestic Violence		Lack of Transportation
Staying the Same	Corruption	Market too far away	No Training Opportunities
Getting Better	Employment Opportunities		

Adapted from *From the Roots Up: Strengthening Organizational Capacity Through Guided Self-Assessment,* Peter Gubbels and Catheryn Koss, World Neighbors, Oklahoma, 2000.

PLANNING ADVOCACY

Purpose

This framework helps analyze problems by making the links between causes, effects and solutions. It encourages discussion of a wide range of solutions and emphasizes the need for social and political, as well as policy, strategies.

Process

(Time: 1-2 hours)

This analysis is best handled in small groups that allow each individual to contribute. If your group is working on several problems, divide the groups up by the problems that interest them.

1. For each problem, make a chart with three columns. The headings of the columns are: "Causes," "Consequences," and "Solutions."

2. Begin by identifying the causes of the problem. Write each cause in the first column of the chart.

> The consequences column shows how problems affect people's lives. This helps in identifying constituencies. It also helps later on in choosing the targets and messages for outreach.

3. Repeat the process for consequences, and then solutions. Sometimes there are not clear cause-effect relationships between causes and consequences. So the cause, consequences, and solutions do not have to be linked or related horizontally. That can be done later.

Discussion

- Are the causes listed the *main* causes of the problem?
- What are the social attitudes and power dynamics that contribute to causing this problem?
- How do the causes and problems affect people's lives? Who is affected and how?
- What are the main solutions proposed? Do any of them address social attitudes?

Tips

- Before beginning the analysis, go through the process in plenary with a different problem to show how the framework works. (See example on next page.)
- Before starting, explain how causes and consequences are different – a consequence is the result of a problem, while a cause helps create the problem.
- This framework can be extended by adding a fourth column which shows who is responsible for each solution and, if there are scarce resources, which are the priorities for them to focus on. If the advocacy will involve government, an international donor agency, the private sector, or somebody else, the fourth column can be used to link solutions with different decisionmaking arenas and institutions.
- During discussion, always look for the main causes. For example, sometimes groups focus on low funding as a cause when, in fact, it is not the primary cause.

Example

The matrix below is an example of how a Ugandan NGO working on debt relief and budgets applied this tool to a big problem – corruption.

PROBLEM: Corruption		
CAUSES	**CONSEQUENCES**	**SOLUTIONS**
-Widespread poverty -Greed, profit-centered priorities -Competition for resources -Lack of transparency -Desire for power and domination -Lack of checks and balances -Lack of effective laws and regulations to punish -Desire to manipulate the system -Breakdown of moral values -Peer pressure -Inappropriate inherited systems	-Increased poverty and marginalization of the poor, the powerless, and minorities -Loss of confidence in the system by the people/ growing indifference -Unsustainable debt burden -Poor social services -Breakdown of moral values -Growth of powerful -Donor dependence -Emergence of dictatorship -Wasteful spending on white elephants	-Increased transparency and accountability -Increased community participation in decisionmaking at all levels -Civic education for family and community -Stiff punishment for offenders -Political consciousness -Increased media involvement -NGO advocacy

Winning drawings from a nationwide art competition in the primary and secondary schools on the problem of corruption in Uganda

PLANNING ADVOCACY

Purpose

This exercise is used to analyze the root causes of a problem and to identify the primary consequences. The tree provides a visual structure for the analysis.

Process

(Time: 1-2 hours)

This activity is best handled in small groups so that each person in the group has an opportunity to participate. If time makes this impossible, a large group can be divided into two groups, with the first group working on causes and the second group examining consequences.

If you are working on more than one problem, assign each group a different problem. Take one problem and go through the process once together before dividing into groups. (Time: 1-2 hours)

1. Explain the problem tree. Point out the different parts of the tree and what each represents:
   - Roots = Root *Causes* of the Problem
   - Trunk = the *Problem*
   - Branches = *Consequences* of the Problem

2. Ask a participant to draw a tree on flipchart paper. Write the problem on the trunk of the tree. Ask all participants to list the causes of the problem. If possible, let each participant who suggests a cause write it on a card and tape it to the roots of the problem tree. If this is too time-consuming, the facilitator can write what the participants say on the tree. Encourage people to explore social, economic, and political causes including attitudes, behavior, and other factors.

3. Repeat the same process with the consequences.

Discussion

First ask questions about the problem itself, then follow up with questions about the solutions.
- What are the most serious consequences?
- Which causes will be easier to address? More difficult to address? Why?
- Which causes and consequences can the government help address? Where can international agencies help? What can people do?

Example

The example on the next page of a problem tree is from an Egyptian coalition advocating for the elimination of the practice of female genital mutilation (FGM) under the auspices of the National FGM Task Force.

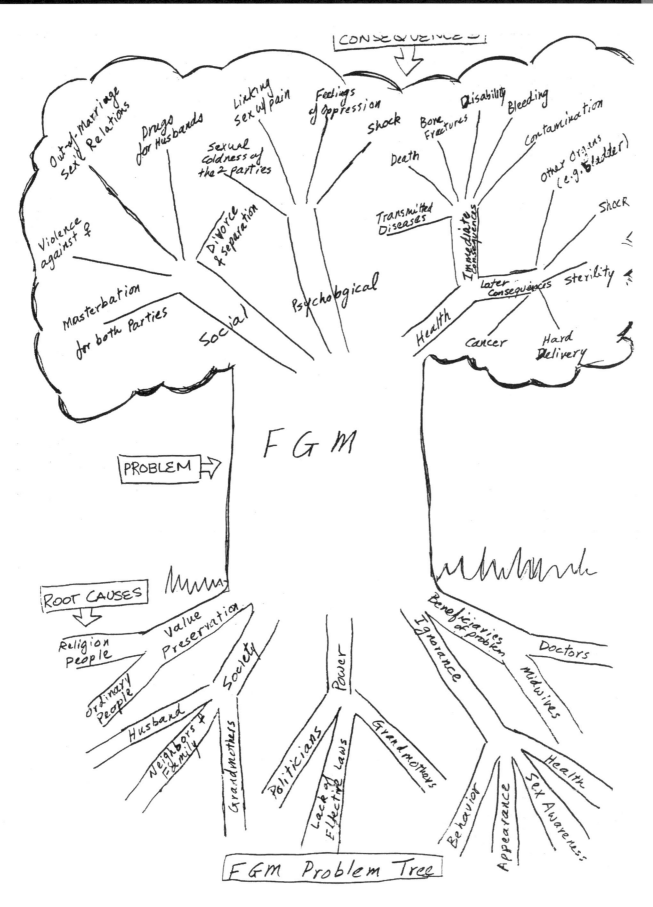

CONSEQUENCES

Out-of-Marriage Sexual Relations
Drugs for Husbands
Linking sex w/ pain
Feelings of Oppression
Shock
Bone Fractures
Disability
Bleeding
Contamination
Death
other Organs (e.g. Bladder)
Transmitted Diseases
Immediate Consequences
Shock
sexual coldness of the 2 parties
Violence against ♀
Divorce & separation
Psychological
Later Consequences
sterility
Masterbation for both Parties
Social
Health
Cancer
Hard Delivery

F G M

PROBLEM ⟹

ROOT CAUSES

Religion
People
Value Preservation
Beneficiaries of problem
Ignorance
Doctors
Ordinary People
Society
Power
Midwives
Husband
Neighbors & Family
Grandmothers
Politicians
Lack of Effective Laws
Grandmothers
Behavior
Appearance
Sex Awareness
Health

F G M Problem Tree

The tree was documented by the Task Force's advocacy advisor, Nader Tadros.

PLANNING ADVOCACY

Purpose

This exercise probes more deeply into the systemic causes of a problem by looking at economic, political, and socio-cultural factors. This type of analysis shows how the political system may contribute to a problem and can potentially contribute to its solutions. It also shows how people's attitudes and beliefs can perpetuate a problem despite policy change. The exercise is a form of structural analysis that examines inequality and power dynamics. (In Chapter 7, the *Structural Analysis* exercise looks at the broad political landscape and not a concrete problem.)

Process

(Time: 1-2 hours)

1. Before the analysis, it is important to define a common understanding of economic, political, and socio-cultural in terms of how these shape a problem. Adapt the descriptions below and distribute them as a handout. (See Chapter 8, for more in-depth descriptions of market, state, and civil society.)

Economic Dimension: This refers to the opportunities for work and for basic survival. Economics is about structures of ownership, wealth, production, and resource distribution. The economic level also refers to socio-economic class – where an individual or group stands on the ladder from poverty to wealth. In addition, this dimension involves the economic context of a country at a particular moment – job and income opportunities, wages, and the economic policy of the government.

Political Dimension: This refers to the rules and procedures that organize economic, social, and cultural life. For example, minimum wage is a rule that affects earnings of workers. The political level refers to decisionmaking and rights. Politics determines who makes laws and policies, how laws are enforced and what budgets are spent on. Politics is not only about government. It refers to all organizations that have power, including structures in the private sector and internationally.

Socio-Cultural Dimension: The socio-cultural level refers to the values, beliefs and attitudes of a society. It also refers to what society believes about itself, the values that are publicly promoted, and the structures which promote them, such as schools, churches, and media. For example, many societies believe that unmarried women are tragic while unmarried men are free and fortunate. Whether this is true is irrelevant — it is what people believe. In many ways, socio-cultural aspects are the most difficult of the three levels to change. For example, the law may be changed to give women more rights, but people may still see women as inferior.

2. Divide into small groups. Each group chooses a facilitator and a note taker. Ask each group to look at the economic, political, and socio-cultural roots of their problem.

3. In many cases, categories of analysis overlap. Some causes may be both socio-cultural and political, for example. Give groups a colored marker to highlight the causes that overlap.

Discussion

After the small groups have presented their analysis and answered questions, use the matrix to explore priorities and possible solutions.

- Which causes overlap? For example, how do policies reinforce social beliefs?

- Is one dimension (economic, political, socio-cultural) a stronger factor than the others?

- Which causes, if addressed, would make the most difference on the problem? (The other, less crucial, causes are often called "contributing factors.")

- If more funding were available, would that solve the problem? Why or why not?

Example

The following example is from a group of Ghanaian women's NGOs (1994). They analyzed the disproportionate level of illiteracy among women resulting from the high drop-out rate of young girls.

PROBLEM: Illiteracy and high drop out rate among girl and young women		
Economic Causes	**Political Causes**	**Cultural Causes**
1. School fees doubled under the Economic Structural Adjustment Program (WB/IMF); no money for fees and materials. 2. Families have more children than they can manage financially and favor boys because girls considered a wasted due to marriage. 3. Girl's labor is necessary to supplement the family income for basic survival and to do all the domestic tasks (fetching water and firewood, cooking, cleaning, washing clothes, kitchen, gardens, etc.)	1. Education not compulsory; not a government priority for poor people. Education of girls not a state concern. 2. No programs for sex education or contraception; under law, pregnant girl must leave school. 3. In negotiations with the International Monetary Fund/ World Bank, the government chose to cut subsidies from education and health programs for the poor in favor of military and infrastructure projects that favor more powerful interests. (This practice is no longer approved of by IMF/WB) 4. Too few women in public decisionmaking which contributes to neglect of children's and girl's rights. 5. Parent-Teacher Associations not well organized; not gender aware.	1. Tradition values women's roles as wives/mothers - for which, it is believed, schooling is unnecessary; among the lower classes, people believe schooling makes women troublesome. 2. Early marriages not frowned upon (interrupt schooling). 3. Larger families (among the lower classes) are more prestigious - too many kids to school. 4. Boy children are more valuable than girl children because girls are married off while boys uphold the family legacy, so it is wasteful to spend on girls. 5. Pregnancy among young women not discouraged, pregnant girls forced leave school.

Adapted from Hope, A. and Timmel, S., *Training for Transformation*, Book III, IT Publications, London, revised version 1995, p.45.

PLANNING ADVOCACY

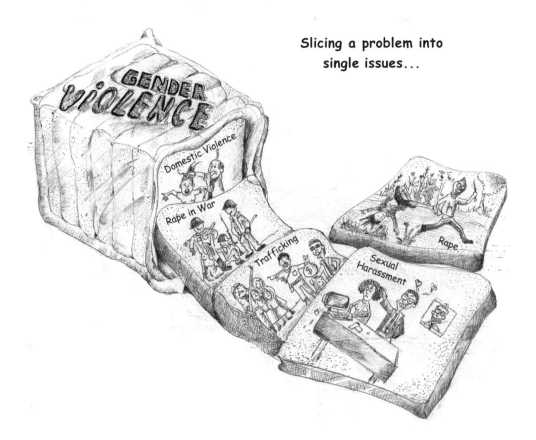

Slicing a problem into
single issues...

From Problems to Issues

Through problem analysis, groups identify a variety of causes of a problem that can potentially be solved through political action. We use the term "issues" to describe the specific aspects of a problem that advocacy addresses. For example, the problem of gender violence needs to be sliced into narrower pieces, such as domestic abuse, workplace harassment, rape, etc. as indicated in the illustration.

Choosing an issue involves several steps. Many of the steps are outlined in this and the previous chapter. They include:

- breaking down a problem by analyzing root causes;

- identifying multiple solutions to start building a holistic strategy;

- defining what makes something a priority;

- comparing different solutions for their potential impact.

Choosing your issue is one of the most difficult tasks, especially for coalitions involving groups with different interests and agendas. As one Ghanaian activist pointed out, "Poverty is so overwhelming, how are we supposed to focus on one issue... it's all an emergency." This is a common feeling, but battles are fought one issue at a time. The issue you start with can build momentum for the next issue you choose.

An organization should choose the issues whose solutions will best further their values, credibility, opportunities, and impact – and, of course, their mission and vision. The *Checklist for Choosing an Issue* can be adapted to suit your context. Some of the criteria cannot be answered fully without more planning, but can guide your information-gathering and be repeated after further analysis.

Purpose

- To define the group's criteria for choosing an issue.
- To apply set criteria for the selection of an issue.
- To assess and explore strategic options.

Before beginning this exercise, the group should have completed a root cause analysis, and at least one analysis of solutions. The more a group has discussed solutions, the easier this task will be.

Advise groups that the criteria will likely stimulate a lot of discussion and debate about potential strategies.

Process

(Time: 2-3 hours)

1. Discuss and adapt the criteria on the checklist. Make sure that everyone in the group has the same understanding of each criterion. Take one criterion at a time, discuss its meaning for the group, and decide whether it is important. At the end, distribute the definitions below as a handout and make the changes that the group has agreed upon.

2. Make sure that all participants understand the issues you are comparing. Quickly review your analysis of causes, consequences, and solutions before applying the checklist. In most cases, the criteria dealing with how the strategy is carried out may be premature at this planning stage.

3. Using the chart on page 162, go through each of the criteria for each issue. Make an X if the issue fits the criteria. After making Xs for each issue, see which issue has the most Xs. Rank your issues #1, #2, or #3 based on how well they meet the criteria, #1 being the highest ranking.

Criteria for Ranking Issues

The solution of an issue should:

Result in a real improvement in people's lives. Some of the important changes that advocacy achieves may not be clearly visible. Seeing and feeling a concrete change is usually the best motivation for people to continue to participate politically. Visible changes also give an advocacy organization credibility for future action. A real improvement in people's day-to-day lives is a sign of citizen victory. Examples include better housing, a women's police station to handle domestic disputes, additional teachers and books for schools, more and better paying jobs, and the establishment of parent-teacher councils to oversee budgetary decisions on local schools. Examples of changes that are not immediately visible in people's lives include constitutional reform, a new NGO law, and more awareness about discrimination.

Give people a sense of their own power. Will the solution involve ordinary people, particularly those affected by the problem, in the advocacy effort? People need to know that they are key to the organizing effort – that it is not just experts or NGO staff running the show. Giving people a sense of their own power demands careful constituency-building through participatory planning and analysis, town meetings, rallies, letter writing, lobbying, consciousness-raising, etc.

PLANNING ADVOCACY

Be widely felt. The numbers of people who care or are hurt by an issue is a good justification for choosing it. Numbers affected will be an important source of power for your strategy. Politicians and decisionmakers can more easily dismiss an issue when it is only felt by a small number of people.

Be deeply felt. To get involved, people must feel strongly about the need for a solution. Anger, frustration, and other emotions are motivators for action.

Build lasting organization and alliances. The issue should lend itself to networking and organization-building. It should present opportunities to strengthen citizens' groups and build linkages across groups, creating a basis for future action.

Create opportunities for women and marginalized people to get involved in politics. A "good" issue presents opportunities for people with less public and political exposure and access to decisionmaking to practice citizenship and leadership.

Develop new leaders. An issue that provides opportunities for new leaders to emerge as spokespeople, coordinators, and planners builds citizen participation. Technical and complicated issues often do not lend themselves easily to the development of new leaders.

Promote awareness of and respect for rights. Is the issue already understood as a right? Can advocacy expand what is understood as a right? Much social justice advocacy is about gaining acceptance that inclusion and fairness are fundamental to human dignity. It is about the right of every person to have a voice in the decisions affecting them, to equal access to education and to job opportunities, etc. These rights are not always recognized and may be difficult to enforce. Some people may not know certain rights exist.

Respect for Rights

Some rights are more widely accepted and recognized than others. Human rights that are already defined in a variety of instruments such as the Convention on the Elimination of All Forms of Discrimination Against Women (CEDAW), the Convention on the Rights of the Child, the International Covenant on Civil and Political Rights, etc. can serve as a powerful advocacy tool. In some cases, if the issue involves a violation of an existing civil or political right, framing the solution in the context of human rights can be useful for demanding government accountability in cases where the government has ratified or committed to respecting these conventions and the rights they protect.

In other cases, there may be an international agreement but no mechanism for enforcing it with governments, like the platforms that were produced at the Beijing 4th World Conference on Women, the UN Conference on Environment and Development in Rio, etc. Often, merely linking your strategy to an international agreement that your government has signed, regardless of whether there are mechanisms for legal enforcement, gives a strategy more clout.

Rights-based advocacy is about expanding the limits of existing rights and making the rights system more responsive to people's needs. (See Chapter 12 for more discussion on using human rights instruments for advocacy.)

Have a clear political and policy solution. If the best way to address an issue is through service delivery — such as in an emergency where people need food and water above all — it is usually not a good advocacy issue. Similarly, if consciousness-raising is the best way to address your issue, it is not a good choice. The solution to your issue must have a clear link with policy and with public or economic decisionmaking.

Have a clear target and timeframe. An advocacy target is the pivotal decisionmaker who can respond to your demands. Personalizing decisionmaking helps make an abstract "system" seem more accessible to change by ordinary people. Also, if you are working with people who are newly active, a definite timeframe helps, as do benchmarks that allow people to celebrate small steps of progress. (See Chapter 15 for more discussion of targets.)

Link local concerns to global issues. "Politics are local," but increasingly many of the causes and solutions to issues involve global decisions. These include, for example, international development, trade policy, and factories moving from place to place which causes unemployment. Linking local concerns to global organizing can be politically powerful, but can also be challenging for organizers to manage multi-level coordination and communication.

Provide opportunities to raise funds. You cannot do much without money. Funds can come from international donors as well as from local supporters. Local support is important because international funding can sometimes discredit local political organizing. If your issue provides opportunities to get money from local people, industry, or others, it shows that there is local support.

Enable you to further your vision and mission. You should not take up an issue that takes you outside your scope of work and your basic values. Advocacy efforts strain organizations, so it is especially important that it contribute to its mission and vision. It is easy to be wooed by an exciting issue and available funds.

Be winnable. Success is the best motivation for sustaining citizen participation. Failure can be discouraging to people. But victory should not be defined only in terms of policy gains. Advocacy, whether successful in the realm of policy or not, can succeed in building organizations and mobilizing public opinion. Make sure that victories are broadly defined and set in modest, step-by-step terms. Then people can celebrate their achievements along the way.

PLANNING ADVOCACY

CRITERIA	ISSUE #1	ISSUE #2
Result in a real improvement in people's lives		
Give people a sense of their own power		
Be widely felt		
Be deeply felt		
Build lasting organization and alliances		
Create opportunities for women and marginalized people to get involved in politics		
Develop new leaders		
Promote awareness of and respect for rights		
Have a clear political and policy solution		
Have a clear target and timeframe		
Link local concerns to global issues		
Provide opportunities to raise funds		
Enable you to further your vision and mission		
Be winnable		

Adapted from *Organizing for Social Change: A Manual for Activists in the 1990s*, K. Bobo, J. Kendall, S. Max, Midwest Academy, Seven Locks Press, California, 1991.

10 Planning Moment #5: Mapping Advocacy Strategies

Choosing the Right Strategy

A lasting solution needs to get to the root causes of a problem. Problems have many causes and many possible solutions. Advocacy strategies attempt to solve a problem step-by-step by getting at its systemic causes and focusing on specific issues. Because of this, advocacy strategies are always multidimensional. They use policy and political change to address the broader socio-economic roots of exclusion and inequality.

For example, if poor healthcare is the problem, one element of your solution may be advocating to increase government resources for clinics and healthcare workers. Would this strategy solve your problem? Perhaps partially, but it is not a complete solution. Poor healthcare can be caused by many things. For example, healthcare for all may not be a national priority. There may be other issues like mismanagement, lack of health education, poor infrastructure, insufficient, expensive medicines, and poverty that are also causes.

No single organization can carry out the complete strategy that addresses all of these factors. Limited resources force a group to choose which aspect to tackle, and then seek alliances with other groups to achieve a broader collective impact.

> "Advocacy is a mindset. Certainty is not a given as we all know. Intuition, feel, the senses count, as does the head. . . Standards of performance and accountability should be open to learning from experience. Put another way, learning from mistakes."
>
> David Cohen, Advocacy Institute, USA

Choosing and planning the right strategy involves exploring and comparing the potential impact and feasibility of alternatives. This chapter presents a series of tools and exercises that help to construct and compare strategies, including:

Factors shaping an advocacy strategy
We discuss some basic ingredients, like timing, context, and organizational capacity that are important to consider in designing and comparing alternative strategies.

Mapping alternative strategies
The *Issue Timeline* helps to trace the political history of an issue, and the *Triangle Analysis* helps to understand how policy, institutions, and social values interact to perpetuate problems and, potentially, solve them.

Drafting a first set of advocacy goals and objectives
We offer basic suggestions for drafting goals and objectives to begin developing strategies.

Dimensions of a citizen-centered advocacy strategy
We discuss the key levels of citizen-centered advocacy using the *Advocacy Action and Impact Chart,* which can help with both planning and monitoring results.

After applying these tools, you will have begun to define your goals, objectives, and strategy. This process will surface a new set of questions and will tell you the information you will need to complete your plan. The next chapters will show how to sharpen the strategy's policy and political dimensions.

PLANNING ADVOCACY

Different Advocacy Strategies for Different Moments

The list of strategies[1] on the next page are some of the ways that groups in different countries have mobilized support and produced change. Advocacy usually involves a combination of these strategies. In Part Three we discuss some of these in more detail.

Pilot or Model Programs

Where it is difficult to influence the public agenda, a successful model intervention can demonstrate to government a better way to solve a problem. This strategy was used especially well by the Undugu Society in Kenya. Undugu used an important international meeting to showcase its innovative housing program for the urban poor with influential

---

The Factors Shaping An Advocacy Strategy

There are some key factors that shape your advocacy strategy. They differ from one place to another, as well as from one issue to another:

Context: Every political environment is different. Each presents its own opportunities and constraints. Governments have different degrees of legitimacy and power vis-a-vis civil society, the private sector, transnationals, and international institutions. Political decisions are made differently depending on the nature of the state, politics, media, etc. In some places, the legislature has more authority. In other places, the Minister of Finance dominates policymaking. Countries have different levels of freedom and access to the public sector. People use these opportunities differently depending on literacy, poverty, social relationships, etc. A society's mix of culture, religion, ethnicity, race, and economic development affects the level of tolerance and openings to social change. In some countries, advocacy at the local or the international level may be more feasible than at the national level. (In Chapters 7 and 12 we provide tools for analyzing these elements of context.)

Timing: Each historic moment presents different political opportunities and constraints. International economic trends may make a country tighten or expand political space. Elections or international conferences may provide opportunities to raise controversial issues. At some moments, a march will draw attention to an issue. At other moments a march may provoke repression.

Organization: In designing your strategy, it is important to be aware of the strengths and weaknesses of your organization. How broad and strong is your potential support? Do you have well-placed allies? Is there a strong sense of common purpose among the leadership? Is the decisionmaking efficient and responsive? What resources can you rely on? Are your aims clear and achievable?

Risk: Not all advocacy strategies can be used universally. In some places, a direct action aimed at a key decisionmaker may be politically dangerous or may lessen the potential for a long-term effort at change. In some countries, pushing for change that affects cultural beliefs may provoke an unmanageable backlash. Sometimes involving people who are usually excluded, like women or poor people, may cause family, social, and community conflict. Challenging relations of power tends to generate conflict, and organizers must have ways of dealing with this. In more closed environments, advocacy often takes the form of community action around basic needs and is not publicly referred to as political advocacy. Whatever the context, sometimes you will decide to take risks because there are no other options. In these cases, everyone involved must understand the implications of those risks.

Adapted from Miller, Valerie, *NGOs and Grassroots Policy Influence: What is Success?*, Institute for Development Research, Vol. 11, No. 5, 1994.

delegates. By doing this, it pushed government officials to make public commitments in front of the visitors about addressing poverty in urban areas.

Collaboration

When there is compatibility and agreement between NGOs, grassroots groups, and government, civil society groups are likely to collaborate directly with government to design and/or implement legislation or state services. Similarly, joint citizen-government monitoring initiatives are becoming increasingly common.

Protest

A demonstration or march relies on numbers and creative messages to gain attention and support. A march of 2,000 people will not usually have the impact of one with 25,000 people. Timing is important. Boycotts are another form of protest often directed at corporations. Vigils and hunger strikes can be less confrontational expressions of protest. Protest is sometimes a tactic of last resort when more conventional strategies of influence fail to open up a policy dialogue.

Litigation

A well-publicized court case can draw public attention to a problem, and sometimes leads to legal reform or fairer enforcement. Some countries have a legal mechanism called "class-action." Where this exists, groups of people affected by abuses of power can use a court case to fight for justice collectively.

Public Education and Media

Education and media strategies build public support and may influence policymakers. Strategies include providing data, articles, and alternative policies to the media, as well as creative messages using music, videos, and songs. Alternative media strategies using theatre, posters, and pamphlets are especially useful in countries where fewer people have

access to radio and television. In some countries, NGOs organize public dialogues to discuss issues. (See Chapters 13 and 14.)

Research

Positions and proposals based on solid information increase the credibility of advocacy. Research provides the necessary information for planning, message development, policy alternatives, and lobbying. Depending on the methodology used, research can also strengthen alliances, build constituencies, and help develop citizenship skills. (See Chapter 8.) Where information is hard to get, research efforts can evolve into "right to know" advocacy campaigns. Advocacy usually benefits from close ties with sympathetic researchers and policy analysts that give advocates speedy access to facts and analysis in the midst of political battles.

Persuasion

All advocacy must be persuasive to a wide range of people. Persuasion has three main ingredients:

- *lobbying* — involves attempts to meet face-to-face with decisionmakers to persuade them to support an advocacy issue or proposal;
- *clout* — gained by the credibility and legitimacy of demands; by showing strength through mobilizing popular support; by working in coalitions and with many diverse allies; by using the media to inform, educate, and be visible;
- *negotiation* — involves bargaining to seek common ground or, minimally, respect for disagreement. It happens aong allies, advocates, and constituents as well as across the table with those in power. To bargain with decisionmakers you need to know your own power and your opponent's, as well as what is negotiable, what is not, and what you will do if negotiations fall apart. (See Chapter 15.)

PLANNING ADVOCACY

Organization and Constituency-Building

The long-term nature of most advocacy efforts demands strong links with constituency groups. Effective advocacy requires alliances between organizations and with key individuals for leverage, legitimacy, and implementation. Organization depends on effective decision-making, shared leadership, clear roles, communication, and members and staff with analytical skills and confidence (discussed in Chapters 16 and 17).

Empowerment

A vital component of all advocacy, these strategies are geared to strengthening people's confidence and understanding of power. People's awareness of themselves as protagonists with rights and responsibilities to participate in and transform political processes is the core of active citizenship.

Timing: Matching the Strategy to the Moment

Developing effective strategies requires careful political analysis of ever-changing opportunities and constraints. The following are some specific political opportunities that can be conducive to advocacy.

Elections are an opportunity to involve a broad base of citizens in public debate, raise issues, criticize officials and current policy, influence candidates, political parties, and policymakers, and present policy alternatives and people's platforms. (See Chapter 14.) The election itself usually happens over a few days. However, you can use advocacy for a year or more before the elections as well as between elections. Unless citizens keep track of political promises by parties and candidates, and sustain pressure on those who are elected, the gains during elections may not last.

Mapping strategies during and advocacy workshop in Nicaragua, 1998

International events and policy meetings, such as UN conferences, World Trade Organization, and G8 meetings, provide opportunities for transnational advocacy and high level dialogue with policymakers that can boost national advocacy. The events can give visibility to alternative perspectives about the impact and process of international policies and demonstrate broad public support for reforms.

Different stages of law or policy formulation provides groups an opportunity to voice positions and propose alternatives. But knowing the timeline for review is essential for effective intervention. Some governments have institutionalized their consultations with civil society on particular issues. While this presents important opportunities, over time it can become exclusive of other issues and people. Similarly, when a policy is debated in Parliament or when a new policy is announced,

there are opportunities for people to express support or opposition. (See Chapter 11.)

A crime or other highly visible tragedy can personalize a political problem and thus generate public attention and demand for a solution. Such tragedies can reveal that marginalized people are more vulnerable to disasters, violence, and exploitation, and force decisionmakers to explore solutions.

Mapping Alternative Strategies

One of the important pieces of background information for developing your strategy is the political history of an issue. The following exercise traces when the issue came to the attention of civil society actors or powerful interests, and what, if anything, they have done to solve it.

Purpose

- To review the public history of an issue, analyzing past political dynamics and identifying key stakeholders.
- To situate an advocacy strategy within the history of the issue.

Facilitator's Tips

- You can have up to four rapporteurs who write on the timeline, depending on the size of the paper
- You can ask a researcher or historian to guide the timeline exercise with detailed information.

Process

This exercise can be applied to a specific local issue, like crime, or to a more general global problem area, such as women's rights or globalization.

1. Working in small groups, draw on flip chart paper a long line with ten evenly spaced marks or boxes indicating the years.

1992	1993	1994	1995	1996	1997	1998	1999	2000	2001

2. Discuss the important political events and shifts during the last decade. Rapporteurs should make notes on the timeline of the key moments that emerge from the discussion.

3. Map a similar timeline for the last one to two years. Divide each year into quarters or months and note key events over this period.

4. If there is time, draw a third timeline that maps anticipated events, policy changes, and reactions over the coming one to two years.

Advocacy timelines from Central America and Mexico

Adapted from *Naming the Moment: Political Analysis for Action, A Manual for Community Groups* by Deborah Barndt. The Jesuit Centre for Social Faith and Justice, 1989.

Discussion

Once the timelines have been completed, discuss what the results mean for advocacy planning. Here are some questions to guide discussion:

- What has worked and what has failed to achieve an impact on this issue?
- Does the timeline help identify forces for and against us? If so, what are they?
- What does the timeline tell us about legislation and policy strategies?
- How can we build on past successes and avoid previous failures?

Example

The following example comes from *Naming the Moment* and the Canadian Jesuit Justice and Peace Center. The Center developed this timeline with a broad-based coalition working on a collective advocacy strategy on legislation affecting refugees.

Reviewing 10 Years

Government bureaucrats informed, not public	Unemployment ("They're stealing our jobs.")	Media campaign against refugees	McLean announced intended restrictions	New law proposed	Passed	Implemented
1978	1982	1985	1986	1987	1988	1989
Boat People	Recession	Refugees from C. Am., Iran, Afgan.	Singh Case	Tamil Boat		

Close-up 2 Years

| | | C-55 introduced | | National state of emergency declared | | C-84 introduced | | Turks deported | | Bills passed | | Elections | | Bills implemented |

Jan '87	Feb '87	Mar '87	May '87	July '87	Aug '87	Sept '87	Oct '87	July '88	Nov '88	Jan '89
				Sikh Boat						

Hawkes proposal rejected in cabinet — Formation of National Coalition for a Just Refugee/Immig. Policy — Bills stalled in Senate — VIGIL and court action

Projecting 2 Years into Future

Government working out the wrinkles of the new system-few deportations		Once public attention has waned, more deportations		Court action decision
Jan '89	April '89	May '89	June '89	1990	1991
Court action launched, VIGIL network formed	Refugee Rights Day	VIGIL conference	Canadian Council on Refugees conference		

Triangle Analysis[2]: Mapping Legal-Political Solutions

This *Triangle Analysis* framework can be used for two main purposes. First, it can be used to analyze how a combination of policies, institutions, and social values and behavior contribute to or perpetuate a problem (issue). Second, the framework can be used to map and clarify strategy options to address each of the three dimensions.

The triangle framework is based on the idea that law and policy affect people's status and rights because they:

- regulate work and social relations; and

- define access to economic resources, opportunities, and political power.

Laws and policies can be unjust in three ways:

- **Content:** The written policy, program or budget can be discriminatory, or may contradict a basic right.

- **Structure:** Policies and laws may not be enforced. Or, if they are, they may be enforced unfairly favoring some groups of people and neglecting others.

- **Culture:** If citizens are unaware of a policy or law, or if social norms and behavior undermine their enforcement, the law does not exist in practice. This is the case, for example, when poor people are unaware of their rights and lack the resources to pursue a legal solution.

The triangle analysis is useful because it highlights the specific aspects of the legal-political system that need to be changed. In some cases, advocacy may need to focus on the content of the law or policy. In other instances, the content may be fine but the law is not enforced, hence the need to focus strategies on getting the legal or other government structures to implement the law. However, whatever the analysis reveals, all strategies must target culture since social norms operate behind the scenes to define power relations and access. By addressing cultural dynamics, policy reform can have a real impact on people's lives.

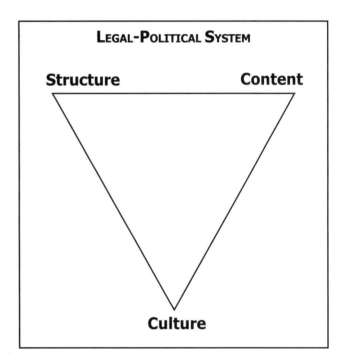

See Marge Schuler, *Empowerment and the Law*, 1986.

Purpose

- To identify how laws and policies contribute to a problem/issue and, potentially, to its solution.

- To understand the legal-political system as a three-dimensional arena where rights, roles, and choices are shaped by the interplay between formal rules and structures of government, social values, and political power dynamics.

- To identify information gaps to complete the analysis and mapping.

Facilitator's Tips

Since this exercise has two steps, it may be easier to break up the steps with a discussion of the analysis before moving on to the strategies. If you choose to do the exercise this way, explain only the analysis task at the beginning. Once the analysis is completed, explain the strategy task. This avoids confusion.

Process

This exercise has two connected parts: (A) analysis and (B) strategy development. Each step will take from 30 minutes to 2 hours depending on how much information is available.

Part A: Analysis

1. Explain the triangle. Hand out written definitions of each of the sides of the triangle (Content - Structure - Culture). Remember that the descriptions for the analysis are different than for the strategy development.

2. Use Example #1 on the next page to illustrate how the exercise works. This example is not an exhaustive analysis of the issue, but it gives an idea of what the framework can produce. Every context would produce a different analysis, although there are some universal obstacles facing some groups.

Meaning of the Sides of the Triangle for Analysis

Content refers to written laws, policies, and budgets relevant to a specific issue. For example, if there is no law to criminalize domestic violence, one part of a solution may be introducing a law. Also, even if a law or policy exist, unless there is funding and institutional mechanisms for enforcement, it will not be effective.

Structure refers to state and non-state mechanisms for implementing a law or policy. This would include, for example, the police, the courts, hospitals, credit unions, ministries, and agricultural and health care programs. Structure can refer to institutions and programs run by government, NGOs or businesses at the local, national and international levels.

Culture refers to the values and behavior that shape how people deal with and understand an issue. Values and behavior are influenced by, among other things, religion, custom, class, gender, ethnicity, and age. Lack of information about laws and policies is part of the cultural dimension. Similarly, when people have internalized a sense of worthlessness or, conversely, entitlement, this shapes their attitudes about and degree of benefit from laws and policies.

Discussion

- *Guiding questions for analysis of content*
    - Is there a law or policy that contributes to the problem by protecting the interests of some people over others?
    - Is there a law or policy that helps address the particular issue you have chosen?
    - Is adequate government money budgeted to implement the policy or law?

- *Guiding questions for analysis of structure*
  - Do the police enforce the law fairly?
  - Do the courts enable men and women, rich and poor, to find a solution?
  - Is the legal system expensive, corrupt, or inaccessible?
  - Are there support services where people can get help to access the system fairly?
  - Do existing programs and services discriminate against some people (even unintentionally)?
  - Does a government or non-governmental agency exist to monitor implementation?

- *Guiding questions for analysis of culture*
  - Are there any political or social values and beliefs that contribute to the problem?
  - Do cultural beliefs contradict basic rights?
  - Do women and men know their rights? Do they know how to access their rights?
  - Do family and social pressures prevent people from seeking a fair solution?
  - Do psychological issues play a role? Do people believe they are worthy of rights?

Example #1

Problem/Issue: Lack of access to credit for poor urban women to initiate small businessess		
CONTENT	**STRUCTURE**	**CULTURE**
- The law requires collateral in the form of fixed assets for a loan. This is beyond the reach of low-income women. - Economic rights are not enshrined in the Constitution. - There is no explicit government commitment to poor women. - There is no regulation of "loan sharks" who charge high interest and harass poor borrowers.	- Creditors require the signature of a male relative because women are not seen as independent producers/ earners - Government and NGO small-scale credit programs are geared to men because men are seen as heads of households. - Low-income people are considered a "bad investment" by private businesses and banks despite evidence to the contrary. - Small business training programs are offered at a cost that is too high for most poor women. It is difficult for women to find time to attend courses.	- Women do not own property in their name because it is unacceptable. The general belief is that men care for women. - Women do not see themselves as producers. Their income is often controlled by their husbands. Women's income is used to cover intangible expenses like school fees and food while the man's income covers the fixed assets, like a house or motorcycle, which can be used as collateral. - Poor people are viewed as ignorant and incapable of running viable businesses. - Poor women may have practical instincts about business, but lack formal training like accounting that enable their businesses to be lucrative.

From Kenyan women's group working on rights and development

Part B: Mapping Strategies

4. The analysis done in Part A lays the groundwork for the group to map possible solutions. Advise participants to explore all the options and not be concerned about the availability of resources at this stage. Later, other tools in this chapter can be used to choose between options. You may want to use Example #2 on the next page as an illustration.

Example #2

Problem / Issue - Domestic Violence: Women are mistreated by partners with whom they have intimate and dependent relationships. They suffer from physical, emotional, and psychological abuse ranging from slaps and threats to severe physical violence.

STEP 1: ANALYSIS

CONTENT	STRUCTURE	CULTURE
- This problem falls between the family and criminal codes because there are no explicit laws applying to abuse within the home between husband and wife or unmarried partners. - A law against domestic violence exists but there are no emergency procedures such as restraining orders to offer immediate protection to women in danger. - The law regards what happens in the "home" as a private matter.	- The law may be adequate but judges and police see domestic disputes as a private matter and do not intervene. - Police and courts encourage couples to stay together even when a woman's life is in danger. The family and children are valued more than women's rights. - There are no alternatives for women to seek protection, for example, safe houses, hotlines, etc. - Hospitals do not report cases of domestic violence.	- Women blame themselves for the abuse and feel ashamed. - The public sees "wife beating" as a problem of poor, uneducated people (they do not see that it also happens among upper classes). Some believe it is caused by alcohol abuse. - Family violence is part of a cycle of violence where power is used to exert control rather than to seek peaceful resolutions. So, men beat women, women beat children, children beat each other and animals, employers abuse employees. - "Minor" abuse is seen as normal or sign of love. - It is believed that men have the right to beat their wives to "keep them in line."

STEP 2: MAPPING STRATEGIES

CONTENT	STRUCTURE	CULTURE
- Reform criminal and family codes to make domestic violence a crime punishable by law. Ensure that the definition includes non-marital relationships. - Define a punishment that dissuades men from using force but does not deprive a woman of economic support unless the problem is severe. (This is a difficult task.) - Make domestic abuse a public crime but give women the right to decide what happens to the perpetrator. - Provide for emergency protection measures such as restraint orders, etc. - Allocate budget funds for legal aid, family dispute centers, safe houses, public education, hotlines.	-Train police and judges about the nature of domestic abuse. - Establish a women's wing at local police stations with trained personnel to deal with psychological aspects of the crime. - Set up safe houses and hotlines for emergency protection. - Train hospital personnel to identify and handle cases of abuse.	- Media campaigns, theatre, demonstrating the impact on women, men, children, and society. Make people see domestic violence as a public concern and a crime. (NOTE: If you denounce domestic violence publicly, make sure that there are support services for women to seek help. Awareness-raising without support for those in need is dangerous.) - Have prominent men speak out against it publicly. Establish men's groups. - Run workshops to teach conflict resolution, confidence-building, etc. - Create community support groups and women's counseling initiatives.

Composite of analysis from Asia, Africa, Latin America, and USA.

PLANNING ADVOCACY

5. After participants have mapped out all of the possible strategies in a second grid, compare this grid of solutions with the first grid from the analysis. Ask:

    *   Do the solutions address all aspects of the problem?

    *   Do all aspects of the problem need to be addressed or do priority solutions exist?

Discussion

Once the mapping is completed, discuss what has been learned from this exercise. Highlight how the interplay between formal rules and structures of government and socio-economic factors define the politics of law and policy.

The Meaning of the Sides of the Triangle for Mapping Strategies

Content responses refer to new policies, laws, or budgets, or changes in existing ones.

Example from the Credit Problem: Change banking laws to lower the collateral requirements or give special tax breaks to banks which provide low-income people with loans.

Structural responses include educating police and judges to make them aware of how their own prejudices cause injustice, introducing sanctions against discriminatory judgments, improving social programs to ensure that they reach marginalized communities, etc. They can also involve the creation of a civil society structure to hold government or business accountable to their promises.

Example from the Credit Problem: Educate loan officers about the special needs of low income people, particularly women. Set up business training programs and support groups for those who need it.

Cultural responses include public education aimed at eliminating discrimination or abuses of rights, and the creation of support groups to help people understand their rights and influence the institutions and laws that treat them unjustly.

Example from the Credit Problem: Programs to educate men and women about women's roles as heads of households and producers; confidence-building programs; using the mass media to publicize women's "invisible" contribution to the national economy; building a coalition of small-scale producers to advocate for better banking laws and fewer regulations on women's businesses.

Comparing and Selecting Strategies

Once you have mapped an array of responses to an issue, you can compare your options and choose the best combination of actions to build your strategy while staying true to your mission and vision.

For example, if your NGO decides to improve girls' attendance in primary school, you could:

- carry out a public education campaign about the importance of sending girls to school;
- work with Parent Teacher Associations to monitor school attendance, and educate communities;
- launch an advocacy initiative to persuade the national government to place more resources in girls' education.

The *best* strategy will use your organization's strengths and take advantage of external opportunities. In the next chapter we introduce tools for identifying external constraints and opportunities.

Strategies vary according to the issue, context, and moment. Those that do not address systemic causes may alleviate some symptoms, but are unlikely to significantly address the problem. At the same time, improving the material well-being of people who are suffering from a problem by addressing the symptoms is an important element of a political solution and key to sustaining constituency involvement.

What Good Strategies Should Be

Appropriate	Will the strategy further your group's vision and mission? Will it make good use of your organization's strengths? Will it fit the community conditions where your group operates? Will your constituency be able to participate? Will it exacerbate or reduce social tensions within the community?
Adequate	Will the strategy be sufficient to address the problem given its magnitude? Does the problem justify the effort and resources you will expend?
Effective	Will the strategy achieve the stated objective? Will the strategy further your mission *and* address the problem in a reasonable timeframe?
Efficient	Will the strategy make optimum use of the organization's material and human resources? What are the strategy's costs in terms of people's time, energy, and materials in relation to benefits?
Sensitive to side effects	Will the strategy increase demand for basic services or resources? Will the strategy generate resistance due to traditions, religion, etc? How can this resistance be minimized? How will those in power respond to shifts in social relationships, demands for change, etc? What will happen if violence breaks out? Will the negative consequences be counterbalanced by the positive benefits?

Adapted from the Institute for Development Research's *Strategic Thinking: Formulating Organizational Strategy. Facilitator's Guide,* 1998, pp. 48-49.

Drafting A First Set of Advocacy Goals and Objectives

Defining advocacy goals and objectives is an ongoing planning task. The goals and objectives that you set at the beginning help you compare alternative strategies. After you choose your strategy, you can then refine your goals and objectives.

The terms "goal" and "objective" have many definitions. For advocacy planning, we define goals and objectives as follows:

- *A long-term goal* describes the social change you want to see. It is your realizable vision.

- *A short-term goal* describes your desired outcome or the proposed advocacy solution to a specific issue.

- *An objective* defines concretely what will be accomplished, with whom, how, and in what period of time. Advocacy strategies usually have a number of objectives that guide different activities.

SMART Objectives

Smart objectives are *S*pecific, *M*easurable, *A*chievable, *R*ealistic, and *T*imebound.

Specific

- Watch out for jargon or rhetoric. Words like "sensitize," "empower," and "conscientize" are vague. They can be broken down into more clearly defined results.

- Watch out for words that can be interpreted in a variety of ways, like reproductive health, empowerment, accountability, transparency, or democracy.

Measurable

- Be as exact as possible about who, what, where, and when. For example, an objective may state, "educate people about their rights." When possible, estimate the num-

ber of people and what they will do as a result.

- Objectives that refer to a state of mind and a process, like "sensitize" or "empower," are subjective and almost impossible to measure. However, process objectives are appropriate for advocacy, particularly when the process is the desired outcome. For example, "bring together grassroots women in small groups to voice their concerns and define common priorities." In many places, that is a major accomplishment. Group formation or strengthening can be a good indicator for process words like those above. When you use words that refer to a state of mind, ask yourself, "What does a gender-sensitized person do? What does an empowered person do?". Use the answers to formulate your objective. Ask yourself, "Sensitize for what?".

Achievable

- The more concrete you are about who, what, where, and when, the more realistic your objective will be. Process goals like empowerment are long-term and elusive. Imagine concrete signs along the way of what an empowered person does and make those your objectives. Feasibility is also defined by the availability of resources.

Realistic

- Changing attitudes and behavior is a very long-term endeavor. Try to be realistic when you decide which and how many people you plan to influence.

- Realistic objectives reflect the limits of available funding and staffing.

- Citizen-centered advocacy demands a balance between idealism and realism to avoid setting yourself up for failure. Objectives are realistic steps toward your greater vision.

Timebound

- Although social change objectives are often impossible to predict in terms of timing, be as precise as possible about your timeline. When do you hope to accomplish your aim?

Tips about Advocacy Goals and Objectives

Long-term goals are more abstract and tend to not change much over time. Short-term goals and objectives are always refined. The more information you have about your political context, target, issue, organization, etc., the more you can sharpen your objectives.

Since effective advocacy demands multi-dimensional strategies, it may be useful to develop objectives and activities for different levels of impact (e.g., policy, public institutions, etc.).

The *Advocacy Action and Impact Chart* on page 181 is a guide to the different layers of influence and change.

Although objectives evolve, it helps to formulate them as clearly as possible from the start. The SMART Framework is useful for formulating objectives, but is not the only one. People have different preferences for formulating objectives. For example, some people prefer a declarative sentence like, "10 citizen monitoring groups created," to one that begins with a verb like, "*To create* 10 citizen monitoring groups."

Objective setting is an important decision-making moment. Participation by the key groups involved generates buy-in and strengthens commitment, and can also be empowering. Participatory objective-setting involves dialogue, debate and negotiation.

PLANNING ADVOCACY

Examples of Ways to Sharpen Objectives

A group in Southern Africa defined a multidimensional strategy to combat domestic violence. The strategy included policy reform, establishing support centers, and public education. Their public education objective was not specific or measurable.

Original Objective

To mobilize and educate women and law enforcement agencies by the year 2001.

Can you see from this objective what the group will do? Which women? Which law enforcement agencies? For what purpose? The group reformulated their education objective as follows:

SMART Objective

To educate rural women involved in savings clubs in three villages about domestic violence and their rights with regard to family law, and to assist them in forming violence prevention groups at the community level within thirty months.

A consumer rights group in India went through a similar process to improve their advocacy objectives.

Original Objective

To create awareness among consumers of the measures they have available to redress grievances.

SMART Objective

To increase the number of disadvantaged people who can effectively use the consumer redress laws and measures in Tamil Nadu to 1,000 by the year 2000.

Using the Triangle Analysis to Set Initial Goals and Objectives

The triangle analysis (content-structure-culture) on page 170 helps define an initial set of goals and objectives. Using the example of domestic violence, some possible advocacy goals and objectives are:

Long-term Goal

- To expand and promote women's legal rights and equality.

Short-term Goal

- To make domestic violence recognized and treated as a crime and a violation of basic rights by society and the legal system.

Content Objective

- To reform the criminal and family codes to make domestic violence explicitly a crime with procedures to protect victims and appropriate punishment.

Structure Objectives

- To provide training to police and judges about the nature of domestic violence and the particular needs of perpetrators and survivors.
- To establish "Women's Desks" in selected police stations on a pilot basis with the involvement of the four key women's NGOs working on violence.
- To persuade government to establish and fund safe houses and hotlines with strict guidelines based on research.
- To create support groups for women survivors to explore alternative ways of assisting women.

Culture Objectives

- To educate the general public through the mass media that domestic violence is a public problem and a crime.
- To establish pilot men's groups to encourage new thinking about violence.
- To conduct training and education programs for women that link human rights, personal self-worth, and the elimination of violence.

Dimensions of a Citizen-Centered Advocacy Strategy

The *Advocacy Action and Impact Chart*[4] on page 181 can be used as a checklist both for planning and for monitoring and evaluation. The framework is shaped by the experience of long time social justice advocates around the world who found that advocacy success needs to produce change in five dimensions – government, private sector, civil society, political space and culture, and the individual.

The **government arena**, the most common arena for success in advocacy, includes changes in policies, programs, officials, elections, laws, processes, budgets, and regulations of public institutions and related interna-

tional organizations such as the UN system, World Bank, and International Monetary Fund.

The second arena, the **private sector**, addresses changes in business policies, programs, and practices. It may be less familiar to some NGOs and grassroots groups, but is an important arena of action for promoting more socially responsible behavior by local and multinational corporations.

The third arena for action and impact involves fortifying **civil society**. Strengthening the authority, voice, agenda-setting, and planning capacities of NGOs and popular organizations is critical to increasing their legitimacy, sustained participation, and voice in public decisionmaking.

A fourth arena of activity and impact entails changes in **political space and culture**. These actions and outcomes help create an atmosphere in which political participation by disenfranchised groups can be effective and carried out, at a minimum, without fear of violence or repression. Possible impacts include increased governmental respect for people's right to participate in decisionmaking as well as increased transparency and accountability on the part of institutions of the State and the media. Other changes might involve shifts in the way society views women's and men's roles, accepting women as legitimate political actors.

The fifth and final arena involves changes at the **individual** level. These actions and changes refer to improvements in a person's physical living conditions such as better access to water or wages. They also include personal changes that are necessary for the development of a sense of citizenship, self-worth, and solidarity.

Drafting objectives for each of the five dimensions can guide planners to think through a comprehensive strategy for change. The following questions can help planners use the chart for developing objectives and activities and identifying areas for further research.

Government

- What needs to be changed in a law or policy to make it more effective, inclusive, and fair?

- What institutional reforms will be necessary for the law/policy to be enforced/implemented fairly and effectively?

- What are the budget implications of implementation?

- What will be needed at different levels of government to ensure accountability?

- What structural reforms are needed to promote transparency and increase people's access to justice?

Private sector

- What kind of corporate policy will help to address this issue?

- What reforms in business practice and behavior are necessary?

- Will training and monitoring be necessary to prevent the issue from recurring?

- How can dialogue and joint problem-solving among government, civil society, and the private sector address diverse interests and needs?

Civil society

- How can education and organizing teach people about government, politics, and rights?

- How can citizens and groups engage constructively and critically with decisionmakers to promote accountability?

- What types of leadership and organization can be developed that foster inclusion and represent a broad range of constituents while retaining political agility and power?

- How can the strategy promote communication, dialogue, and horizontal networks?

Political space and culture

- What can be done to expand the role of citizens' groups in the formal political process? How can governments, corporations, and civil society work together to address injustice and poverty?

- What must be changed about policy formulation or enforcement to create more transparent, accountable decisionmaking?

- What information needs to be made public and accessible? What are the roles of civil society, government, and the private sector in ensuring that people know about things that affect them?

PLANNING ADVOCACY

- What types of leadership and organization will be necessary to promote inclusion and consultation in all arenas?

- What public processes and policies can promote democratic values and ensure that all sectors of society are represented in decisionmaking?

Individual

- How will citizens participate effectively in public debate and policymaking?

- What material improvement will be felt by individuals as a result of the political reform process?

- What kinds of skills, information, and experiences do citizens need to be confident and active and to internalize their rights?

- How can the public education component of the advocacy encourage people to respect differences and to address discrimination?

Example Goals and Objectives (developed during an African training workshop)

Issue: Inadequate health services and education for women that lead to debilitating health problems with negative repercussions for infants and children.

Long-Term Goal: To promote the enjoyment of women's rights for healthier, more productive lives.

Short-term Goal: To ensure the provision of reproductive health services, information, and options to women aged 18-45 living in the northern region of Uganda.

Government Objective: To lobby for a gender-sensitive reproductive health policy in line with the Cairo recommendations. The policy should include guidelines for government and community programs serving women, and designate 24% of the health budget for this purpose.

Private Sector Objective: To call on private health facilities to designate a small percentage of their services to mobile or stationary health clinics for indigent women and children.

Political Space and Culture Objectives:
- To establish a joint committee involving NGO leadership, government, and private sector health organizations to monitor and evaluate the impact of the new policy.
- To promote public dialogue about women's rights and health.
- To use the policy to help political and business leaders better understand the value of gender-sensitive approaches, and the benefits of responding to women's needs.
- To establish community monitoring groups to ensure that quality services are provided.
- To educate the media about reproductive health issues and assist them in doing a series of stories to educate men and women.

Civil Society Objectives:
- To foster horizontal linkages between women's groups and other citizens' groups concerned with social issues through community focus groups.
- To strengthen the leadership and communication skills of development NGO networks.
- To make decisionmaking structures of women's groups and health coalitions more agile and accountable.

Individual Objectives:
- To educate women aged 13-45 through age-specific programs about their reproductive health, their choices and responsibilities, and the right to demand better services.
- To improve the health of women and their ability to make informed choices about their own and their children's health.
- To promote respect and better understanding between men and women regarding the importance and differences of their health needs.

Advocacy Action and Impact Chart	
ARENA	**IMPACT**
1. State / Government Sector	Support for or change in a law, policy, program, practices, person, decisionmaking process, budget, enforcement, access, etc.

National
  -Executive
  -Agencies / Ministries
  -Legislative / Parliament
  -Military / Police
  -Courts
  -Other
Provincial Government
Local Government
International Bodies
  -UN
  -IMF / World Bank
  -Multilateral Development Banks
Other
	Actions and impacts that advance human rights, foster more equitable sustainable development, and promote greater voice and power of excluded populations in public decisionmaking (e.g., women, indigenous groups, the poor, and religious, racial or ethnic minorities, etc.)

2. Private Sector	Support for or change in policy, program, practices, behavior, etc.
Local / National / Multinational	*See actions and impacts under State / Government sector*
3. Civil Society	Strengthen and expand civil society's capacity, organization, accountability, and power; expand knowledge; and increase overall social reciprocity, trust, and tolerance.
-NGOs -Membership Organizations -Community-based Organizations -Ally Organizations / Coalitions -Other	*Actions and impacts that fortify groups and alliances working to advance the rights and improve the living conditions of marginalized peoples to protect the health of societies and the planet overall.*
4. Political Space and Culture	Increase democratic space, expand participation and political legitimacy of civil society, and increase accountability / transparency of public institutions and media; transform norms and customs that lead to intolerance, subordination, and exclusion.
-Political -Social / Cultural -Other	*Actions and impacts that enhance the political and social dimensions of culture in ways that promote the voice and vote of the marginalized in decisionmaking and encourage behaviors and values of cooperation, collaboration, trust, inclusion, reciprocity, and equity.*
5. Individual	Improve concrete living conditions and opportunities for health, education, and livelihood; promote beliefs and awareness of self as protagonist / citizen with rights and responsibilities to participate in change.
-Living Conditions / Opportunities -Attitudes / Awareness -Personal Relationships, etc.	*Actions and impacts that improve the lives and expand the knowledge, political analysis / consciousness, confidence, solidarity, skills, and vision of marginalized populations and their allies; actions and impacts that challenge discrimination / subordination in personal and family relations.*

PLANNING ADVOCACY

How can the people in the background be more involved in political decisions?

Strategic Emphasis

The *Advocacy Action and Impact Chart* can be used after you have begun your advocacy to monitor and evaluate progress. One approach to assessment is to examine whether the focus of your efforts and resources is consistent with your priorities. Resources are limited, and this analysis helps to direct activities in those areas where they are most needed and where they can have the most impact.

The exercise *Focusing Advocacy Resources* on page 184 is one way to do this kind of analysis.

For more information on monitoring and assessing advocacy impact, see Action Aid's *Monitoring and Evaluating Advocacy: A Scoping Study*, by Jennifer Chapman and Amboka Wameyo.

The Advocacy Debate: Changing Policy, Changing People   ○

Why will policy change in itself not bring about social change? Policy change can set up new rules of engagement, shift priorities and resources, or codify rights and commitments. This is significant, but advocacy concerned with social justice, basic rights, and participation has to also address values and behavior that do not change simply because law changes. Changing policy is about changing people — in civil society, government, and in the private sector. Unless strategies are aimed at people explicitly, political decisions will often not be realized on the ground. The case from Zimbabwe below may help groups understand the importance of the different dimensions of advocacy strategies.

In the early 1980s, soon after the Rhodesian apartheid state was dismantled, the new government of Zimbabwe embarked on a number of important legal and policy changes. Influenced by leading human rights lawyers, the country passed the Legal Age of Majority Act which made all women legal adults at the age of 18. Prior to that time, women were perpetual legal minors, unable to have a bank account, get a license, have custody of their children, or make any other legal decision without approval from their husbands or fathers.

The passing of the Act was mired in controversy. By the time news of the new law reached villages, especially in rural areas, many men and women rejected it outright. Many mothers (and fathers) were angry because the law meant their daughters could get married at 18 with or without their permission and whether or not lobola (brideprice) was paid to the girl's family. There was very little public consultation about the Act outside of the main urban areas before it was passed. Rural people felt this was yet another imposition from city folk who did not respect custom and family. Few people – women particularly – understood the law's benefits.

Part of the reason the Act was passed quickly was that the party in power wanted to expand the number of voters; including women and men between the ages of 18 and 21 (before the law men were legal majors only at 21). Unfortunately, the opposition to the new law deepened resistance by women and men to all subsequent women's legal rights-related reforms. This became a serious obstacle to further progress on women's rights for the following two decades. Some people said that the law aggravated the generation gap among women and contributed to conflicts within families. Others argued that these tensions were inevitable, and that legal change was needed sooner rather than later for such an urgent human rights matter.

The following questions provide some ideas on how to conduct discussion on this case as it relates to policy and social change.

- What does this story tell us about social values and legal change?
- What does this story tell us about the impact of legal change on the public? On custom and cultural beliefs?
- What alternative legal reform strategy might lessen the possibility of backlash and resistance?

PLANNING ADVOCACY

Purpose

- To identify, once you have begun your advocacy work, in what dimensions advocacy activities have been developed and what their impact has been.

- To determine if and how the focus of your advocacy strategy should be adjusted.

Process

This exercise is done in small groups. Each group should be made up of people who have worked together on a particular advocacy initiative.

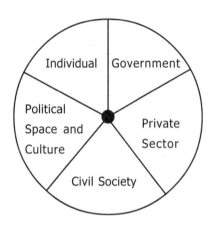

1. Explain to each group the meaning of each of the five dimensions: government, private sector, civil society, political space and culture, individual (see page 178-179). There may be some confusion about the fact that "culture" is a separate dimension because it is also part of all the other dimensions. Remind the group that this exercise is a tool to reflect on the focus of advocacy activities, and that it is important that activities focusing directly on political culture are not overlooked.

2. Ask each group to make a list of the major activities they have carried out to effect change in each of the five dimensions.

3. Using the list as a guide, the group should estimate the comparative size of each dimension in terms of effort and resources expended and draw a pie chart to reflect their analysis

Discussion

Discuss what the analysis means for future advocacy work. Questions to guide this discussion may include:

- What dimensions have been left out of our current and past advocacy work? Should we try to address that dimension?

- Has our action in the different dimensions been consistent with our analysis of the problem?

- Have the dimensions we have been working on the most shown a corresponding impact?

The chart has five different dimensions. However, a group may decide that it is unable to impact all of these dimensions because of limited resources or because of the political context. Nevertheless, it is important not to forget that all the dimensions exist. Eventually, the advocacy effort will probably need to address each of them to produce long-term success.

Examples

The following examples were developed during a Latin American training workshop and are illustrative of how different groups divide their resources. The analysis of this exercise will involve much more in-depth questioning and detail than is shown here.

This chart was made by a group in El Salvador addressing the problem of sexist education in the school system. The impact chart shows a relative balance of activities in the five areas.

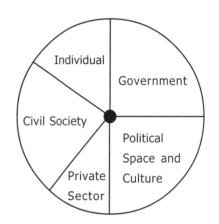

Government: Research on sexism in education; public debate with the Ministry of education; development of an urban model and materials for non-sexist education; distribution of publications and stories; mobilization and pressure.

Political Space / Culture: Public debates; group reflections; interviews on radio stations, TV, and in newspapers; course on feminist debates; public campaigns; marches; parties; video fora.

Private Sector: Public and video fora; seek support for information campaigns.

Civil Society: Alliances with teachers' organizations; establishment of a documentation, information, and communication center for communities and teachers; activities to encourage rural women to organize themselves.

Individual: Group reflection based on personal experiences; different kinds of impact on education for girls and boys.

The chart below reflects the advocacy work of a group from Honduras. In their case, the National Health Secretariat had approved a policy on sexual and reproductive health. However, the policy was in danger of being overturned by powerful opponents and the group was advocating to protect it. After making the chart, the group recognized that none of their activities targeted the private sector, an important potential ally, and that most of their advocacy concentrated on the government.

Government (particularly the National Health Secretariat): Participation on a commission of "dignitaries;" preparing information for the government to use to support the new policy; lobbying and awareness-raising activities.

Political Space / Culture: Participation in radio and TV programs; distribution of information.

Civil Society: Coordination and alliances with other organizations; fora for debate and discussion; conferences; information dissemination.

Individual: provision of information to individual women and spaces for reflection and analysis.

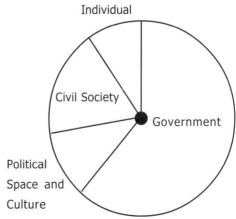

NOTES

[1] Adapted from Miller, Valerie. *NGOs and Grassroots Policy Influence: What is Success?* Institute for Development Research, Vol. 11, No. 5, 1994.

[2] Adapted from Schuler, Margaret, "Conceptualizing and Exploring Issues and Strategies" in *Empowerment and the Law: Strategies of Third World Women*, OEF International, 1986.

[3] Adapted from Institute for Development Research. *Strategic Thinking: Formulating Organizational Strategy. Facilitator's Guide.* Boston, 1998.

[4] Developed and refined by Valerie Miller and Lisa VeneKlasen; see also V. Miller, ibid.

11 Finding Policy Hooks and Political Angles

In order to sharpen your advocacy plan, your group will need more information about:

- the policy and political arenas where you focus your strategy; and

- possible policy hooks to advance your issue.

Analysis of the formal political system, the policymaking process, and its internal power dynamics helps you identify entry points for influence. It can also reveal the limits and possibilities of policy change.

Policy Hooks

A policy hook is the link between your advocacy issue and specific policies, people, and/or institutions in the formal political arena. Advocacy aimed at the private sector may need to combine public policy hooks with strategies focused on corporate policy and practice.

Once you have identified your policy hook, you can identify your targets—the key decision-makers with the power to deliver on your issue. You can also identify possible opponents and allies.

Research and information-gathering are important tasks for fleshing out the remaining elements of your advocacy plan and for finding your policy hook. Involving citizens in this task also brings them into contact with government and other powerful entities. For example, the Highlander Center (USA), a 65 year old school for grassroots organizing and social justice, set up a participatory research process and training program with poor people displaced by floods to investigate who owned the land in their communities and how much they paid in taxes. Their discoveries and analysis fueled a multi-year citizen advocacy battle in several Appalachian states to take large property owners to task for not paying taxes. The process expanded and strengthened local organization and citizen leadership.[1]

Some research may require the expertise of a trained researcher or someone who manages information in government. These experts or insiders can be useful allies in your advocacy as long as the research agenda continues to be driven by the advocates.

This chapter offers an outline of political and policy dimensions to help guide your information-gathering and is divided into the following sections:

- *Different Political Systems and Entry Points*

- *Phases of Policymaking and Refining Policy Objectives*

- *Other Policymaking Arenas*

- *Budget Analysis and Advocacy*

- *International Policymaking and Advocacy Opportunities*

As we discussed in the previous chapter, policymaking is not the only formal political hook for advocacy. Elections and citizen-government fora also present advocacy opportunities. However, we focus this chapter solely on policymaking.

Different Political Systems and Entry Points

Each phase of policymaking involves diverse players, procedures, and institutional structures and can also involve different, often interconnected, levels – international, national, or local. The national level is sometimes overlooked in international advocacy. This is unfortunate, because ultimately it is up to national governments to implement international policies. The importance of local level advocacy depends on the degree of decentralization and specific authority of the local government.

This overview focuses on the national level and provides some basic elements that groups will need to examine critically in order to understand the specifics of their own political institutions and processes.

National Policymaking

The key *formal* political structures which can be targets at the national level are usually:

- the Legislature – Congress / Parliament;
- the Executive – President / Prime Minister;
- the Judiciary – courts;
- bureaucracy – appointed leadership and staff in government offices;
- political parties;
- police and military.

These players and structures respond to other policy players, including the local and international private sector, donors, citizens, and each other. How they operate depends in part on the type of political system in which they live. In some countries, the military can operate as a separate branch of government.

A Presidential system works differently than a Parliamentary system. In the next section, we describe some of the differences of the two systems, and discuss how these systems work in theory. In practice, they often operate differently. In some countries there is a mix of a presidential and parliamentary system.

The Courts

Legal decisions determine what a law means in practice. When a change in the law itself is not possible, sometimes groups can use the courts to make changes in how the law works by establishing legal precedents (if the constitution upholds the rights they wish to enforce). For example, when women's rights advocates in Zimbabwe compared possible strategies for establishing women's equal rights to inheritance, they saw two possible alternatives: 1) seeking an amendment to existing law through Parliament or 2) bringing a case to the superior courts. The Parliament and President at the time were opposed to any proposal that "tinkered with African culture." But the Supreme Court was recognized for its independence, fairness, and respect for international human rights standards. The choice was therefore simple, but the task was difficult. The advocates needed a solid court case where the judgment would clearly change law and where the plaintiff was willing to endure public scrutiny. (For more information, see *The Advocacy Debate: Changing Policy, Changing People* on page 183.) In some legal systems, "class action" allows a group of people to be the plaintiff. This reduces the individual isolation and exposure.

Differences between the Presidential and Parliamentary Systems

Presidential System

In its purest form, there is strict separation of legislative and executive powers. Neither is dependent on the other for policymaking. Their terms of office are also different.

In the *legislature*, formal power resides in a few key individuals. If there are two chambers – such as the House of Representatives and the Senate in the United States — each has its own leadership. In many countries, the main leaders are the Speaker and Deputy Speaker or President Protempore. Also important are the political party Whips and Majority and Minority Floor Leaders who are responsible for keeping their party colleagues in line and shaping the agenda. Often the most important policy formulation take place in committees of legislators. In some countries, there are expert staff to assist the committees who often have a lot of influence over policy.

The President is the *executive* and has a set term in office. She/he is a policymaker, budget chief, head of political appointments, and implementer. Traditionally, the President reveals her/his policy agenda to the public at the opening of a legislative session and works with legislators and others to push through legislation or block it. She/he can also issue executive orders and has veto power. The national budget is primarily an executive responsibility but involves bargaining with ministries and legislators. The President makes key appointments, including to the Cabinet and regulatory agencies, to top positions in ministries and departments. Since enforcement involves discretionary decisions, the President can play a large role in ensuring enforcement.

Parliamentary System

In this system, the executive and legislative branches are fused. The legislature elects from its members the Chief Executive, usually called the Prime Minister, who is often the leader of the majority party or coalition. The Cabinet is chosen from among Members of Parliament. The Prime Minister can dissolve Parliament and call for new elections. On the other hand, a motion of no confidence by Parliament either leads to the Prime Minister's resignation or to holding of new elections. Theoretically, the Prime Minister and Parliament are equal in power. In practice, often the Prime Minister and Cabinet have more power than Parliament.

The Prime Minister is responsible for the overall direction of policy. The ministries formulate specific policies for their respective areas. Parliamentary committees cannot themselves change bills referred to them, but can recommend changes to the executive. Bills originate from the executive who also indicates priority matters. In a parliamentary system, there is more debate on the floor when a bill is tabled than in a presidential system, where votes are often lined up before a bill comes to the floor.

Regardless of the type of political system, the *national legislature,* when it has a measure of real power, can be an important focus for the policy component of an advocacy strategy.

Based on Socorro Reyes, "Navigating and Mastering the Policy Arena", chapter for the first draft of the *Action Guide*, 1997.

PLANNING ADVOCACY

Bureaucracy

Presidents and Prime Ministers use their power of appointments and place people they trust in leadership positions to move their political agenda forward. In numerous countries, many of the critical issues are deter- mined by the Ministry of Finance, Planning Unit, or its equivalent. In countries where the multilateral donors have a big hand in economic and budget policies, the Finance Minister can be nearly as powerful as the President. In many countries, well-placed civil servants can be either points of influence or key informants and allies for advocates. It is usually the bureaucracy that ensures that policies are translated into real programs. They can have considerable discretionary power and sometimes play a significant role in determining policy. Advocates need to know who's who in the relevant ministries and departments affecting their issue, and who shapes decisions long before they come to a vote in the legislature.

Political parties

Part of the current worldwide political trend is a shift to multiparty politics. Many people expect multiparty politics to generate more political competition and, therefore, more responsive governance. On the one hand, the emergence of parties can give advocates more opportunities to influence policy and electoral processes. On the other hand, established political parties are often hierarchical, exclusive, and resistant to change — especially the changes promoted by new voices and players in the political game. While the party system is meant to create more choices for citizens, often a few parties dominate the political scene and do not adequately represent excluded groups.

In some places people are trying to reform political parties and to find alternative systems that enable more citizens to participate in the

political process. For example, in the Philippines, the Party List System Act of 1995 reserves 20% of the total number of seats in the House for any organizations and political parties that garner at least 2% of all votes cast. Those seats are then apportioned accordingly. The Act aims to promote the representation of disadvantaged groups such as women, peasants, workers, and fisherfolk. Chapter 14, page 274-276, provides a case study on advocacy in the Philippines using the Party List Law.

Several countries have affirmative action policies. These require that a certain percentage of all candidates and people elected represent a particular group, such as women or ethnic groups. Different countries have differ-

> "In order to get beyond racism, we must first take account of race... and in order to treat some people equally, we must treat them differently."
>
> Justice Harry A. Blackmun,
> U.S. Supreme Court Justice, 1978

ent kinds of quotas. The box on the following page describes some of these differences.

Despite their problems, political parties are important points of influence and change, particularly during elections. Advocates can put pressure on parties to include key issues in their election platform.

Levels of Policymaking Arenas and Processes

Different kinds of policies are formulated at the international, national, and local levels. Transforming written policies into public programs and real changes in people's lives happens primarily at the national and local levels, but all three levels are increasingly interconnected. For example, national budget, trade, and

> "Political parties are the gatekeepers in democratic governance. They choose and decide who will run for office, what flagship issues they will be identified with, where the campaign funds will be sourced, and how the election will be won. Once they acquire power, they steer the 'ship of state' in the direction provided in their party platform and program of government."
>
> Socorro Reyes
> Center for Legislative Development, Philippines

Correcting Imbalances in Politics: Quotas and Affirmative Action

"Many countries have gender quotas and affirmative action policies to increase women's participation in politics. In some cases, quotas are established by national legislation and in others, by political parties. According to the Inter-Parliamentary Union, in 1998, 56 parties in 24 countries used quotas. Their success depends on the specifics of the quota policy. In Argentina, the law on statutory quota requires political parties to reserve 30% of electable positions for women, and to have a woman occupy every third place on the list or party slate. In less than ten years, this law has increased women's representation from 6% to 25%. In contrast, the electoral law in Costa Rica requires 40% overall representation of women in party slates. Yet, it is not as successful as the Argentinian approach since it does not require that parties place women high up on the ballot or list.

In South Africa, there is a penalty for political parties that fail to nominate a woman delegate to all parliamentary committees and international delegations. In Eritrea, 30% of seats in the national and regional assemblies are reserved for women. The 33% quota for seats in local government bodies in India has brought over a million women into local self-governing bodies like the panchayats.

Initially, problems such as lack of training and campaign funding for women, inexperience, fear of politics and prejudices about women as public leaders reduced the impact of these affirmative action policies in many countries. But as women gain experience and training, and enter politics in record number, the problems are disappearing and women's voices are making formal democratic structures more representative."

From "Women Around the World", Center for Legislative Development, Philippines; for more information see www.cld.org and WAW6.htm.

PLANNING ADVOCACY

environmental policy can be heavily influenced by international policy.

For most issues, the national and local levels will be the primary focus for social and political change. However, the ultimate target may be the international policymaking bodies. For example, environmental battles can lead to the international arena where international financial institutions and transnational corporations are, along with governments, the focus for change. Alternatively, international agreements and bodies can provide leverage for national advocacy.

The scope of decisionmaking at the *national level* depends on the extent of decentralization in a given country. Throughout the world, there is a growing trend toward decentralization with both positive and negative results. On the positive side, by having policymaking more

accessible, citizens are able to see the direct impact of politics on their lives and can be more motivated to get involved. On the negative side, local government is often subject to local prejudice, inexperience, and control by local elites. Further, decentralization can lessen the possibilities for redistribution between wealthier and poorer parts of a country. Even where the system is decentralized, some

In most countries, making the *policy process* more transparent is an important goal of citizen advocacy. Advocacy battles for increased transparency and the "RIGHT TO KNOW" demand that governments and corporations make their decisionmaking processes and information accessible to the citizens. The measures that accomplish this task are often called *Sunshine Laws* because they open up policymaking to the light of day.

policy decisions remain at the national level. These include most legal matters, defense, international affairs, and key budget issues.

The local level can encompass several different layers of decisionmaking. These include regions, provinces, states, districts, municipalities, villages, and neighborhoods. In many countries, the local levels are charged more with implementing than with making policy. In some countries, the local levels are simply administrative branches of the higher levels.

It is important to find out exactly which decisions are made at which level before determining the targets and strategies for advocacy.

Phases of Policymaking

The policymaking process has four different overlapping phases: agenda setting, formulation and enactment, implementation, and monitoring and evaluation. Each phase is shaped by different power dynamics and involves different players, both inside and outside the formal political process.

Although the policymaking process is often explained as a step by step logic, it is rarely linear and predictable. For example, after a policy is formulated, it may not be implemented if there is strong opposition. Similarly, sometimes policy is enacted, but lack of money and other factors prevent enforcement. At times your advocacy will aim to stop a policy from getting passed once it reaches the legislature. In the best democratic circumstances, citizens can

find out about, monitor, and influence the process at each stage. But powerful stakeholders can often make it difficult for outsiders to find out what is going on. Frequently, the public is unaware of pending policy changes until they come up for a legislative vote or until an executive order is issued. In many countries, policies and laws are decided before they get to the legislature.

Agenda Setting

Power dynamics and political forces put an issue on the policymaking agenda. Getting your issue on the agenda is often the toughest part of advocacy work. Constituency-building and mobilization use the power of numbers to attempt to get on the agenda. Where agenda setting is tightly controlled, lack of access can sometimes lead to large-scale public protest.

Formulation and Enactment

Once on the agenda, policies and laws are developed through research, discussion of alternatives, technical formulation, and politics.

Phases of Policymaking

Agenda-Setting
Getting an issue/problem on the policy agenda

Formulation and Enactment
Developing a policy that responds to the issue and getting it passed by the relevant agency or branch of government

Implementation and Enforcement
Putting the policy into action and enforcing it when necessary

Monitoring and Evaluation
Monitoring and assessing the policy's application and impact

Valerie Miller and Jane Covey, Advocacy Sourcebook, IDR, 1997

There are many players involved, and the process varies significantly between countries.

After formulation, enactment can happen in different ways. When enactment happens through a vote in a legislature, opportunities for influence are optimum. But sometimes policies are passed quickly because negotiations happen behind the scenes before passage. Lobbying skills are important in this phase, and a strong base of citizen support on the outside increases your clout on the inside. (See Chapters 14 and 15.)

Implementation

The agencies and individuals who are responsible for implementation vary from issue to issue, but will always be targets for advocacy and influence. Implementation often involves the development of social programs, retraining or hiring new government staff, and setting up regulations or enforcement mechanisms. Budgets are therefore a critical ingredient. If policies are approved, but there is no budget allocation, they are unlikely to have any real impact. Policies without resources attached are called "unfunded mandates," and bureaucrats are, understandably, reluctant—or simply unable—to implement them. Advocacy efforts sometimes seek to *block* implementation of a particular policy or law.

Monitoring and Evaluation

This phase involves assessing a policy's impact on the problem it was intended to solve. Without public pressure, this phase is often overlooked by governments or international policymaking bodies because it involves resources and time. They may also avoid this phase because it shows where policies have been unsuccessful or reveals the corrupt diversion of resources. Sometimes the impact of a policy can be a motivating starting point for broad-based constituency-building and citizen education because it is felt concretely.

This phase has increasingly become the focus of advocacy. Sometimes citizens groups propose the establishment of joint citizen-government monitoring boards. These are increasingly popular in some parts of Latin America where enforcement is getting new teeth. State and local governments are passing citizen monitoring laws that require governments to systematically get input and approval from civil society to ensure enforcement.

PLANNING ADVOCACY

Exercise: Mapping the Policy System

Purpose

This two-part exercise is designed to help advocates identify and evaluate the key policy players in different phases of policymaking and develop appropriate strategies to influence them during each phase.

Process

(Time: 1–2 hours)

The first framework lists the key institutional and individual players in each phase of the process and spells out their interests and positions. It can be used in conjunction with the *Mapping Power* (page 219). The second combines the *Policy Map* with the *Advocacy Action and Impact Chart* (page 181). By combining the frameworks, you can plan the aims and activities that will be part of your advocacy in each phase. The "dimensions" show which actors and systems you will target or engage at different moments.

Policy Map

Issue/Policy:				
PHASES	Institutions	Individuals	Interests	Positions
Agenda-Setting				
Formulation and Enactment				
Implementation and Enforcement				
Monitoring and Evaluation				

Adapted from *Advocacy Sourcebook*, Miller and Covey, IDR, 1997.

Setting Objectives for Phases of Policymaking

Dimensions	Agenda-Setting	Formulation and Enactment	Implementation and Enforcement	Monitoring and Evaluation
Government *National* -Executive -Bureaucracy -Courts -Legislature *Local Councils* *International Agencies* (World Bank/ IMF, UN, etc.)				
Private Sector				
Civil Society				
Political and Social Culture				
Individual				

PLANNING ADVOCACY

Budget Analysis and Advocacy

Over the last decade, there has been growing citizen interest in budget policy. Budgets are the most powerful policy that governments make because they determine whether other policies or laws get implemented or not. Budgets reveal the true priorities of governments. They may be skewed in favor of vested interests at the expense of those with less voice in the political process. Budgets are therefore important targets and tools for social justice and rights advocates. Politicians rely on the fact that most people are intimidated by budgets.

Budget advocacy projects ideally combine research and analysis with advocacy. Most existing initiatives challenge corruption and critique budget imbalances that favor elites. Some take a pro-poor perspective, some take a gender perspective, and some combine these. Most push for budget transparency and the "right to know" about the budget-making process and the data used to make choices. However, there are important differences among budget advocacy projects in terms of how the advocacy agenda is set and who participates in the process. Below are two broad distinctions that can be found among strategies that offer some lessons for linking advocacy and budget analysis.

A notable model of participatory budgets comes from Porto Alegre, Brazil. In the 1990s, the city government legislated citizen involvement in deciding and monitoring budgets. Citizens now gather in town halls and soccer stadiums to debate budget priorities. The process has been refined over the years, with ever greater numbers involved.

Research-led

Many budget initiatives have policy research as their starting point and emphasis. In these mostly national-level projects, NGO think tanks and researchers produce valuable analysis for advocates or government reformers. Where the research is directly tied to an ongoing campaign or policy change, the information boosts advocacy significantly. However, if the research is not directly linked to a citizen action agenda from the outset, it can be difficult for citizens' groups to figure out how to use the information. This is especially true when research looks at the entire budget because citizens' groups may have difficulty finding an entry point.

Advocacy-led and Problem-centered

Some budget initiatives are led by citizen-organizing and advocacy groups. In these

---

Budget Analysis

Budget analysis looks at:

Inputs — the money appropriated (tax and other revenues) and spent;

Activities — the services planned and delivered (e.g., health services, industrial support services, tax collection services);

Outputs — the planned and delivered take-up of the activities (e.g., patients treated, businesses supported, taxes paid);

Impacts — planned and actual achievements in relation to broader objectives (e.g., healthy people, competitive businesses, sustainable growth of national income).

Elson, Diane, *Gender Budget Initiatives as an Aid to Gender Mainstreaming*, OECD Conference on Gender Mainstreaming, Competitiveness and Growth, November 2000.

cases, the research often starts with problems that people face in their daily lives and issues that are the focus of ongoing advocacy. These projects typically target local as well as national government, and work with research groups to develop the information and analysis related to their specific cause. Participatory or action research methods are used to engage communities in their own analysis, linking a problem to a policy to a budget allocation. Some of the projects place as much emphasis on gathering and using information to build citizen participation as on using it to change the allocations and priorities in the budget. In connecting budgets to real life and accountability, projects look at budget impact as well as allocation.

In both kinds of projects, people, legislators, and government reformers sometimes work side by side. In this way, government and elected officials gain the skills and information they need to do their job more responsively while citizens gain the capacity to influence the budget process.

A problem-centered approach combines participatory methodologies and gender analysis and includes five steps:[2]

1. a description of the situation and problems faced by a marginalized group in a specific context (or sector) and a prioritization of problems;

2. an assessment of government's policies and programs in relation to these priorities, including the extent to which they are responsive to excluded groups;

3. an assessment of the extent to which the allocation of financial and other resources is adequate to implement the policies and programs;

4. monitoring of the extent to which the resources are used for the intended purpose and reach the intended beneficiaries;

5. an evaluation of the impact of the resources on the problems identified in the original situation analysis of step one.

Budget projects that focus on women or gender use gender analysis to help groups priori-

Understanding the meaning of budgets

tize problems and pinpoint how budgets and other policies are discriminatory, thus shaping those problems as well as potentially solving them. Using a gender lens often exposes the unequal and inefficient collection and distribution of resources. But a full analysis of budget priorities calls for a combination of gender with class, age, race-ethnicity, and regional perspectives as well.

Certain political factors are conducive to the kind of citizen budget work that gives voice to marginalized populations such as women and the poor. Those factors include:

1. political openness and a government commitment to clean up corruption and increase transparency (negotiations around debt cancellation often create an opening for budget advocacy at the national level);

2. a group of reformers within key ministries such as Finance or Planning;

3. a group of reformers in Parliament or local councils;

4. a combination of NGOs concerned with accountability and social justice that include policy expertise, membership- or community-based groups, development agencies, research or academic institutions, and rights and advocacy groups.

Often, budget projects that emphasize citizen-centered advocacy:

- are citizen-led, including the research activities. The budget analysis is a process of citizen education that enables people to demystify, analyze, and influence the allocation of public resources.

- use participatory methodologies for defining community priorities;

- are oriented to solving problems in an equitable way. By combining technical expertise and practical experience, they

strengthen the capacity of government to address people's needs equitably;

- use gender as a tool for analysis and action;

- highlight the right to participate in decisions that affect one's life and have equitable access to public resources;

- promote constructive dialogue and collaboration among communities, advocates, and government.

International Policymaking and Advocacy Opportunities

In the last decade, international policymaking has been both a target and tool for citizen advocacy. Major policy questions of trade, foreign debt, financial flows, corporate responsibility, the environment, and development strategies are defined at the international level. Although the impact on ordinary people is enormous, the international decisionmaking processes still tend to be less responsive and open to outside voices and interests. Global advocacy has called for increased transpar-

> ". . . as many governments and international organizations have found to their dismay in recent years, secretive decisionmaking by small elites can no longer be sustained. Contrary to the claims often made by central bankers, government officials, and even some in the World Bank and the IMF that decisionmaking on technical or complex subjects is best left to the experts, without informed participation by all those affected, policy decisions will fail to take into account important information and interests and will lack the legitimacy that only public voice can bring. Decisionmakers should not try to sneak even a good public policy past the public."
>
> Ann M. Florini [3]

ency and representation as well as specific policy change.[4]

At the same time, international policies, commitments, and conventions can be valuable tools that legitimize local demands. The advocacy processes around these can also draw upon regional and international advocacy networks. The language in the international agreements can produce new points of leverage for advocacy with policymakers at the national and local levels, and can help define a policy hook and message. When national laws and policies are unlikely to be passed on a difficult issue, a resolution with international backing can be an effective angle for reaching policymakers. We look at some of the international hooks below. (In Chapter 15 we address advocacy on economic and trade policy in more detail.)

International Rights Advocacy

A rights-based approach to advocacy implies many different meanings and strategies. Two of these involve: a) using international conventions to push for the enforcement of rights at the country or local level; and b) expanding the definition of rights to include social, cultural, and economic issues by amending agreements and creating mechanisms for enforcement. In these cases, international agreements are the *policy target* or the *policy hook* for advocacy.

Until the early 1990's, most human rights advocacy focused on civil and political rights, such as freedom of speech, of association, or of religion. Advocates continue to denounce abuses of these rights, particularly in conflict situations and repressive political environments, using instruments such as the International Convention on Civil and Political Rights.

PLANNING ADVOCACY

Headlines on Rights

"On April 23, 2001, the United Nations Commission on Human Rights reaffirmed its political commitment to women's rights to land, property, housing, and inheritance. After a showdown on the 'right to adequate housing' between Mexico and the US, the Mexican delegation won and the resolution was adopted through consensus by this important human rights body. For the second consecutive year, the delegation of Mexico—supported by close to 50 government delegations from both the North and the South—put forward for adoption a resolution entitled, 'Women's equal ownership of, access to and control over land and the equal rights to own property and to adequate housing' (E/CN.4/2000/L.53).

"Although the content of the resolution is only slightly stronger than last year's, there are important new additions. For example, the resolution encourages all human rights treaty bodies, in particular the Committee on Economic, Social, and Cultural Rights and the Committee on the Elimination of Discrimination Against Women, to 'regularly and systematically take a gender perspective into account in the implementation of their mandates, and to integrate the contents of the present resolution into their work, as appropriate.' The resolution also remains an important affirmation of women's right to inheritance.

"This resolution would not have been adopted without the support of many NGOs in countries around the world. These same supporters must now ensure wide dissemination of the resolution, transform it into a popular advocacy tool, and translate it into local languages. The advocates will need to develop creative means to use the resolution so that it assists in domestic struggles for women's rights to land, property, housing, and inheritance."

Excerpt from the AWID RESOURCE NET, from The Association for Women's Rights in Development (AWID) at www.awid.org.

Using UN Conferences and Their Related Declarations

During the 1990s, there were seven UN conferences that are important for the international social justice movement. These conferences are commonly referred to by the cities where they took place:

- New York (1990), World Summit for Children
- Rio de Janeiro (1992), UN Conference on Environment and Development
- Vienna (1993), World Conference on Human Rights
- Cairo (1994), International Conference on Population and Development, including women's reproductive rights
- Copenhagen (1995), World Summit for Social Development, including social policies and rights
- Beijing (1995), Fourth World Conference on Women
- Istanbul, Habitat II (1996), UN Conference on Human Settlements
- Hamburg (1997), UN Conference on Adult Education

Critics of the conferences complain that often policy changes do not follow smoothly from the declarations generated by the meetings. They are also concerned that preparations and participation consume a lion's share of the resources and time available for NGO advocacy. This often leaves very little for local organizing. Some organizations are now rethinking their investment in the UN arena. Instead, they are refocusing their energies on strengthening constituency groups and grassroots leadership. The challenge is to find ways in which the different spheres of political action—local, national, and international—can create synergies for change.

Some of the important outcomes of UN meetings include:

New and strengthened networks: To prepare for UN conferences, many NGOs and advocates have organized first at the local level and then nationally. This enables groups to agree on what they want to see in the official government and international platforms. Monitoring and follow-up activities after the conference provide opportunities for building linkages. For example, after the Beijing conference, there were extensive cross-border e-mail discussions on women's equity, political power, health, and other issues.

Exchange of new skills and knowledge: The shadow NGO conferences that run parallel to official conferences create spaces for activists to come together. The process is sometimes nonhierarchical and a significant shift from usual domination by Western industrialized countries.

Legitimacy: The preparatory processes for each conference strengthen the legitimacy of the official and NGO country delegations. If conducted in a participatory way, the preparatory processes should also strengthen accountability.

New government commitments. After conferences, some governments introduce important reforms in keeping with their commitments. NGOs can use these commitments to monitor progress and press for further change.

Reforming international institutions and policies: The shadow NGO fora demonstrate to international institutions that civil society is not only capable of participating in policymaking, but is essential to the process. As a result, many UN agencies are now more open to working with civil society.

Improved advocacy and policy knowledge: The conferences have multiplied the capacity of NGOs worldwide, particularly in areas like advocacy and policymaking. This has led to unprecedented levels of informed citizen involvement at the global and national levels.

Adapted from the *Advocacy Learning Initiative, Volume I: Reflections on Advocacy*, David Cohen, Advocacy Institute-Oxfam America, Draft 11/19/99.

Questions to Analyze Your Human Rights Policy Hook

- Does your problem involve a violation of a protected right (e.g., one covered in some legal instrument)? What is the right?
- Is the right defined in the national constitution? Explain.
- Is the right defined in international human rights conventions? Explain.
- Is the right defined through common practice? Explain.
- Do national laws conform to international human rights standards? If not, what do they need to do so?
- How is the right being violated?
- Who is/are the violator(s)?
- Can the state be shown to be directly or indirectly responsible for the violation?
- How will you prove the violation? Are there documented cases that can be used to demonstrate the violation?
- Does the public understand that the problem involves violation of human rights?
- Has this problem been challenged through courts or national-level human rights mechanisms? If so, can you use these challenges for this case?
- Could you use international mechanisms to address the problem?
- If yes, do you have access to international mechanisms or must you put pressure in other ways?
- What kind of remedies do international mechanisms offer?
- What do you think you can achieve by working on this problem? Write out your desired outcomes as separate sentences.
- Does some practice need to be stopped or does positive action need to be taken to comply with human rights standards? Explain.
- Are you demanding something of the government? If yes, what exactly and specifically must the government do?
- What would constitute satisfactory action by the government?

From *Advocate's Strategy Workbook* (draft), by Margaret Schuler, Women, Law and Development International, 2001.

PLANNING ADVOCACY

There are many political challenges in using other international rights agreements in advocacy. Although governments sign the agreements, they usually do so with formal reservations and may not ratify them. They also may not take the obligations seriously.

It has been more difficult to advocate on a broader range of economic, social, and cultural rights. While there is a universal definition and international enforcement mechanisms for political and civil rights, these do not exist for economic, social, and cultural rights. As a result, many forms of discrimination and exclusion that appear to be serious violations of

rights may not legally be defined as such. Yet considerable gains have been made and incorporated into many agreements related to children, women, labor, health, etc.

For example, despite the growing condemnations of violence against women, in many cases, international mechanisms to protect women are not enforceable unless it is proven that the state is in some way responsible for the continuation of violence. In most cases, there are national laws that criminalize assault and abuse, but they may not be enforced for a variety of reasons. In Brazil, in response to extreme levels of violence against women, human rights organizations monitored actions taken by the police and justice system and found extensive impunity and discriminatory treatment in favor of the perpetrators. State negligence was proven to be deliberate and systematic—constituting a violation of international human rights standards. The Brazilian government was sanctioned by the Inter-American Court of Human Rights.

A valuable lesson from the Brazil case is that the definition of human rights standards and enforcement is evolving, and that working to gain recognition of rights is an important advocacy project. Here, much can be learned from the women's movement.

Women's Human Rights Advocacy

Women, Law and Development International (WLDI) describes the task of women's human rights advocacy in the following way:

> Despite promising advances at the international level, it is clear that women the world over confront a daily reality characterized by the denial of their fundamental human rights . . . Realizing the potential of human rights in

the lives of a broad constituency of women is a major, pressing challenge for the global women's rights movement. Making sure that human rights norms ratified at the international level have practical impact in people's lives involves advocacy . . . WLDI understands women's human rights advocacy as citizen-initiated efforts to:

- Amplify the definition and understanding of human rights to include abuses of women that are not yet generally acknowledged as human rights violations;
- Expand the scope of state responsibility for the protection of women's human rights;
- Enhance the effectiveness of the human rights system in enforcing women's rights and holding abusers accountable.[4]

The frameworks (on the following page) from WLDI describe the women's human rights advocacy process. These frameworks can be used to explore how your women's rights advocacy can use a rights policy hook or target. (See the WLDI *Advocates' Strategy Workbook* and *Facilitator's Process Guide* for more guidance.)

Making Formal Rights Real Rights

Which rights?	Where are they found?	Advocacy Challenges
All rights that apply to both men and women.	Rights found in general human rights instruments	To ensure that these rights are consistently applied to both sexes.
Rights that are specific to women or that need to be expanded to ensure basic rights for women's situation.	Rights covered in specialized instruments, such as CEDAW.	To ensure that these rights are treated with equal seriousness as the general human rights.
Evolving rights.	Not yet defined or covered in any treaty or instrument.	To press for the explicit definition of these rights.

Women, Law and Development International and Human Rights Watch Women's Rights Project. *Women's Human Rights Step by Step*, Washington DC, 1997.

The Dynamics of Human Rights Advocacy

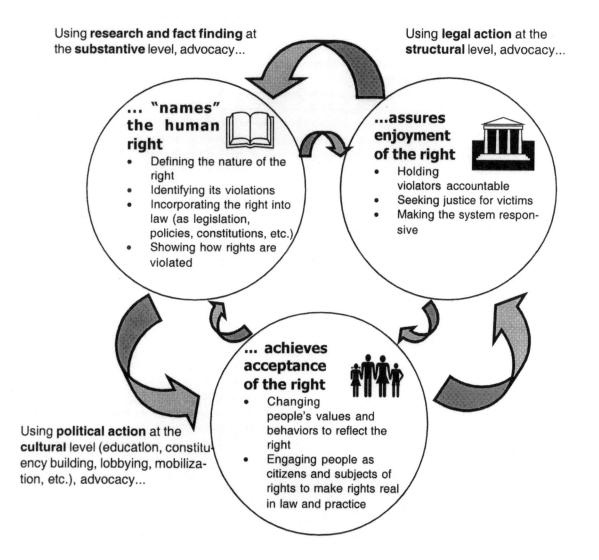

Using **research and fact finding** at the **substantive** level, advocacy...

Using **legal action** at the **structural** level, advocacy...

... "names" the human right
- Defining the nature of the right
- Identifying its violations
- Incorporating the right into law (as legislation, policies, constitutions, etc.)
- Showing how rights are violated

...assures enjoyment of the right
- Holding violators accountable
- Seeking justice for victims
- Making the system responsive

... achieves acceptance of the right
- Changing people's values and behaviors to reflect the right
- Engaging people as citizens and subjects of rights to make rights real in law and practice

Using **political action** at the **cultural** level (education, constituency building, lobbying, mobilization, etc.), advocacy...

From *Advocate's Strategy Workbook* (draft), by Margaret Schuler, Women, Law and Development International, 2001.

PLANNING ADVOCACY

	CONCEPT	DEFINITION	EXAMPLE

Example Framework for Defining ESC Rights and Obligations: Right to Health

CONCEPT	DEFINITION	EXAMPLE
Core content of a right	The specific individual entitlements that make up a right	In the area of health, the right to immunization against preventable epidemic or endemic diseases
State obligation	The responsibilities of the state to respect, protect, promote and fulfill the entitlements under the right	The state is to develop policies and programs to meet obligations. In the case of the right to health, policies and programs of promotion, prevention, treatment, and rehabilitation.
Obligation of conduct	Obligation to undertake specific steps (acts or omissions)	For example, developing immunization campaigns
Obligation of result	Obligation to obtain a particular outcome	Decrease in mortality from epidemic or endemic diseases

From *Circle of Rights: Economic, Social and Cultural Rights Activism,* by the International Human Rights Internship Program and Asian Forum for Human Rights and Development, 2000.

Economic, Social, and Cultural Rights Advocacy

Despite many challenges, advocacy on economic, social, and cultural (ESC) rights has advanced considerably in the last decade. However, while policymakers are increasingly open to rights language, advocacy for the right to housing, food, a decent wage, basic healthcare, and a voice in decisionmaking generates firm opposition from policymakers. Disagreement takes shape around the elusive legal and budgetary challenges of enforcement and ideological differences about who is responsible for addressing poverty and inequality. Advocates for the formal recognition of ESC rights argue that a person cannot enjoy political rights without freedom from hunger, poor health, and exploitation.

In some countries, advocates can use language from the many agreements and conventions that establish ESC rights as part of their strategy.[5] (See following cases.)

ESC Case Study #1: Nigeria, A Case Study on Education

"Arbitrary and discriminatory imposition of fees may result in a denial of equal access to education and therefore constitute a violation of the state's obligations. For example, in a class action filed on behalf of the National Association of Nigerian Students (NANS), the Social and Economic Rights Action Center (SERAC), a Nigerian nongovernmental organization, is asking the court to determine whether the arbitrary increase in fees as applicable to tertiary institutions by upwards of 1,000 percent was compatible with the right to education. The suit is founded on the grounds that the policy would impede access to higher education; that it constitutes a violation of the principles of equality and nondiscrimination due to its selective application to schools mostly in Southern Nigeria; and that the policy is unjustifiable given the rapid decline in quantitative and qualitative standards in higher education."

International Human Rights Internship Program and the Asian Forum for Human Rights and Development. *Circle of Rights: Economic, Social, and Cultural Rights Activism,* 2000, p. 306, 416.

ESC Case Study #2: The Assembly of the Poor and the Power of the People in Thailand

"Negative effects of economic and industrial development led to the merger of disadvantaged groups in one of the most powerful people's movements in the history of Thailand. On 10 December 1995, representatives of people affected by dam projects and land and forest conflicts as well as representatives of the urban poor and industrial workers, met to chalk out a strategy for dealing with their problems. They were joined by students, NGOs and representatives of people with similar problems in other Asian countries. On 14 December 1995, in a special village established in protest against the Pak Mool Dam, a declaration was adopted creating a network called 'Assembly of the Poor,' which would provide mutual support to the various member networks and strengthen their bargaining power. The next day, thousands of people submitted an open letter to the Thai prime minister at a meeting of the heads of governments in the Southeast Asian region. This attracted domestic and international media attention. The Thai government ignored this as well as subsequent demonstrations by the Assembly of the Poor.

"On 25 March 1996 more than 10,000 people from twenty-one provinces assembled in front of Government House in Bangkok; they established a 'Village of the Poor' in the heart of the city. The government opened negotiations with representatives of the Assembly, but no progress was made. After one hundred days, the Assembly decided to disperse and reconvene again with a bigger rally. On 25 January 1997, the Village of the Poor was reestablished with participation from an even larger number of people. Nearly 20,000 people filled up a more than one kilometer stretch near the Government House in Bangkok.

"The Assembly was a nonviolent, creative expression of protest by people who had long been ignored. It was a model of organization, with different committees taking responsibility for ensuring the smooth stay of nearly 20,000 people. The long effort of the Assembly achieved success with the newly elected government, which announced its willingness to negotiate. After ninety-nine days, the government agreed to many of the Assembly's demands and twelve committees were established to monitor the implementation of the various aspects of their agreement."

International Human Rights Internship Program and the Asian Forum for Human Rights and Development. *Circle of Rights: Economic, Social, and Cultural Rights Activism*, 2000, p. 306, 416.

Advocacy on Corporate Policy and Practice

One result of globalization is the increasing power and geographic reach of corporations. Today transnational corporations shape the working and living conditions for people in many countries. They have brought opportunity and resources in some cases. Yet growing poverty and the rapid movement of capital in and out of countries often create instability that has been devastating for people's basic survival.

The transnational corporations that produce everything from jeans to music can also make competition difficult for many local, and especially smaller, businesses. At the same time, local businesses, which now compete in the global marketplace, argue that they have to keep wages low to survive, and rationalize deplorable working conditions in the name of competition.

It is increasingly difficult for national governments to regulate transnational corporations. They are conflicted between their desire to protect their citizens from the negative side-effects of globalization while also taking steps to encourage foreign investment. Corporations that ignore working conditions in their factories or turn a blind eye to the environmental impact

Do You Know People Who Shop in a Supermarket?

One example of an innovative corporate advocacy campaign is "The Great Supermarket Till Receipt Collection" organized by Christian Aid, a charity organization in Great Britain. The supermarket campaign was developed to pressure supermarkets to establish and meet standards for their store-brand products to ensure basic worker rights, and fair pay and conditions.

As a faith-based charity, Christian Aid appeals to church members to collect as many supermarket receipts as they can. The receipts are regularly sorted and then given to the corresponding local supermarket managers with the explanation that the people who spend all that money care about the way workers in developing countries are treated. In this way consumers are demanding that supermarkets play an active role in ensuring just labor conditions for the workers who supply their products. Campaign participants regularly return to the supermarkets to ask about the progress being made.

The supermarket campaign has collected over £15 million worth of supermarket till receipts and generated extensive coverage in the local press. The campaign has also worked with other groups including businesses and unions to press major supermarkets to join the Ethical Trading Initiative (ETI). ETI is a government-sponsored initiative through which members must adopt a minimum standard for their codes of conduct for ethical training. Thanks to the supermarket campaign and other efforts, seven of the ten top UK food retailers have become members of the ETI.

The supermarket campaign continues because the ETI has yet to deliver real change in conditions for overseas workers.

For more information on this initiative, see http://www.christian-aid.org.uk/campaign/supermar/supermar.htm

of their operations have often been targets of advocacy. Effective advocacy strategies to foster improved corporate social responsibility have included both protest and incentives. (See Chapter 14, p 272 for the case of Via Campesina.) Consumer groups have used their buying power to persuade corporations to seek a better balance between people's wellbeing and profits in their decisionmaking.

As with all other issues that are potential targets for advocacy, it is crucial that strategies focused on corporate policy and practice involve the participation of those affected by the problem. It is easy to feel indignant at corporate use of sweatshop labor or inhumane working conditions. However, outside groups that have little or no connection to the workers they are trying to help may end up causing more harm than good if their efforts are not linked to local groups with knowledge regard-

ing the context and the alternatives available for the workers. Transnational corporate policy requires a transnational advocacy approach so that local groups and individuals in the affected areas have a voice in decisionmaking around the advocacy.

We talk more about strategies for action in Chapter 15, Outreach and Mobilization, that are applicable to corporate advocacy.[6]

A Note on Formulating Policy Alternatives

Just as your policy hook will help you determine the targets for your advocacy, it also will guide you in developing policy alternatives. With more information about the policymaking process that corresponds to your particular policy hook, you can refine your proposed solutions into policy alternatives. A policy alternative spells out exactly how a concrete problem will be solved and specifies the role of government in the solution. It should take into consideration both how the solution can be implemented in concrete terms, and how and where the budget necessary for its implementation can be found.

In some cases, developing a policy alternative may be a rather technical process, for example, if you want to propose or amend a law. In these cases, advocates should carefully analyze the time and resources they have available to dedicate to this activity. Groups may find it more efficient to engage someone with expertise in this area to assist them in

drafting the formal policy alternative so that they have more time to dedicate to other aspects of the advocacy. In any case, the group must have a clear idea of what they expect the policy alternative to achieve and work closely with the people developing the proposal to ensure that it accurately reflects the solution they are proposing. Whatever the situation, members and constituents need to be involved in defining the parameters of the alternative to guarantee accuracy, buy-in, and follow-up. Once finalized, the alternative will need to be presented in formats appropriate for policymakers, constituents and the broader public.

Sensitivity to Different Contexts for Effective Global Advocacy: The Case of Child Labor

One area of corporate practice that has been the target of numerous advocacy efforts has been the use of child labor. Yet generalized assumptions regarding the problem of child labor have led to many advocacy mistakes and problems. In some countries, childhood is considered a period during which a child is dependent on, and protected by adults and child labor therefore considered a violation of this norm. However in other countries, work is seen as an important part of a child's socialization, and also as an often necessary contribution by the child to the family and community. In fact a 1998 ILO document acknowledges that in some contexts "the absence of work . . . can condemn the child to a variety of social, moral, and health risks."

Increased awareness of and consideration for these varying cultural norms is leading to greater recognition of a distinction between child work and child labor, where "child labor' categorizes less acceptable practices involving exploitation and dangerous working conditions.

While taking contextual norms and standards into consideration is important, advocates must also be cautious about validating culture for culture's own sake where it may be violating the rights of certain groups. This example again emphasizes the importance of the active participation in advocacy of those affected by the problem so that the solutions developed are viable and appropriate to their needs.

Debbie Budlender

Assessing Entry Points: Questions about Policy Engagement

Although a key advocacy goal is to create opportunities for citizen's groups to be directly engaged in policy processes, engagement does not always impact policy decisions in the end. It is easy to believe that access to policymakers will translate into influence, but in practice this is rarely true. Policymakers sometimes construct these policy spaces to educate citizens about the choices they have made or to appear consultative, thus diffusing public criticism. But they may have no intention of changing their agendas. For this reason, many activists worry about being "co-opted" by policy engagement. Some NGOs that work closely with governments are criticized for losing their independence and connection with people when working with government consumes all of their energy and time. So a plan to engage should include the option to disengage if the political costs outweigh the benefits.

Deciding when and how to engage with policy processes is not straightforward or simple. Many different factors usually have to be considered and weighed against each other. Once the decision is made to engage, it must be reassessed continuously as the process unfolds. Among the many questions to explore are:

*   Is the policy space "created" or "invited?"* If you come to the decisionmaking table as a result of political pressure generated by your efforts — a created space — you may be in a stronger position to influence policy choices. In contrast, when policymakers invite citizens' groups into the policy process, transforming the space into a meaningful opportunity for change will often involve demonstrating your power once you get there. However, citizens' groups may not be fully aware of the power dynamics and so behave like guests invited to a dinner party, not wanting to offend the "host" with more demands.

*   What are the opportunity costs of engagement? How much time and resources will the meetings, research, and other activities consume? To what alternative activities could those resources be dedicated? If more could be gained from other advocacy activities, then perhaps the policy opportunity has lost its value, and another strategy is more appropriate.

Impact is another important issue to assess when deciding if and how to engage. Again, this is not so straightforward, and there are several issues to compare, such as:

*   Are you making an impact on policy priorities and choices? As groups involved in UN conventions and Poverty Reduction Strategy Papers have seen, influencing a policy document does not necessarily have a real impact on policy. It may be the first step in a long process of change, or it may be a waste of time.

*   Can the policy opportunity be used to educate people about their rights and the political process, and to build your constituency for the long-term? Although you may not have a real impact on policy, the opportunity to engage may stimulate dialogue and give your organizing efforts increased focus, public visibility, and credibility. However, people may expect something concrete from the process beyond learning and organizing, and then can become disillusioned if a project or more resources do not materialize.

*   Will the policy opportunity translate into real change on the ground? If the opportunity to engage leads to new programs, new opportunities, and new resources, then the risks of engagement may be counterbalanced by these gains.

While these questions provide some ways of looking at engagement, there is no formula or substitute for strategic, critical thinking. As groups engage with power, they should be vigilant and may need to remind themselves to whom they are ultimately accountable in order to make sure the process is worthwhile. If it is not, remember that advocacy is about creating more promising spaces for engagement where citizens are able to advance their agendas with policymakers.

* See Brock, Karen, Andrea Cornwall and John Gaventa, *Power, Knowledge and Political Spaces in the Framing of Poverty Policy*, IDS (draft), September 2001, and the workshop report from *Making Change Happen: Advocacy and Citizen Participation*, December 2000, produced by IDS.

NOTES

[1] See Gaventa, John, *Power and Powerlessness*. Urbana: University of Illinois Press, 1980.

[2] Adapted from Debbie Budlender, project documents and materials, The Asia Foundation.

[3] Ann M. Florini, Carnegie Endowment for International Peace, *Does the Invisible Hand Need a Transparent Glove? The Politics of Transparency*, 1999.

[4] Women, Law and Development International and Human Rights Watch Women's Rights Project. *Women's Human Rights Step by Step*, Washington DC, 1997.

[5] *Circle of Rights: Economic, Social, and Cultural Rights Activism*, produced by the International Human Rights Internship Program and the Asian Forum for Human Rights and Development (2000), is a useful resource for this purpose. The publication contains exercises and information for understanding the conventions and mechanisms as well as examples of advocacy.

[6] There are also many websites where you can find information about corporate practice, and potential hooks for advocacy. One example is Verité, a nonprofit organization that promotes independent monitoring of factories, linking with local humanitarian and advocacy organizations to both evaluate and address workplace conditions (www.verite.org). Other related sites include the Centre for Innovation in Corporate Responsibility at www.cicr.net, Global- Exchange at www.globalexchange.org, or Maquila Solidarity Network at www.maquilasolidarity.org, to name just a few.

12 Forces, Friends, and Foes

Once you know the policy focus of your advocacy, you will have a better idea of the institutions, individuals, and interests you will be engaging. You will need to continually weigh the political forces both for and against you. Initially this process will help you identify your targets, allies, and potential opponents.

This chapter has frameworks and exercises for carrying out this power analysis. Some of these are adapted from strategic planning processes, and others combine elements from the field of negotiation and conflict resolution.

- **Identifying the Forces:** The first set of tools will help you to name and measure internal and external constraints, opportunities, friends, and foes.
- **Classifying Friends and Foes:** The second set of tools will help you choose and assess the relative power of your targets, allies, and opponents.

Identifying the Forces

An assessment of political forces for and against your advocacy is sometimes called a "Stakeholder Analysis," a term which can be misleading because it suggests an even playing field. In practice, the playing field is very uneven, and advocacy requires navigation of different power dynamics. So a crucial element of this analysis is weighing who has more power, who has less, and what kind of power the different actors use. The following tools can assist you in sizing up the forces.

Each tool offers different levels of detail. All of them, used in sequence, will help you to build your advocacy strategy. They are:

- *The SWOT Analysis*
- *The Forcefield Analysis*
- *The Power Map*

The SWOT Analysis: Internal and External Forces[1]

The SWOT analysis is a tool from strategic planning methodologies. It provides a simple way to assess the *internal* forces that determine your organization's potential to carry out a strategy, and the *external* forces that will help or hinder you.

The SWOT analysis uses a grid that separates the internal, organizational assessment of strengths and weaknesses from external opportunities and threats.

1. Internal ➡ **S**trengths
                Weaknesses

2. External ➡ **O**pportunities
                Threats

Strengths	Opportunities
Weaknesses	Threats

1. Internal Capacities: Strengths and Weaknesses

This analysis builds on the organizational self-understanding exercises in Chapter 6. At times

PLANNING ADVOCACY

organizations set out to achieve something that they do not have the technical resources, skills, or time to pull off. In advocacy, being realistic is key. An internal assessment helps you figure out who you will need as allies to expand your forces and complement your strengths and weaknesses.

The following questions will help you assess internal capacity. The questions may need to be adapted slightly for membership, grassroots, and nonprofessional groups:

- What does your organization do best? What programs are effective and strong? In what areas do the staff excel?
- What are the key capacities of your leaders, members, staff, and allies?
- What do staff and members see as problems? What programs need improving?
- What is missing?

In measuring your organization's capacity, think about each of the areas below. Consider gender, age, ethnicity, and other differences. For example, do both men and women have opportunities to take on leadership roles? Are there hidden obstacles? Are younger people taken seriously?

Leadership

Do the leaders coordinate work well? Do they communicate openly? Are decisionmaking mechanisms clear and transparent? Do leaders respond to staff and program problems? Do they encourage initiative? Do they have the support of the board, staff, and members? Are they representative of the diversity in the staff, members, or communities with which they work?

Technical skills

What is the technical capacity of staff or members and is it sufficient to meet the needs? Are staff trained to do their jobs? Does the

organization seek outside help when it needs it?

Funds and other material resources

Does the organization have enough funding, equipment, and other resources to achieve its plans? Does it use its resources efficiently? What percentage of the organization's time is spent on raising money? Is there a perception that money is the only important resource? Are the programs driven more by donors and the availability of funds than by opportunities and concrete needs?

Clarity of purpose and programs

Are the aims and activities of the organization clear to all the staff? Are the vision, mission, goals, and objectives of the organization written down? Who developed them? Are there mechanisms to monitor program implementation and adjust to new developments?

Commitment and participation

Does the staff care about the work they are doing? Do the members or beneficiaries feel part of the organization? Are plans developed jointly or delivered top-down?

Organization and operations

Is there adequate planning, evaluation, and program design? Are tasks fairly distributed? Does everyone know their responsibilities? Does the structure of the organization facilitate its work? Does the organization have good relationships with other organizations?

Interpersonal relations

Do the members and staff get along with each other? How are conflicts handled? Is there agreement about decisionmaking procedures? Are there hidden obstacles for personal advancement? Does everyone feel free to express their concerns? Do they feel confident they will be taken seriously? Are differences of opinion respected?

Relationship with members or beneficiaries

Does the organization have members or clearly defined beneficiaries? Are the staff, leaders, and board accountable to members? Do members or beneficiaries have some say in what is provided to them? Are there sufficient members? How many members have left the organization and for what reasons?

After identifying your organization's strengths and weaknesses, think about how much they hinder or help you to pursue your advocacy goals.

2. Your External Environment: Opportunities and Threats

In identifying your external opportunities and threats, some of the analysis generated from Chapters 7 and 8 will be helpful. Opportunities and threats may relate to:

- the issue you are addressing;
- the availability of resources for your work;
- the political/policy space you operate in;
- your allies and opposition.

> Social change work generates conflict. For example, working with women may provoke hostility from men or fundamentalist religious groups. Working with labor may provoke antagonism by powerful business interests, etc. At the same time, work with these groups may suddenly generate an outpouring of support from churches, civic groups, and other potential allies. Managing the tensions and dynamics produced by change is a perpetual balancing act.

The issue you are addressing

Are other organizations addressing this issue? Are there similarities in how you are addressing it? Differences? Are there forces that will prevent your group from ever solving this problem? These may include forces that you did not know existed when you first developed your strategy. How controversial is your issue?

The availability of resources

Is there support from donors for this type of activity? Are there technical services available to help you do what you want to do? Are other organizations competing for the same resources?

The political and policy space

Does government see your advocacy as a threat? Do they seek your involvement to legitimize a set agenda? Will any of your planned actions provoke strong opposition or backlash? Is there any risk of repressive action in response to what you are planning? If your group has been invited to be part of the policy process, what will you need to do to be taken seriously? How will you assess the potential for impact? How will you retain independence and a critical perspective while collaborating? Are there trends or other social, political, economic, or cultural forces that may affect your potential for success?

Allies and opposition

Are there other groups or individuals who might threaten or support what you are doing? How powerful are your allies? How powerful are opposition forces? What might they do to prevent your success? What can you do in response?

PLANNING ADVOCACY

Purpose

To assess the internal and external factors that may hinder or facilitate your group's advocacy strategy in order to refine your goals, objectives, and activities.

Process

(Time: 3 hours)

Using the explanation on pages 211-213, make sure that everyone fully understands the SWOT tool. Use examples to illustrate. Begin with the *External Factors: Opportunities and Threats*, then move to the *Internal Factors: Strengths and Weaknesses*. If participants are working in small groups, separate the two tasks with plenary discussion to make sure everyone is engaged. Be sure to have a clear understanding of the advocacy problem and goals. The following questions and grids can help you in the analysis.

External Factors: Identifying Opportunities and Threats

1. Brainstorm the external forces that will impact your strategy, including:

   - groups and structures relevant to the *issue* that the strategy addresses.

   - organizations that are sources of *resources*. Remember that resources can be financial, technical, human, political, etc.

   - trends and groups that influence the *political and policy space* in which you will advocate. Include cultural, ideological, and religious forces in both the public and private realms, particularly if the issue relates to women's rights. Include key events if relevant.

   - *other* groups or forces that affect your strategy.

   Include both the positive and negative forces. Organize the forces you come up with in this grid:

External Forces Affecting:			
The Issue	**Resources**	**Political/Policy Space**	**Other**

2. Mark the forces that are threats with a T and those that represent opportunities with an O. In some cases, the group may see a particular force as both a threat and an opportunity. In such a case, mark as both.

3. Take a vote on the two or three most important opportunities and the two or three most important threats. Mark these with a ++. Do a second vote on the 2–3 next most important opportunities and threats. Mark these with a +.

Internal Factors: Assessing Organizational Strengths and Weaknesses

4. Using the grid below, list the strengths and weaknesses of the organization. Then rate with ++ and + how important each strength and weakness is for your strategy.

Strengths	How important for the strategy?
Weaknesses	How important for the strategy?

Example

Below are examples of what you may identify in a SWOT Analysis.

Internal

- *Strengths*: staff skills, links with the community, funding base, commitment, common purpose, political credibility
- *Weaknesses*: lack of staff skills, uncertain funding, internal squabbling, low morale, limited community support, no common vision of advocacy and organization's purpose

External

- *Opportunities*: elections, a reform process, new policy initiatives, international conferences, important visitors, incidents that have caught public attention
- *Threats*: lack of coordination among NGOs, religious or political forces which go against social change, limited political freedom, lack of transparency in the political process, cultural views about roles, policy opportunities that derail and coopt your organization without creating any real chance for influence

Discussion

List the implications of the SWOT analysis for your advocacy strategy. The following questions can help the group think about the implications:

- How can we build on our strengths to further our strategy?
- What must be included in our strategy to minimize our weaknesses?
- What must be included in our strategy to take full advantage of the opportunities?
- What must we do to reduce the impact of the threats?

Adapted from *Strategic Thinking: Formulating Organizational Strategy Workshop*, Facilitator's Guide, Institute for Development Research, Massachusetts, 1998.

PLANNING ADVOCACY

Purpose

To identify the forces in the political, economic, and ideological/cultural arenas that will impact your advocacy strategy. This exercise builds on the analysis of the external environment that began with the SWOT. It looks in more detail at the forces that will affect your strategy. These forces will vary depending on your issue and your strategy. This analysis is especially useful when preparing for negotiations.

Process

(Time: 3+ hours)

Before the group begins, explain the task. Ask people to think about why this analysis is important for advocacy. Some possible responses include:

• We need to know who is with us and who is against us. We need to know how much power each player has.

• The analysis helps us figure out the most controversial arenas and prepare for conflict.

• The analysis looks at important current events and players influencing our advocacy.

• The analysis will help us plan more carefully think about allies, our message, and the timing.

1. Write at the top of a flipchart the short-term and long-term goals you are working toward. Make three columns, one each for the economic, political, and ideological/cultural arenas. In each column, list the forces that are with you, against you, and uncommitted. Mark those with you with RED, those against you with BLUE, and those uncommitted with GREEN.

Short-term Goals: Long-term Goals and objectives:		
Under *Economic*, you may think of: -Corporate entities (e.g. shoe factory, insurance company, etc.) - Chamber of Commerce - Business associations - Individual business leaders - Financial institutions (i.e., banks, investment houses, World Bank, IMF)	Under *Political*, you may think of: - Government (Ministers, civil servants) - Legislators, President, etc. - International financial institutions and donors (IMF, World Bank, etc.) - Political parties - Trade unions - Advocacy groups in civil society	Under *Ideological/Cultural* you may think of: - Churches/religions - Media- Trends (like "multi-culturalism", fundamentalism, feminism, consumerism) - Value-oriented movements (Muslim Brotherhood, Moral Majority, Women's movement) - Schools

2. For each actor, note on the chart her or his short-term and long-term interests in relation to your issue.

3. Make a new chart like the following one. In the "Forces With Us" column, include short-term allies. In the second column, list the "Uncommitted." If there are any you will be able to win

FORCES / ARENAS	FORCES WITH US	UNCOMMITTED	FORCES AGAINST US
Ideological/ Cultural			
Political			
Economic			

over, mark them in red. Under the "Forces Against Us" column, put those forces you will not be able to win over. Put in parentheses any actors about whom you need to do further research.

4. Decide on the balance of forces—who is winning, who is losing, and why, and how this will affect your advocacy. This analysis will help to round off this task. Later in this chapter and in the next chapter, we look at additional elements that you need to consider in planning.

Tips

- The listing and classifying of the actors may not be straightforward. Your group may debate who goes in which column of both charts. This debate is helpful and serves to deepen the analysis. You may also want to include some expert analysts in your deliberations.

- Sometimes forces that are against or for you in one arena may be working in the opposite direction in another arena. For example, Canadian groups working on a strategy on racist police brutality debated where the women's movement stood. They felt that the movement was a "force against" in the "ideology" sphere because it did not do enough to expose racism within the movement. But they felt that it was a "force with" in the economic sphere because of its fight for equity. In the ideological sphere, the Canadian groups first thought that multiculturalism would be a "force with." After discussion, they placed it in the "force against" column because they felt that multiculturalism often hides racism.

- Sometimes the "uncommitted" will include groups that seem sympathetic but are not doing enough to support your issues. For example, the Canadian group listed liberals and some trade unions as uncommitted. They felt these groups did not take explicit actions against racism.

- Some actors may support your short-term goals but oppose you on your long-term goals. These are "tactical" allies that can be used for short-term purposes but are not usually part of your long-term strategy. For example, some corporations will be an ally in supporting the promotion of human rights but are unlikely to support steps that directly affect them.

- Your analysis will be more precise if you identify real people associated with the different institutions and organizations. Individuals often tell you more about the politics of a group. Identifying individuals is also useful when you choose your advocacy "targets" and for negotiations.

Adapted from *Naming the Moment: Political Analysis for Action, A Manual for Community Groups* by Deborah Barndt, The Jesuit Centre for Social Faith and Justice, 1989.

PLANNING ADVOCACY

12

The Power Map: Identifying Players and Positions

Advocacy planning demands a forecast of the political players who will care about, fight over, and be affected by your strategy. This information is needed to forge alliances and build support, and also helps in assessing risk. The *Power Map* complements the *Forcefield Analysis* by focusing attention on influential individuals.

The *Power Map* will also show you what further information you need. Many groups getting involved in political action for the first time do not know much about government or economic and international decisionmaking structures and officials. Without this information, it is difficult to work out a good strategy.

In the mapping process you will look at:
- *Who is at the table*: formal decisionmakers;
- *What is on the table:* the issues and policies they are discussing;

- *What and who are under the table:* the players and agendas that exert influence from behind the scenes.

In one workshop, Zimbabwean groups did a power map on the issue of land reform. Their preliminary conclusion was that all of the stakeholders favored land reform. One participant then asked, "So why can't we get the land policy passed?" The participants then realized that the public opinions of players may be different than their private ones. Further, sometimes players in the private sector or elsewhere have more power than the public decisionmakers sitting at the table. And in some cases, international interests wield more influence than a national government on particular issues. Finally, sometimes policy change opportunities are presented to appease or distract citizens' groups when those in power have no intention of letting change happen.

Who is under the table?

Illustration from *Naming the Moment*

Purpose

- To identify the institutions, groups, and individuals with influence, power, and an interest in the changes your strategy seeks on a particular issue.
- To identify the public and private positions of these actors in order to determine allies, opponents, and targets.

Process

(Time: 2–3 hours)

1. Begin by explaining the chart on the next page. Expand the boxes to give more room for notes and make sure that the categories match the context.

   - The first category of players in the chart refers to structures and individuals within the formal arena of public or state decisionmaking. This includes officials, legislators, the executive, and appointed personnel.

   - The second category contains all other influential players in the private sector and civil society. These two categories should include both national and local players.

   - The third category contains international actors.

2. In the first column, write the institutions (e.g., Ministry of Finance, local councils, chamber of commerce) that have a stake in your issue and advocacy. In the second column write the names of individuals who are leaders and decisionmakers in those institutions in relation to your issue. Use the results of the *Forcefield Analysis* on page 216 to feed into this exercise.

3. In the last column, note the viewpoint of the identified player with respect to the issue. If the viewpoint of the institution and the individual are different, mark both. Note any differences between their public and private stances. For example, AIDS activists argue that pharmaceutical companies may publicly support a bill to fund AIDS prevention, but their real interest (under the table) is to involve the government in subsidizing drugs for people who cannot afford them to avoid having to reduce prices.

4. Next to the institution and name of the individual, categorize them as follows:
   - O = Opposed
   - S = Supporter
   - U = Uncommitted
   - ? = Don't know

5. Rank the power of the player on a scale 1–4, with 1 being the most powerful and 4 the least powerful.

Discussion

- Who are your immediate allies? Who will you need to persuade to support you?
- Who are your strongest opponents?
- Who is the key formal decisionmaker on this issue? Who is the key decisionmaker under the table? Which of the two is more powerful?

PLANNING ADVOCACY

- What do the positions of the various players tell you about how you must craft your messages to the public? To government? To legislators? To other key actors?
- How does this analysis change your short-term goals and objectives? Does it help you define the types of activities you will be doing in your advocacy strategy? Does it tell you when you need to do different activities?

Short-term Goal:			
Long-term Goal:			
MAJOR PLAYERS	**INSTITUTIONS/STRUCTURES**	**KEY INDIVIDUALS**	**OPINION-INTEREST/RANK**
1. Government Decisionmakers and Actors			
National			
Provincial/State			
Local/District			
Other			
2. Other Influential Actors			
Business/Corporate			
Media			
Political Parties			
NGOs			
Community Groups			
Membership Groups			
Labor			
Religious Institutions			
Academics and Professionals			
Other			
3. International Actors			
Donors and Foundations			
NGOs and Support Groups			
UN Bodies			
World Bank and IMF			
Other Governments			
Banks			
Multinational Corporations			
Other			

Classifying Friends and Foes: Targets, Allies, Opponents

Your advocacy will generate friends and foes. There are people and institutions who share your values or will benefit from your advocacy, and they may support you. For a variety of reasons, other people and institutions will oppose you.

But friends do not always remain friends, and enemies do not always remain enemies. The political landscape is constantly shifting. These shifts must be factored into planning.

Using the *SWOT*, the *Forcefield*, and the *Power Map*, we classify friends and foes as targets, allies, and opponents. We define these as:

- **Targets:** Individual decisionmakers with the power to respond to your advocacy demands

- **Allies:** Influential individuals and organizations that support your advocacy in different ways and degrees

- **Opponents:** Influential people and institutions who oppose your advocacy—from outright enemies to mild dissenters

Constituents are also critical to the forcefield, however we have discussed constituents in Chapter 4 and many times in Part Two.

Targets

Development organizations use the word "target" for beneficiaries, as in the "target population" or "target audience." In advocacy, a *target* is the person with the power to respond to your demands and to move the political process toward addressing your issue. Some of your advocacy activities should be directed at persuading your target that your issue is worth addressing.

It is often difficult to identify a single individual as the target. But this is an important step because it pinpoints the person with the most power to facilitate change. Unless this individual feels the pressure of your efforts, he or she is unlikely to consider your issue seriously. Without that person, it is unlikely you will achieve change. Personalizing decisionmaking can also be empowering for citizens who are intimidated by politics. They see that the "real people" responsible for policy can be reached and influenced while at the same time, they recognize that power dynamics are complex.

Sometimes citizens may not have the possibility of reaching the main target. This is why there are two types of targets—primary and secondary.

Primary target

This is the decisionmaker with the most power to address your issue. However, you may not have access to this person, or there may be too great a political risk in putting him or her on the spot.

Secondary target

This is an individual who does not have the power to solve the problem, but who is close to the primary target. If you can pressure this person, they can in turn pressure the primary target.

For example, in countries with a Presidential system, the President usually has a lot of power over most decisions. But a citizens' group will not usually be able to reach the President. Instead, these groups can choose a secondary target—a key advisor or Minister—and reach the President through that person. For example, in one country, NGOs reached the President on the issue of land reform by using an association of commercial farmers, who had access to the President, as their secondary target.

Review your *Power Map* and identify primary and secondary targets. To choose your targets, ask yourself, "Who has the power to make a decision on this issue?".

Often the person who appears to be the decisionmaker is not. For example, if you want to reinstate subsidies for basic health services, your target may not be the Minister of Health. The decision may depend more on the Finance Minister. In such cases, mapping decisionmaking is complex but critical to identifying your target.

Legislators are usually not primary targets because they generally approve or reject policies that are developed prior to reaching the floor of the legislature. You may target a key legislator as part of your *lobbying strategy*, but your main target will be the person who determines whether your issue reaches a legislature. For example, in the USA, the power to agree to the ban on landmines rests with the President, so the President is the primary target. But the President is influenced by other players, particularly high level military officials. These officials are the secondary target. The land mine campaign includes a legislative lobbying strategy, but the strategy is ultimately geared to reach the President.

Once you have identified your target, you will need to gather some basic information on him or her. The tool on the next page will guide your research about your target.

Allies

Allies are prominent individuals and institutions sympathetic to your cause and organization. Your allies will play very different roles in your strategy depending on their motivations:

- some will support your advocacy because they will personally benefit from the changes you seek;

- some will share your values and may endorse you publicly but will not use their resources or get involved;

- some will easily be persuaded to support you out of some common interest; and

- some will collaborate directly with you and will share responsibility for the advocacy effort because they have a direct stake in the solution and the process.

Individual allies

Individual allies can be opinion leaders, influential insiders within the structures you want to influence, and other powerful individuals who are sympathetic to your cause. They may include current and former public officials, well-known business and religious leaders, prominent professionals, academics, and others.

I can't believe we are asking a priest to speak at the rally on Saturday . . . with the Church's conservative position on women.

True, but Father Diego promoted women's rights and political participation for years, even at the risk of being criticized by the Bishop.

Statement explaining your advocacy position:

_____

_____

_____

Target's Name:

After doing your research, rank your target on each of the following (1 is low, 5 is high):

1. Level of knowledge of your organization	1	2	3	4	5
2. Level of knowledge of your cause	1	2	3	4	5
3. Level of agreement with your cause	1	2	3	4	5
4. Level of previous support for your cause *(if totally opposed, mark 0)*	1	2	3	4	5
5. Level of your communication to date	1	2	3	4	5
6. Level of mutual trust	1	2	3	4	5

Describe your previous contacts with the target:

_____

_____

_____

_____

Other considerations (for example, declared or undeclared interest that your target has in the issue):

_____

_____

_____

_____

Level of influence you may have over your target suggested by the responses to the previous questions:

_____

_____

_____

_____

PLANNING ADVOCACY

Adapted from Nader Tadros

Some Tips on Individual Allies from Activists

Do not make assumptions about your allies' opinions: You should not rely only on what people have said in the media or what they stood for in the past. Most leaders are concerned about retaining their status. This may mean that their political stance shifts. Make sure that you understand what they mean when they express support for a broad cause.

Arrange a meeting with the person: Prepare for the meeting carefully. Discuss your advocacy proposal and solicit their input and guidance. They may be offended if you tell them what to think or do. Instead, ask them whether and how they might support you.

Involve your allies strategically to reach specific aims and audiences: Particular opinion leaders may influence the opinions of some groups but be controversial with others. For example, a business leader is less likely to reach a group of traditional leaders or union leadership than a former public official.

Be specific about what you want your allies to do and say: While you should not tell an opinion leader directly what to say or do, you should know exactly what they plan to say and do to ensure that it advances your cause. Discuss the objectives of the activity the opinion leader will be involved in and what role he or she will play.

Keep your allies informed of your progress and solicit their suggestions: This communication must be included in your planning. Neglect can cause bad feelings and loss of allies.

Well, he said he was with us.

Individual allies are different than constituents because of the influence they have on your target and on public opinion.

Important things to know about these allies are:

- How strongly do they support your advocacy efforts?

- What do they really think about the issue and about what should be done?

- How far are they willing to go to express support?

- What are their misgivings about your efforts?

- How involved will they want to be to remain your ally?

- What will they gain from supporting your campaign?

- What, concretely, can they do for your advocacy efforts?

Organizational allies

Relationships with organizational allies are a vital part of advocacy. We deal with them in detail in Chapter 17. Constructing and maintaining alliances is difficult even with like-minded organizations. However, it is a worth-while investment because alliances increase

---

Charting Support from Allies

The chart below can help you to gather information on your allies systematically. Where you list organizations, include names of key contacts. Depending on the answers to the questions, there are several ways that you can ask individual allies to support your advocacy, such as:

- speaking at a public event or press conference in support of your efforts;
- writing and signing a letter to key decisionmakers promoting your cause;
- writing an article for the newspaper, speaking on radio or TV;
- joining a highly visible advisory board;
- helping to raise funds;
- talking to other leaders privately to persuade them to support your cause.

Name of person/organization	Level of support	Motivation/agenda	Degree of influence

---

your political leverage and strengthen citizen voice. Organizational allies vary as much as individuals. For simplicity, we discuss only two types of organizational allies here.

Primary allies

These are organizations that share your values and commitment to the issue, and could benefit from the advocacy effort. This alliance may be more formal and involve some shared decisionmaking, authority, and responsibility for planning, implementation, and fundraising. These relationships tend to be long-term.

Secondary allies

These are organizations that are sympathetic to your cause, are willing to endorse your efforts publicly or offer limited resources, but will not be directly involved. Organizations that have a large membership or are well-known are valuable secondary allies. Groups of professionals, trade or commerce associations, women's clubs, and charities are some examples. They should be treated similarly to

individual allies by using their support strategically and selectively.

Opponents

Change inevitably causes conflicts. Social problems are often created by extreme imbalances of power. If advocacy challenges this imbalance, it can provoke a reaction from those in power or with different values and agendas.

Rarely does anyone give up power without a fight. Individuals and groups may oppose your advocacy efforts for various reasons, such as:

a) They disagree with your **values** about society. For example, they may believe women should not be able to seek a divorce, that workers should not form unions, or that citizens are too uninformed to be involved in policymaking.

b) In their eyes, a **victory for you represents a loss for them**. For example, if workers form unions, managers/investors see workers' demands as a threat to profits.

PLANNING ADVOCACY

c) They are **ideologically** opposed to anything that changes current institutional
arrangements or social roles. For example,
public interest campaigns in favor of an
increased regulatory role for government
reflect a different ideology than those
focused on liberalization.

It is important to know your opponents and
assess their level of opposition. Opponents fall
into three broad categories:

Primary opponent
These are firm opponents because they stand
to lose something from your advocacy success or because your efforts call into question
their values. You should know these opponents
well.

Secondary opponent
These oppose you but may not take any action
against you. Secondary opponents do not
perceive your work as a direct threat.

A fence rider or fence sitter
This is a potential opponent who could be
persuaded by your advocacy efforts.

Some important questions to ask about your
opponents include:

* Why do they oppose you? How actively will
they oppose you?

* How much power do they have? (e.g.,
money, credibility, contacts, access)

* What level of force are they likely to use
against you? Is it life-threatening?

* What are their organizational structures,
policies, etc.?

* What are their agendas, strategies, and
tactics? What will they do to challenge
you?

* With whom do they have influence?

* Is there anything on which you might
agree? If so, can you find common ground
on some issues and agree to disagree on
others?

Your answers to these questions provide a
measure of your opponent's strength. This will
help you factor your opponent into your plans.
For example, if your opponent is vehemently
against you but is generally seen as a predictable nay-sayer about anything involving
change, you may choose to do nothing regarding their opposition. In other cases, your
opponent may be so powerful that criticizing
their views in public can be risky for your own
credibility. This is true in some contexts where
religious leaders and institutions are influential
and powerful. The following two grids *Charting
Opposition* will help you, first, to classify your
opponents, and second, to define your tactics
and their risks. The risks refer to the intensity
and impact of their reaction against you.

Chapters 13 and 14 discuss some tactics for
handling opposition. But before designing
these, you must weigh the need to engage
your opposition against the risk it poses to
your strategy and your organization. Remember that risks may involve physical danger, but
risks also include questions of opportunity
costs. For example, how time-consuming and
resource-intensive engagement may be in
comparison to other important advocacy tasks.

Charting Opposition

Name of person or organization who opposes you	Level of support behind them	Their motivation/agenda	Their degree of influence

Name of opposition	Your objectives to counter their influence	Your tactics	Risks

PLANNING ADVOCACY

NOTES

[1] Adapted from *Strategic Thinking: Formulating Organizational Strategy Workshop*, Facilitator's Guide, Institute for Development Research, Massachusetts, 1998.

PART THREE
DOING ADVOCACY
BUILDING CLOUT: MESSAGE, TACTICS, AND ORGANIZATION

Advocacy involves both thinking and doing. The *thinking* aspects, described in Part Two, include participatory analysis, information-gathering, dialogue, and planning. Part Three looks at ways of *doing* advocacy. The thinking and doing are part of a cyclical process where thinking informs action, and action, in turn, informs further thinking. The cycle builds a deeper understanding of politics and a greater ability to influence political and policy change.

The chapters in this Part are about communication and media, outreach and mobilization, lobbying and negotiation, and organization and leadership. Advocates use all of these strategies and actions to influence and educate the public and decisionmakers. At the same time, creative strategies for building clout provide opportunities to enhance citizen participation and so bring about permanent changes in how public decisions are made.

This Part has very few exercises. Instead, we provide examples to inspire you to design creative actions for your own situation. There are five chapters:

Chapter 13: Messages and Media, Reaching and Educating

A vital piece of advocacy is a compelling message tailored and disseminated specifically for a defined audience. This chapter covers a variety of approaches for engaging, educating, and persuading audiences using the mass media and alternative media.

Key concepts:

- Message development
- Message delivery

- Mass media advocacy
- Alternative media for citizen outreach and education

Chapter 14: Outreach and Mobilization

While advocacy should build citizen participation, success also depends on the power that organized numbers of people can wield in the political arena. In this chapter we look at how outreach and mobilization serve to achieve both a policy objective and strengthen citizens' voices.

Key concepts:

- Designing outreach and mobilization strategies
- Actions and activities for mobilizing with impact

- Mobilizing moments and actions

Chapter 15: Lobbying and Negotiating

The potential and success of your lobbying and negotiation strategies depend greatly on your organizational strength and all the other activities involved in advocacy, from defining your vision to constituency-building to media work. This chapter is about getting to the decisionmaking table and advancing your issue once you get there. Engaging directly in discussions to persuade decisionmakers is an important part of successful advocacy and provides important lessons about politics and power.

Key concepts:

- Familiarize yourself with the corridors of power
- Classify the players
- Inform, educate, and build relationships
- Get attention, show strength, persuade

- Different approaches to negotiation
- Dealing with opposition
- Shadow negotiation

Chapter 16: Advocacy Leadership

Advocacy requires strong groups and leaders that understand power, people, and process. Advocacy leaders face a perpetual juggling act of promoting collaboration and encouraging new leadership on the one hand, and giving direction and vision on the other. These require different skills and styles. This chapter focuses on the aspects of leadership that facilitate broader participation and organizational collaboration.

Key concepts:

- Formal and informal leadership
- Shared responsibility
- Transformative leadership
- Leadership styles and approaches
- Leadership and teamwork
- Productive meetings
- Feedback for strengthening self and group

Chapter 17: Alliances and Coalitions

Coalitions and alliances can greatly enhance advocacy by bringing together the strength and resources of diverse groups to create a more powerful force for change. But, they are also difficult to form and sustain. This chapter focuses on their dynamics and ways to strengthen them. We examine how to improve communication, decisionmaking, conflict management, and accountability.

Key concepts:

- Pros and cons of coalitions
- Considerations for building advocacy coalitions and alliances
- Coalition decisionmaking structures
- Dealing with conflict in coalitions

13 Messages and Media: Educating and Persuading

Communication is central to effective advocacy. First, good interpersonal communication is vital *inside* the advocacy effort itself — among colleagues, leaders, constituents, allies, etc. Second, we need communication strategies to reach, educate, and persuade *external* audiences, from policymakers to communities.

In this chapter, we cover the following areas in media advocacy and education strategies:

Message development and delivery
This section focuses on identifying and knowing the audience you want to reach, and tailoring your message according to their profile. We also discuss the pros and cons of different ways to deliver your message. In later chapters, we give more examples of message delivery as it relates to outreach and mobilization, lobbying, and negotiation.

Mass media advocacy
We offer tips and strategies to engage and utilize mass media that reach large numbers of people (newspaper, radio, TV, etc.). We also discuss some of the challenges of working with both private and publicly-owned media, where the owners' interests may conflict with your advocacy goals.

Alternative media
We discuss and give examples of strategies for engaging your audiences in dialogue and public education. Such community-based and popular media use theater, song, workshops, and other direct forms of communication.

Why Media Advocacy?

Media advocacy is important to:
- get on the political agenda;
- make your issue visible and credible in policy debate;
- inform the public about your issue and proposed solution;
- recruit allies;
- change public attitudes and behavior;
- influence decisionmakers and opinion leaders;
- shape policies, programs, and the conduct of public and private agencies;
- raise money for your cause.

A *media advocacy plan* spells out:
- what message you want to convey;
- who you want to reach with the message;
- how you will reach this audience;
- how you will utilize each type of media;
- how this will boost your overall advocacy effort;
- how you will time your media effort to complement your other strategies;
- how you will measure success.

Like all aspects of advocacy, media advocacy requires clear goals and carefully planned strategies.

Message Development

Your advocacy message is what you choose to say about your issue, its solution, and who you are. To develop a message, you will need information to back up the arguments you use.

The following are some basic principles of message development. Not all of these principles are universal. For example, if the media is government-owned, some principles may not apply. Some principles depend on whether you are using the mass media or alternative media. In general, to develop an effective message, it is important to:

1. Know your audience.
2. Know your political environment and moment (controversies, big issues, fears, and what is considered left, right, and center).
3. Keep your message simple and brief.
4. Use real life stories and quotes.
5. Use precise, powerful language and active verbs.
6. Use clear facts and numbers creatively.
7. Adapt the message to the medium.
8. Allow your audience to reach their own conclusions.
9. Encourage audiences to take action.
10. Present a possible solution.

1. Know your audience.

Find out who cares – or could be persuaded to care – about your issue. In Chapter 12, the *Power Map*, the *SWOT,* and the *Forcefield Analysis* help you identify key stakeholders in relation to your issue. Your "audiences" are these same stakeholders, as well as potential sympathizers. When you develop your messages, you can refer back to this analysis, but you may also need to sharpen your profile of each audience.

The box below shows different categories of potential audiences with a range of interests and perspectives. The particulars of your issue will direct you to the specific type of person or organization you want to engage. For example, if your issue has to do with land rights for poor women and men, your audiences will be those who have influence and interest in land issues. In this case, your audiences might be grouped according to locale of operations and include:

- *local level:* your main constituents – peasant and farmer's associations as well as large and small-scale farmers, extension and other agricultural service workers;

- *national level:* associations concerned with agro-business, agricultural development, and the environment; journalists covering development and agriculture; politicians representing rural constituencies; decisionmakers with influence over land and agriculture, such as the Ministers and top officials in Agriculture, Justice, Trade, and Finance; agricultural professionals; related academics; and concerned citizens;

Potential Audiences

Local and National
- Decisionmakers – politicians and policymakers
- Opinion leaders
- Donors
- Journalists
- NGOs and grassroots groups
- Issue-specific researchers and professionals
- Trade unions
- Constituents and social movements
- Private sector
- The general public

International
- Bilaterals and Multilaterals (the World Bank, etc.)
- Donors
- NGOs
- Corporations
- UN Agencies
- Social movements

Information/Analysis ——→ Position ——→ Argument ——→ Message

Using solid information and analysis, groups develop their position on an issue, create compelling arguments, and design a message that conveys all of this in a nutshell.

- *international level:* institutions shaping trade and agricultural policy, like the World Trade Organization, the World Bank, and the International Monetary Fund; NGOs concerned about globalization and food; influential donors.

Find out what your audiences know, their concerns, their values and priorities, and what kind of language they use. To capture people's attention, you need to know their interests, their situation, and their vocabulary. This involves listening to their ideas and concerns. For some audiences – like citizens – you may need a focus group (see Chapter 8). For opinion leaders and decisionmakers, their background and positions on issues are usually publicly available. Study media stories and existing research on social and political issues to find out more about your audiences. (See *Getting the Message Right: Using Formative Research, Polling and Focus Group Insights on the Cheap*, The Advocacy Institute, Washington, DC, 1998.)

2. Know your political environment and moment.
Many contextual factors will shape your message. These include the level of political openness and public attitudes about controversy. In countries emerging from conflict or economic crises, messages that express hope may work well. When a government is broadly under fire, it may be more acceptable to criticize explicitly. In a time of war, critical messages become less acceptable. Often it helps to link your message to another issue that has public attention. Comparisons with other well-known

problems help audiences understand the seriousness of your issue.

For example, after the US government found two Chilean grapes with cyanide on them, it stopped all imports of Chilean fruit. Tobacco control advocates used this incident to compare the much larger amount of cyanide in one cigarette with that in several bushels of tainted grapes.[1]

3. Keep the message simple and brief.
Make sure the information can be easily understood by someone who does not know the subject. Jargon is confusing and should be avoided. Even common terms like "sustainable development" and "civil society" are obscure to most people.

Illustration from *Naming the Moment*

4. Use real life stories and quotes.
Political debates are often reduced to facts and sweeping social analysis that may not reach most audiences, even policymakers. The human element makes a problem real. Quotes and personal stories bring to life the challenges of a problem in a way that general explanations cannot.

DOING ADVOCACY

5. Use precise, powerful language and active verbs.

Advocacy groups often use language that may not work with all audiences. For example, the general public message of an African women's advocacy campaign to reform inheritance laws was, "Put an end to property-grabbing. Support women's equal rights to inherit." The message was then tailored for rural women, suggesting a concrete action and using an image showing the need to be vigilant: "End property-grabbing: Write a will and cry with one eye open."

6. Use clear facts and numbers creatively.

Good information boosts the clout of any advocacy. But the facts you choose and how you present them is important. The last chapter discussed some of the information needed for advocacy planning. That same information can be used for your media strategy. Concretely, what is the problem/issue? What are the causes? Who is directly affected and how? What are the financial and social costs? Who is to blame? What is the solution, and what can a citizen or policymaker do to help?

Messages that reach citizens are....

In a workshop with African advocates in 1998, participants gave the following reasons from their experiences why certain messages worked:

- Humorous
- Use popular expressions
- Adaptations of popular songs, metaphors, stories, and poetry
- Brief, rhythmic, and witty
- Reference to a respected person or institution
- Appeal to children who help to inform parents and other adults

---

The answers to these questions require credible research from reliable sources. Although some issues require new research, usually there is a lot of information already available. What you will add is a new way of understanding the facts and figures in line with your advocacy objectives.

7. Adapt the message to the medium.

Each medium has its own possibilities and limitations. For example, radio relies on sounds, so you should use different voices, backgrounds sounds, and music to make your message more compelling. For television, make full use of the visual element and reduce written and spoken information. For street theater, engage the audience by asking questions, inviting responses, speaking to individuals, and making people laugh.

8. Allow the audience to reach their own understanding.

Provide the basic details and allow the audience to develop their own understanding of the issue. Too much explanation appears dogmatic. Longer explanations are useful once you have your audience's attention.

9. Encourage the audience to take action.

Your audience – whether it is policymakers or the general public – needs to know what they can do to support your cause. Offer simple suggestions, like "visit your local councilor" or "discuss this matter in your Parent Teacher Association" or "vote 'yes'" or "call the Campaign for a Living Wage to register support."

10. Present a possible solution.

Tell your audience what you propose to solve the problem. Keep the solution simple, such as, "The government needs to show its commitment by providing adequate funding" or, "New laws are needed to keep people safe."

Framing Your Message

How you frame your issue and solution is one of the most critical factors in advocacy. To help you present the information with the message development principles in mind, we recommend you:

- start with your advocacy campaign's **core message;**
- **tailor the message** to reach distinct audiences;
- put your **frame** around the issue.[2]

A "**core**" **message** is one or two brief, direct statements that reflect:

- your analysis of the issue;
- the causes of the issue;
- who is responsible for solving the issue;
- your proposed solution;
- the actions you ask others to take in support of the solution.

A **tailored message** is created for a specific audience based on an analysis of:

- what will be most persuasive;
- what information the audience needs;
- what action you want the audience to take.

This analysis will determine the message's:

- content;
- form (words, images, etc);
- length;
- medium;
- messenger.

Tailor your message to different audiences by:

- tapping into the audience's priorities, values, and concerns;
- giving relevant human examples;
- choosing the appropriate medium and moment for delivery;
- including a "what you can do" appeal that enables the audience to respond.

To **frame** the issue:

- translate individual stories into larger social and political problems;
- assign primary responsibility for the problem;
- present a clear solution;
- spell out your proposals;
- develop images that highlight your values.

A Framed Message

"*Frames are the boundaries that highlight specific parts of an issue, place others in the background, and leave out some entirely. The frame influences how an audience thinks about an issue, including who is responsible for the cause and its possible solution... You need to frame the issue in a way that is as compelling as the opposition's frame, and shifts the audience's attention to your perspective.*"[3]

DOING ADVOCACY

The matrix on the following page can help you frame your message by guiding you through an analysis of the available media and the concerns of the audiences you wish to reach.

Pretesting Your Message

Pretesting your message helps to ensure that your intended audience understands and is engaged by it. Yet for many reasons, advocates rarely pretest their message to make sure it appeals beyond the "converted." Often, they assume that if the message sounds good to activists, it will sound good to everyone. Unfortunately, this is rarely the case. Advocates often have their own language that may not be easily understood by others, even those who may care about the issue.

Being on the political defensive can make advocacy groups forget that they need to reach and persuade others. For example, during the World Bank protests in Washington,

DC in 2000, a small group of activists was asked what they wanted to communicate to the average American citizen. They answered: "Guilt. Americans should feel bad for what's happening in the rest of the world." Trying to make people feel bad is not a good way of gaining support. Poorly designed messages can confuse or alienate potential supporters.

The most common way to pretest a message is through focus groups, which were discussed in detail in Chapter 8. To conduct a focus group for this particular purpose, you will want to bring together individuals representing the audience you want to reach and ask what they like and dislike about the message, and how they understand it.

Message Delivery

Message delivery involves careful attention to:

- how the information will be transmitted – the *medium;*

Different Frames, Different Solutions

In her book, *Prime Time Activism: Media Strategies for Grassroots Organizations,* Charlotte Ryan offers an example of how one event can be framed in many ways. The different frames affect the event's meaning. Consider these three frames for the same event:

- "An infant left sleeping in his crib was bitten repeatedly by rats while his 16 year old mother went to cash her welfare check."
- "An eight-month old South End boy was treated yesterday after being bitten by rats while sleeping in his crib. Tenants said that repeated requests for extermination had been ignored by the landlord. He claimed that the tenants did not properly dispose of their garbage."
- "Rats bit eight-month old Michael Burns five times yesterday as he napped in his crib. Burns is the latest victim of a rat epidemic plaguing inner-city neighborhoods. A Public Health Department spokesperson explained that federal and state cutbacks forced short-staffing at rat control and housing inspection programs."

The first version, by emphasizing the age and actions of the mother, suggests that the problem is irresponsible teenagers having babies. The solution would be discouraging such irresponsible behavior. In the second version, the issue is a landlord-tenant dispute about responsibility for garbage. The solution depends on the reader's perspective. Some readers will say there must be stronger enforcement of landlords' responsibilities. Others will say that the laws must make it easier for a landlord to evict tenants. Only the third version looks at larger issues such as how cuts in funding for basic services affect low-income communities.

From *Advocacy for Social Justice: A Global Action and Reflection Guide,* ibid. p 105.

Framing Messages for Different Audiences

AUDIENCE	CONCERNS	POSSIBLE MESSAGES	MEDIUM
Decision-Makers (Political and economic) - Ministers - Chief of Police - Legislators - President & executive staff - Chief executive officers - Board of Directors/shareholders			- Major newspapers - Television channels - Radio - Business journals - Issue briefs
Donors - Foundations - Bilateral agencies (e.g., SIDA, DFID, USAID) - Multilateral agencies (e.g., World Bank, regional development banks)			- Major newspapers - Television channels - Radio - Business journals - Issue briefs - Intl. development journals - Internal updates, etc.
Journalists - Reporters - Foreign correspondents - Editors - Feature writers - Columnists - Economics & labor reporters - Women's issues reporters			Local & international print & electronic media
Civil Society Groups - NGOs - Trade Unions - Development agencies - Grassroots groups - Church groups - Research groups & think tanks			- Major newspapers - Television channels - Radio - Posters - Pamphlets - Bumper stickers - Listserves - Newsletters - Conferences & workshops - Issue briefs
Issue Relevant Practitioners - Individual professionals - Trade associations			- Major newspapers - Television channels - Radio - Posters - Pamphlets - Bumper stickers - Listserves - Newsletters - Conferences & workshops - Issue briefs - Professional journals
General Public			- Major newspapers - Television channels - Radio - Posters - Pamphlets - Bumper stickers
Opinion Leaders - Religious & church leaders - Chiefs & traditional local leaders			- Major newspapers - Television - Radio - Conferences & workshops

Adapted from *TB Advocacy: A Practical Guide*. Global Tuberculosis Programme, World Health Organization, 1998.

DOING ADVOCACY

- who or what will convey the message – the *messenger.*

Choices about delivery differ depending on the audience, the country, and the community. For example, a 1991 study in Zimbabwe found that for most rural people the primary source of trusted information was a respected visitor – often a government extension worker who was in the area on a regular basis. In places where access to electronic or printed information is limited, people trust information they receive face-to-face from a person they regard as knowledgeable. Other information sources simply do not reach them. In contrast, the primary source of information for many people in Indonesia is television.[4]

Many countries have two faces – one of poverty and isolation where information is scarce and personalized, and another resource-rich side where the electronic and print media bombard people with information. In places where public interest organizations are strong, some concerned citizens might depend on a newsletter or internet communication. Increasingly, a key source of information for people around the world is electronic. Often the source is international, like the TV network CNN. But the electronic sources rarely reach poor or excluded groups.

Multiple information strategies are needed if you have diverse audiences. Some of the many different options for delivering a message include[5]:

Person-to-Person
- one-on-one;
- lobbying visits (discussed in Chapter 15);
- group or community meetings (discussed in Chapter 14);
- seminars, workshops, and conferences;
- public hearings (discussed in Chapter 14);

- protests and public demonstrations (discussed in Chapter 14).

Print
- newspapers and magazines;
- journals, bulletins, newsletters, updates;
- posters, leaflets, fliers, action alerts, pamphlets, bumper stickers;
- reports, studies;
- letters to decisionmakers.

Electronic
- radio;
- television;
- videos and films;
- Internet.

Drama and folk art forms
- street theater;
- songs, music; and poems;
- dance.

Choosing the Right Medium

Your choice of a medium to deliver the message depends on who you are speaking to, what you want to say, your purpose, and your ability to work with that medium. Here are some questions to guide the selection:

For each audience, ask:
- What are the audience's primary sources of information? Who or what do they listen to? What do they read? What do they watch? What appeals to them?

- What are the audience's characteristics (age, gender, class, employment, race, etc.)? Where do they live? Work? What languages do they speak? Do they read? Do they buy newspapers? Do they have access to television and the internet? Do they listen to radio?

Purpose

To apply the principles of message development to a slogan in order to better understand how different audiences require different messages.

Process

(Time: 30 minutes)

1. Divide participants into small groups according to the advocacy issue they are addressing. Give them the following instructions:

   - If your group does not have a slogan, write one that communicates a message about your issue. Clarify who your audience is and how you will test the slogan.

   - If your group has already developed and used a slogan, identify the intended audience, describe how the slogan was developed, and say how you knew if it was effective or not.

2. After they have finished, the groups can share their slogans in plenary.

Discussion

- What purpose(s) can slogans serve in advocacy?
- What are the characteristics of the most effective slogans? Why are some slogans ineffective?

Examples of Slogans in Different Contexts

Slogans can reach large numbers of people but their impact varies widely from context to context. A consumers' group in India developed the slogan, "Sterlite sterilizes life," to create public awareness about the deaths and illness caused by gas leaks from a company named Sterlite. When the organization analyzed its slogan, they found several problems. First, the word sterilize has more than one meaning. On the one hand, it can mean to make something clean. On the other hand, it can mean to make a person impotent. Second, only people who read newspapers knew about the accidents caused by Sterlite since they had not been covered on the radio or television. So the impact of the slogan was limited.

In Nepal the slogan, "When the mountains fade, daughters be alert," was used to warn young girls about the danger of being lured across the border into forced prostitution. The slogan seems abstract, but it was turned into a more explicit song that was broadcast throughout the country and became popular.[1]

The Uganda Debt Network (UDN) developed the slogan, "Debt is death for children." The slogan was intended to convey the consequences of negative macroeconomic policies on the most vulnerable of the population. A small working group designed this slogan to reach policymakers from the World Bank, IMF, and from government as well as the general public. Information accompanying the slogan explained that a nine million dollar debt (generated primarily by a dictator in the 70s and 80s) was paid each year by the Ugandan government to international financial agencies while only three million dollars were spent on health each year. Organizers of the campaign argued that debt caused the death of children because it reduced spending on public health. The posters were placed in front of the local World Bank offices one week before elections, and banners were placed in the streets. In addition, a petition was sent to the World Bank; its President sent a response thanking UDN for their work.[2]

From GWIP Asia TOT and *GWIP Africa TOT*

DOING ADVOCACY

- What are their political views? Their jokes? Expressions? Religious and cultural sensitivities? Are there differences based on race, age, gender, and other factors?

For each medium, ask:

- How do we access this medium as advocates? Will it cost money? Will we need assistance from specialized people? Will we need influence that we currently do not have? Who owns it? Who controls the information it transmits?

- Will they be willing to convey our message and, if they do, will they distort it?

To assess your group's capacity to work with the medium, ask:

- What skills are needed?
- What resources are needed?
- If we do not have the skills and resources internally, can we get them easily?

Mass Media Advocacy

Mass media can be both a tool and a target of advocacy. On the one hand, because it reaches so many people, it is a powerful tool to inform and build support around your issue. On the other hand, its influence over public opinion and values makes it a prime target.

Working with media that reach large numbers of people, such as newspapers, television, radio, and magazines, requires good relationships with the journalists and editors who will choose whether and how to cover your issues.

Assessing the Mass Media in Your Context[6]

Assessing the media is part of your overall contextual analysis (see Chapter 7). This combines a general analysis of the media in your context with more specific research about different media organizations, and should answer these questions:

- What are the main sources of information in the geographic area where you are operating? And what are the main sources of information for your key audiences?

- What is the mix of privately-owned, government-owned, national, and international media?

- What are the politics of each of the key media outlets (organizations)?

Then, looking more specifically at each media source, the basic information you need is:

- Who are their main audiences?
- What is their likely position regarding your issue and proposed solution?
- Who owns and runs the organization? Is there a department or specific journalist who covers your issue?
- Which individuals inside the media may be possible allies?
- What are the coverage options (articles, editorials, columns, political cartoons, letters to the editor, op-eds, radio talk shows, etc.)?
- How much advance time (hours, days) is needed to get each option into the media?

Through observation you can also assess:

- how often and how your issue is covered;
- the likelihood that your message will be covered or distorted;
- who is held responsible for your issue;
- whether solutions are presented;
- what kinds of people write and are quoted.

Key Steps in Mass Media Advocacy

1. Develop a list of names and contact information for the different news organizations, their editors, and key journalists.

2. Based on your contextual assessment of the media, develop a hierarchy of those who are most important to contact.

3. For the top news agencies, establish relationships with journalists and editors. For the more sympathetic ones, the relationship should enable you to regularly inform the media staff about the progress of the campaign.

4. For each agency and audience, know what is considered "newsworthy." (See page 243.)

5. Track news coverage and public opinion on relevant matters. Keep press clippings so you can see how the issue is portrayed over time and in different sources.

6. Look out for upcoming events where your issue might be highlighted.

Networking with Journalists

This task varies depending on where you are operating. In Zimbabwe, where leading press is government-owned, NGOs usually have to cover reporters' expenses to persuade them to cover their issues. In countries where there is freedom of press and the media is privately owned, mainstream journalists are lured by a well-substantiated claim, the relevance of the issue, the human interest aspect and the likelihood it will advance their career. The work of journalists is also shaped by the business interests of the media outlets that employ them.

The following tips come from US reporters with international press experience.[7]

- Sobriety, balance and data, data, data – in other words, the more "facts" the better.

- Be able to substantiate what you say and respond to counter-arguments.

- Offer well-researched information that points out specific problems or offers practical solutions. Use examples as much as possible.

- Be honest about your agenda and whether or how the issue affects you personally.

Challenges Journalists Face

"Members of the media face many challenges. . .

- **Partisan control of the press** is a problem around the world. Governments usually have some way of exerting pressure on the media. Sometimes the control is very direct. For example, in Indonesia, . . . [g]overnment often asks newspapers to censor what they write. In other countries, government controls what happens through strict licensing laws. In Malaysia the newspapers, magazines, and printing presses must renew their operating licenses yearly. Malaysian media organizations that are critical of the government have trouble renewing their licenses.

- **Private media ownership** can also jeopardize the freedom of the press, especially when the media is owned by large corporations. A daily newspaper in China experienced this kind of corporate control when a group of Malaysian businesspeople with interests in the sugar industry bought the Hong-Kong based *South China Morning Post.* The businesspeople wanted to sell their sugar to lucrative Chinese markets and put their business interests first. They changed the editorial board of the newspaper, and hired new reporters. Activists reported that the paper subsequently became more hesitant in covering human rights issues.

- **Threats of libel suits** can limit what the media and individual journalists say. In most countries, an individual who feels defamed has the right to sue for libel. Even if the newspaper or station is in the right, defending it can be costly."

From *Making the Most of the Media: Tools for Human Rights Groups Worldwide.* Center for Sustainable Human Rights Action, 2001, pp 12-13.

DOING ADVOCACY

How a Journalist Writes a Story, in Nine Steps

A Kenyan journalist who works for a weekly newspaper outlined nine steps in writing a story. Once he
1. gets a tip for a story, he
2. researches the history and past coverage of the issue. He then
3. makes a list of questions and
4. calls sources who might be able to give more information. Once he has heard different points of view, he
5. verifies the facts and
6. asks other sources to confirm or deny the details he has received. To write a strong story, he
7. looks for good quotes. When he has sufficient details, quotes, and different sides of the story, he
8. begins to write, and
9. rechecks the facts as his deadline approaches.

Making the Most of the Media: Tools for Human Rights Groups Worldwide, Center for Sustainable Human Rights Action. 2001, p. 11.

- If you don't know, say you don't know. If you can't talk about it, say you can't.

- Get the people affected by the problem to talk about it themselves.

- Be aware of media deadlines and work within them.

- Build a relationship of trust with journalists by being honest.

A US journalist covering Asia for the New York Times has these tips for dealing with media:

- Journalists are usually not interested in promoting specific organizations. Focus on the issue, not your organization.

- If a story is not immediately relevant, make linkages between your issue and the reality of the readers.

- Locate your issue in the broader social, economic and political trends of the time.

Often a journalist may share your interest in informing people about a social issue. However, journalists have to prove the issue is worth covering. Where the media is private, they must prove that readers want to hear about this type of issue.

There are other factors to consider when building media relationships. How a journalist's story gets published depends on the politics of the editors and owners of the media. If the issue is controversial, the journalist's words may be changed to reflect corporate or government interests. When working with journalists on controversial stories, do not automatically blame them if the coverage seems distorted.

The Politics of Mass Media: Being "Newsworthy"

An independent media is an important pillar for democratic governance. It facilitates open political debate and keeps the public aware of injustices, corruption, and issues of national importance. There are many examples of how the media has helped social justice and accountability advocacy, ranging from the impeachment of former Filipino President Estrada to the tobacco control campaign in the US.

But there are many forces that undermine the independence of the media. The media often reflect the same power dynamics that shape policy issues. For example, even in the most independent media agencies, the voices of women, poor people, and minorities are extremely rare or coverage is slanted by social stereotypes. Women's issues are considered "soft" while stories of war and business are "hard" and so more worthy of coverage. Politics and economics also shape what is considered newsworthy. In many countries, people or institutions with political power may prevent a controversial issue from being covered so that their part in it remains invisible and less open to scrutiny.

The exclusion of certain social issues is also related to "the bottom line," especially where media organizations are profit-driven corporations. Media outlets may try to avoid alienating investors or sponsors, or spend more time marketing products rather than ideas. The need to sell news can sometimes compete with the desire to offer balanced coverage.

What makes news "newsworthy" depends on the political context, the nature of the mass media, and the politics of the particular issue. There are some things that may boost your chances for coverage, such as:
- controversy, conflict, and scandal;
- deception or injustice on a massive scale;
- broad interest to many people;
- things that are mysterious or unusual;
- celebrities and opinion leaders as spokespersons;
- individuals affected by a problem telling their story;
- compelling images.

Making an issue "newsworthy" depends on how you package your message, who delivers it and whether you can persuade the media that it is newsworthy. This is all political.

Mass Media Tools

The most common tools for getting publicity from the mass media are:

- press releases;
- media events: news conferences and press releases;
- letters to the editor;
- television or radio interviews;
- radio dialogues and educational soap operas.

Press release

Press releases aim to attract journalists to cover an upcoming event or one that has just occurred. Some journalists receive hundreds of releases a day, which makes the competition to be interesting steep. This means that the wording of the headline and first sentence must be compelling.

Content of the release
- Make sure the headline, first sentence, and first paragraph are newsworthy.
- The first paragraph should have the 5 Ws:
  - *Wh*at is happening?
  - *Wh*en is it happening?
  - *Wh*ere is it happening?
  - *Wh*o is involved and who is speaking?
  - *Wh*y is it important?
- Use a direct quote in the first two paragraphs.
- Use one fact or numbers to show it is important.
- Be specific.
- Attach a fact sheet so that the release is not too long.

Style of the release
- Use short sentences of no more than 25 words.
- Use paragraphs containing no more than two to three sentences.
- Keep the length to one or two pages.
- Use a simple, jargon-free style.

DOING ADVOCACY

- Avoid lots of adjectives and adverbs.

- Use active verbs, e.g., "Twelve women who witnessed and survived the horrors of trafficking testified. . ." rather than: "The horrors of trafficking were described by twelve women."

- Proofread.

Layout

- Put the date and release details at the top of the page. Say whether the information is "FOR IMMEDIATE RELEASE" or "EMBARGOED FOR RELEASE." An embargo means that the information must not be released until a specified date and time.

- At the end of the release, put - *END* - and list contact names and numbers where the journalist can get more information.

On the following page is a sample press release from the Supermarket campaign organized by Christian Aid (UK).

Practicing a Press Release in Ghana

Draft - "The population of Ghana doubled in nine years. This has put a strain on all economic resources. There are inadequate health services, water supplies, and food to meet the growing numbers. A big factor is escalating teen pregnancy. A thousand women from around the country are meeting to discuss how better family planning services can halt this dangerous trend."

Rewrite - "A thousand women from across the country gathered in Accra today to devise solutions to Ghana's escalating population growth. . ."

Media events: news conferences and press briefings

A news conference lets you announce a news story to a number of journalists at once. Usually it involves articulate speakers making presentations followed by questions from journalists. The checklist on page 247 can simplify conference organizing. But first be sure that your story warrants holding a news conference, as they can be costly to organize and will be disheartening if few people attend.

In some cases, you can achieve the same results and be more cost effective by handling the story from your office. For this, you need to send journalists your press release and briefing materials with an embargo until the date of the launch. The briefing materials should also inform them who is available to interview.

Journalists cover hundreds of stories and may not know anything about your issue. If you want them to produce accurate stories, they need to be properly briefed. Consider organizing an informal press briefing. This can also help build good relations with journalists. For example, invite selected journalists to attend a briefing at your offices in advance of your planned event, or offer to meet them in their own offices. Brief them on key developments relating to your issue and what your organization is doing about it. You can do the briefing as a breakfast meeting and provide refreshments. Take along briefing materials, such as fact sheets, to distribute.

Press release
THE GREAT SUPERMARKET RECEIPT COLLECTION

Local churches challenge supermarkets

Photo opportunity:

Receipts will be handed in to

_____

manager of

_____

supermarket

at _____

on _____

at _____ am/pm.

Local churches have issued a challenge to supermarkets to ensure that the Third World workers who produce many of the products they sell are fairly paid and properly treated.

The challenge is part of Christian Aid's ongoing campaign _Change the Rules_. As part of this campaign, Christian Aid is calling on supermarkets to adopt a code of conduct to protect vulnerable workers in the Third World. Christian Aid believes implementation of this code should be independently monitored.

Churchgoers at _____ are collecting till receipts from local branches of supermarket chains. They are now handing in receipts with a total value of _____. These will be presented to supermarket managers at

_____

_____ as proof of the level of concern about the lot of workers in developing countries, some of whom work under appalling conditions for long hours and very little money.

"This isn't a threat to the supermarkets. But as their customers we want to say to them: 'We're spending a lot of money in your shop, and we want to know we can be absolutely confident that the people who produce the things you sell us are guaranteed basic, minimum conditions and fair pay,'" explained _____, _one of the local organisers._

Martin Drewry, Head of Campaigns at Christian Aid, said: "Christian Aid is already involved in negotiations with the supermarkets nationally. We believe they might be prepared to adopt codes of conduct to ensure workers are fairly treated – providing we can show them that their customers do really care.

"The magnificent response of all those who collected together their till receipts shows beyond any shadow of a doubt that shoppers do care, and want to know that the goods they buy are not produced by workers who are exploited or unfairly treated."

For more details phone _____ (local contact)

or Martin Drewry, Head of Campaigns at Christian Aid, on 0171-523 2264.

London: PO Box 100, SE1 7RT **Belfast:** PO Box 150, BT9 6AE
Cardiff: PO Box 21, CF4 2DL **Edinburgh:** PO Box 11, EH1 1EL
Dublin: Christ Church, Rathgar Road, Dublin 6

Registered charity no 258003   CAP1

Christian Aid
We believe in life before death

DOING ADVOCACY

Examples of Mass Media Advocacy

Truth Speaks to Power in the Philippines

How does a corrupt, incompetent President get impeached? An experience from the Philippines demonstrates that organized citizens' groups can move the media even when powerful interests are against change. The Philippine Center for Investigative Journalism was at the heart of the advocacy that led to former President Estrada's impeachment. The Center did careful research and produced a series about the President's corrupt business practices. Initially, their information was not carried by most major newspapers due to political pressure. But as discontent and advocacy expanded, the information added momentum to the impeachment campaign. It convinced many sectors of the Philippine society that the impeachment allegations were credible and demanded action.

Helping Journalists See All Angles in Croatia *

A story from Croatia illustrates how groups can work to change images of women in the media.

"My name is Kristina Mihalec. I am the International Communications Liaison at Be active, Be Emancipated (Budi aktivna, Budi emanipirana or B.a.B.e.) in Zagreb Croatia. We are a strategic lobby NGO working for women's human rights in Croatia. One of our main projects is *Women in Media*. We at B.a.B.e. monitor the media daily. We don't have to search for sexist examples in advertising because it is pushed into our faces. Sexism in visual and printed media is the norm. Female opera singers are reported on only if they take a 'sexy' pose in their underwear. The covers of newspapers never show women unless they are half naked, a model or a victim. Jumbo public posters show fully naked women advertising a car. Bare breasts are used to sell everything, be it beer, jeans, kitchen faucets, cars, medicine, juice, etc. Yet when we try to take out sexism, the women at B.a.B.e. are called extremists.

There is no government monitoring or regulation of sexism in the media. So, we have designed several projects. We give workshops to female journalists on what sexism is. We teach them to develop journalist skills from a gender perspective. We use all forms of media in training journalists: gathering information on the internet about women or the Croatian government, analysis of pictures and art. At the last workshop participants expressed the need to invite men to our workshops, since they need to be educated too. So, in the future we will hold workshops for women and men journalists. This will be very difficult, but necessary.

Here are more examples of our media work:

- We did very successful street actions. On public sexist signs we placed large stickers which read 'this offends women,' 'sexism,' and 'STOP.' This form of graffiti was an inexpensive and fun way to convey a message to the public.
- The women at B.a.B.e. monitor all the Croatian newspapers. Every day, newspapers are read, all sexist articles and pictures concerning women are cut out and filed for our research library.
- We campaigned against a food store for its sexist advertisements through writing to the manager and educating store owners. Since then, their advertisements have drastically improved.
- We have done research on gender stereotypes in schools. The results are distributed to schoolteachers, media, and government bodies.
- We have analyzed the portrayal of homosexuals in the media.
- We have published two booklets on the portrayal of women in Croatian media.
- For the 16 Days of Activism Against Gender Violence last year, we commissioned a female rap group to do a rap and video. This was very successful. Finally, young female musicians were given coverage. They received much publicity on the national radio, TV, and newspaper. Their CDs were distributed throughout Croatia and Europe, and can be found on MP3 format on the internet."

* This story from Croatia was part of a list-serve dialogue on Women and Media coordinated by UNDP during the Beijing plus 5 preparations; for more information contact babe@zamir.net.

Rationale

___ A big, newsworthy story

___ New information relating to a big story being followed by the news media

___ A statement by an important figure on a controversial issue

___ Participation of high profile speakers

___ Release of important new findings

___ Launch of a major new initiative

___ Announcement of something important locally

Location and Set Up

___ A central, well known location, convenient for journalists and appropriate to the event

___ Avoid large rooms that give the appearance that few people attended

___ Make sure the noise level of the room is low

___ Reserve space at the back of the room for television cameras, possibly on a raised platform

___ Reserve a quiet room for radio interviews following the news conference

___ Ensure light and sound systems are in working order

___ If possible, have fax, phone, and email available

___ Make sure there is a podium and a table long enough for all spokespeople to sit behind

___ Consider displaying large visuals, such as images, logos or charts

___ Have a "sign in" sheet for journalists

___ Consider serving coffee, tea, and light snacks following the event

Timing

___ Hold the event in the morning or early afternoon of a workday, or with enough time for reporters to meet deadlines

___ Check that you are not competing with other important events on the same day

___ Start on time - do not keep journalists waiting

___ If you distribute materials beforehand, use an embargo to prevent journalists from publishing before the event

___ Wait until the event to release some information. This creates an element of surprise and rewards those who attend

Possible Materials

___ Press release

___ List of news conference participants

___ Executive summary of report

___ Case studies and stories

___ Fact sheets

___ Biography and photos of speakers, and copies of speeches

___ Pictures

___ B-roll (broadcast quality video background footage)

___ Consider putting all of the materials together into one "press kit"

Inviting Journalists

___ Keep an up-to-date mailing list of journalists

___ Make sure you know who the relevant journalists for your issue are

___ Focus on getting the most influential media to attend

___ Remember to invite foreign media

___ Inform journalists of the event at least a week before the day

___ Make a follow up call to check that the right journalist received the invitation

___ Build interest for the event without giving out the story

___ Consider offering "exclusive" angles to key media

Preparing Speakers

___ Select speakers who are articulate and authoritative

___ Brief speakers carefully on the message of the event

___ Prepare speakers in advance on how to answer difficult questions

___ Ideally, each speaker should present for only three or four minutes

___ Make sure that each speaker makes one or two important points. Try to get speakers to make different points

___ Keep speeches simple and non-technical, aimed at a general audience

___ Select a moderator who will manage questions from the floor after the presentation

___ Encourage questions and keep answers short

Follow-Up

___ Within a few hours of the end of the conference, get the information to important journalists who were unable to attend.

___ Advise the person who handles the phone in your organization where to direct follow-up calls.

___ Gather news clippings of the coverage that results from the news conference. Distribute these to coalition partners and policy makers.

DOING ADVOCACY

From *TB Advocacy: A Practical Guide.* Global Tuberculosis Programme, World Health Organization. Copyright 1998 by the WHO.

Letters to the editor[9]

Most newspapers and magazines have a "letters page" which gives readers the opportunity to express their views or correct previously published information. Letters are widely read and provide a good opportunity to promote a cause or debate issues.

Letters should be short and to the point. Those over 500 words are unlikely to be published. Short letters of 100 words can be very effective. A letter should make one main point and end on a challenging note, with a call to action.

Make sure you refer to your organization. The impact can be increased if letters are signed by more than one signatory, representing different organizations or interests. If your letter is responding to an article in a daily newspaper, you should submit it to the paper within a couple of days.

Television or radio interviews

Activists in many countries say that getting on television is nearly impossible and costly, especially when it is government-run. But where possible, appearing on radio and television can be one of the best ways to get your message across to a broad audience.

Before you agree to an interview, make sure you know:[10]

Sample Letter to the Editor

The following letter to the editor was published in the *Wall Street Journal* on July 17, 2000.

Rain Forest Devastation Is Real

Philip Stott's July 10 editorial-page commentary "The Rain Forest Doesn't Need Saving" creates the illusion of scientific controversy where none exists. Mr. Stott claims that because "rain forest" is an imprecise term that includes diverse ecosystems, its destruction is "hype." This is like saying that since cancer is not one but various diseases, we need not concern ourselves with it.

Wishing to portray the issue of rain forest conservation as a fad, Mr. Stott fails to mention, much less address, the very considerable mainstream scientific consensus that exists on tropical deforestation. He does not explain, for example, that 2,000-plus climate scientists of the U.N. Intergovernmental Panel on Climate Change concur that tropical deforestation is responsible for 20%-30% of the emissions of greenhouse gases globally; nor that in 1997 more of the earth's surface was on fire than in any time in recorded history, largely because of burning rain forests; nor that biologists overwhelmingly concur that half, and possibly as much as 90%, of the species of plants and animals on the planet are in the 6%-7% of the earth's surface that is tropical forest.

It is a self-serving distortion to allege that concern with forest destruction arises only in "the rich, self-indulgent countries of the North." Much of the forest devastation benefits corrupt governments, corporations and oligarchs at the expense of forest peoples. This is why grass-roots leaders from the Amazon to Indonesia have risked and at times lost their lives to stop the destruction. A national public opinion poll in Brazil recently found that 88% of the public thinks that forest protection in Brazil should increase, not decrease.

Thomas E. Lovejoy
Stephan Schwartzman

(Mr. Lovejoy is chief biodiversity adviser to the president of the World Bank and counselor to the Secretary of the Smithsonian Institution for Biodiversity and Environmental Issues; Mr. Schwartzman is a senior scientist of Environmental Defense.)

- what the program is;

- whether it is live or pre-recorded;

- who the interviewer is, what their interview style is (confrontational, conversational, etc.), and if possible, their views on your issue;

- what information they have, the reasons they want the interview, and whether or not they have your press release and other relevant materials;

- what you are likely to be asked and how long you will be given to talk.

Select spokespeople who will come across well – people who are knowledgeable, articulate and appear confident. Less experienced people will need to think carefully through what they want to communicate. Facing a camera can make anyone jumpy and go off the topic. Practicing the message over and over again can help the speaker avoid getting diverted.

Radio dialogues and educational soap operas

Public education programs that aim to change attitudes and behavior often depict a familiar human story and illustrate alternative ways of seeing and resolving common problems. Women's groups in Latin America and Africa have developed and used radio and television soap operas in this way. In some cases a human drama unfolds over several episodes of a series. Surveys indicate that audiences find them enjoyable and thought provoking. Rather than preaching, these stories show real life dilemmas and the consequences of stereo-types, prejudice, and hidden injustices.

Radio can also be used to generate citizen dialogue and debate. Call-in shows allow listeners to comment and debate indirectly with one another about issues. Many citizen educa-tion initiatives combine radio with structured face-to-face discussion to deepen the learning.

Preparing for Television Interviews

Selecting speakers for live programs on television and radio is tricky. Sometimes you may choose citizens who are affected by the issue. Although they may not be as confident speaking in public as an "expert," the human aspects of their story are often more compelling. The emotion in their story makes a powerful and lasting impression on the public and policymakers. Radio and television interviews also give constituents an opportunity to learn new skills and gain confidence.

Preparing for Television Interviews[11]

- Focus on one main message and come back to that message again and again in different ways.
- Do not allow the interviewer to sidetrack you from your main message.
- Do not use jargon, do not make too many technical points, and keep your answers simple.
- Be yourself. Rely on the strong points of your own personality.
- Be enthusiastic about the subject. People will usually remember your passion for an issue more than what you say.
- Look at the interviewer when talking with him or her. If there is an audience, look at them when appropriate.
- Do not pretend to know the answers to all the questions.
- Do not become defensive or angry.
- Ask the producer what you should wear – dress is part of the message.
- Sit up straight and lean forward slightly.
- Rehearse, rehearse, rehearse.
- Be prepared for confrontational questions.

DOING ADVOCACY

Purpose

To practice and examine key elements of media strategies involving press releases and television talk shows.

Process

(Time: 1½ hours)

1. Divide the participants in two groups and ask each to do a role play illustrating the use of a different media strategy (either real or invented).

   • One group focuses on the print media and writes a press release on their issue. The role play must show the process used to write the release, who and what information sources they consult, how they try to get the story or information placed with a media outlet, and the problems they encounter.

   • The second group focuses on appearing on a television show. The role play must show the steps they take to prepare, the appearance itself, the problems the show presents, and how they respond.

Discussion

Analyze the approach each group used. Emphasize the elements of the strategy that worked and those that did not. Identify ways that the group could have changed their strategies to be more successful. If necessary, prepare handouts of the tips on press releases, media advocacy, and talk shows.

Example for Facilitators

Print media

In an Asian training-of-trainers workshop, the *print media* group's role play was about developing a press release on the problem of bride burning.* The release was written by three human rights organizations in consultation with a woman journalist. The human rights groups tried to get the story placed in the media by sending it to newspapers and talking with an editor. They wanted the story on the first pages of the papers, the name of the victim omitted, and an emphasis on the demands the three human rights groups were making of the government. Ending on a realistic note, the story appeared in only one paper, on the last page and it mentioned the victim's name.

The participants suggested ways to engage the media more strategically. They said that the groups could have asked the woman journalist to investigate the case herself, or taken her to the location where the woman was burned. The group also discussed some of the challenges of writing effective press releases. Press releases appear simple to do but are not. Editors and journalists may not read beyond the first sentence, so that sentence has to be intriguing. An opening sentence stating that three human rights organizations are concerned about burnings may not be as compelling as one that gives the startling figures and reasons for bride burning.

---

* In South Asia, a significant number of alleged accidents have surfaced where it is later uncovered that in-laws and husbands burn new brides with cooking fuel in order to pressure them to increase the dowry or have cause for divorce to seek another wife for more dowry.

Television Show

The *television show* group acted out a TV talk show in which a women's rights activist discussed domestic violence and the court system. The activist wanted to illustrate the problems underlying the case of a woman beaten to death by her politically influential husband who was tried and found innocent. A legal expert on the show supported the activist's arguments. However, the moderator gave more credence to a conservative newspaper editor who dismissed the points. As a result of the show, the activist received many calls of support.

The participants raised a variety of issues. Getting on television can be difficult, especially when it is controlled by the government. Even in more open political contexts, effective communication through television requires a great deal of preparation. Effective spokespersons maneuver the discussion so that their message gets across. They present the message in a way that has impact. Facts and figures can be powerful, as can human interest stories. Visual aids are also useful.

Radio Promoting Common Ground: Studio Ijambo in Burundi

In May 1995, Search for Common Ground and Common Ground Productions established Burundi's first independent radio studio, Studio Ijambo ("wise words" in Kirundi). This happened at a time when hate radio was promoting fear and mistrust, and had encouraged the massacre of hundreds of thousands in neighboring Rwanda.

Studio Ijambo employs Hutu and Tutsi staff to produce about 15 hours a week of news, public affairs, and cultural programming. The studio also produces a radio drama featuring a Hutu family and a Tutsi family who live next door to each other. Entitled *Umubanyi Niwe Muryango (Our Neighbors, Ourselves)*, the production describes the conflict between these neighbors and how, in the end, they reconcile their differences. A survey found that an estimated 87% of Burundians listen to the radio drama. It found that 82% of those surveyed believe that Studio Ijambo's programs help reconciliation.

Studio Ijambo reaches beyond Burundi, to an estimated 12 million people throughout the Great Lakes region in Africa. It has earned a reputation for unbiased reporting, and its broadcasts are used regularly by other news organizations such as Reuters, the BBC, and Voice of America. Studio Ijambo has also helped to decentralize the media in Burundi and build local capacity for news coverage. Studio Ijambo was seen as so innovative that it became the subject of a story by the United States ABC-TV news program *Nightline*.

Source: www.sfcg.org

DOING ADVOCACY

Alternative Media for Citizen Outreach and Education

With the mass media, communication is usually in one direction, thus less controllable and measurable. Without two-way dialogue, you do not know how the message is received and whether recipients will take action for or against your advocacy. Alternative media, in addition to helping you reach people without easy access to mass media, can also be more effective for probing complex issues and for engaging people in advocacy. Alternative media can also be simpler and less costly.

We will briefly discuss each of these alternative forms of media:

- Internet;
- newsletters;
- talking points and issue briefs;
- conferences, seminars, and workshops;
- posters and bumper stickers;
- pamphlets, comic books, and photonovels;
- street theater and songs.

Internet

Global policy advocacy has benefited from the use of international communication technology (ICT) to engage citizens' groups in dialogue and planning for coordinated action. The International Campaign to Ban Landmines has relied on communication and education through the internet, as do the global protests on economic and trade policy. These demonstrate that virtual forms of organizing can work. Emergency action alerts to mobilize protests against violations of human rights often depend on the speed and reach of the internet. Issue-focused listserves bring together activists, practitioners, donors, and policy makers in dialogue around UN conferences and other global policy events.

Innovative internet-radio connections offer new ways for activists to communicate with each other and reach larger audiences. For example, FIRE, the Feminist International Radio Endeavor, covers a range of concerns important to women advocates. It broadcasts dialogues with activists from major international events such as the UN Conferences in Beijing and Durban. Radio journalists at these meetings record FIRE's programs and send them through the internet for rebroadcast locally in their countries. (See www.fire.or.cr.)

Newsletters

Brief updates in print or via the internet are used by NGOs and citizens' groups to inform allies and other stakeholders about issues.

The Internet as a Tool for Democratization?

Many people are enthusiastic about the potential of the Internet to democratize the policymaking process, and provide citizens with information and an avenue to make their voices heard. However, potential is one thing and reality another. In *Internet . . . Why and What For?* Ricardo Gomez of the International Development Research Centre (IDRC) of Canada and Juliana Martinez of Costa Rica's Fundacion Acceso, looked at the experiences of about 50 IDRC-funded information and communication technology (ICT) projects in Costa Rica since 1997. Collectively, these projects were worth more than CA$4 million. Gomez and Martinez conclude that ". . . Connecting the masses is not by itself enough to foster democracy. . . a social vision of the Internet in Latin America has to involve three things: *equitable access,* which involves basic training and reasonably priced connections; an *ability to make meaningful use of ICTs*; and *social appropriation* — ICTs should help people solve concrete problems and transform current realities. Otherwise, ICTs will just reproduce and increase the social divide. . ." [emphasis added]

www.idrc.ca/reports

Some newsletters ask for reader feedback to encourage an exchange of ideas and to facilitate consultative planning.

Talking points and issue briefs

These are useful for educating and lobbying decisionmakers. Issue briefs are 3-10 pages long and highlight crucial facts and analysis. They assist the media and policymakers to understand the issue and your proposed solution with minimal energy on their part. Talking points are generally shorter than briefs and are used to guide advocates in making their case in 3-5 minutes to a decisionmaker. We discuss this in more detail in Chapter 15.

Conferences, seminars, and workshops

The audiences for conferences, seminars, and workshops can vary in size, but these fora can be an effective way to educate specific groups of people. Many NGOs use community-based workshops for citizen training and education as part of their legal rights and policy advocacy efforts. Conferences with high level speakers or compelling topics can also draw mass media attention. In many countries, a gathering of international visitors will attract media coverage. When the workshop involves people who are not used to speaking to the press, the workshop program can include time for preparing and rehearsing media statements.

Posters and bumper stickers

One of the cheaper ways to get a simple message out to the general public is with posters and bumper stickers. With a clever slogan, a captivating illustration, and basic information, posters can reach more people than most other media. This is particularly true where there is a low level of literacy and poor access to the mass media. The choice of image and words can be more difficult than in other media tools because a poster must reach many different people and be self-explanatory.

A good poster will captivate, energize, provoke and educate. Bumper stickers are useful in countries where there are many individually owned cars. In some countries, caps and T-shirts can also spread the word. The use of these different channels depends on your budget and your audience.

Pamphlets, comic books, and photonovels

Pamphlets and other simple materials can help with follow-up to a one-off event. They can be cheap and, where information is scarce, will likely attract an audience, depending on literacy levels. The challenge is making the content and design educational and entertaining. Many NGOs put out pamphlets to educate communities about different topics. In some cases these pamphlets are not read, either due to low literacy levels or the complexity of the language. Comic books can be more effective reaching certain audiences as can photonovels, which are short stories depicted through photos with simple text, similar to comic books.

Street theater and songs

Street theater and songs can reach a wide range of people. Again, they are particularly useful in situations where the mass media reaches only a fraction of the population. The combination of entertainment, real life dramas, thought-provoking information, and interaction engages people in a way that no other media can. Street theater and songs work for both literate and non-literate populations. By depicting real life situations and using humor, drama and songs, they can encourage public discussion of controversial cultural and religious issues without appearing to directly criticize values and beliefs. In addition, street theater and song can be tailored to local needs and available resources. (See the case from Cambodia on the next page.)

DOING ADVOCACY

Example: Public Education through Street Theater in Cambodia

The Project Against Domestic Violence (PADV), the Women's Media Center (WMC), and the traditional *ayai* Prom Mahn street theater troupe – headed by one of Cambodia's most popular stage personalities – developed a play that was performed nightly in 36 remote communities in five provinces to raise awareness about family violence. The play attracted as many as 30,000 people in some districts.

The drama compares the experiences of two neighboring families. One family enjoys a high quality of life, which is attributable to the loving relationship between the husband and wife. The other family suffers from repeated incidents of domestic violence. Prior to each performance, a public awareness team from PADV and Women's Affairs contacted local NGOs and officials for support. Before the show, a team member spoke about domestic violence and explained where families could find local help. Each play informed the public of the law and the local services available to victims, including interventions from the police and community officials, legal aid, and domestic violence shelters. In the play, the heroine takes action to end the abuse by turning to the services available in the area where the play is performed.

Through the story, the performance:
- showed that domestic violence is a public problem, not just a family matter, by highlighting its harmful effect on women, children, families, and society;
- raised awareness that domestic violence is a human rights violation and against the law;
- encouraged community intervention in cases of domestic violence; and
- informed the public of the available local services and legal remedies.

After the performances, local organizations reported an increase in the number of women seeking assistance. The project also stimulated the formation of broad coalitions of human rights and women's organizations to advance women's rights. PADV and WMC also gained the support of the Ministry of Women's Affairs, which ensured the security of the performing troupe and the cooperation of local authorities. Through press releases, PADV gained media coverage for performances, expanding the reach of the performance.

Source: The Asia Foundation

NOTES

[1] Adapted from Advocacy Learning Initiative, Vol II, page 90, draft 11/99.

[2] Adapted from Advocacy Learning Initiative, Vol II, page 91, draft 11/99.

[3] Adapted from Advocacy Learning Initiative, Vol II, page 93, draft 11/99.

[3] International Foundation for Electoral Systems (IFES), Indonesia poll, 2001.

[5] The list is adapted from the Advocacy Learning Initiative, VolII, Oxfam and the Advocacy Institute, Draft copy, 11/99. (To be published by Kumarian Press.) p. 99.

[6] Adapted from Advocacy Learning Initiative, ibid., p 105.

[7] In "Media-Advocacy Relationships: The View from the Other Side, by Amanda Rawls in *CHANGE EXCHANGE*, Part 1, Issue #6, "Common Threads", October 1999, the Advocacy Institute, Washington, DC.

[8] ibid. p. 18.

[9] *TB Advocacy: A Practical Guide.* Global Tuberculosis Programme, World Health Organization. Copyright 1998 by the WHO.

[10] *TB Advocacy: A Practical Guide.* Ibid.

[11] *Advocacy Guide.* International Planned Parenthood Federation, Western Hemisphere Region. IPPF/WHR Regional Council. September 30 - October 1, 1994. Aruba.

DOING ADVOCACY

This *Guide* talks a lot about the differences between advocacy where organizers *speak on behalf of the "voiceless,"* and advocacy where organizers work with the *"voiceless" to speak for themselves*. In this chapter, we describe outreach and mobilization activities that build citizen participation and enable excluded groups to advance their rights and hold decisionmakers accountable.

But outreach and mobilization activities are also important for policy advocacy where citizen participation is not a core objective. Some *policy-centered* efforts focus on the need to prove numbers of supporters with less concern about what those numbers think or gain by collaborating.

However, on a practical level, policy gains without broad-based organized support are unlikely to be implemented. When advocates lobby "on behalf of" communities, they are often perplexed when their efforts fail. In some cases, they alienate constituents and can even generate hostility to "outsiders." People, even in poor communities, do not like others telling them what they need and think.

In contrast, *citizen-centered* outreach and mobilization strategies focus on empowerment and citizenship. They educate and activate. However, as discussed in Part One, generating involvement in advocacy can mean breaking through ingrained patterns of withdrawal or resistance to change, which takes time and resources. It requires dialogue, education, and action designed to practice new forms of citizen behavior and build organization. This is why the *planning* aspect of advocacy described in Part Two is as crucial as the *doing* aspect discussed in Part Three.

> "Just as mobilizing without consciousness leads to narrow victories, so too, awareness-building without organizing to win concrete victories can lead to frustration, a reinforcement of a sense of powerlessness, or a critique of the world that is perceived as inaccessible or irrelevant to the everyday lives and realities of ordinary citizens."
>
> Julie Fisher, *The Road from Rio*, 1993

Outreach and mobilization are closely interconnected. In this chapter, we look at the following aspects of outreach and mobilization:

- **Different Ways to Do Outreach and Mobilization:** exploration of types and the role that outreach and mobilization play in advocacy.

- **Designing Outreach and Mobilization Strategies:** considerations in structuring ways to involve people.

- **Mobilizing Moments:** a review of moments that present political opportunities for mobilization.

The last part of the chapter is a case study on the experience of a federation of community-based women's organizations in the Philippines. This case shows how an organization

Outreach includes a wide variety of strategies – participatory planning and organizing, media, education, mobilization, and direct recruitment – that aim to gain the support and direct involvement of constituencies and to build their capacity as active citizens.

Mobilization engages people as political protagonists and includes activities that build and use the strength of numbers and organization.

Constituency-building Strategies that Link Thinking to Action

Critical Consciousness
Developed through:
- Problem Identification
- Analysis and Reflection
- Strategy Planning
- Information Gathering
- Making Choices

+

Action, Organization, and Leadership
- Outreach
- Public and Policy Dialogue
- Political Education
- Mobilization
- Citizen Events

=

- **Empowered Citizenship**
- **Engagement with Power**
- **Expanded Public Space**
- **Accountability**

made choices based on their principles and what those choices meant for their outreach and mobilization, as well as their advocacy more generally.

Different Ways To Do Outreach and Mobilization?

Outreach and mobilization include a diverse range of activities that:

- transform people's concerns into the organized expression of rights and specific proposals for change;
- recruit sympathetic and affected people to be involved;
- enable people to practice citizenship and public leadership.

Outreach and mobilization strategies can also:

- expand public and political support for specific advocacy efforts;
- demonstrate citizen support for your issues;
- increase legitimacy and leverage to reach and be persuasive at the negotiating table;
- generate broad ownership of a campaign;

- create new forms of practicing and expressing citizenship;
- strengthen the bond between the grassroots base of a campaign, organizational leadership, and lobbyists.

Organizers who see constituency-building both as a practical strategy for leveraging power and as a way of promoting inclusive participation will devote sufficient time and resources to do it. But in many cases, outreach and mobilization are reduced to the bare minimum necessary to advance a policy agenda and appear legitimate.

Different Ways to Do Outreach

There are many ways to do participatory outreach. The Guide focuses on four main strategies:

Participatory planning and organizing
The strategies described in Parts One and Two that engage constituents in analyzing their situation, choosing priority issues, information-gathering, exploring solutions, planning strategies, and understanding power dynamics are all valuable ways of doing outreach. Asking

people what they think, what is important to them, and what they want to do gets people involved.

Media

In Chapter 13, we describe different ways to reach out to concerned citizens, policymakers, politicians and others through the media. Some media strategies involve citizens in the creation of public messages. Others transmit messages to inform and motivate action.

Events

Strategies that bring concerned citizens together – like a town meeting, a music concert with a political message, an "accountability session" (all described on the following pages) – can convince other citizens to join your ranks.

Direct recruitment

Recruiting new supporters can be a part of the three strategies above, or it can be a separate initiative. The polling, canvassing, and door-to-door strategies (discussed in Chapter 8) aimed at finding out what people care about are an opportunity to recruit. During mobilization events, it is important to have an information table to let people know about a campaign and how to get involved. (See *Organizing for Social Change: A Manual for Activists in the 1990s* for detailed advice on recruitment strategies that can be adapted for different contexts.)

Since participatory planning and organizing, media, and direct recruitment strategies are discussed elsewhere in the Guide, this chapter focuses on mobilization.

Creative outreach strategies

Designing Outreach and Mobilization Strategies

Designing ways for people to participate in policy debate and political processes takes some imagination. In particular, disadvantaged groups may feel skeptical, even fearful, about getting involved in politics. In some cases, traditional kinds of citizen engagement, such as Parent-Teacher Associations, can be empowering and effective. In other cases, new forms of citizen action, like accountability sessions with government and corporate leaders, stakeholder juries, scorecards for candidates and parties, and street theater, have a greater impact on both the citizens involved and the individual and institutional targets of advocacy.

It may be difficult to think creatively about activities that involve constituents equally as leaders and organizers. In some cases, NGO leaders are unsure if grassroots people are able to speak directly to a public official when they themselves are nervous about doing it. While the constituents in your advocacy efforts may not speak like professional lobbyists, the

In advocacy, NGOs have legitimacy when speaking about issues they work on or specific interests they have as organizations. Concerns are raised, however, when NGOs speak on behalf of people who have not given them the authority to do so.

fact that they *live* the problem being addressed gives their voice *power and legitimacy.*

Citizens need to be prepared before they mobilize. They need:

- clarity and agreement about the issue they are addressing and why;
- knowledge of how the political system can help address their issue;
- strategies and skills to articulate demands and alternative solutions;
- organization to give them a base of collective power from which to speak;
- a sense of identity with a broader campaign, and an understanding of how their actions link with other advocacy strategies;
- an understanding of the power dynamics in which they operate and the risks they may face;

Downward Accountability

Grassroots democracy — Activism 'from below' — Downward accountability.

All these terms . . . deal with a fundamental part of our mandate: who do we speak for? It is fine for civil society organizations (CSOs) to advocate for the poor and marginalized, but unless CSOs can demonstrate a real link with their constituency, those in power are unlikely to listen. CSOs have a role beyond advocacy: they are interlocutors, facilitating communication between the disenfranchised and those in power. To play that role, they need legitimacy, which feeds back into the need to connect: governments will not listen if they believe CSOs do not have a constituency, and marginalized people will not let CSOs advocate for them if the latter do not represent them accurately. A further issue is how much CSOs are willing to integrate their constituency into their organization, in order to achieve this representation. Some CSOs are afraid a democratic practice will interfere with maintaining a coherent mission and operational effectiveness. But this is a tension that must be resolved in favour of increased democracy if organizations want to maintain the trust that their constituencies have placed in them. Ultimately, that trust is the measure of how well CSOs fulfill their mandate to strengthen civil society.

Kumi Naidoo, Secretary General, CIVICUS, from *Working for pro-poor social, economic and development policy, the advocacy work of the South African National NGO Coalition,* www.civicus.org/main/server_navigation/skeletons/ Civicus_01/framework/navigation.cfm?contentid=3C85E92C-7D55-11D5-A9CF00508BDFD42C.

What is an ACTION?

We use "action" here as it is used in "citizen action organizing"(see *Organizing for Social Change: A Manual for Activists in the 1990s*). Actions involve a group of people affected by an issue who make known their concerns to those who have the power to change things. A good action gets the attention of those with power, generates public support, and, above all, provides constituents with opportunities to practice organized citizenship.

How confrontational an action is will depend on the political environment, the risk of political repression, the capacity of the constituency groups, and accessibility of the target. If your issue is highly-charged or the political environment repressive, actions must call attention without bringing on unnecessary risk.

"In mere days, the use of actions can cut through months, and sometimes years, of bureaucratic red tape. More important is the impact on participants. People come away with a heightened sense of their own power and dignity, while their opponents are made to appear smaller and more vulnerable. At the same time, relationships of power are clarified because problems that might have been attributed to misunderstanding or lack of communication are seen sharply for what they really are — the conflicting interests of public good against private greed. In the process, loyalty to the organization is build up because people see it actually working for them and realize that their participation is essential to its success."

Adapted and quoted from *Organizing for Social Change: A Manual for Activists in the 1990s*, p.48.

- a clear, tested message to communicate to the public and decisionmakers.

Criteria for Designing Mobilizing Actions

Below are some criteria for designing actions. If possible, actions should:

- *present opportunities to learn new skills* — such as planning, defining clear demands, public speaking, going door-to-door to get others involved, running a meeting, etc.;

- *offer practice in leadership* — encourage new leaders to emerge, and build their leadership skills;

- *demystify politics and power* — by exposing people to how public decisionmaking works through direct contact with decisionmakers, research about how decisions are made, etc.;

- *have a concrete and feasible aim* — constituents must be able to see their victories and assess their losses;

- *boost morale* and give constituents a sense of their collective possibilities;

- *encourage people to try new things* — if they have never spoken publicly before, they should be encouraged and helped to do so.

Actions should also:

- *be thoroughly planned* — careful planning increases confidence;

- *be fun* — people's lives are full of demands and duties, so advocacy has to be more than just exhausting;

- *take account of the political environment* — to ensure that your constituents do not take unnecessary risks.

Sometimes it is not possible to check off everything on this list. In reality, there are times when it is more important to take action quickly than to wait until there is a common argument.

One of the strengths of the global protest movement that emerged in the late 1990s to influence international economic policy has been its ability to mobilize quickly on a global

PLANNING ADVOCACY

scale. Distinct groups with diverse agendas and tactics converged to protest at high-level meetings about trade and economic policy in different cities. The groups were loosely held together by the common aim of making the governments and international agencies more accountable to people's interests. There are pros and cons to this strategy. Diversity, the scale of mobilization, and the element of surprise gave the protestors the power to prevent consensus among the governments and institutions at the meetings. Turning this into a real opportunity to present alternatives and to expand the policy dialogue has been more difficult. It is here that the lack of a common agenda or proposal is a problem.

Mobilizing Moments

In this section we describe different kinds of actions that use different political moments to mobilize constituents and capture the attention of decisionmakers.

During Elections

Elections are an ideal time for mobilizing because parties and candidates are competing for votes, and the voters are looking for infor-

mation. The power of the vote can be the ultimate leverage citizens have over decisionmakers — the power to remove them from office. Additionally, the vote provides organizing opportunities where people's collective interests can influence the election process. For example, you can involve constituents in the following actions:

Voter education and "get out the vote"
Constituents can choose the issues that are most important in selecting parties and candidates, and they can organize voter participation around those key issues. The example on the next page is from South Africa, where the Tshwaranang Legal Advocacy Centre produced a local government elections brochure to educate citizens about what local governments need to do to end violence against women.

Referenda
In some countries, it is possible to place an issue on the ballot so that citizens can vote directly on policy questions. This is, for example, common at the state level in the US. You can use this method even when it is not part of the formal political process. Citizens can run a voting campaign parallel to the

Reflections on Mobilizing

No mobilization is perfect. Naomi Klein responded to the criticisms about global economic protests in the following way:

"Maybe the protests in Seattle and Washington look unfocused because they were not demonstrations of one movement at all but rather convergences of many smaller ones, each with its sights trained on a specific multinational corporation . . . a particular industry (like agribusiness) or a new trade initiative (like the Free Trade Area of the Americas). These smaller, targeted movements are clearly part of a common cause: They share a belief that the disparate problems with which they are wrestling all derive from global deregulation, an agenda that is concentrating power and wealth into fewer and fewer hands. Of course, there are disagreements—about the role of the nation-state . . . about the speed with which change should occur. But within most of these miniature movements, there is an emerging consensus that building community-based decision-making power—whether through unions, neighborhoods, farms . . .— is essential to countering the might of multinational corporations."

Klein, Naomi, "The Vision Thing", The Nation, July 10, 2000.

VIOLENCE AGAINST WOMEN AND LOCAL GOVERNMENT: STEPS TO END VIOLENCE AGAINST WOMEN

1. What is violence against women? Did you know. . .?

- Violence is any act or threat that causes physical, psychological or emotional harm to women or men.
- Violence against women takes different forms including sexual violence (rape — forced sexual intercourse, sexual harassment — unwanted sexual acts in the work place)
- Domestic violence (violence in the home) is: sexual abuse; physical abuse — slapping, kicking, punching; emotional abuse — intimidation, name calling, etc.; and femicide — killing of women by husbands or boyfriends.

2. What can we do to address violence against women at local government level? Did you know . . .?

Through citizen participation, individually and collectively, we can make our communities safe from all forms of violence? Some examples of how we can address violence against women include:

Participation — By registering and voting in local government elections. Ensuring that the political party you vote for has specific programmes that address violence against women.

Information — By obtaining and sharing information about what local government services impact on addressing violence against women.

Monitoring — By attending regular public meetings to ensure that political parties /councilors carry out programmes on violence against women. By writing letters to newspapers to inform others in community if councilors are not fulfilling their obligations.

Reporting — By reporting all cases of sexual, domestic or femicide to police and at community policing forums. Joining or supporting women's organisations that offer services to abused women. Examples include volunteering your time for counseling, assisting in fundraising for shelters for abused women. Setting up Neighborhood Watch in your street to monitor any criminal activity.

3. Which local government services address the problem of violence against women? Did you know.. .?

The following local government services or functions can address violence against women in communities:

Street Lighting: Police reports show that women are more likely to be raped by strangers in areas with poor lighting. To prevent rape and other crimes like mugging and assault, communities need to ensure that all streets have adequate lighting. ACTION: Report faulty lights to municipality. Where lighting is not sufficient, make request for adequate lighting to municipality.

Public transport buses and trains: The problematic nature of public transport system places women in a vulnerable position by creating an unsafe environment. Police reports and research show that women are often raped, assaulted or mugged in deserted taxi, bus or train station. ACTION: Report unreliable bus or train services to transportation department. Draft petitions calling for speedy regulation of the taxi industry. Challenge bus and train price increases if these are not matched with improved services.

Housing: Council houses and flats. The lack of alternative housing or accommodation (e.g., safe houses or shelters) is often one of the reasons why women stay in abusive relationships. Shelters are limited and supported by non-government organizations. ACTION: Communities should ensure that women (single or married) with children are given first preference or priority for council housing. Communities should support local shelters and provide accommodation for women who choose to leave abusive relationship.

Municipal Health Clinics: Health services offered by some municipal clinics do not provide service for sexual and domestic violence. Counseling, a mental and emotional health service is often not provided by clinics. Counseling, of raped and abused women, can assist mental and physical healing. Clinics often claim that there are no financial resources to provide counseling. ACTION: Individuals can volunteer their time to providing counseling at municipal clinics, (provided that they are trained as counselors).

Parks: Rape (and other forms of sexual abuse) by strangers can take place in deserted areas like parks at night. ACTION: Communities need to monitor parks and ensure that parks are locked at certain times. Communities need to embark on awareness programmes of public safety and rape.

From brochure by Tshwaranang Legal Advocacy Centre, South Africa

PLANNING ADVOCACY

elections where they ask voters to register their views on a specific topic. In this way, you take advantage of the run-up to the elections to gain support for your issues.

Create an issue platform

Worldwide, citizens have developed issue platforms to educate voters and candidates. There are many examples of environmental platforms, fair trade platforms, health platforms, etc. In several African countries, women have spelled out their priority demands through the creation of a "Women's Platform." The platform is used to educate voters, candidates, and parties and assess which candidates and parties to support. A platform can be used to pressure parties to improve their own platform on your issues. (See the example from Benin in Chapter 8 and the example from Botswana in the box below.)

Electoral scorecard

A fun way of educating voters is by grading candidates and parties through a standard school report card. In some places, a giant report card has been presented in a public forum to challenge candidates on their position. The example on the next page is from South Africa.

For an in-depth look at another example of outreach and mobilization during an election, see the case study from the Philippines at the end of this chapter.

During Policy Review

Policy can be made at the local, district, state, regional, or national level depending on the form of government. Often constituents relate more to their local council than to the national legislature. Further, many countries are decentralizing government, giving local governments increased power. However, while local policymaking may be more directly accessible, local governments often have narrow mandates, few resources, and can be parochial and prejudiced. In some cases, lack of clear procedures and technical know-how com-

The "Women's Manifesto"

In Botswana, the day before the political parties were to announce their platforms for the 1994 elections, Emang Basadi, a national women's group, announced the "Women's Manifesto" at a public ceremony attended by advocates and press. The 20-page document described eight priority issue areas affecting women. These issues came out of community consultations and dialogue with women's groups, NGOs, political leaders, government, and activists. The Manifesto was later used in voter education programs to measure candidates and political parties against criteria that included commitment to gender equality, women's rights, and social justice.

Women from various political parties, women's NGOs, Emang Basadi members, marching to the district commissioner's office to present the first copy of the Women's Manifesto (2nd Edition) to be sent to the President of Botswana July 1999.

From *Together For Change: The Botswana Consultation*, African-American Institute - Emang Basadi-UNIFEM, 1995
Photo from Keboitse Machananga, Emang Basadi

Example Report Card: The United Democratic Movement (UDM)

A coalition of South African women's groups issued the following report card on one political party's local election platform. The party in question, United Democratic Movement (UDM), received a failing grade on gender and women's issues.

Evaluation: F [Failing]
"The UDM's Local Government Manifesto: 'We Care and Deliver', claims to be a better plan for the future. The manifesto promises free water for 'deprived areas,' 'access to electricity' in rural areas, and basic services, safe streets and reasonable rates in urban areas. Included in the party's urban issues is 'proper schooling' although this is a provincial and national government function. The party also promises 'respect for traditional leadership' in rural areas. The manifesto does not clarify what the party means by this and does not take into account the problematic nature of many traditional beliefs with regard to women's equality. This omission is of concern to anyone with a gender perspective. In a document titled *Local government in Crisis, Innovative Solutions: the UDM Approach* the party further explains its local government policy. The party states its mission as 'uniting communities at the local sphere of government by stimulating and creating a stable and orderly environment for growth and development, the rendering of equitable, sustainable and cost-effective services and eradicate poverty and imbalances in communities. This will be achieved through optimal consultation and co-operation with all stakeholders without bias to either the rural or urban areas and in consultation with traditional leaders where they exist.' This document does not talk about women, women's issues or gender. All references made to the role of the mayor are made in gender specific terms – male of course, while references to the voter are made as 'he/she'. . . we might be accused of nit-picking, but if a party can't even get the language right when it costs nothing and doesn't require any real action – what can we expect from them as our representatives?"

pound the problems. On the other hand, the fact that decisionmaking may not yet be entrenched at the local level can create openings for citizens.

Creation of a citizen's advisory group
The creation of a citizens' advisory group on an issue under policy debate provides an opportunity to articulate issues and propose solutions. In some cases the group may be officially sanctioned and provide formal input. But even when it is not, it can play a role educating the public and policymakers. When the advisory body includes regular citizens – for example consisting of a domestic worker, a rural farmer, a doctor and a businessperson – it demonstrates a broad base of support. Experience shows that citizen groups also need to be vigilant when joining government-sponsored bodies to avoid wasting scarce time and resources on an effort that will not affect decisions.

Hearings
In some countries, governments have provided opportunities for NGOs and grassroots groups to participate in hearings on the content of legislation. Even if your government does not do this, a mock hearing can be organized to imitate an official one. Mock hearings can be entertaining for the media and the public when they take a humorous jab at the proceedings and behavior of leaders. In India, citizens groups have used public hearings successfully to challenge corrupt officials. Key elements of successful hearings include: time (the longer the hearing, the less likely the press will remain throughout), who testifies, and topic (testimonies should be brief, interesting, and delivered by someone tied to the issue).

Citizen policy juries
Citizens' juries engage people in making judgments that feed directly into policy. Although the details differ, the basic approach involves a

government or sponsoring agency and 10 to 20 citizens randomly selected to consider a policy matter. The citizens are given information, resources, and time to reach their own conclusions. In some places, the selection process ensures a diversity of perspectives. Like legal juries, the jurors are expected to come up with a common position about what the government should do about an issue. In the UK, citizens' juries have debated such diverse issues as education policy and decency in television. In Scotland, citizens' juries were complemented by "stakeholder juries," made up of representatives from agencies able to take action on the citizens' recommendation. The process can be empowering for citizens and for policymakers, as well as produce better policy.[1]

Town meeting

A town meeting typically brings together citizens with political leaders from a community to discuss problems. The gathering can be called by citizens' groups or by officials, but should always involve some decisionmakers with power over the solution. In the meeting, citizens ask questions, make demands, or propose solutions. A town meeting can attract good media coverage.

International Events

The same strategies mentioned above, such as citizens' juries and hearings, can be adapted for international events.

UN conferences

In Chapter 11, we describe how different UN conferences have become moments for citizens' groups to combine mobilization with lobbying (see page 200). A strategy of parallel NGO fora has now been institutionalized for UN conferences that enable the official discussions to take into account NGO views. A number of NGO representatives have also gained official status to observe, and sometimes participate in, their country's delegation.

International policy meetings

In the last fifteen years, activists have used the occasion of World Bank, International Monetary Fund, G-8, and World Trade Organization meetings to mobilize and influence these institutions. Groups have used policy research and parallel citizens' fora to get the attention of key leaders and the public. The growing frustration by advocates with the institutions' lack of responsiveness have sometimes escalated into widespread protests. See "Activism In the Economic Sphere" on page 271.

Visits by international VIPs

Most governments and corporations like to present a good front for Very Important Persons (VIPs) visiting from other countries. These VIP visits are usually covered by the press and thus provide a great opportunity to get attention for an innovative program or a social issue that is the subject of advocacy.

Other Citizen Events for Key Moments

Accountability session[2]

This is a community meeting held for the purpose of holding public officials accountable. An accountability session requires a high turnout of people and a carefully presented list of specific demands, such as legislation, funding, reparations, ser-

vices, etc. In Nicaragua during the 1980s, the government held gatherings called Face the People (*Cara Al Pueblo*), where government leaders listened to citizen complaints and demands and made commitments for follow-up. Government-initiated accountability sessions are increasingly used in Brazil and Bolivia where citizen participation is mandated by law.

Ideally, a citizen-initiated accountability session convinces policymakers to agree to take measures to address your problems. Events should be professional and serious, but should also be fun. Ideally, they should end with a clear decision on further action.

You can adapt the following *Checklist for Holding an Accountability Session* to plan your own actions.

You said that we'd have street lights in November. Well, it's now May and we still don't have them!

Accountability session

PLANNING ADVOCACY

___ Are your key leaders on the planning committee?

___ Have you used the strategy chart (see pg. 171) to plan the accountability session, taking into account your power?

___ Do you have main demands (usually substantive), a list of demands, and some fallback demands (usually procedural)?

___ Are the proposed date and time for the accountability session suitable for your constituency?

___ Have you confirmed the date and time with the target?

___ Do you have an appropriate site that is accessible, centrally located, and equipped to handle your needs?

___ Have you made a realistic "turnout" plan? Are there enough people assigned to work on "turnout"? (Turnout refers to the number of people who will come to the event.)

___ Is there a good press plan? Have you arranged for the:

    ___ Initial press release

    ___ Follow-up calls to media

    ___ Press packets at the session

    ___ Visuals for photographing

    ___ Press table and person staffing it

    ___ Special area for television crews

    ___ Post-session press release

    ___ Calls to press people who did not attend

    ___ Thanking press people who covered the session

___ Does the agenda demonstrate power over the target and give your leadership visible roles?

___ Does the agenda include the following components:

    ___ Welcome and purpose

    ___ Opening prayer, song, or words that inspire

    ___ Community residents speaking

    ___ Collection

    ___ Demands and target's response

    ___ Summary statement

    ___ Adjournment

___ Have you taken care of logistics? Have you arranged for:

    ___ Refreshments

    ___ Room set-up

    ___ Room decorations (posters, banners)

    ___ Music or entertainment

    ___ Baskets or buckets for collecting money

    ___ Words for chants or songs

    ___ Demands scoreboard

    ___ Audiovisual equipment

    ___ Microphones

    ___ Extension cords

    ___ Sign-in sheets and sign-in table

    ___ Room clean-up

___ Will you provide child care? Is there a good room available?

___ Are there carpools or transportation arrangements available?

___ Do you have a dress rehearsal schedule?

___ Is someone assigned to greet the target as she or he enters the building?

___ Are your key leaders and staff assigned to the following roles?

    ___ Chair (leader)

    ___ Chair's messenger (leader or staff)

    ___ Scorekeeper (leader)

    ___ Chair's organizer (leader or staff)

    ___ General organizer (leader or staff)

    ___ Target greeter (leader)

    ___ Press contact (leader or staff)

    ___ Press spokesperson/s (leader)

    ___ Speakers on the program (leaders)

___ Have you recruited other volunteers and emerging leaders for the following roles:

    ___ Ushers

    ___ Microphone holder

    ___ Person with the sign-in sheets

    ___ Person to distribute handouts

    ___ People to collect money

    ___ Refreshment servers

    ___ Music or entertainment fill-ins

    ___ Child care

    ___ Applause and audience participation starters

___ Does your follow-up include:

    ___ Sending a confirmation letter to the target

    ___ Sending thank you notes to everyone who helped

    ___ Celebrating key people

    ___ Checking attendance lists against those who said they would come and/or deliver people

    ___ Meeting with the planning committee to evaluate the session

    ___ Adding names, addresses, numbers from attendance list to your potential membership and fundraising lists

PLANNING ADVOCACY

From *Organizing for Social Change: A Manual for Activists* in the 1990s, Midwest Academy, 225 West Ohio, Suite 250, Chicago, Illinois 60610, p. 67.

Public information meetings

A public information meeting focuses on one issue. With enough publicity, and if the problem is widespread, you can attract many people. It is important to prepare a list of demands before the meeting and be sure to have accurate facts, quotes, etc. The information should be presented simply and concisely.

Citizen evaluations

Similar to citizens' hearings, this involves a meeting to evaluate a government policy or program. It allows for people to express their views and make proposals. A simple house-to-house survey before the meeting can recruit people to attend the meeting and give some insight into people's concerns.

Petitions

Gathering signatures provides opportunities for constituents to meet each other, talk about issues, and gain a sense of support. Petition drives can be followed by a town meeting or accountability session to publicize and dramatize the support for your cause.

Awards and Booby Prizes

Inventing awards for particularly good or bad behavior can be a fun way to educate people and attract media attention. For example, the Peruvian NGO, Centro de la Mujer Peruana Flora Tristán, developed two media awards. "*Fem TV*" was for the best commercial presenting women in positive roles. "*Sapo* (toad) *TV*" was for the worst commercial presenting women in degrading roles. One publicity firm that received the "*Sapo TV*" award was so concerned by the negative publicity that they made a different kind of commercial and a few years later received the "*Fem TV*" award.

Rallies, marches, and vigils

In many countries of the world, grassroots constituents participate in advocacy through street marches, rallies, or vigils. When organizing such events, there are several things to consider:

- Are there opportunities for participants to do more than simply walk or stand with others? Are there ways in which they can

The power of numbers

play a more active role, for example by speaking or organizing?

- What are the political risks involved in a mass-based event? Is it legal?

Large numbers of people chanting, marching, or holding candles can draw the attention of decisionmakers and the general public. However, if you overuse mass gatherings, they may not be taken seriously. Some important ways to enhance their impact include:

- Get enough supporters to make a visual impact. A poor showing suggests that you do not have support.

- Have a clear purpose and message. Everyone involved should have a basic understanding of what the issue is and what is being proposed.

Activism in the Economic Sphere

In response to growing poverty and the gap between haves and have nots that have accompanied economic globalization and liberalization, citizens' groups are focusing their advocacy more on international corporations, investment groups, and economic policymaking. Economic issues at the forefront of advocacy include consumer rights, agricul-

tural productivity, food security, environmental degradation, workers rights and labor conditions, and the unregulated movement of factories, jobs, and financial investments that contribute to boom and bust instability in poorer countries in the world.

The economic sphere offers many strategic moments for mobilization, including investors meetings, CEO retreats, stockholder meetings, meetings of the international economic and trade policy groups, and others.

In some cases, people are mobilizing around consumer rights. For example, groups are taking action against corporate mishandling of healthcare services, labeling of food, genetic engineering, and poor quality products. These activists argue that governments are not regulating the market sufficiently, thus forcing citizens to use their power as consumers to persuade corporations to be more socially responsible. Local and international boycotts, media campaigns, protests, pressure on CEOs and Boards of Directors, monitoring labor conditions, and educating venture capital institutions are among the strategies being used. See the examples from student and peasant organizing efforts in the following two boxes.

PLANNING ADVOCACY

Student Alliance to Reform Corporations and United Students Against Sweatshops

There are two well-organized national student groups based in the US that are focused on corporate responsibility: Student Alliance to Reform Corporations (STARC) and United Students Against Sweatshops (USAS). USAS was founded in 1998 and has stopped many universities from buying sweatshop-produced apparel for sports teams and campus shops. USAS has chapters at more than 160 campuses in the United States and Canada. STARC was officially launched in 2000. It has a database of about 2,000 members and a presence at 130 schools. STARC's projects include pressuring colleges to invest in socially responsible companies. Both STARC and USAS harness students' power as consumers and investors to influence corporate policy. They have used the Internet for posting information and training packs, fact sheets, and logistical information to facilitate their nationwide organizing efforts.

Summarized from http://ns.rds.org.hn/via/

Via Campesina

Via Campesina is an international movement that coordinates the global advocacy of peasant organizations, agricultural workers, rural women, and indigenous communities from Asia, Africa, America, and Europe. It was constituted as a world organization in 1993 and works on issues such as food sovereignty, agrarian reform, credit and external debt, technology, women's participation, and rural development. The primary objective of Via Campesina is to develop solidarity among members in order to promote economic equality and social justice.

Via Campesina is very creative in how it mobilizes constituents around the world to participate in campaigns. For example, Via Campesina organizations from India, Brazil, Colombia, and Western Europe participated with more than 450 farmers in an international caravan that passed through 12 European countries to make their demands known through protests in front of the head offices of transnationals. Via Campesina's mobilization around the WTO meeting in Seattle in 1999 included:

- planting a tree in a city park to symbolize the peaceful struggle for a healthy environment;
- organizing a demonstration in front of a fast food restaurant to protest the use of transgenics and hormoned meat;
- a gathering in front of an alternative producers market to support fair and local markets, controlled by agricultural workers;
- participating in demonstrations and holding regular press conferences.

Summarized from http://ns.rds.org.hn/via/

Purpose

To assist groups in developing strategies for citizen mobilization.

> See Chapter 16 for tips on running meetings to plan and evaluate your action.

Process

(Time: 2 – 3 hours)

1. Using the questions below, design a mobilization plan. You must identify the what, why, who, where, and when of the action and weigh the potential risks and opportunities for your organization. If the action involves risks, specify how you will minimize them. The following questions review much of what was covered in the planning chapters and may help you design your mobilization plan.

   - What is our issue? Who does it affect and how? Do we need further research to find out more about it? (See the exercises and tools in Chapters 8 and 9 if you have not done this.)

   - What is our proposed solution?

   - Who is responsible for the problem and what would we like them to do?

   - Which government agency or department deals with this problem? Which official in that agency makes the decisions affecting this problem? Who are the other stakeholders? Who would oppose or support a solution? (See Chapters 10, 11, and 12.)

   - What can we do to get the attention of the relevant officials? What is the political risk involved in different options? Are there ways to lessen the risks? What can we accomplish by each of the different options?

   - What do we need to do to prepare for the action? How many people should be involved? Do we need resources?

   - What do we want to communicate and how? If it is a public event, who should speak for the group? What should they say? (See Chapter 13 on messages and media.)

   - What are the different tasks and who will be responsible for each task?

   The following chart on large paper can assist planning and coordinating.

Mobilization Goals/Objectives:			
TASK	**WHEN**	**WHERE**	**WHO**

2. If your plan involves public speaking, practice first until the speakers are confident. Then carry out the plan. Does everyone know his and her responsibility and role?

3. After your action, evaluate. What impact did your activity have? Did we achieve our goal? What did we learn from planning and carrying out the activity? Next steps?

Adapted from *Organizing for Social Change: A Manual for Activists in the 1990s* by Bobo, K., J. Kendall, and S. Max. Midwest Academy, 1991.

PLANNING ADVOCACY

Introduction

Founded in 1987, the Democratic Socialist Women of the Philippines (DSWP) is a national federation of community-based women's organizations scattered across nine regions of the Philippines. DSWP's members are drawn from the marginalized communities of Philippine society – peasants, workers in the formal and informal sectors, youth, urban poor, fisherfolk, indigenous peoples, and Muslims. DSWP's objectives are:

- to fight against all forms of discrimination against women;
- to promote a form of development that recognizes the role that women can and do play;
- to raise women's level of consciousness, self-confidence, and economic independence;
- to increase women's participation in all levels of decision-making;
- to work together with other women's and mixed organizations to promote common goals and objectives.

Electoral Advocacy: Constituency-Building for the Party List Law

As in many other countries, marginalized groups in the Philippines have been excluded from effective political participation. To address this problem, organizations pressed the Filipino legislature to enact a law that would guarantee fuller representation of these groups in Congress. In 1995, the Party List System Act was signed, and in 1998 it was implemented for the first time. The law reserved 20% (52 seats) of the total number of seats in the House of Representatives for organizations and new political parties which get at least 2% of the total votes cast at the national level. Women were among the sectors identified as eligible for representation under the law.

DSWP followed the debates and process related to the Party List Law closely. They held meetings with other mass and rural-based organizations to both critique the law and explore how it could benefit them. In these meetings, initially grassroots leaders were concerned about how they could play a role in the organizations that had already decided to participate in the elections. The women were concerned about the background, composition, and track record of these groups, and challenged their commitment to grassroots women.

Finally, DSWP decided to organize BABAYI, a national alliance of grassroots, community, and sector-based women's organizations involved in political issues. DSWP reached this decision together with several rural-based groups outside of the federation when it became clear that all other women's party list groups were dominated by middle-class, educated, or elite women. The grassroots leaders wanted an organization that would not treat them as mere supporters. They wanted to be active participants and play a role in decisionmaking for the party. They felt this would not be possible in the other organizations. At the same time, they recognized that the Party List Law presented the possibility of expanding the concept of representative politics.

BABAYI was an experiment – it was an entirely new experience in the history of Philippine politics. There was a range of inevitable difficulties which women confronted pragmatically. These included:

- lack of financial resources;
- lack of political or electoral experience;
- lack of connections with national political figures or the media;
- lack of public recognition.

These difficulties were compounded by the fact that the electorate hardly knew the Party List Law existed, and many disadvantaged sectors were skeptical about the value of elections.

There were, however, also strengths to balance these difficulties. The major strength was the idealism of the women which motivated them to work hard and dedicate scarce resources to BABAYI. They were uncompromising in their opposition to exclusive politics and committed to creating a more inclusive type of politics.

Unlike other party list groups, BABAYI had a built-in constituency at the national level. Enormous effort went to gaining the support and participation of thousands of other rural-based women's organizations. Eventually, BABAYI had more than 3,000 local women's groups – poor women's organizations – as its members.

Another difference from other women's party list groups was the manner in which BABAYI selected nominees for its House of Representatives list. BABAYI ensured that there was geographic and sectoral diversity. BABAYI's list of nominees was the only one that included ordinary women.

BABAYI ran its campaign on the basis of women's ideals of what politics should be. BABAYI's positions, even on controversial issues, were never compromised, even if it meant antagonizing some people and losing votes. The campaign was seen as a rare moment when the public was inclined to listen to poor women.

BABAYI developed and publicized its legislative agenda as well as informational materials on the party list law. It established core groups at the village level and engaged people through local meetings, forums, women's rallies, and house-to-house campaigning. It also carried out election and post-election monitoring.

These electoral efforts led to:

- A better understanding among DSWP members as well as other rural-based groups of the concept of "authentic" politics and the importance of women's participation in politics.

- An increase in the number of women, and specifically community-based women, who ran for local office. More than 260 DSWP local leaders ran and won in the 1997 barangay (village) elections.

- Accreditation for BABAYI by the official agency for party list elections as a grassroots, women-led national alliance. The campaign period was used to do consciousness-raising on women's issues and advocacy for laws and policies for women.

- A significant number of local women's groups are represented on the Local Special Bodies in many areas of the country.

- Aconstructive relationship between DSWP chapters and local government units (LGUs) in many areas. It is now common for LGU officials to consult women's organizations in their areas about LGU programs.

- An increased interest in women's issues by LGU officials. DSWP members find that sometimes the LGUs are not opposed to women's issues, but they may not know what to do.

Since the elections, the DSWP has been involved in lobbying for more gender-sensitive legislation and policies. To this end, DSWP has conducted advocacy training and has lobbied for electoral reforms, improved legislation and services for women workers, and bills on sexual harassment and rape.

Challenges and More Challenges

Despite some important advances, DSWP's approach to advocacy is not without its weaknesses and problems.

The holistic approach is time-consuming and entails a lot of human, material, and financial resources. Although the federation has many leaders who are committed to working for it on a voluntary basis, because of the nature of DSWP's membership, the federation does not have enough leaders with technical skills and expertise. DSWP will have to invest more resources into technical capacity-building.

Material and financial resources are always scarce. The federation cannot depend on its membership for all of the material and financial resources it needs for its work. The DSWP needs to find ways of raising funds that make the work sustainable.

Attempting to work on several problems is also taxing, time- and resource- consuming, and overwhelming. At times other groups perceive DSWP as lacking focus because of its involvement in so many issues. Nevertheless, the federation needs to keep abreast of what is happening on all fronts to meet the interests and needs of its members.

Attempting to influence men – even the "progressive" ones – can be frustrating. While men may accept the importance of women's issues at the ideological level, translating this into concrete action, especially in their organizational and personal lives, is a different matter.

PLANNING ADVOCACY

DSWP's use of participatory approaches sometimes prevents quick action. This is especially true with respect to more controversial issues, which require thorough discussion.

DSWP Insights from Doing Advocacy

For advocacy to be effective, a holistic approach is critical, particularly if the advocacy is to get the direct involvement of the women it aims to serve. Some of the lessons are:

Organizing and constituency building is a must. To be effective, advocacy on women's issues must be supported by a critical mass. Ordinary women must not only understand the issues, they must own them. This means that poor women's issues must be at the forefront of the advocacy. If this is so, community women and women's groups will *lead*, and not simply support, the advocacy.

Public education is essential. Advocacy success depends on support from the broader public. This demands information and education. Use of the media is indispensable because it reaches all corners of the country.

The participatory approach needs to be balanced with outputs. While participatory methodologies are critical to ensuring that women steer the advocacy process, advocates equally need to be able to respond quickly to specific situations. This is especially true for legislative advocacy, which needs to be closely synchronized with the legislative process. To this end, constituencies need to give lobbyists a mandate to maneuver quickly. Constituencies must agree on a minimum and maximum position to define the parameters of negotiation.

National means the whole nation. National level advocacy must be truly national. Activities must not be concentrated in the urban areas. When advocacy does not have a meaningful base across the country, it is easily dismissed by decisionmakers as the actions of a few noisy, urban troublemakers.

Negotiating skills are a must. Negotiations inevitably happen at some stage in successful advocacy. The advocates need to be armed with negotiating skills, a clear grasp of the issue at hand, a clear position, and the data necessary to back up that position. Tact and articulateness are important qualities. Women advocates need to assess when being "irritating" can work for the advocacy and when it can harm it. Advocates must keep in mind that there will be future advocacy campaigns, so they must avoid needlessly antagonizing people who are in a decisionmaking role.

Advocacy requires common sense. Doing advocacy can be frustrating. It brings the advocates eye-to-eye with the people and institutions who perpetuate the status quo. The idealism of advocates needs to be tempered with pragmatism. If one attempt at advocacy fails, there are always lessons to be learned. Advocates can try again and use other strategies to achieve their desired gains. The important thing is the recognition that advocacy is a never-ending task. As long as there are advocates with a desire for change, there will be advocacy.

Summarized from a case study written by Elizabeth Cunanan-Angsioco, National Chairperson, and Eva Cayanan, Educator, Democratic Socialist Women of the Philippines, for the Global Women in Politics Program of the Asia Foundation.

NOTES

[1] For a detailed description of the process and cases see *Citizens' juries: Reflections on the UK Experience*" by Clare Delap, in PLA Notes, #40, IIED, February 2001.

[2] See *Organizing for Social Change: A Manual for Activists in the 1990s*, Midwest Academy, 1991.

Maneuvering on the Inside: Lobbying and Negotiating

This chapter is about getting to the decision-making table and advancing your issue there. Your success at the table depends on your organizational strength and all your other advocacy activities, from defining your vision to constituency-building to media work. Engaging directly in discussions with decisionmakers is a part of all successful advocacy. Engagement also provides people with learning experiences about politics and power. This chapter includes tips and stories that cover:

- **Lobbying—Getting to and being persuasive at the table:** What you will need to do to articulate your issues, demands, and proposals effectively.

- **Negotiating—Advancing your issue:** How to present your position, bargain, deal with opposition, and manage the power plays that go on over and under the table.

Who Is a Lobbyist? Who Is a Negotiator?

Not all social justice activists make good lobbyists and negotiators. Everyone can learn the basic skills, but certain personal traits are also important. Lobbyists and negotiators need to be:

- good listeners;
- not easily upset or distracted;
- willing to let the other person talk and take the lead;
- persistent, but not pushy;
- able to think on their feet;
- able to faithfully represent the views of others while still being flexible;
- able to say, "I don't know";
- able to keep a sense of humor;
- able to identify concealed agendas;
- able to know when to retreat and try a new angle.

Heading to the Corridors of Power

As with so many other advocacy activities, to be effective in your lobbying and negotiation efforts you need:

- a clear issue including analysis of why it is a problem, who it hurts, what the social and economic costs, and realistic solutions are;

- specific policy demands and proposals;

- a map of power, including who is at the table, who is under the table, and who has influence on all these players;

- the legitimacy and clout that come from visibly representing a broad constituency, and diverse allies and interests;

- an analysis of the political and policy environment, the controversies surrounding your issue, and the political possibilities of your effort.

With these ingredients, you are ready to plan your lobbying and negotiation strategies. If your advocacy relies on a broad coalition, select your lobbyists and negotiators carefully. Lobbying and negotiation are challenging tasks. There is often a tension between representing the diverse people involved, and responding to opportunities as they arise in the fast-moving political arena. The individuals selected must remain true to their "pact" with allies and constituents.

Planning for lobbying and negotiation should not only involve the lobbyists and negotiators. Lobbying and negotiation depend on all of the different groups and individuals that move advocacy forward. Lobbyists and negotiators will need information and preparation to be ready for the unpredictable and to feel more confident when addressing people in decision-making and influential positions. As they get closer to power, the pace is fast and there is little margin for error. It is critical to make a good impression with every encounter. A broad base of support and a strong organization are both key to the lobbyist's ability to convince decisionmakers.

Lobbying: Getting to the Table

Lobbying involves direct one-on-one communication with decisionmakers and others who have influence on decisionmakers. It is aimed at educating and convincing them to support and advance your agenda. The primary targets of lobbying are the people with the power to influence a policy change on your issue.

The term "lobbying" comes from the word "lobby" which refers to an entrance area or meeting place. In the case of advocacy, it refers to conversations and meetings where people get access to and seek to persuade those in power.

Lobbying can occur either:

- formally, through visits to and briefings of decisionmakers and others;
- informally, through conversations in corridors, restaurants, parking lots, etc. as decisionmakers go about their daily lives, or at events that are not directly related to your advocacy.

There are four key steps, discussed below, which will help your lobbying advance to serious negotiation. They are:

1. *familiarize yourself with the corridors of power,* the system, procedures, timelines, and key leaders and players;

2. *classify the players* on the basis of where they stand on your issue and how much influence they have either as key decisionmakers themselves, or in persuading others (such as civil servants);

3. *inform and build relationships* through visits and briefings to help them understand your issues and to gain their trust in you as both a reliable source of quality analysis and as a representative of people's voices;

4. *get attention and show your power* by timing your media, outreach, and mobilization activities in such a way that decisionmakers are aware of the support behind your proposals.

STEP 1: Familiarize Yourself with the Corridors of Power

You can begin by reviewing your analysis from the tools in Chapter 11 (*Finding Policy Hooks*) and Chapter 12 (*Forces, Friends, and Foes*). You may need to deepen this analysis by researching the rules, processes, committees, and people that are most important to your issue. The rules are both written and unwritten. Remember that things seldom happen as they are supposed to—that includes the timing of debate and policy approval as well as the shifting positions of different actors.

Familiarizing yourself with the corridors of power involves figuring out how best to maneuver the maze. The frustrating part is that the maze always seems to change. In addition, different political systems present a different configuration of actors and possibilities. We discuss tips for getting to know presidential and parliamentary systems in the box on the next page. However, the situation will differ according to a country's particular political context and culture.

Knowing the Players

In a Presidential System

Players are found in the legislature and the executive (see Chapter 11). To get to know the legislative players, it is important to:

Know the leadership of the majority and minority parties, their socioeconomic and geographic origins, education, party and religious affiliation, organization linkages, positions on issues, and voting records.

Study the committee system and its leadership. Congressional committees are legislative work groups engaged in research and oversight. They also decide the fate of legislation. Committee chairs have a lot of influence because they set the agenda. Some committees have more power than others. For example, the Rules Committee is responsible for deciding which bills are heard and in what order. The Appropriations Committee reviews all legislation with a budget component. Identify which committees, chairs, and members are concerned about your issue.

Get to know congressional staffers. In many countries, legislators do not have staff support. But where they do, these staffmembers are often gatekeepers to their bosses. In some countries, they are policy experts who work on the nitty-gritty of legislation. In these situations, it can be useful to focus on the staffers working for the most powerful players related to your issue.

On the Executive side, you should:

Know the President's agenda to determine whether your issue is part of his or her priorities, or whether he or she will oppose it.

Identify the ministries and departments that have jurisdiction over your issue. In many countries, the Ministry of Finance is a big player. Sectoral ministries have a lot of control over programs and funding allocations in their sectors. Determine their positions and interests regarding your issue.

In a Parliamentary System

In contrast to the presidential system, committees cannot alter bills that are referred to them. They can only recommend changes that will be accepted or rejected by the ruling government. But when a bill hits the floor, the debate is a source of information about who's who and what they think. It is also a place to get your issues heard through the words of supportive decisionmakers. Members of parliament rarely have legislative staff. They usually carry out their own research, but also rely heavily on their political parties for guidance.

In a parliamentary system, it is crucial to understand the ruling party's plan. Often political parties, ministries and the Prime Minister's cabinet are important targets for lobbying.

Political Parties

In both systems, it is crucial to know the thinking, leadership, and dynamics of the dominant political parties. If the political system has many minor parties that could form an alliance on your issue, then you must get to know them too. Once you know the platform, key positions, and leadership structure of the parties, your lobbying can hone in on the influential people.

Other Arenas and Players

Similar information gathering is necessary to prepare to lobby decisionmakers at the international level in UN fora, and in bodies such as the World Trade Organization and World Bank. You can find the formal structures and leaders through the Internet. Much more time will be necessary to find out about the unwritten rules and hidden agendas of the different actors and to determine who potential allies are.

For corporate lobbying, the same kind of profiling is necessary regarding the Chief Executive Officers, lead advisors, boards, and key shareholders.

Adapted from *Navigating and Mastering the Policy Arena: A Manual*, Dr. Socorro Reyes, Center for Legislative Development, Philippines, 1999.

DOING ADVOCACY

STEP 2: Classify the Players

This classification process described here deepens the analysis gleaned from the Power Map on page 219 and the discussion about allies, opponents, and targets in Chapter 12. Both informal (under the table) and formal (at the table) decisionmakers need to be lobbied. At this stage, it helps to classify players according to:

• where they stand on your issue;

• how much power they have to influence the target (key decisionmaker) and others.

Some activists also distinguish between decisionmakers and pressuremakers. *Pressuremakers* have the power to pressure decisionmakers, other opinion leaders, and public opinion, although they do not have formal decisionmaking power. Some international examples include prominent figures such as the Pope and Nelson Mandela. Every national and international policymaking arena has its own pressuremakers. These people need to be taken into consideration as you classify the players related to your advocacy.

Ranking decisionmakers

Advocates sometimes rank decisionmakers using numbers from 1 to 5 as follows:

#1. definite supporter of your advocacy proposal

#2. potential supporter

#3. fence sitter

#4. likely opponent

#5. definite opponent

If your lobbying strategy involves a vote in a policymaking body, it is important to estimate votes and then focus your lobbying on those who are most likely to be won over (those

---

Politicians Are Not Always the Best Focus for Lobbying: Lessons from Budget Advocacy

Usually discussions of lobbying mainly focus on the ins and outs of lobbying elected politicians, such as parliamentarians. When you are lobbying around budget issues, elected politicians may not be the only or the best target.

In most countries, the national parliament has relatively little decisionmaking power over budgets, although local elected bodies sometimes have more power. In many countries the national parliament must either accept the budget as presented or reject it completely. They cannot make smaller changes such as shifting money from line item or sector to another. Total rejection of the budget calls the whole political setup into question, and most parliaments will try to avoid this.

If this is the situation in your country, and you are lobbying on a budget issue, it might be better to target a civil servant working on the issues you are concerned about and responsible for developing budgets. Civil servants often deny that they have much power—they say they are just carrying out instructions. This is not usually true. Often civil servants are the source of new policy ideas or policy changes. Even more often, they determine the detail of how policies are implemented and what budgets look like.

Many of the principles of lobbying remain the same whether you are lobbying elected politicians or civil servants. But there are some differences. In particular, with civil servants it often helps to make your arguments more technical. Civil servants work on a daily basis with the policies and programs. They know all the details and will have all the excuses for not making changes. If you can show them that you also know the details, they will find it less easy to wrap the wool around your eyes.

Debbie Budlender, *Women's Budget Initiative*, South Africa, 2001

ranked as #2s or #3s), drawing on the firm support of your #1s.

STEP 3: Inform and Build Relationships

Lobbying requires a series of formal and informal one-on-one contacts with decisionmakers, and a steady stream of concise backup information. Over time, you may want to establish yourself as a resource for policymakers working on relevant issues. To establish a good relationship, lobbyists advise not to approach a decisionmaker solely when you need something. Combine one-on-one visits with briefings, mailings, and invitations to general events your group may be organizing. We offer some advice on how to do these below.

Although it may not be possible due to distance and cost, one-on-one visits can be extremely effective. Personal time helps establish familiarity. Personal visits can be complemented with visits by small groups. A group of constituents affected by the issue can often make a convincing case, particularly if they are voters in the geographic area the decisionmaker represents. Constituents acting as lobbyists can be as powerful at the international level as they are at the national and local levels. Often, international policymakers are detached from the problems people face, and directly hearing the voices of people affected is persuasive. Sometimes, it helps to include supportive researchers and analysts who can complement the stories of constituents with facts and figures. Group visits require preparation to coordinate roles and statements of each member of the group.

Feel confident. As a citizen, you have the right to voice your opinion. You do not have to be an expert. You just need to know what you want and what people in power can do on your issue.

Tips for a lobbying visit

Here are some general tips for lobbying compiled from activists and advocacy manuals from the United States.[1] You can adapt them to your particular context.

Rehearse difficult questions and responses. using a timer (no more than five minutes each). For group meetings, plan who will open up the discussion, who will speak when, and who will answer what kinds of questions.

Introduce yourself. If you are alone, introduce yourself. If you represent a group, give a one sentence description of the group. If members belong to different organizations, indicate their affiliation. There is usually no time for personal introductions unless you have someone well-known in the group.

Express appreciation. If possible, praise the decisionmaker for past support. Also, thank him or her for making time to see you.

Be personal, when possible. Try to relate what you are saying to something the decisionmaker has done or said. You may also want to congratulate him or her on a recent occurrence, such as the birth of a child, an appointment, etc.

Make it clear that you are willing to help with information and support. Mention relevant briefings, reports, or additional information that you or others plan to produce.

Be prepared for a conversation. Be prepared to present your "talking points" (see box on next page), but remember that the decisionmaker may want to have a conversation rather than hear a presentation. Pausing between the points will allow for discussion.

DOING ADVOCACY

Talking Points

In a 5–15 minute discussion, be prepared to say what you have to say simply and clearly. You can review Chapter 13 about message development to help you think through your message. The brief statement, or talking points, that you include in a conversation with a decisionmaker usually covers four main categories of information:

1. what the issue is, and what the social, political, and economic costs are;
2. who or what is primarily responsible;
3. what your concrete policy demands and proposals are;
4. what the decisionmaker can do to help, and how might it be worth his or her while to do so.

The talking points should be presented slowly, pausing to see whether the person with whom you are speaking has a question or comment. A slightly longer version of no more than two pages should be left behind after the visit. It should have your contact information and a short description of your organization.

But try to make all of your points before the meeting ends. Listen carefully to pick up on words that give you clues about the decisionmaker's interests and positions.

Do not avoid controversial topics, but remain calm.
Debate, but avoid being combative. Provide clear and succinct answers to questions. If you do not know the answer, say you will get back to the decisionmaker with the necessary information after the meeting.

Try to get a commitment from the decision-maker.
If you want the decisionmaker to support or oppose a piece of legislation, policy, or event, try to get a firm answer. If she or he seems to be avoiding taking a stand, you can ask directly, "So, can we count on your important support/opposition for . . . ?"

Leave information about your efforts.
Offer brochures or fact sheets on your organization and work for future reference. Stress that you would be happy to provide additional information.

After you leave, make notes and evaluate your visit with colleagues.
Make sure that you share all of the details, including the language used, with your co-advocates. Your lobbying visits provide important information about power and politics.

Send a thank you note.

Briefings[2]
A good way to educate policymakers and bureaucrats about your issue is to hold periodic briefings for them or their staff. Briefings usually feature experts talking about the latest information on your issue and its importance.

- Have handouts so that policy people can read them at their leisure or pass them on to their staff. Short fact sheets are especially good.

- Have participants sign in before the briefing so you can send thank you notes to everyone who attended and build a list of interested people.

- Follow up with a phone call to ask if they need more information or to request a meeting to discuss your efforts in depth.

Guidance on Briefing Sessions: International Planned Parenthood Federation

The International Planned Parenthood Federation (IPPF) offers the following guidance for activists interested in lobbying for a family planning youth clinic. IPPF suggests that a briefing session on this topic with local policymakers include the following elements:

- describe, with statistics and anecdotes, why you believe such a clinic is needed;
- invite an expert familiar with youth clinics to explain their work;
- list the organizations and individuals you have consulted, such as social workers, teachers, parent groups;
- outline your plans and how you will evaluate the clinic's achievements;
- display the materials (pamphlets, posters, videos, etc.) that will be available;
- introduce the staff who will be directly involved, and identify those who will be available for further information;
- provide a fact sheet as well as a briefing kit with fuller information and samples of the educational materials;
- reassure policymakers that you will keep them in touch with all developments, and invite them to the official opening.

From the International Planned Parenthood Federation, Western Hemisphere Region. *Advocacy Guide*, 1994.

Letters[3]

When you are unable to meet face-to-face with policymakers, letters can be a good way to communicate your position. The following guidelines may help draft one.

- Be brief and to the point. State why you are writing in the first sentence.

- Be personal. Include an anecdote about your issue.

- Provide a convincing rationale for why the policymaker should support your issue and why it is important for you, your community, and your country that s/he support it.

- Include a brief description of your organization and indicate how many people are involved in your advocacy effort.

- Tailor your arguments to the policymaker's personal background and interests.

- If you are unhappy about something the policymaker did or said, do not antagonize or threaten, but be clear that you are not pleased and why.

- Do not shy away from controversial topics. Provide arguments for your position without apologies.

- Provide examples of how the policy you want the policymaker to support has already worked previously or elsewhere.

- Offer to provide the policymaker with additional information.

DOING ADVOCACY

Purpose

To help participants understand what it takes to plan, prepare for, and do lobbying.

Process

(Time: 1½–2 hours)

1. Divide participants into two groups. Instruct the first group to develop a role play of the planning and actual lobbying at a formal visit to a decisionmaker. The role play should include how the advocates set up the meeting, and how they decided what to say and who would say what.

2. Ask the second group to role play the planning for and lobbying of a decisionmaker as he or she walks to a meeting.

3. Give each group five minutes to act out its role plays. After the presentations, ask participants to comment.

Discussion

- Was there adequate planning for the lobbying? If not, what other preparation should have been done?

- What were the two most challenging aspects of the lobbying encounter?

- Was different preparation needed for the formal than for the informal lobbying?

- What was effective about the visit? What needed to be changed?

General Tips for Lobbyists

- Treat staff members like the policymaker.
- Pop in to say hello; get to know personal interests and drop off related information.
- Remember there are no permanent friends and no permanent enemies.
- Dress and present yourself in a way that shows respect.
- Remember that you are there to establish a long-term relationship for the next advocacy battle too.
- Do not denounce anyone until you are absolutely sure he or she will never support you on anything.

Purpose

To help groups craft an argument and understand policy debates and political differences from people's and government's perspective.

Process

(Time: 1 ½ hours)

1. Distribute the following case study and read through it as a group.

The Grootboom Case – The Right to Shelter

In South Africa, socioeconomic rights are written into the Constitution and bill of rights. In particular, the Constitution says that every person has a right of access to adequate housing and protection against arbitrary evictions and demolitions. The Constitution says that government must "respect, protect, promote and fulfill" the rights in the bill of rights. In terms of fulfilling, the Constitution recognizes that this will take time and money. It says that the government "must take reasonable legislative and other measures, within its available resources, to achieve the progressive realization" of the rights.

Rights for children are even stronger than those for adults. The Constitution says that children have an absolute right to basic nutrition, shelter, basic health care services, and social services. These rights do not depend on government's resources.

The Grootboom case was one of the first cases to test government's responsibility to protect the socioeconomic rights of citizens. The case started when about 900 adults and children (one of whom was named Grootboom) from the Wallacedene area of Cape Town said that the government had a duty to provide them with adequate temporary shelter or housing. The case first went to the High Court.

The Facts

The applicants had lived in Wallacedene for many years. They moved onto vacant private land to have better living conditions. After moving, they were evicted from the land by the owner. The municipality wanted to buy the land and assisted the owner with the eviction. After eviction, the applicants could not return to Wallacedene as their previous shacks were now occupied by new residents. Further, during the eviction, the materials they had used to build their shacks were destroyed by employees of the sheriff and the police. The people were left without any shelter or housing materials.

The people camped on a sportsfield next to the community centre. They asked for, and won, a temporary court order. The order said that all the children and one parent for each child who needed supervision must be given accommodation in the Wallacedene Community Hall.

In their application for a final court order, the *people* argued:

- The government must provide them with temporary shelter as part of their right of access to adequate housing and children's right to shelter.
- This was the government's minimum duty while it took steps to progressively realize their full right to adequate housing.

The *government* said:

- The government has policies and plans in place to realize these rights, but these do not include a right to temporary shelter.
- The government does not have the money to provide temporary shelter.
- The applicants have no right to "jump the queue" for housing assistance.
- Children's shelter rights in the constitution mean a place of safety—not housing that includes the family.

The *High Court* ordered government:

- To provide the children with shelter until the parents are able to provide shelter for their children.
- Also to provide the parents of the children with shelter, as this is in the "best interests" of the children.
- To present reports to the Court on the steps they had taken to implement the order within three months from the date of the court order. The Court said that the minimum kind of shelter includes tents, portable latrines, and a regular supply of water.

The *Court* also said that:

- The group of people who brought the case must have an opportunity to comment on the proposals made by the government on how to provide shelter.

The Court said that to win a case against government on these socioeconomic rights, applicants must prove that government is not implementing a "rational" or "good faith" program which will help to advance the realization of the rights concerned. The Court said that to win the case, the government must present "clear evidence that a rational housing program has been initiated at all levels of government in the context of the scarce financial resources."

The government was not happy with the judgment and took it on appeal to the Constitutional Court. What budget and other arguments would you use in arguing before the Constitutional Court if you were representing (a) the government and (b) the community?

2. Divide participants into two groups—one representing the community and the other the government. Ask each group to choose one member to be its legal representative in the court. The groups must then develop the arguments that their representatives would present to a courtroom. Give the groups 20–30 minutes preparation time.

3. When the participants are ready, each group role plays the Constitutional Court process, with the facilitator playing the role of the Constitutional Court president. Each side has a chance to present its case. Groups then have a short time to caucus, after which they give a five minute response to the case put forward by the other side.

4. After both responses, ask all participants to vote, as judges, for the stronger argument. Remind participants that they must vote on the basis of the arguments, and not on the basis of their emotions or values. (Note: in reality, decisionmaking is never free of values and emotions.)

Discussion

Facilitate a plenary discussion in which participants discuss their experience of the debate and the strengths and weaknesses of how each side presented its case. Also explore what it felt like to play each role and what lessons the exercise offers for lobbyists.

Source: Debbie Budlender, Women's Budget Initiative, South Africa, 2001.
The case is also described in *Circle of Rights: Economic, Social and Cultural Rights Activism: A Training Resource* by the International Human Rights Internship Program and Asian Forum for Human Rights and Development, 2000.

Step 4: Get Attention by Showing Strength

In order to persuade decisionmakers, usually visits, briefings, and letters need to be complemented by other strategies that demonstrate your organizational power.

Letter-writing campaigns [4]

One way to get the attention of policymakers is to bombard them with letters from your supporters—the more letters, the better. Letter-writing campaigns are coordinated efforts to deliver handwritten, personal letters to decisionmakers urging support of an issue.

Avoid form letters. Each separate letter, while emphasizing the same issues, should be individually expressed. Personal letters are taken very seriously by many elected officials, especially when they are accompanied by petitions of signatures.

If you are trying to set up a meeting with a decisionmaker, get your supporters to start sending letters a few weeks before the meeting. When you attend the meeting, bring your petitions to show the breadth of support.

Other ways to get the attention of decisionmakers

In the previous chapter, we describe ways that citizens have mobilized to get the attention of decisionmakers. Here are some additional tips for getting attention:

Show the power behind your demands.
Ways of doing this include:

- petitions with thousands of names of supporters;
- statements of support from opinion leaders;
- a large turnout by your supporters at a key event.

Be creative.
In countries where opportunities to influence policies have recently emerged, advocacy efforts are often overly serious. Advocacy *is* serious, but if you want to win the public's and media's attention, do something imaginative. In some countries, it may be too risky or culturally unacceptable, but humor or a dramatic action can often be the most persuasive tool in your advocacy.

A signature campaign dramatizes the number of signatories

DOING ADVOCACY

Advice for Getting to the Negotiating Table

Your lobbying should bring you closer to the negotiating table. The following advice from an international activist reminds us of all the different elements that make reaching the table possible.

"In order to achieve your goals, the work done before getting to the negotiating table is as important as what takes place at the table. In our work in the International Campaign to Ban Landmines, perhaps the key element of success of our ban movement has been the close and effective partnership between NGOs, governments, the International Committee of the Red Cross, and UN agencies at both the strategic and tactical levels. NGOs have been full partners in the ban process, actively involved in drafting language of the Mine Ban Treaty, as well as formulating strategies for its success. But in order to get to that partnership, the NGO movement was built on the following:

1. The ability to provide to governments and the entire international community expertise on the issues involved and credible documentation to back up the expertise;

2. The ability to articulate our goals and messages clearly and simply;

3. The ability to maintain a flexible coalition structure—inclusive and diverse—while still managing to speak with one voice on our issues;

4. The ability to recognize that most coalitions operate based on the extensive work of a committed and dedicated few, supported by the many;

5. The ability to communicate key developments to members of the coalition itself as well as to governments and other agencies involved in the issue;

6. The ability to organize a strong power base—expertise in an issue itself does not necessarily translate into expertise in forming a coalition and moving it forward; it is critical to recognize the difference and use individual skills appropriately;

7. The ability to formulate action plans with deadlines—and always follow up so that the goals of the action plans are achieved, building momentum and excitement."

Jody Williams, International Campaign to Ban Landmines and Nobel Prize Laureate, reflections, 2001.

Organizing for Social Change gives some examples of creative approaches. In one case, advocates used an enormous thermometer to demonstrate that "people are really hot about this issue." In another case, advocates offered a decisionmaker a glass of polluted water to show that not even he would drink it.

Shocking actions can also be powerful. In Kenya, mothers protesting the political detention of their sons resisted a police round-up by disrobing, using a cultural taboo against seeing older women naked as their defense.

Use personal contacts to reach a decision-maker.
Often personal contact can break through red tape. As you plan your lobbying activities, find out whether anyone in your group knows someone close to the target and use these connections to open doors.

Negotiation: Advancing Your Issue

Negotiation does not only occur when groups sit down at the decisionmaking table. It is a constant feature of work within organizations, constituencies, and coalitions. However, in this chapter we focus on negotiating with public and corporate decisionmakers. In Chapter 17 we turn our attention to negotiation within advocacy organizations.

Different Approaches to Negotiation

Negotiation can be defined as a process to resolve conflicts when someone else controls what you want. Through the give and take of negotiation, groups try to agree on a solution that both sides can live with. The process involves bargaining, good communication, an understanding of the relative power and interests of all stakeholders, and a willingness to dialogue and compromise.

Negotiation theory[5]

The theory and practice of negotiation has been shaped by the world of business, trade, and labor disputes, on the one hand, and by public disputes and peace initiatives, on the other. One popular approach to negotiation emphasizes win-win strategies. However, there are many kinds of conflicts around the world where compromise of any kind is very difficult, if not impossible, especially in the short run.

Conflict has become a common feature of countries in political transition. It is not surprising that conflict emerges as the political space opens up. Differences (ethnicity, race, religion, etc.) and resentments (historic exclusion or abuse) emerge that have long been repressed by tight controls and fear. Sometimes they erupt violently, and this violence only heightens when measures are not taken to validate and discuss festering disagreements or injustices. Some of these conflicts are familiar to social justice advocates because they are the

---

Constructive Confrontation

"Unlike those who seek resolution for the sake of resolution, we seek justice, fairness, good decisions, and good solutions. Sometimes this means working to resolve a conflict, while sometimes it means continuing the conflict, but doing so in a more constructive way.

One goal of constructive confrontation is to help disputants develop a clear understanding of the dimensions of the problem—both from their own perspective and from their opponents'. A second goal of constructive confrontation is to enable people to separate the core conflict from the complicating factors—the unnecessary and confounding aspects of the conflict that divert attention from the core issues.

[Another] goal is the development of a conflict strategy (which may or may not be a resolution strategy) that will best serve the party's interests.

Since it is almost always in the interest of both parties to act in a way which limits destructive outcomes (e.g., violence, escalating hatred, and distrust) this strategy seldom makes a conflict worse, and it usually encourages constructive results—improved relationships, better understanding of the issues from all points of view, and a better understanding of the confrontation and resolution options and the likely results of both. Thus, the strategies usually work to the advantages of both sides. They are unlikely, however, to go far enough to resolve the conflict.

The ultimate goal is the constructive transformation of conflictual relationships. Such a transformation allows individuals, organizations, and the society as a whole to realize the benefits of conflict. "

Consortium on Conflict Resolution, University of Colorado (For more information on intractable conflicts, see the Consortium of Conflict Resolution's online course dealing with power and strategies of constructive confrontation. www.colorado.edu/conflict/peace), 2001.

DOING ADVOCACY

product of discrimination, severe power imbalances, and disparities in wealth.

A group of conflict resolution experts[6] describe these as *intractable conflicts* and classify three different types. These are disputes where:

- there are major differences in values and religious beliefs, such as abortion and other women's rights issues;

- the dispute involves distribution of resources, such as land ownership, housing, economic policies, etc.

- there are questions of domination, i.e., who has more power, wealth and status in society.

With intractable conflicts, those involved need to go beyond traditional compromise-oriented negotiation approaches to address serious power imbalances in order to lay the foundation for a lasting solution. Empowerment strategies that help people to analyze and voice their issues and organize around solutions, for example, can help to make the playing field more level and increase the possibility for a settlement. This approach is grounded in the view that some conflicts are long term and difficult to solve. They must be mutually understood and validated and, ultimately, transformed into constructive confrontation (see box on the previous page) or engagement. A key tool for this approach is a conflict map which is used by the interested parties to identify actors, interests, positions, and relative power. These maps are similar to the one described in this Guide in Chapter 12.

> "The people in the village . . . first asked, 'shall we build a new hotel?' Some said yes, some said no and the battle was joined. They began to make progress when they backed off and posed the problem as 'what is the best use of the vacant land?' and 'how do we provide accommodations for visitors?' . . . Whenever possible, an issue should be defined as a mutual problem to be solved . . ."[7]

Two negotiation strategies

In developing negotiation plans, the following two strategies can help you deal with the tensions and opportunities which negotiation produces.

Mini-Maxi

This strategy refers to what your group wants (the maxi) and the least it is willing to accept (the mini). To define your Mini-Maxi you must separate out all the elements of your proposed solution into negotiable pieces and rank them in order of importance. This gives you a range of options and sets a minimum floor for your bargaining.

BATNA (the Best Alternative To A Negotiated Agreement)[8]

This defines what your group is prepared to do if the negotiation process falls apart. It is your Plan B or trump card. It keeps you from feeling trapped into compromises that will not solve your issue.

Key Points for Developing a Negotiation Plan

- Conflicts are a mix of procedures (rules), relationships (people), and substance (information).
- To find a good solution, you must understand the problem.
- You need sufficient time to develop and implement a negotiation strategy.
- Besides solid information, there must be positive working relationships.

    "Although accurate and consistent data are needed to understand complex public issues, data alone will not resolve them. Information is of little value unless people are able to use it to solve a problem. Parties in a dispute must be willing to exchange information, make agreements and keep their word. But people who are caught up in the dynamics of conflict reach a point where they stop talking with each other. . . . Sooner or later the parties must start to trust each other if commitments are to be made and solutions found."

- Negotiation begins with a constructive definition of the problem.

    "The parties must agree on what the problem is before they start resolving it. It is important to avoid using a problem statement that can be answered with a yes or a no."

- Parties should help design the solution.
- Lasting solutions are based on interests and needs, not positions.

    "Traditionally, each side in a negotiation takes a position knowing that it will not get all that it asks for. The positions become realities in themselves separate from the original issues. The positions, not the problem, determine the direction of the bargaining, especially if they have been stated publicly. . . . But positions are a poor foundation on which to build a successful resolution of differences, composed as they are of anxieties, resentments, desires, public pronouncements, face-saving, and playing to constituents. Positions limit the range of opportunities for solutions. . .

    "An alternative way to find solutions is to persuade the parties to disengage for a moment and do something that will be unfamiliar and even uncomfortable at first: talk with each other about their interests—what they need in an agreement for it to be acceptable. Focusing on interests forces contending parties to back off from their stated positions and perform a straightforward task—talking among themselves. When they talk about themselves, they lose their adversarial tone, and their opponents begin to understand why they have the positions they have. People in a dispute may have one position but many interests, some more important than others. The stand they take is often determined by a combination of motives rather than a single clear objective. . . . Most interests are reasonable and can be described."

- The process must be flexible.
- Think through what might go wrong.

From Carpenter and Kennedy, *Managing Public Disputes*. San Francisco: Jossey-Bass, 1988.

DOING ADVOCACY

Exercise: Negotiation Simulation

Purpose

- To help participants experience the dynamics of negotiation;
- To develop participants' ability to take a position, define their minimum and maximum agenda, and negotiate with other players.

Process

(Time: 2 hours)

Role plays are a quick way to become aware of the challenges of negotiation. This role play can be adapted for your real issue, where the actors represent the actual parties in the dispute.

1. Divide the participants into four groups with equal numbers of members representing:
   - Women activists (proponents of the bill)
   - Conservative women
   - Conservative legislators
   - Progressive legislators

2. Give each group a copy of the following situation. (If groups want to use an actual issue they are facing, this step is unnecessary.)

Eleven women's groups came together to form an advocacy coalition to advance their concerns through the law. The first issue in their advocacy agenda was violence against women and, more specifically, rape. They reviewed the existing law on rape, which was patterned after the Spanish Penal Code. The law: (a) classified rape as a private crime; (b) limited the definition of rape to penile penetration; and (c) did not explicitly recognize marital rape. After thorough research and consultation, the coalition drafted an Anti-Rape Bill which:

1. reclassified rape from a private to a public crime punishable by law;
2. expanded the definition of rape from penile penetration of the vagina to include the use of any object, instrument, or any part of the body;
3. made marital rape a punishable crime;
4. excluded the victim's sexual history as part of the evidence that the defense can use in court;
5. prohibited media disclosure of the identity of the victim and coverage of the trial; and
6. provided survivor victims of rape with medical, legal, financial, and counseling services.

The proposed bill triggered heated debates inside and outside the legislature. With a few exceptions, the men in Parliament opposed the bill. The women members were divided—some strongly supported the bill, others rejected it. The President endorsed the bill as a priority measure. Traditional and conservative women's groups found the bill too radical. Religious organizations were concerned that the bill would promote sexual promiscuity.

Case developed by Socorro Reyes, Center for Legislative Development, Philippines.

---

3. Ask each group to:
    - discuss the issues involved in the measure;
    - analyze the arguments for and against the bill;
    - define their interest and prepare their position;
    - prepare flyers and banners to support their position and post these around the room.

4. Bring the groups back together to report their positions and interests in plenary. Presentations should be made as if each group were promoting its position in a public rally.

5. Reconvene the four small groups to consider the positions and interests of the other groups in developing answers to the following:
    - What do we want? What is our minimum-maximum position on the bill?
    - What do others want? How can we change their positions?
    - How can we counter some of our opponents' arguments?

6. Mix the groups. Construct new groups, each of which contains a woman activist, conservative woman, conservative legislator, and progressive legislator. Each group must negotiate and come up with a final version of the bill.

Discussion

After 30 minutes, bring everyone back together in plenary to discuss the following questions:
- What was the process involved in deciding a minimum-maximum position in the small group?
- What happened in the mixed group?
- Whose interests were best reflected in the negotiated bill and why?
- What were some of the barriers to negotiation? After identifying these barriers, a discussion about the characteristics of public disputes and intractable conflicts can help to deepen the learning. Also the following tips can help in dealing with strong opposition.

Dealing With Strong Opposition

You will seldom win over everyone, so opposition is inevitable. Sometimes, the opposition may be loud and powerful. The following are some tips for dealing with opposition:
- In most cases, the best strategy is to avoid direct engagement with your opponents, especially if it will produce open hostility or danger. Strong disagreement inevitably stirs up strong emotions. There is nothing wrong with these feelings, but they may prevent you from reaching a large segment of the public or decisionmakers.
- Avoid getting defensive. Do not personally insult your opponents in public. Instead, challenge their assertions on the basis of facts.
- Develop clear, simple arguments to counter their arguments. Be straightforward about what your demands are and why. Avoid ideological judgements. You may want to place your argument and the opposition's side by side in an issue brief for decisionmakers to contrast the two positions easily.
- If your opponents bully you, you may want to tell the media about it.

Remember, sometimes your opponents discredit themselves by their words and actions without any effort on your part.

Doing Advocacy

Preparing for Negotiation

Successful negotiation requires a careful appraisal of where you stand and what you can do to improve your situation. Below are some steps to prepare yourself:

1. Take Stock: List the skills and experience you bring to the table. Often you will find hidden resources you are not using. Look at what makes you feel vulnerable. Then you can plan ahead to compensate. Ask yourself:

- What do you have that the other group wants or needs?
- What are the factors that have helped you succeed in past negotiations?
- What do you know about the other party and situation that you can use to influence them?
- In what areas are you vulnerable?

2. Learn as Much as You Can: Lack of information creates anxiety. Collect the facts that support your case, but also learn as much as you can about the other group and their circumstances.

- *Factual information:* With the facts on hand, you will not get unsettled or tense when you are asked questions or challenged. You can provide specific reasons why your proposal is valid and important.
- *Scouting information*: Find out about the people on the other side and the political environment in which you are both working. The tools discussed in Chapter 12 can be useful for this purpose. The information you gather will allow you to anticipate problems and increases your control over negotiations. Sometimes, the best way to prepare is by putting yourself in the other side's shoes.

3. Develop Alternatives: Use the information you acquire to formulate alternatives and assess what the other party will do. You can then better decide whether to make a deal or walk away. Understanding both sides' options provides you with a clearer idea of your cards and your possible moves.

- *Find a variety of ways to meet your needs.* When the other party believes that you have no options, he or she will usually compromise as little as possible.
- *What is the worst that can happen?* Your fallback position may be to let things remain as they are. If you cannot make a deal at least you will not lose anything.
- *Analyze the other party's alternatives.* When you know the other party's options and the constraints under which they are operating, you are less inclined to grab any offer they put on the table.

4. Get Fresh Perspectives: At times we get trapped in our own thinking. Talking to others whose judgment you trust often helps you see the situation in a new light.

Kolb, Deborah and Judith Williams, *The Shadow Negotiation: How Women Can Master the Hidden Agendas that Determine Bargaining Success*, 2000.

Engaging Your Counterpart[9]

It helps to develop as amenable a relationship as possible with your counterparts. By demonstrating an appreciation for their circumstances, feelings, and opinions, you increase your opportunities for action. Asking counterparts to expand on their ideas helps build relationships and also encourages them to reveal more information.

For an effective negotiation relationship, protect everyone's "face" and do not threaten another person's self-image. For example, when people back themselves into a corner, allow them to retreat. Otherwise they may dig in their heels and become entrenched in their positions. Find a way for them to retreat gracefully and without appearing weak.

Collaborative working relationships are a two-way street. They take time and energy to develop. However, not everyone has the personality to engage in a mutually respectful way. Also, the nature of the issue and balance of power may prevent productive interaction. In such cases, it is important to recognize when to back off and pursue other strategies.

> "As bargainers try to turn the discussion of the problem to their advantage . . . they size each other up, poking here and there to find out where the give (vulnerability) is. They test for flexibility, trying to gauge how strongly an individual feels about a certain point." [10]

Dirty Tricks and Calculated Moves

While effective advocacy depends on establishing basic levels of cooperation, the dynamics are not always straightforward. You may face a reluctant bargainer, or one who is unscrupulous. The manipulations in the shadow negotiations complicate the bargaining process, especially for traditionally marginalized groups. It is important for groups to recognize and understand how power plays and dirty tricks operate in order to develop ways of addressing them.

Shadow Negotiations and Other Lessons from Experience [11]

Negotiations work on two levels: 1) substance and 2) relationships. While people are negotiating over concrete issues, they are also conducting a less visible parallel negotiation on the terms of their relationship—how cooperative they are going to be, whose needs and interests will be more prominent, how power will operate. This "shadow negotiation" occurs below the surface and is often unrecognized.

Negotiators need to be aware of these shadow negotiations, because they affect the negotiations over substance. The impressions that

---

Negotiating on an Uneven Playing Field

All negotiations take place in a context of social values and unequal power where various forms of bias are often invisible factors. The way power is played out around gender in negotiation offers insights into how it also plays out along class, race, age, and other factors that define exclusion. As a result of subordination, women often are unaware of their own power. They therefore trip themselves up during negotiations in a variety of ways. These include:

Opportunities for negotiation are not recognized. They accept no for an answer, not seeing a negative response as just one point in an ongoing dance of give and take.

Seeing assertiveness as pushy, aggressive, and "not nice." Many women feel the pressure to be accommodating to others. These invisible norms of niceness constantly tell women to put the needs of others before their own. A need to smooth differences over can lead women to cede on points of negotiation.

Seeing only weaknesses; expecting to lose. Doubts affect the ability of women to negotiate and so become self-fulfilling prophecies.

Bargaining ourselves down. Self doubts lead many women to make concessions even before a negotiation has begun. Their starting point is then lower and the goals less ambitious.

Adapted from "Ways That Women Often Trip Themselves up in Negotiations" Kolb, ibid.

DOING ADVOCACY

groups create in the shadow process help determine how much negotiating room they have over issues. If an organization appears unprepared or in doubt over the legitimacy of their demands, they will have a difficult time convincing others. Groups need to be prepared not only to advance their interests, but also to block any effort to challenge their credibility.

Bullying Tactics

One of the toughest challenges in negotiation is when those in power belittle the demands of citizens groups. In some cases, they attempt to undermine the legitimacy of citizen concerns to prevent the negotiations from occurring. It is important for groups to know the kinds of bullying tactics they may face and to develop strategies to counter them. See the box *Tips for Shifting the Balance of Power in Negotiations* on the next page for ideas.

Sample Bullying Tactics

Here are common strategies used by some government and corporate leaders to stave off public inquiry and negotiation:

The Stonewall
Keep quiet, evade answering questions or conceal incriminating information.

The Whitewash
Use public relations tactics to minimize the negative impact of government or corporate actions; downplay people's concerns.

The Smokescreen
Hide the truth, raise doubts, form research organizations that claim to be independent in order to promote viewpoints as scientifically valid.

The False Front
Lobby under false pretenses—fund "independent" advocacy organizations to lobby public officials; as a legislator, support a bill knowing that it will be killed in committee.

The Block and Blame
Block action by blaming someone else for the problem.

The Slash and Burn
Attack citizen groups, brand them and their leaders as naïve, ignorant, troublemakers, or terrorists.

Susskind, Larry and Patrick Field. *Dealing with an Angry Public: The Mutual Gains Approach to Resolving Disputes.* New York: The Free Press, 1996.

Tips for Shifting the Balance of Power in Negotiations

These are some useful tips for creating a more even playing field when facing reluctant bargainers and "dirty tricks."

Hold out incentives so the other party sees you have something of value:
- make sure you have something the other person needs;
- make your value visible.

Step up the pressure to demonstrate the costs of not reaching a settlement:
- issue a credible threat (e.g., media exposure, protest, boycott, etc.);
- force a choice on the other party;
- make consequences tangible to the other person.

Establish your authority and credibility:
- secure an explicit mandate from your constituency;
- maintain the backing of your side;
- consider authorization from your constituency an ongoing activity.

Enlist support and show clout:
- use allies as intermediaries to get to the negotiating table;
- use allies as strategic partners to maximize resources and respect;
- use allies as sources of pressure to gain access and visibility.

Exercise control over the process:
- anticipate reactions of the other party;
- plant the seeds of your ideas by sharing information carefully and strategically;
- build support behind the scenes for your agenda by talking with their allies as well as your own.

The moves you make to address power differences generate reactions from the other party. Their counter moves will attempt to exploit your weaknesses or provoke you. They are intended to put you on the defensive and change the dynamics of the negotiation. Rather than ignoring them or counterattacking, redirect the other party's moves, as follows:

Interrupt the other's move:
- take a break;
- call a time-out;
- change the pace.

Correct the move:
- shift the focus to the positive;
- supply a legitimate motive;
- counter stereotyped images.

Name the move:
- reveal the move's ineffectiveness;
- expose the move's inappropriateness;
- highlight the move's unintended consequences;
- characterize the move as counterproductive.

Divert the move:
- look ahead, not to past mistakes;
- substitute a better idea;
- shift from the personal to the problem.

Source: Kolb and Williams, *The Shadow Negotiation: How Women Can Master the Hidden Agendas that Determine Bargaining Success*, 2000.

DOING ADVOCACY

NOTES

[1] *Advocacy for Social Justice: A Global Action Guide*, Oxfam and Advocacy Institute, 2001, and *Advocacy Guide*, International Planned Parenthood Federation, IPPF/WHR Regional Council, 1994.

[2] *Advocacy Guide*, International Planned Parenthood Federation, Western Hemisphere Region, 1994.

[3] Ibid.

[4] Bobo, Kim, Jackie Dendall, and Steve Max, *Organizing for Social Change: A Manual for Activists in the 1990s*, second edition. Midwest Academy, 1996.

[5] Miller, Valerie, "Understanding Conflict and Negotiation for Social Justice Advocacy and Citizen Participation", 2001, unpublished.

[6] University of Colorado/Consortium on Conflict Resolution: Heidi and Guy Burgess, codirectors (www.colorado.edu/conflict/peace).

[7] Ibid.

[8] Larry Susskind, Urban Policy and Planning Department, Massachusetts Institute for Technology.

[9] Kolb, Deborah and Judith Williams, *The Shadow Negotiation*, 2000.

[10] Ibid.

[11] Ibid.

16 Advocacy Leadership

Social justice advocacy depends on the support and involvement of many people. Consolidating and using this kind of citizen power depends on good leaders. There are many different leadership roles and tasks necessary for building advocacy, from community organizing and public speaking to running a meeting and lobbying. Some of these involve more visible and formal roles, while others are less visible and informal. All of them demand a wide array of skills and talents that are rarely found in a single person. That is why advocacy needs a range of different kinds of leaders in different roles. The one core element for all types of advocacy leaders is a clear understanding of and sensitivity to power dynamics in the personal, organizational, and policy arenas.

For example, leadership for advocacy can mean giving direction to actions and, when necessary, being able to recognize opportunities for changing direction. We discuss these assertive forms of leadership more in Chapter 15.

Another kind of advocacy leadership involves being able to communicate ideas and plans in a way that inspires, persuades, and informs. We discuss communication skills in Chapter 13 and in the Annex.

Advocacy leadership is also about facilitating the growth and leadership of others. Long-term commitment and participation in advocacy is sustained in part by giving people opportunities to try new things, develop new talents, gain confidence, and grow. We discuss this kind of leadership in more detail in Chapter 4 and in Part Two.

One of the most challenging yet important leadership tasks in advocacy is coordinating and managing the work of others. These special talents are what make organizations and advocacy initiatives successful. In this chapter, we focus on these kinds of leadership tasks and skills. We look especially at:

- leadership roles and styles;
- promoting teamwork and accountability;
- giving and receiving feedback.

Leadership Roles: Formal and Informal

Leadership is often defined in individual terms, yet leadership happens in relation to others. It is a collective process based on reciprocity and shared responsibility. In addition to *formal* leadership, there are also *informal* day-to-day acts of leadership that form the backbone of effective advocacy and strong organizations. Whether recognized or not, we all take on leadership roles at certain times. These roles range from providing ideas in small group discussions to developing budgets or holding colleagues accountable. The small acts of informal leadership and good teamwork help ensure effective action and build the next generation of leaders. So leadership is not just about the visible leaders of organizations, it is about all of us.

At the same time, formal and informal leadership tend to demand different kinds of qualities and skills that are found in different people. Certain individuals – often those who are more comfortable with decisionmaking or more experienced communicators – tend to be formal leaders, while others who work behind-the-scenes as facilitators tend to be informal leaders. Although advocacy depends on both types, the formal hierarchies that inevitably bring more recognition and affirmation to formal leaders present serious challenges, particularly for advocacy concerned with inclusion and generating alternative kinds of power.

Leadership and Shared Responsibility: "Affidamento" and Pacts

Helpful insights about leadership and organization have come from women's movements around the world.[1] For example, the commonly held assumption and myth that all women are equal (and therefore the same) can make women uncomfortable with leadership roles.

Such discomfort, whether on the part of leader or led, can paralyze action. Conflicts will inevitably arise in any organization. The all-are-equal problem makes conflict difficult to address since taking on leadership roles, no matter how consultative or participatory, is seen as a betrayal of principles of sisterhood, solidarity, and equality. A similar phenomenon occurs in people's movements and social justice work where people may be uncomfortable with hierarchies.

The other problem that comes from the denial of or discomfort with hierarchy is that some of these same leaders fail to recognize when their own behavior is domineering and exclusionary. Without alternative models of leadership, many NGO and grassroots leaders simply repeat the top-down pattern of traditional power and authority.

Lessons from women's movements emphasize synergy and diversity. Since individuals have different identities and strengths, they need

each other to advance their common concerns. Recognizing that women are not all equal, this approach allows women to deal with conflict, power, and hierarchy more realistically. It also allows them to assume roles as formal and informal leaders and use their differences to their advantage.

This perspective emphasizes the importance of mutual accountability. It is based on building trust and mechanisms of evaluation and on accepting differences in roles and certain forms of hierarchy. This new vision of leadership based on reciprocity and joint responsibility is also called "affidamento" by some activists.

"Affidamento" is a helpful concept for dealing with leadership and structures in advocacy. On the one hand, it acknowledges that some people will have major decisionmaking authority, especially to meet the fast-paced demands of changing circumstances so common in policy work. At the same time, "affidamento" stresses that effective decisionmaking and implementation are interwoven and require joint agreements on responsibilities. This interdependency demands a level of accountability and trust that is often implicit, but needs to be explicitly affirmed at different moments.

In the Framework for the Guide on page 74, there are two moments where leaders, organizers, and constituents affirm their pact of trust and accountability by discussing plans, next steps, risks, and responsibilities. The participatory planning processes described in Part Two are geared to forming these kinds of "pacts" of trust and accountability. We discuss the notion of political accountability and responsibility in organizations in more depth in Chapter 17.

Transformative Leadership

Transformative leadership is a relatively new term, but one that is important for social justice advocacy. It defines leadership in a context of more equitable relations of power and encompasses a vision of social change.

The Association for Women's Rights in Development (AWID) explored the idea of transformative leadership in its 1999 forum . They emphasized that this type of leadership "goes beyond putting women into formal positions of power."

> Feminist leadership is "*transformative* in the sense that it questions and challenges existing power structures; *inclusive* in the sense that it takes into account the views and fosters empowerment of the most marginalized and poorest groups of society; and *holistic* in the sense that it addresses all forms of social injustice. [It] can be practiced by both women and men, and as such, is more than just women's leadership."[2]

Developing Local Leaders

Building and strengthening grassroots leadership can be a long, in-depth process sometimes involving 10 to 15 years of working closely with people in skill-building, critical reflection, confidence, organizing, problem solving, and other forms of accompaniment. Rarely does leadership happen as a result of workshops alone. It involves a continual systematic process of examining and interacting with one's own community and context in ever changing ways. This process of change is both empowering and painful for leaders as they challenge themselves and the status quo in many aspects of life.

Outside organizers and NGOs often identify potential leaders through workshops or community projects where opportunities for prolonged conversation and familiarization exist. Leadership promise can be demonstrated through a variety of qualities and characteristics – anger and impatience in the face of injustice, optimism, confidence, commitment to honesty and action, a critical sense of one's own history and personality traits, a trust in people, and an ability to listen and inspire others. Poor women face additional challenges in becoming leaders because of their multiple work responsibilities in the family and outside the home, as well as social pressures to play traditional roles. Developing their leadership capacities usually requires more time and creative strategies to accommodate their schedules, needs, and constraints. Generally, leadership development is significantly different for men and women because they encounter and use power so differently.

Leadership development involves a combination of approaches from structured learning activities such as workshops, courses, and in-service training programs to more informal approaches, such as apprenticeships and accompaniment. Structured programs include a mix of topics – self-reflection and personal awareness; knowledge of laws, political systems, and human rights; and skills in facilitation, communication, team building, organizational development, planning, analysis, and persuasion. Grassroots organizers stress the importance of applying this learning to real life experiences and then analyzing those experiences to gain a deeper knowledge.

Some programs start with people telling their personal histories, analyzing those stories in the context of their community, neighborhood or village social structure, and then expanding the analysis to include provincial, national and global systems. They then structure learning around concrete efforts to solve local problems – from holding community meetings to meeting with government officials.

DOING ADVOCACY

Transformative leaders mobilize people in ways that encourage collaboration, respect, shared values and action. Transformative leaders know both how power and conflict work and how their own needs, aspirations and identities interact with those of others. They are active learners and listeners and create the space for others to learn, make decisions, and act. They accept certain responsibilities that come with being a leader, but recognize that success depends on engaging others as informed decisionmakers.

Who Is a Leader?

It should never be assumed that the apparent leaders in a group are the only, or ideal, leaders for advocacy. Sometimes leadership can emerge through the process of advocacy and is not immediately apparent in the first stages. One veteran citizen organizer from the US says that he listens for passion among the people who speak last. The clearer the anger about the issue, the more motivated the person will be to fight. He says the combination of anger and compassion makes leaders. His experience shows that leaders are rarely the people who speak up first.

Ernie Cortez, Industrial Areas Foundation, personal conversations.

Advocacy Leadership: Combining Styles and Approaches

There is no simple recipe for good leadership, but a few basic rules and skills help. Sometimes advocates are catapulted into leadership positions as the coordinators of organizations or coalitions due to their good communication skills and strategic, quick thinking. However, in some cases, they have no background in the basics of management, interpersonal communication, or organizational decisionmaking. So, making time for leaders to develop a full range of capacities is one important rule not to be overlooked.

Leaders involved in social justice advocacy balance contradictory demands. On the one hand, they are concerned about team building, participation and empowerment. On the other, the pace of politics and the scarcity of resources demand efficiency, quick decisions, and impact. While some tasks, like sustaining a shared vision and commitment, are continuous and common across advocacy efforts, different contexts call for different leadership approaches. The following examples illustrate four different kinds of leadership useful at different moments.

- **Facilitative** leadership encourages people to participate and pursue their own potential; leaders encourage others to assert themselves and have faith in their own judgment; they delegate responsibility.

- **Assertive** leadership gives direction, states positions, and helps others move toward agreements.

- **Supportive** leadership backs other people's positions, makes them feel validated, and maintains group cohesion;

- **Disruptive** leadership shakes people up and helps the group think critically, disagree, and challenge constructively.

With experience, leaders learn to match the appropriate approach to the right circumstances. This is crucial because using the wrong approach can cause divisive organizational misunderstanding and conflict. Not every leader has the capacity to use all of these approaches, but they learn to rely on others to complement their strengths.

How decisions are made within advocacy organizations and alliances is critical to their survival. Again, the tough balance between participation and clear lines of authority is important. While decisions about issue priorities and general strategies can and should be participatory, the implementation of strategies involves different roles and responsibilities. A leader needs to ensure that people fulfill their tasks and obligations while encouraging their creativity and initiative.

Some basic rules about what makes organizations work well can help. Organizations can thrive based on the extent a leader promotes:[3]

- *shared understanding,* by sustaining the vision and giving a group a sense of the "big picture," clarifying aims, and facilitating broad involvement in goal setting, problem analysis and strategic planning;

- *teamwork,* by helping individuals to join forces and to be part of a process where they feel a sense of belonging;

- *rewards,* by recognizing people's individual contributions and growth in tangible or intangible ways;

- *autonomy,* by delegating and respecting the ability of each individual to decide the best way to accomplish a task within some general guidelines;

- *accountability,* by clarifying responsibilities and establishing a process for feedback and evaluation; by demonstrating responsibility to a group through minimizing action without consultation unless absolutely necessary.

Effective leadership is also difficult because personal needs, anxieties, pressures, and backgrounds can get in the way. For example, if a person is very insecure, it is difficult to be a supportive leader. People assuming leadership positions need to understand their own personal experiences with subordination and find ways to address the negative impact this can have on their leadership style.

The exercises on the next few pages may help to stimulate reflection on these issues.

Participants for the Global Women in Politics Asia-Pacific Regional Advocacy Training of Trainers in Subic Bay, Philippines,

DOING ADVOCACY

Purpose

To help participants analyze different styles of leadership and identify some characteristics of effective leaders.

Process

(Time: 1½ hours)

Divide participants into small groups. Give each group one of the case studies below or your own. Ask them to develop their role play based on the case and to present the situation in a way that allows everyone to get a sense of the group dynamics. The aim is not to present answers to the problems, but rather to give an overview of the situation.

<table>
<tr><td>Tips for Facilitators</td></tr>
<tr><td>Talking about current leaders and their styles in a workshop can be difficult, especially if more than one person from an organization is present. Participants may be reluctant to talk frankly in case what they say gets back to the leader. There is also a risk of personalizing the issues in a way that makes objective analysis difficult. Using role plays can help people examine problems more dispassionately before analyzing leadership styles in their own organizations.</td></tr>
</table>

Discussion

After the groups present their role plays, the following questions can assist in analyzing the skits.

- Describe the types of leadership presented? What made the leadership effective or not?
- What were the differences and similarities among the leadership approaches?
- What are the strengths and weaknesses of the different approaches?
- What other leadership styles have you seen? In what kinds of circumstances?
- What kind of leadership is needed for social justice advocacy? What kind of skills and attitudes are required?

Case Examples of Leadership Styles[4]

Case 1: Thandiwe is chairperson of Paso Women's Rights Group. She is the founder and has been the chair for the entire seven years that the group has been in existence. At a meeting of all members and staff of the group, she explains that there are several tasks to be carried out. She calls out names of some members and assigns each one a task. She tells them what to do and how to do it. She also gives them the time within which the task should be completed. She warns several of the members not to mess up their tasks like they had done the last time. All the members are quiet throughout the meeting.

Toward the end of the meeting, Winnie puts her hand up. She explains that she was glad to have the task assigned to her but thought it could be carried out with better results in a different way. Thandiwe replies that she has been the leader of the organization for seven years and that is how they have always done the task.

She asks if there are any further questions. There are none. She walks out of the room. The members start complaining among themselves about the way they are treated.

Case 2: Falomo Development Association is an organization that seeks to raise the awareness of rights among women in Falomo. Mumo is the leader of the Association. She is very interested in democracy and participation of all members. At a recent meeting to plan activities for a six-month period, she asked for ideas. Sosi wanted the organization to conduct public meetings in all the districts of Falomo. Kuka preferred to publish a series of booklets and distribute them. Several other suggestions were given. Each contributor was so convinced that her idea was the only good one, Mumo did not know how to proceed. The meeting broke up. Neither Mumo nor the other members understood what was agreed upon.

Being an effective leader, especially one committed to building citizenship and empowerment, requires an understanding of one's own personal qualities and skills and relations with others. Providing people with opportunities to discuss leadership and identify their own leadership potential can help them recognize their own abilities and consider taking on new responsibilities.

Purpose

- To explore effective leadership and identify individual potential for leadership.
- To assist people in reflecting on their own strengths and weaknesses as leaders and in determining what aspects of their leadership could be improved.

Process

(Time: 1 hour)

1. Divide participants into small groups and ask them to brainstorm what qualities and skills an effective leader should have.

2. Ask the groups to report back on their lists in plenary, record their answers on newsprint, and then ask the group to add any that may be specific to leadership focused on advocacy and constituency building.

3. Give each participant five small stickers and ask them to prioritize the qualities and skills named in the list by placing a sticker next to the five they consider most important (small dot stickers work well).

3. In plenary, compare the lists and identify the top 10 qualities and skills.

4. Ask everyone to reflect on these different characteristics and write down some of their own strong points and some that need improvement or further development. Make a list of new skills and attitudes they feel they need to acquire.

5. In small groups, have everyone discuss one of their strengths and one of their weaknesses, as well as ways that they might improve or develop their qualities to become more effective leaders.

> For another version of this exercise see
> *From the Roots Up: Strengthening Organizational Capacity through Guided Self-Assessment*, World Neighbors 2000.

DOING ADVOCACY

Leadership and Teamwork

Effective organizations depend on strong leadership and teamwork. Promoting teamwork is an important responsibility of a leader. It requires self-knowledge and an understanding of our strengths and weaknesses in working with others. What motivates us? What are our core values? How have our life experiences shaped us? In the Appendix and in Chapter 7 you will find different exercises for self-exploration that can be adapted for leadership training and development. The following four questions can help you to examine how you work with others and can be used with the chart *Group Maintenance and Task Needs* in Chapter 17 (page 316) for a fuller discussion:

- How do I act in a group?
- What positive and negative roles do I play?
- How does my behavior contribute to group process, creativity, solidarity, and decisionmaking?
- What skills can I learn to help increase group effectiveness?

Tips for Promoting Teamwork

- Clarify roles, relationships, and responsibilities.
- Share leadership functions within the group and use all member resources.
- Tolerate uncertainty and a seeming lack of structure.
- Take interest in each member's achievements as well as those of the group.
- Remain open to change and creative problem solving.
- Be committed to focusing group communication while permitting disagreements.
- Promote constructive criticism and feedback.

A Note on Group Process

Frequently people in groups get so involved in *what* they are doing that they lose sight of *how* they are doing it. Similarly, people are often unaware of how their own behavior affects a situation. They are so busy trying to finish a task that they do not realize their behavior may be contributing to misunderstanding or conflict.

- Foster trust and commitment in the group.
- Encourage members to support and respect one another.[5]

The skills of listening and asking questions are key to good leadership. The chart *Types of Questions* on the next page provides examples that have been effective in promoting teamwork and problem-solving.

Productive Meetings

Meetings, meetings, meetings. They are a tedious but important part of effective advocacy. Knowing how to facilitate a productive meeting is a critical leadership skill. The following guidelines[6] provide some general rules.

1. Attend to the basics.
Prior to the meeting, check with those who will be presenting information to review their key points. Arrive early to ensure the room is set up appropriately. Start on time. Where appropriate, have participants introduce themselves.

2. Develop an agenda.
Prepare an agenda, including all unfinished points that emerged from the previous meeting if relevant. When possible, members should receive the agenda in advance of the meeting. If you do not have an agenda beforehand, the group can spend 5 - 10 minutes at the beginning of the meeting to draft one on newsprint so that everyone can see it.

Types of Questions for Promoting Teamwork		
This chart provides a typology of questions that can help promote teamwork and problem-solving		
TYPES	**PURPOSE**	**EXAMPLES**
Factual	To get information To open discussion	What, where, why, when, who, and how?
Explanatory	To get reasons and explanations To broaden discussion To solicit additional information	In what way would this help solve the problem? What other aspects of this should be considered? Exactly how would this be done?
Justifying	To challenge old ideas To develop new ideas To get reasoning	Why do you think so? What other ways are there to think about this? What evidence do you have? How do you know?
Leading	To introduce new ideas To advance a suggestion of your own to others	Could this be a possible solution? Would this be a feasible alternative?
Hypothetical	To develop new ideas To suggest a possibility, unpopular idea, or change in the course of the discussion	What would happen if we did it this way? Another group does this. . . Is this feasible here?
Alternative	To make a choice between alternatives To get agreement	Which of these solutions seems best, A or B?
Coordinating	To develop consensus To get agreement To take action	Can we agree that this is the next step? Is there general agreement on this plan? If this is so, then what do we need to move forward on this?

Adapted from *Working Together*, by Bob Biagi, Amherst, MA: Citizen Involvement Training Project, 1978.

Agendas should include the topics to be discussed and can also include the reasons the issues are included, the presenters, and approximate time limits for discussion. It may help to indicate which items require a decision.

3. Follow the flow.
Meetings usually start with an acknowledgment of new participants, taking attendance, and reviewing the agenda. You may want to read minutes from the last meeting and review action items from the prior meeting. Agenda items should be discussed in order, and the meeting should conclude with a decision on the priorities, time, and place for the next meeting.

4. Use a facilitator.
Meetings tend to run more smoothly when they are coordinated by a facilitator or chairperson who keeps the discussions focused, prevents anyone from dominating, encourages participation from everyone, summarizes key points and seeks clarification on confusing ones, and brings discussions to an end. In a network, this role can be rotated among members.

At certain times, an outside facilitator may be more appropriate, for example when a coalition is dealing with an issue that may produce conflict.

DOING ADVOCACY

5. Keep a written record.

At each meeting, notes should be taken regarding attendance, key items discussed, the main points raised, all decisions made, and topics to be addressed in the future. The record should include who has agreed to take responsibility for what and the timeline for doing things. A written record can serve as an accountability mechanism that allows a group to review decisions and fulfillment of obligations. In a network that has no secretariat, note-taking can be rotated.

6. Celebrate personal and organizational achievements.

When appropriate, include a time during meetings to recognize individual and organizational achievements. This can be useful for building the team and sustaining energy. Some groups also include an inspirational moment in their meetings, like a song, poem, prayer, poignant story, or funny anecdote.

7. Draft the next meeting's agenda.

At the conclusion of each meeting, list items that need to be included in the next meeting and clarify, if necessary, who will develop the complete agenda.

8. Evaluate the meeting.

End by reviewing the process and progress of the meeting. In some cases, groups assign process observers at the beginning of a session. These observers watch the dynamics of the meeting and report briefly at its conclusion. Other groups use an open-ended approach. Feedback should include discussion of helpful and unhelpful behaviors and suggestions for improving the process and achievements.

Feedback

Getting and giving feedback is an important leadership task. Feedback about performance and behavior helps us learn more about our-

Celebrate accomplishments

selves, change unhelpful behavior, and increase group effectiveness. Each of us has blind spots about ourselves – good and bad. Feedback allows others to help us identify them. Since feedback can touch on personal issues, it is important to handle negative issues sensitively.

There are direct and indirect ways to get feedback.[7] For example, observation provides indirect feedback – are people staring out the window as we speak? Do they leave the room early when we are leading meetings? Do groups implement plans that we design with them? But, observation can also be misleading. A person staring out the window may appear bored, when in fact she is simply worried about something. Asking others for their opinions provides more reliable feedback as long as people are prepared to be open and direct, even with negative information. This varies significantly from culture to culture.

The following are tips for giving and receiving feedback. Groups should determine which of these are appropriate to their own cultural contexts and adapt them accordingly.

Tips for Giving Feedback[8]

- Give feedback in a climate of trust.

- Provide feedback when a person wants it. Feedback can be offered but never forced.

- Speak in the first person. "I felt. . . or "When I heard you say. . ." In this way, you do not claim to represent everyone.

- Present negative feedback as your own problem and explain how it affected you personally. "I felt disrespected when you interrupted me and wouldn't let me finish my comments."

- Provide feedback on people's behavior, not their motivation.

- Give feedback about both positive as well as unhelpful behaviors. For example, if someone sounds condescending in one part of a presentation but is engaging at another time, speak about the positive style, tone or body language.

Facilitator's Tip on Feedback

One way to practice principles of feedback is to have people review the tips on feedback and then ask for volunteers who want to practice their skills. The volunteer can choose the people from whom they want to receive feedback.

The following questions can guide the process:
- What do I appreciate or find helpful about your participation and behavior in the group?
- What do I find difficult or unhelpful about your behavior or participation?
- What would I like to ask of you so that your participation and teamwork is more effective?

To start off, the facilitator might say, "I like the way you are always willing to volunteer for jobs that need to be done." Ask those providing feedback to start with helpful behaviors. After three or four people have given feedback, move on to the next volunteer and repeat the process.

Ask people what was difficult about this experience as 1) a giver of feedback and 2) a receiver of feedback. Ask them what they found easy or useful.

See *Training for Transformation* Volume II, London: IT Publications, revised version 1995.

- Give feedback only about behaviors that can be changed.

- Ask questions that clarify reasons for behavior or action. For example, "Why did you decide to do. . .? In this way you credit people with judgment and validate critical thinking.

- Acknowledge your connection to the problem. For example, statements such as, "This is helpful for us/me to think about because. . ." allow people to understand they are not alone.

- When possible, suggest alternative responses. For example, "Have you thought about. . . ."

Tips for Receiving Feedback

- Direct your own feedback. Whether in a group or one-on-one setting, ask people directly what has been helpful and unhelpful about your behavior.

- Listen carefully to comments. Try not to get defensive or explain away behavior that people find unhelpful. Accept the positive comments.

- Have someone take notes if you are in a group so you can review the feedback later. If someone else takes notes, you can also listen more carefully.

- If one person is especially negative about a behavior, check with others to see if it is a common problem.

- Stop when you have had enough. Thank everyone, and assure them you will think about their comments.

NOTES

[1] Marta Lamas, "Feminismo y Liderazgo", in *Mujeres al Timon,* Agende, Flora Tristan, et al. (eds.). Mexico, D.F.: Equidad de Genero, 1998.

[2] Marleen Nolten of The Netherlands Organization for International Development Cooperation (Novib).

[3] Adapted from leadership workshop materials, The Support Center of Massachusetts, 1991.

[4] Adapted from *Legal Rights Organizing for Women in Africa: A Trainer's Manual,* WILDAF, Zimbabwe

[5] Adapted from Robert Moran and Phillip Harris. 1982. *Managing Cultural Synergy.* Houston, TX: Gulf Publishing Co. in *Networking for Policy Change.* The Policy Project. Washington D.C. 1999.

[6] Drawn and adapted from Michael Doyle and David Straus. 1976. *How to Make Meetings Work.* New York: Berkeley Publishing Group. Peter R. Scholtes. 1998. *The Team Handbook: How to Use Teams to Improve Quality.* Madison, Wisconsin: Joiner Associates and The Policy Project 2000. *Networking for Policy Change.* Washington, DC.: The Policy Project, 1999.

[7] Ibid.

[8] Hope, A. and S. Timmel. *Training for Transformation II.* London: IT Publications, revised version 1995, p. 66-67; *Educating for a change,* p.130-131.

Coalitions and alliances bolster advocacy by bringing together the strength and resources of diverse groups to create a more powerful voice for change. They help people get to the decisionmaking table. But coalitions and alliances are also difficult to form and sustain. This chapter focuses on their dynamics and ways to strengthen them, specifically how to improve communication, decisionmaking, conflict management, and accountability.

Coalitions and alliances often have difficulty managing differences. They sometimes suffer from unrealistic expectations, such as the notion that people who share a common cause will agree on everything. As they evolve, members of coalitions and alliances often realize the importance of not only finding points of agreement, but also agreeing at certain times to disagree.

Coalitions, Alliances, and Networks

For our purposes, it helps to have some basic definitions that distinguish coalitions, alliances, and networks. But in practice, these terms are used flexibly.

Coalitions often have a more formalized structure, an office, and full-time staff. They usually involve long-term relationships among the members. Their permanence can give clout and leverage.

Alliances generally involve shorter-term relationships among members and are focused on a specific objective. Being limited in time and goal, alliances tend to be less demanding on members.

Networks tend to be loose, flexible associations of people and groups brought together by a common concern or interest to share information and ideas.

Okay, we know we disagree on labor issues, but we're together on the environmental clause of the trade agreement.

DOING ADVOCACY

There are different types of coalitions and alliances. Geographically, they may be local, national, regional, or transnational. They may be formed to achieve one short-term objective. For example, the National Women's Coalition in South Africa was set up to influence the gender content of the post-apartheid constitution. But, coalitions may also be set up to address one or more long-term issues. Examples include the Coalition to Save Rainforests and national NGO coordinating committees that work to advance the common interests of their members in many countries.

Coalitions and alliances also differ in terms of structure. Some may be formally organized and highly structured with headquarters and permanent staff. Others are informal and flexible, relying on volunteers.

Donors who support advocacy are often eager to support coalitions. Coalitions have, in some cases, been promoted as the "magic bullet" for NGO collaboration. As a result, some coalitions are donor-initiated or donor-created. But coalitions are usually strongest if they grow organically out of common interests. Experi-

Pros and Cons of Coalitions

Groups can examine the pros and cons of coalitions and the myth of coalitions as magic bullets through a simple brainstorming process. Generating a list of advantages and disadvantages allows organizations to analyze the advisability of joining coalitions.

Below is an example of common responses received during advocacy workshops in Asia and Africa.

ADVANTAGES	DISADVANTAGES
- Generates more resources to accomplish your goal: alliance members can pool human and material resources and so achieve much more.	- Distracts from other work: the demands of the coalition can lead to neglect of other organizational priorities.
- Increases credibility and visibility: decisionmakers and the broader public are more likely to pay attention to a force of ten organizations than they are to one or two.	- Generates an uneven workload: weaker members of the coalition benefit from the hard work of the stronger members who may become resentful.
- Produces safety in numbers: it is more difficult for the state to crack down on several groups than it is to harass one.	- Requires compromises to keep the coalition together that some members feel dilute their objectives.
- Broadens your base of support: joining forces brings together the different constituencies that each member works with.	- Causes tensions due to inherent inequalities of power: because members differ in terms of resources, skills, experience, etc., there are imbalances of power; a few powerful organizations may dominate, even when weaker ones have a lot to offer.
- Creates opportunities for new leaders: when existing leaders assume positions in the alliance, they can create opportunities for others.	
- Creates opportunities for learning; Working together on an issue provides lessons in democratic culture.	- Limits organizational visibility: each member may not be recognized sufficiently for what it contributes.
- Broadens the scope of each organization's work: working in coalition adds to the activities and potential impact of each organization.	- Poses risks to your reputation: if one member has problems, there can be guilt by association; one member can hurt the coalition as a whole.
- Contributes to long-term strength of civil society: the more networking that exists among actors in civil society, the more it is capable of holding decisionmakers accountable.	

ence shows that they are unlikely to survive if they are externally imposed.

Groups form alliances and coalitions for a variety of reasons. Some of these reasons are general in nature and some are specific to advocacy.

General reasons include:

- to share information and resources;
- to provide training and technical assistance;
- to respond to a local crisis;
- to facilitate more coordinated planning and implementation;
- to avoid duplication or fill gaps in service delivery.

Advocacy-specific reasons include:[1]

- to publicize an issue and educate constituencies;
- to strengthen political voice and power;
- to ensure a consistent message and widen the coverage for community-based civic, voter, and legal education initiatives;
- to support policies or political candidates;
- to achieve a political victory that might not happen otherwise.

The Difficulties of Coalitions and Alliances[2]

Coalitions offer many advantages for groups that need to combine strength and resources to advance their cause. If not organized well, however, they can drain resources and undermine members' advocacy efforts. The headaches associated with being in and maintaining coalitions and alliances are so serious that it probably is not advisable to join or create one unless you have done a careful analysis of the major pros and cons.

Before joining a coalition or alliance, organizations should consider the following challenges:

Communication barriers

These can include technological barriers such as unreliable phone systems or the lack of a common language. Without good, ongoing communication, some members will be uninformed and excluded from decisions. This can cause the break-up of the coalition or the departure of the marginalized members. To address these kinds of differences among groups, the core members may have to use resources and time to reach out to those lacking technology or a common language.

Credibility

Organizations will not want to be formally associated with groups that may harm their reputation.

Undemocratic decisionmaking

Decisionmaking in advocacy rarely flows in a smooth, predictable pattern. Generally, processes and relationships tend to work better when they are more democratic. However, in ever-changing environments, decisions sometimes need to be made quickly without consultation. There needs to be some agreement about this among the coalition members. In general, when groups feel marginalized from decisionmaking, they tend to withdraw. While not an easy task, the decisionmaking system must address both representational concerns and the frequent need for quick decisionmaking in advocacy.

Loss of autonomy

Smaller organizations may be reluctant to join a coalition for fear that they will be overwhelmed by the collective.

Competition between a coalition and its members

Coalitions can become counterproductive if their activities become too similar to those of

Tips: Decisionmaking / Consensus-Building

Decisionmaking is crucial to develop solid advocacy plans and strong organizations and coalitions. We present two ways that can help groups set priorities and reach more informed collaborative decisions. Groups may want to adapt these to fit their own cultural or organizational circumstances.

Building Consensus

1. After a group has had sufficient time for discussion about a particular topic and proposed decision, ask all group members to indicate where they are on the decision (see *Levels of Consensus* below). They can do this by raising their hands or by standing along an imaginary line that indicates their position. If a quick scan of the group reveals all ones and twos, then the group can see that consensus has been achieved. If there are significant numbers in the three and four categories, or if there is even one five, then more discussion will be needed to reach full consensus.

2. Whatever the result of the poll, it is useful to ask if there is a need for further discussion or comments.

3. If even one person is in disagreement with the decision, the group needs to consider that person's viewpoint. If he or she cannot agree, then the group needs to decide whether the decision will be postponed to provide time for more thinking or research, whether discussion will continue until an acceptable solution is found, or whether to use a fall-back decisionmaking method such as voting.

Levels of Consensus

"1. I can say an unqualified 'yes' to the decision. I am satisfied that the decision is an expression of the wisdom of the group.

2. I find the decision perfectly acceptable.

3. I can live with the decision; I'm not especially enthusiastic about it.

4. I do not fully agree with decision and need to register my view about why. However, I do not choose to block the decision. I am willing to support the decision because I trust the wisdom of the group.

5. I do not agree with the decision and feel the need to stand in the way of this decision being accepted."

Multivoting

Multivoting is helpful for prioritization once a group has generated and discussed a list of items.

1. Write all items on a flip chart. Be sure there is clarity about the meaning of each point on the list. Where there is agreement, combine similar items.

2. Each person gets the same number of votes. People can cast votes in several ways, including raising their hands, making a checkmark or placing colorful dot stickers beside the items, or voting by secret ballot. Using checkmarks or dots gets people out of their seats and generates more energy and interest in the group.

3. Explain the method for vote distribution. There are two common ways. One is to say that no item on the list can receive more than one vote from one person. For instance, if individuals have four votes then they would vote for four items. The second option is to say that people can distribute their votes any way they please, placing all votes on one item or distributing them across the board. A further option is to color code the choices, for example, using red for top priority, blue for second, and so on.

4. Once the votes are counted, be clear about what happens to all the items on the list. Do not assume those points receiving fewer votes will be totally discarded. Sometimes the group will want to keep them as part of their report.

5. To determine the appropriate number of votes, use the N/3 method. N stands for the number of points on the list; divide that number by 3.

See Dee Kelsey and Pam Plumb. *Great Meetings: How to Facilitate Like a Pro.* Portland Maine: Hanson Park Press, 1999.

the member groups. In such instances, instead of adding value, the coalition can usurp members' functions and funding base.

Money tensions

Money is often a source of distrust in coalitions and is one of the most common reasons for their break-up. Often, groups are unwilling to share information about funding sources. Sometimes those with greater fundraising skills feel entitled to more control.

Expectation of unity

In some cases, coalition members assume they share similar principles, perspectives, and priorities beyond the issues that bring them together. When differences arise over message, tactics, or goals, they may view disagreements as political betrayals. These kinds of ideological tensions can create stubborn divisions that undermine citizen power.

Considerations for Building Advocacy Coalitions and Alliances[3]

Setting up a working relationship with other organizations involves dealing with many practical matters. For example, it is important to define group roles and relationships while maintaining the integrity of each member organization. The structure should allow for the active participation of all members in both decisionmaking and action whenever practical and possible. At the same time, a coalition must be stronger than its constituent parts to sustain active membership and attract new organizations. Members need to feel there is a high return on their investment.

In a larger, more formal or permanent coalition, a board of directors may be helpful to determine roles and responsibilities and to monitor the coalition's program, finances, and management. They may also need to create a secretariat with separate staff to coordinate coalition operations. Such coordinating structures can serve as "honest brokers" and facilitators that represent the concerns of all members. In an informal, short-term alliance, a board of directors may not be necessary unless the alliance seeks outside funding. Instead, an advisory board can be useful for visibility, credibility, and liaison with others.

Time is often a key factor in determining the arrangements of the relationship. In many advocacy campaigns, groups come together informally in response to a political opportunity or threat. Then, with time, success, and relationship-building, they may adopt a more formal structure. There are occasions when groups may jump straight into a formalized structure, but this can be risky because it can truncate the ability of groups to build trust and effective operating relationships.

Tips for Establishing a Coalition

There is no single way to form a coalition or alliance, but the following guidelines[4] may be useful:

1. Be clear about the advocacy issue proposed as the focus of the coalition. A written issue or problem statement (see Chapter 8) can be helpful for this purpose.

2. Develop membership criteria and mechanisms for including new members and sustainability. These criteria can help members decide whether organizations or individuals can join, whether individuals must represent a particular segment of the community, and other guidelines. Mechanisms for sustaining the interest and active involvement of the membership are key for survival.

DOING ADVOCACY

3. Resolve what the coalition will and will NOT do. Invite potential members to come together to determine, as a group, the alliance's purpose, scope, and priorities. Decide how it will make decisions.

4. If the group is large, select a steering committee of five to seven people that is representative of different membership interests or member organizations. Use the steering committee to facilitate advocacy planning and strategy decisions, ensure communication and consultation among members, resolve problems, and conduct outreach. It is important to set up a process for ensuring that the steer-

ing committee is accountable and responsible to the broader group. Avoid designating the steering committee or any single person as the sole spokesperson for the coalition. Rotating opportunities for visible leadership can avoid resentment about who gets credit.

5. Establish task forces to plan and coordinate different activities, such as advocacy priorities, specific agendas, publicity, outreach, lobbying, fundraising, and procedural matters. Involve all members of the coalition in at least one committee and encourage development of new leadership.

Group Maintenance & Task Needs

In order to work together, groups within a coalition have to be aware of and address a variety of needs to accomplish their goals and stay together. These needs fit into two categories: *task needs* – those related to completing the task, and *maintenance or relationship needs* – those related to maintaining the group. Some of these roles are outlined here.

TASK NEEDS	MAINTENANCE NEEDS
- **Starting the process** by helping the group begin a task or discussion.	- **Supporting**, being friendly, responding to suggestions made by others, showing appreciation and acceptance.
- **Assisting members** to set goals.	- **Giving everyone** a chance to speak, take on leadership roles, and be recognized.
- **Asking for information** Asking what information group members have and need, and where information can be found on the topic.	- **Recognizing and sharing** people's feelings.
- **Providing information** when group members do not have all the relevant facts.	- **Encouraging silent members** to express their views.
- **Seeking opinions** and ideas.	- **Resolving arguments**.
- **Explaining and defining** by giving practical examples or definitions to make a point clear.	- **Recognizing and accomodating differences** on all levels while affirming common interests.
- **Clarifying and summarizing** by repeating what has been said clearly and in a few words.	- **Promoting creativity** in the group.
- **Checking** to see whether everyone agrees.	- **Sharing responsibilities**.
- **Analyzing the problems** under discussion.	- **Developing the confidence** and skills of all members.
- **Making creative suggestions** to resolve the problems.	- **Setting standards** (for example, that no one speaks more than twice and dominates).
- **Having and following a clear process** for making each decision.	- **Checking** to see whether people are satisfied with group process.
- **Evaluating strengths and weaknesses** of the group's work to see how it can be improved.	- **Diagnosing difficulties** and admitting errors.
	- **Relieving tension** by bringing a problem out into the open or making a well-timed joke.
	- **Compromising and offering different proposals** to help people find common ground.

See *Training for Transformation*, Volume II, Mambo Press, Zimbabwe 1996.

6. Assess progress periodically and make whatever changes are necessary. This assessment should examine decisionmaking structures, the effectiveness of the coalition in meeting the advocacy objectives, opportunities for constituents to take on leadership roles, and other relevant areas. Assessment is often neglected, but it can be a useful opportunity for building shared understanding and commitment to a coalition's directions and activities. Ongoing consultation among members helps avoid duplication of activities and acrimony caused by misunderstanding of actions and motives.

7. Develop a code of conduct to ensure mutual respect and responsibility. If this is drawn up collectively, member organizations can more easily be held accountable without finger-pointing and resentment. Remember that each member will have different strengths. Ensure that your rules of collaboration acknowledge diversity in capacity and resources.

Ideally, coalitions operate on the basis of written principles. In particular, clear policies on leadership and decisionmaking should be established from the beginning. Coalitions may want to allow members to opt out of positions taken on specific controversial issues.

Facilitator's Tip: Assessing Teamwork

For individuals, use the chart *Group Maintenance and Task Needs* on the previous page as a way for people to assess their own behavior in groups. Identify and assess other behaviors that affect teamwork such as blocking, dominating, being silent, talking too much, not listening, having a hidden agenda, etc.

For groups, ask members to assess their own effectiveness as a team by asking themselves:

Task Functions:
- How clear are the goals of the team/group?
- How strongly involved do we feel in what this team is doing?
- How well do we diagnose our team problems?
- How do we usually make decisions and how effective is the process?
- How fully do we use the resources, talents, and creativity of our members?

Maintenance Functions:
- How much do members enjoy working with the others in the team?
- How much encouragement, support, and appreciation do we give to one another?
- How freely are our personal and group feelings expressed?
- How constructively are we able to use disagreement and conflicts in our team?
- How sensitive and responsive are we to the feelings of others, especially those not being explicitly expressed?

DOING ADVOCACY

Three examples from the Philippines show how decisionmaking structures affect a coalition. Democratic structures help establish common purpose, responsibility, and ownership as well as help to hold together ideologically diverse groups. Decisionmaking structures also determine effectiveness. Coalitions that employ separate secretariats do not drain as much time from member organization personnel but require more resources and a longer time frame. The secretariats are more easily seen as representing the concerns of all members. The following coalition snapshots illustrate different approaches.

Example 1: Urban Land Reform Coalition

The Urban Land Reform coalition was able to make rapid decisions and respond in a timely fashion to advocacy opportunities but lacked formal accountability and represen-tation structures. When a decision was needed quickly, the coalition secretariat would convene a meeting, and which-ever members were present made the decision by voting. This *ad hoc* process allowed for prompt responses but did not ensure full representation. The secretariat was account-able for the decisions taken by those present at a given

> "Attention to who is making decisions and who holds power in a coalition is extremely important. . . . Coalitions should be operated as models of shared power, which means that special efforts need to be made to include all groups and perspectives in the decisionmaking body."
>
> From the Ground Up, 1995

meeting, but there was no mechanism of accountability to the coalition as a whole. The secretariat's commitment to keeping members informed and involved provided an informal channel for participa-tion. However, important groups were not always represented in crucial decisions, which generated serious tensions and resentments among the members.

Example 2: Coalition of Fisherfolk for Aquatic Reform

The nationwide Coalition of Fisherfolk for Aquatic Reform (NACFAR) developed a decisionmaking mechanism that incorporated speed, flexibility, and a more direct process of representation and accountability. Its governing board included the elected officers from member fisherfolk federations and was responsible for making key decisions. Board members, together with four secretariat staff members, made up NACFAR's advocacy and lobby team. Working within the coalition's general guidelines, this team made and implemented decisions on advocacy strategies. Because of its small size, it was able to respond quickly to the political dynamics of the campaign. With account-ability and representation structures and an efficient secretariat, NACFAR was able to ensure effective participation and a high degree of member commitment. Among the coalitions studied, it was the most successful in winning policy gains and in strengthening its membership base.

Example 3: Congress for People's Agrarian Reform

The Congress for People's Agrarian Reform was a coalition of peasant federations. It had a much slower, more formalized decisionmaking process with strict adherence to consensus building. To make important decisions, each federation consulted its members internally and then had to reach consensus with all other member federations. This process held the ideologically diverse coalition together. However, despite an excellent secretariat of professionals and peasant leaders, the lengthier decisionmaking structures and processes made quick responses and effective advocacy difficult.

Valerie Miller, *NGOs and Grassroots Policy Influence: What is Success?* Institute for Development Research , Boston, MA 1994.

Purpose

To identify some challenges of decisionmaking in coalitions and alliances and to develop recommendations to address those challenges.

Process

(Time: 1 ½ hours)

1. Divide the group into three teams, each representing a different organization. Their task is to develop a decisionmaking process and structure for a new national coalition that will advocate for greater legal protection for street vendors. There are 18 organizations that are considering becoming members of the coalition. They range from service organizations, groups of lawyers, and advocacy groups to vendor's associations and research institutes. The three organizations have been asked to come up with recommendations for a decisionmaking structure for the coalition.

   • **The first team** consists of representatives of a street defense organization that provides temporary shelter to migrant and homeless vendors. This group has extremely limited resources and consists of a few paid staff members and many volunteers, including vendors. They make decisions by consensus and include in the process everyone who works in the organization. They are concerned about how vendors, especially the poorest and women vendors, can represent themselves and have a voice in decisions.

   • **The second team** is a nonprofit group of lawyers with elected officers and a professional staff. Decisions are made by senior management with staff input. The board makes decisions affecting fundamental policy. This group wants to ensure that legal issues are taken seriously by the other members.

   • **The third team** is a small advocacy organization that focuses on a range of issues affecting the urban poor. Decisions on issues, positions, and strategy are decided by vote of professional staff in monthly meetings or whenever necessary. This organization wants to ensure that decisions are made in a timely and effective fashion, and that strategies do not conflict with their efforts to promote justice and political power for the other affected groups that are part of the urban poor.

2. Each group meets separately and responds to the following questions.

   • Who should make decisions for the coalition regarding key issues such as coalition budget, content of legislative proposals, legal battles, advocacy strategies?

   • What should the process be for making those decisions? Be specific. For example, if it is by vote, what percentage of the membership will be required?

   • Who will make decisions on day-to-day tactics such as lobbying, public relations, media? How will timeliness be ensured?

   • How will the coalition handle disagreement?

3. In plenary, share results, note points of agreement and difference, and develop recommendations for the full coalition to consider. Use the *Tips for Establishing a Coalition* on page 315 to highlight key points.

DOING ADVOCACY

Conflict in Coalitions and Alliances

To maximize the likelihood of success in a coalition or alliance, there must be a clear process and commitment to preventing and handling misunderstandings that produce divisive conflicts. When conflicts arise, they need to be dealt with in a constructive way. Different countries and cultures deal with conflict and conflict resolution very differently. What is constructive for someone in Nicaragua might be completely unacceptable for someone in Thailand. There are similar differences within countries when people from different cultures are brought together. Effective communication helps in resolving disputes and managing differences. In fact, there is considerable evidence from research on coalitions that strong alliances rely on the superb interpersonal skills of their leaders. (See the Annex for tips for improving communication.) However, good communication skills are required at all levels of an organization or coalition to ensure effective negotiation of institutional commitments, interests, and resources.

Pacts and common statement of principles

Coalitions and alliances can create pacts or agreements that spell out common principles, expectations, and processes of group interaction and responsibilities. Pacts help members develop systems that facilitate problem solving and decisionmaking and avoid misunderstandings and conflicts. They also avoid false assumptions about group solidarity. As we discussed in chapter 16, poor people, women, and other excluded groups are not homogenous and do not necessarily share the same goals or values. Experience indicates that collaboration needs to be based on commonly shared concerns and principles, as well as take into account members' strengths, weaknesses, and relative power. Pacts can also streamline decisionmaking by providing the leadership of a coalition clear guidelines, thus

---

Advocacy Coalitions and Alliances: Political Responsibility

In building advocacy alliances, participating groups confront political and ethical challenges. In particular, certain members will face greater risks and repercussions than others. Certain members will commit more resources and have greater responsibilities than others, although everybody may benefit from the successes. Some members will do more behind-the-scenes work while others will have more visibility. These differences pose a number of challenges to alliances. When campaigns involve a mix of NGOs and popular organizations, such as peasant movements or community groups, those challenges increase.

Global advocacy coalitions work in local, national, regional, and international arenas and tap the expertise of member organizations that can best operate in each of these different arenas. In using this expertise, the coalitions have an obligation to be responsible to members. International activists emphasize that risks must be "assumed only in regard to the burden that can be borne by the most vulnerable." To address this concern, agendas and strategies need to be developed collaboratively, taking into account the potential risks facing all members.

It helps when coalitions acknowledge differences among the members, both with regard to what each group brings to the coalition and the responsibilities they handle. Problems arise when the members closer to policymaking and information become more important than the groups doing grassroots organizing. Part of the task of accountability and responsibility is ensuring that each type of role that is performed in a coalition is validated and recognized.

See "Political Responsibility in Transnational NGO Advocacy" by Lisa Jordan and Peter Van Tuijl in *World Development* Vol. 28 No. 12, pp 2051–2065, 2000.

enabling them to make certain kinds of decisions when fast-moving politics demand urgent responses.

Conflict Management and Coalitions[5]

Even when groups come together around a common issue, conflict is unavoidable. The dynamic nature of advocacy and the frequent changes in politics and coalition size, membership, interests, and other areas will often result in conflict. Yet conflict is a natural part of coalitions, advocacy, and politics and is not something that should be avoided, but rather, recognized and managed. Again, different cultures and social groups have different norms and approaches to conflicts which makes it hard to provide a one-size-fits-all formula for dealing with them.

Conflict management is essential for coalition development. "Bargaining, trade-offs, negotiating, compromise, and agreement are basic coalition-building strategies. Coalitions really function as mediating structures, balancing differences among their members, and striving, not for unanimity, but for a way in which their members can work together."[6]

The following guidelines offer useful suggestions for managing conflict in a coalition[7]:

- Preserve the dignity and self-respect of all stakeholders.
- Listen with empathy.
- To maximize understanding, ask clarifying questions.
- Disagree with ideas, not with people. Do not accuse or blame. Do not make personal attacks.
- Always define the issue as shared. For example, it is best to say, "We do not agree about the division of labor," rather than, "John refuses to do his share of work."

- Do not polarize the conflict by posing it in terms of mutually exclusive positions. For example, it is more effective to say, "We need to figure out how to reach the most people in the shortest time," and not, "Gloria wants to go door to door and Jose thinks a mailing will be better."
- Allow time to resolve conflicts. If discussions in regular meetings do not solve the conflict, set up a special process for dealing with it.

Despite good conflict management, sometimes differences will be unresolvable and certain organizations will resign from coalitions. In the long run, this may lead to more unified positions and more effective advocacy.

Styles of Conflict Behavior

There are different ways in which you can behave when there is conflict:

- you can approach the conflict competitively;
- you can attempt to cooperate, while acknowledging the existence of a conflict; or
- you can try to ignore the situation and maintain the status quo.

People use a variety of strategies to respond to conflict. Some approaches produce gains for all involved; others do not. Generally coalitions do best when they use "win-win" strategies in which all groups are satisfied with the solution. However, sometimes strategies that do not result in clear victories for everyone are appropriate. Such "win, lose, or draw" approaches may be useful when ceding a point or smoothing over a disagreement in order to advance the agenda. These different strategies are elaborated in the box on the following page.

DOING ADVOCACY

Conflict Response Strategies for Organizations

Creative use of conflict is possible when you are flexible in your approach. Effective coalitions change the style of conflict resolution behavior according to the situation.

"Win, Lose, or Draw" Strategies

Avoiding

Withdraw from the conflict situation or refuse to deal with it. This is useful to buy time and when damage caused by confrontation will outweigh benefits.

Smoothing

Preserve relationships by emphasizing common interests or areas of agreement and downplaying areas of disagreement. This is useful when maintaining harmony is important. However, if this approach is always adopted, you lose the possibility of a more mutually satisfactory solution.

Accommodation

Agree to the other partys solution. This is useful when the issue means more to the other party, when harmony is important, or when you are open to a solution other than your own.

Domination

Force compliance or resist. One side causes the other to acquiesce and gets what it wants at the other's expense. Common mechanisms are yelling, physical force, punishment, and sarcasm.

"Win-win" Strategies

Nonresistance

Offer no resistance to the other party's views and find ways to blend your ideas with theirs.

Co-existence

Establish a way in which both parties can maintain their differences but still work together.

Decision-rule

Set rules for how differences will be handled. This can be win-win if everyone helps to set the rules.

Compromise

Each side obtains part of what it wants and gives up part. For example, you can split differences, make trade-offs, or take turns. This approach achieves a temporary settlement when there is limited time and when you have mutually exclusive goals.

Problem-solving

Agree to cooperate and find a solution that will meet the needs of both sides. This approach is useful when concerns are too great to compromise, when solutions have long term effects, and when the decision will greatly affect all involved.

Adapted from *From the Ground Up*, 1995 and *Resolving Conflicts at Work*, 2000

General Approaches For Dealing with Conflict

When conflict erupts in a coalition, determine what it is really about. If the conflict is over issues, deal with the issues. If it is personal, try to improve the relationship. Conflicts over values can be addressed by reaching some understanding about what each party believes. If the conflict is not being expressed directly, bring it out in the open.

There are several general strategies that can help resolve conflicts:

- helping people vent feelings, raise questions, and clarify issues through the use of special feedback meetings or retreats;
- finding areas of agreement and opportunities for collaboration;
- focusing on common ground and playing down differences;
- arranging opportunities for the organizations involved to talk about their differences, remove misunderstandings, and build relationships;
- helping members to recognize the conflict and to explain conflicting views;
- deciding in advance on criteria for decisions and using these as a basis for conflict resolution;
- discussing acceptable and unacceptable aspects of each position;
- breaking down broader conflicts into manageable elements and obtaining agreement incrementally;
- working with facilitators who help create a safe environment, suggest processes for resolving conflicts, and make sure each side is really listening to the other.

Adapted from AHEC/Community Partners, *A Workbook on Coalition Building and Community Development,* Amherst MA, 1995

When Coalitions Break Up

Coalitions do not last forever. There will be times when individual organizations decide to leave because differences become irreconcilable. There may also be times when coalitions themselves decide to fold because of changing circumstances. These occurrences can be a sign of success and, if less positive, should not be seen necessarily as failures. They may in fact represent strategic choices. If possible, breakups should be dealt with in a way that facilitates future cooperation.

The third example on page 318 from the Philippines[8] also illustrates how departures can be handled in a way that makes future coopera-

tion possible. In the early 1990s, some members of the Congress for People's Agrarian Reform decided to leave the group because they felt the government was responding to their needs. The remaining members believed that the government was co-opting the departing groups with empty promises. But, rather than criticize or attack those leaving, the coalition leadership decided to end the relationship with a party celebrating the victories they had won together. The leaders believed that it was important to maintain good relationships because when circumstances changed in the future, there would be new opportunities for alliances with the departing groups. By not cutting off relations, they left the door open for future collaborations.

DOING ADVOCACY

Purpose

To analyze a conflict situation in an organization and identify strategies for addressing it.

Process

1. In plenary, ask participants to think about a past or present conflict in their coalition or a conflict in other coalitions.

2. Divide the participants into small groups and ask each group to develop a role play portraying a particular conflict. The role play should include the key characters, the context, and whatever background information is needed.

3. In plenary, have the groups present the role plays. Analyze each one using the following questions:

   - What are the critical issues?
   - What is each party's stake in this conflict?
   - What conflict behavior and style are being used?
   - How open and accurate is communication between parties?
   - Do the parties have any misunderstandings or lack important information?
   - How can this conflict be managed? List all possible solutions.
   - What will the final agreement look like? What will each party agree to?

Dealing with conflict by competing

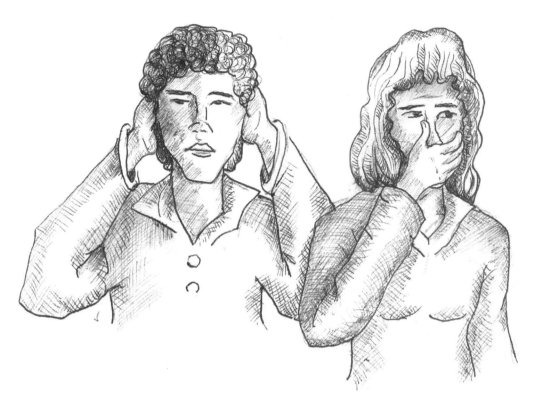

Dealing with conflict by ignoring it

Dealing with conflict by collaborating

Adapted from *From the Ground Up*, 1995, Illustrations by Marcelo Espinoza, 2001

DOING ADVOCACY

NOTES

[1] Adapted from *Organizing for Social Change*, ibid.

[2] Adapted from *Human Rights Institution-Building*, published by The Fund for Peace in association with the Jacob Balustein Institute for the Advancement of Human Rights.

[3] Adapted from SEGA, ibid.

[4] The book *From the Ground Up* provides valuable insights on how to manage conflicts in coalitions and is the major source for this section.

[5] Ibid.

[6] Ibid.

[7] Ibid.

[8] Part of the reason that all of our coalition examples are from the Philippines is that this country is particularly well-known for alliances and coalitions, and partly, because Valerie Miller has had the opportunity to work with and document them closely.

Additional Tips for Planners and Trainers

> The Annexes include additional tips, exercises, and discussion.
> - Annex 1 provides tips for running productive workshops and using the Guide;
> - Annex 2 includes more on Understanding Power (continued from Chapter 3);
> - Annex 3 is a bibliography of resources used in this Guide.

First Steps for Training and Planning

We think that all advocacy planning or training should begin with two important steps:

1. **A team-building and personal reflection activity** that allows participants to say something about themselves and learn about others in the group. This builds personal connections between people, creates an open environment, and boosts confidence. See Chapter 6 for a more in-depth explanation of why this is important. On page 333, we include a section on *Creating a Conducive Learning Process* which contains a selection of exercises for this purpose.

2. **A discussion of what advocacy is** and what the important results of effective advocacy should be. Without a common definition, some confusion and disagreement will inevitably arise and make participatory planning difficult, or even impossible. See Chapter 1 for more about defining common terms.

Besides these two important steps, advocacy planning and training should also include:

- **Review of the purpose** of a specific meeting or workshop.
- **Clarification of expectations** about what people want to gain from the overall planning or training. This will allow facilitators to

clarify which expectations are realistic and appropriate given the time allotted and the program goals. It will also help identify any potential problems due to different expectations that facilitators and organizers need to consider.

- **Review of agenda** times, items, and activities. This gives participants an opportunity to understand the logic of the process in light of the needs and goals and to contribute suggestions to the program.
- **Development of ground rules** to ensure that everyone is treated equally and fairly. To get buy-in, the facilitator asks participants for concrete suggestions. (See box on next page.)

Sample Ground Rules to Consider

- No side conversations
- Share the floor
- No interruptions
- Encourage everyone to participate
- Debate ideas, not individuals
- No evaluation during brainstorming
- Stay on the subject
- Be constructive
- Begin and end on time

Any advocacy training program should be based on a **needs assessment** that incorporates a review of participant and organizational needs. Rather than provide fixed curricula, we opted to highlight the sections of the book that

---

Hints for Establishing Ground Rules

Groups are often resistant to establishing ground rules, either because of the time it takes or because they feel it is childish to define good behavior. A sense of humor, a declaration that you, as facilitator, need the ground rules, and a promise to keep the process of generating ground rules 'crisp' usually is enough to engage the group.

To generate ground rules, we use this process:
1. Ask for suggestions for ground rules. All ideas are welcome.
   Example: A group member says, "I want everyone to be polite."
2. Define the suggestion in terms of behavior. Asking, "what would it look like if . . ." helps.
   Example: The facilitator says, "John, what would it look like to you if everyone were being polite?"
   John: "No one would interrupt anyone and there would be no personal attacks."
   Facilitator: "So you are proposing two ground rules; no interruptions and no personal attacks."
3. Check with yourself to see if the ground rules really serve the group. If not, explain your concern to the group and offer an alternative.
4. Check for consensus on the ground rule.
5. After the ground rules are written, confirm that everyone can abide by them.

See Kelsey, Dee and Pam Plumb. *Great Meetings: How to Facilitate Like a Pro.* Portland Maine: Hanson Park Press, 1999.

---

have been helpful to us as planners and trainers to enable you to review, select, and arrange them according to your needs and goals. We have divided this section into three subsections: Using the Guide for 1) *focused analysis*, 2) *focused planning*, and 3) *training / learning about advocacy.*

Using the Guide for Focused Analysis

Careful ***analysis*** of problems, contexts, interests, and power are an essential feature of good planning, and critical to advocacy success. They also lessen the risks and conflicts related to political work. The following parts of the Guide are especially useful for carrying out the different types of analysis. The exercises and sections of the book that are listed are sequenced in an order that has worked for our purposes, but you will have to choose which ones are the most applicable for your situation.

Power Analysis

We have found that it is helpful to begin a power analysis with a clear issue and a draft set of advocacy objectives for addressing that issue. The more you know about your aims and strategy, the better you will be able to assess the power dynamics and conflicts your actions may confront. The following tools and frameworks guide power analysis.

Power Analysis	
The Power Flower	p. 94
Conceptual discussion about power	Ch. 3
Structural Analysis	p. 111
Naming the Powerful	p. 114
SWOT Analysis	p. 214
Force-field Analysis	p. 216
Mapping Power	p. 219
Discussion of different kinds of conflict	p. 289

Problem Analysis	
Anatomy of a Problem	p. 128
Tips for Developing a Problem Statement	p. 127
Causes-Consequences-Solutions Analysis	p. 152
Triangle Analysis	P. 171
Discussion on prioritizing and defining the issue including the Checklist for Choosing an Issue	p. 159
The SWOT Analysis	p. 214

Advocacy Planning	
Power Flower	p. 94
Structural Analysis	p. 111
Naming the Powerful	p. 114
Historical Analysis of Political Landscape	p. 118
Vision of Political Decisionmaking	p. 99
Discussion and examples about Vision, Mission, and Strategy	p. 97-98
Discussion and exercises for prioritizing issues	p. 147
Tips for developing a Problem Statement	p. 127
Causes-Consequences-Solutions Analysis	p. 152
Triangle Analysis and Mapping of Strategies	p. 171
Advocacy Impact Chart	p. 181
Different Advocacy Strategies for Different Moments	p. 164
Levels of Policymaking Arenas and Processes	p. 190
SWOT Analysis	p. 214

Contextual Analysis	
Vision of Political Decisionmaking	p. 99
The Power Flower	p. 94
Conceptual discussion about power	Ch. 3
Structural Analysis	p. 111
Naming the Powerful	p. 114
Historical Analysis of Political Landscape	p. 118

Using the Guide for Focused Planning

Similar to the Focused Analysis above, we have listed exercises and sections of the book that are relevant to the broadly defined *planning* tasks below. Again, you will want to select from these in order to design the combination of steps and tools that best suit your purposes. Most of the planning proposed below will require about three full days, but the constituency-building piece may take four to five days.

Planning Policy Work

Policy work is part of a more comprehensive approach to advocacy that includes citizen education and organizing, media and other strategies. It is important to affirm this at the beginning and end of policy planning. The *Advocacy Action Impact Chart* and the *Vision of Political Decisionmaking* can be helpful for that purpose. The following selection can assist in planning and designing policy-focused work.

Planning Policy Work	
Problem Statement	p. 127
Triangle Analysis and Mapping of Strategies	p. 171
Chapter 11: Policy Hooks and Political Angles, especially Levels of Policymaking Arenas and Process, International Rights Advocacy and A Note on Formulating Policy Alternatives	Ch. 11
Lobbying: Getting to the Table	p. 278
Formal and Informal Lobbying	p. 282
Tips for a Lobbying Visit	p. 281
Talking Points	p. 283
Presenting Your Case to Decision makers	p. 285
Two Negotiation Strategies	p. 290
Negotiation Simultation	p. 92
Political Responsibility and Accountability	p. 320

Media Planning	
What is advocacy? What is citizenship?	Ch. 1 and 2
What is Political Consciousness? Fostering Political Consciousness	p. 61
Features of Participatory Learning	p. 66
Legal Rights and Citizen Education Programs: Reflections from Participatory Learning	p. 63
Anatomy of a Problem	p. 128
Problem Statement	p. 127
Causes-Consequences-Solutions Analysis	p. 152
Forcefield Analysis	p. 216
Review Entire Chapter 13: Media and Message Development	

Planning constituency-building	
What is advocacy? What is Citizenship?	Ch. 1 and 2
Vision for Political Decisionmaking	p. 99
What do we mean by constituent?	p. 60
How Constituency-building Changes Strategies	p. 60
What is Political Consciousness? Fostering Political Consciousness	p. 61
Features of Participatory Learning	p. 66
The Importance of Participation in Advocacy Planning	p. 85
Making Participation Work	p. 86
Constituent Credibility checklist	p. 107
Anatomy of a Problem	p. 128
Some Guiding Questions to Get Specific About Problem	p. 130
Participatory Approaches for Defining Problems	p. 134
Knowing your constituents	p. 130
Some thoughts on power differences within groups	p. 136
Constituency-building Ways to Identify Problems through the end of Chapter 8	Ch. 8
Analyzing for Priorities	p. 149
Causes-Consequences-Solutions Analysis	p. 152
Triangle Analysis and Mapping of Strategies	p. 171
checklist for Choosing an Issue	p. 159
Dimensions of a Citizen-Centered Advocacy Strategy	p. 178
Message Development	p. 231
Message Delivery	p. 238
Alternative Media for Citizen Outreach and Education	p. 253
Developing Local Leaders	p. 301
Political Responsibility and Accountability	p. 320

Using the Guide for Training/ Learning about Advocacy

The following lists are a few general designs for different types of training workshops. The exercises and sections of the Guide are sequenced in a way that has worked for our training purposes. Again, these reference lists are meant to inspire and focus your use of the Guide, but not as a curriculum per se.

Lobbying Training: 3 days	
What is advocacy?	Ch. 1
Perceptions of Power and Political Change Strategies	Ch. 3
Heading to the Corridors of Power	p. 277
Lobbying: Getting to the Table	p. 278
Ranking Decisionmakers	p. 280
Formal and Informal Lobbying Exercise	p. 284
Tips for a Lobbying Visit	p. 281
Presenting Your Case to Decisionmakers Exercise	p. 285
Talking Points	p. 283
Advice for Getting to the Negotiating Table	p. 288
Key Points for Developing a Negotiation Plan	p. 291
Two Negotiation Strategies	p. 290
Negotiation Simulation	p. 292
Dealing with Strong Opposition	p. 293
Maneuvering Power in Shadow Negotiation	p. 295
Tips for Shifting the Balance of Power in Negotiations	p. 297

Intensive Advocacy Training: 10 days	
What is advocacy? What is citizenship?	Ch. 1 and 2
Vision of Political Decisionmaking	p. 99
Naming Assumptions	p. 96
What is Power?	p. 39
Chart on Power, Political Participation and Social Transformation	p. 50
Features of Participatory Learning	p. 66
The Importance of Participation in Advocacy Planning	p.85
Making Participation Work	p. 86
Constituent Credibility Checklist	p. 107
Anatomy of a Problem	p. 128
Some Guiding Questions to Get Specific About Problems	p. 130
Participatory Approaches for Defining Problems	p. 134
Problem Statement, Causes-Consequences-Solutions Analysis	p. 127, 152
Triangle Analysis and Mapping of Strategies	p. 171
Dimensions of Advocacy Strategies	p. 178
Draft Goals and Objectives	p. 163
SWOT Analysis	p. 214
Forcefield Analysis	p. 216
Power Map	p. 219
Message Development	p. 231
Mass Media Advocacy	p. 240
Lobbying: Getting to the Table	p. 278
Presenting Your Case to Decisionmakers	p. 285
Negotiation Simulation	p. 292
Affidamento	p. 300
Pros and cons of coalitions	p. 312
Political Responsibility and Accountability	p. 320

Introduction to Advocacy: 2.5 days	
Advocacy Stories (Chad, DSWP, Via Campesina)	p. 60, 274, 272
What is advocacy?	Ch. 1
What is citizenship?	Ch. 2
Vision of Political Decisionmaking	p. 99
Naming Assumptions	p. 96
Discussion of democracy, power, and empowerment	Ch. 2 and 3
Problems - Issues - Advocacy Strategies	p. 126
Causes - Consequences – Solutions Analysis	p. 152
Triangle Analysis and Mapping of Strategies	p. 171
Factors Shaping an Advocacy Strategy and Different Advocacy Strategies for Different Moments	p. 164
Dimensions of an Advocacy Strategy and Charting Advocacy Impact	p. 178

Media for Advocacy Training: 3 days	
What is advocacy?	Ch. 1
Vision of political decisionmaking	p. 99
Chart on Power, Political Participation, and Social Transformation	p. 50
What is Empowerment?	p. 53
Chapter 13: Messages and Media: Reaching and Educating, especially Message Development	Ch. 13
Framing Your Message	p. 235
Message Development Exercise: Slogans	p. 239
Mass Media Advocacy	p. 240

Constituency-building and Citizen Participation Training: 6 days	
What is advocacy?	Ch. 1
What is a Good Citizen?	p. 31
Citizenship as "Makers and Shapers"	p. 29
Perceptions of Power and Political Change Strategies	p. 34
Vision for Political Decisionmaking	p. 99
What Do We Mean by "Constituent?"	p. 60
How Constituency-building Changes Strategies	p. 60
Fostering Political Consciousness	p. 63
Features of Participatory Learning	p. 66
The Importance of Participation in Advocacy Planning	p. 85
Making Participation Work	p. 86
Constituent Credibility Checklist	p. 107
Anatomy of a Problem	p. 128
Some Guiding Questions to Get Specific About Problems	p. 130
Participatory Approaches for Defining Problems	p. 134
Knowing your constituents	p. 134
Power Differences Within Groups	p. 136
Constituency-building Ways to Identify Problems through the end of Chapter 8	Ch. 8
Analyzing for Priorities	p. 149
Causes-Consequences-Solutions Analysis	p. 152
Triangle Analysis	p. 171
Checklist for Choosing an Issue	p. 159
Advocacy Action and Impact Chart	p. 181
Message Development	p. 231
Alternative Media	p. 252
Developing Local Leaders	p. 301
Political Responsibility and Accountability	p. 320

Creating a Conducive Learning Process: The Personal is Political

In education and organizing work, it is important to begin with exercises that affirm people's sense of self and build their connection to others. We weave the personal with the political to create the shared commitment that provides the foundation for successful group collaboration. Our experience has shown that several of these exercises need to be included at different moments in a course or workshop in order to strengthen relationships and communication.

The approach of each kind of activity should be tailored to different audiences. More professional and university educated groups, such as human rights lawyers or researchers, initially may resist these types of personal exercises, especially exercises that use art or creativity as a starting point. Once they have participated in them, however, they usually appreciate the cooperative and reflective climate such exercises produce. It is best to begin with exercises that are more comfortable or less threatening.

Basic communication and listening skills can also help enhance group learning and effectiveness. We present some exercises and simple tips on the next few pages that focus on these areas.

Personal Reflection and Team-Building Exercises

Introductions

Personal introductions are essential at the start of a workshop. They break the ice, develop a sense of community, and build trust. Asking people to share something positive about their lives or work can set a good starting tone. Sample discussion questions include:

- Think about a person who inspired you to become involved in this work – what is one important quality about that person?
- Think about your organization – what is one of the things about the organization that makes you proud to be a part of it?
- What has been one major event in your life that drew you to work on advocacy and human rights?

Personal posters/photo collages

Creating a collage that represents a person's life is a visual way to describe and affirm an individual's sense of self and connections to others. The approach is especially appropriate if a group is going to be spending an extended period of time together. Even in situations where people supposedly know each other, this type of exercise can be useful. Unless organizations are very small, people rarely have a sense of the richness of their colleagues' lives or talents. Before the event, ask individuals to bring photos or other images that represent different aspects of their lives – personal, professional, political, community, etc. During one of the first evenings together, provide participants with colored paper, tape, and markers to create their collage. For those who do not have images, provide a selection of magazines. After everyone has finished, place the posters on the wall and have each person explain the highlights.

Personal storytelling

Simple storytelling can deepen bonds between people and affirm individual life journeys. Storytelling can also be the starting point for developing leadership and examining the effect of power on people's lives. Conversation in an informal setting gives everyone a chance to share their stories in a relaxed way. Specific questions to guide stories should be tailored to different groups, such as:

- What got you involved in advocacy?
- What got you involved in social justice work?
- What are the major turning points in your life that have made you who you are?

This exercise can also be done as a drawing using the image of a river to represent the directions and flow of life.

Personal sources of inspiration

Sharing sources of personal inspiration reinforces group relationships and helps address burnout. Before an event, ask participants to bring something that inspires them in their work and that they draw strength from in moments of discouragement. For example, they could bring a piece of poetry, prose, song, a painting, a photo, a story, etc. In a relaxed setting, have people share their examples. This can lead to a deeper discussion on survival strategies that people use to counter the pressures and risks of political participation.

Paper quilt

Working together on a paper quilt allows people to combine their individual expression with the group's and build a special sense of community. Each person first designs their own square, choosing symbols that relate to a specific theme. They then combine their square with others to create a complete quilt. The theme for the quilt will vary according to the group. For example, people can design a piece to represent why they are involved in advocacy or what a workshop has meant to them. Provide participants with a pre-cut square and an assortment of materials to draw or construct their square. After everyone has explained the meaning of their square, the group works to place the pieces together. When everyone is satisfied with the overall design, the pieces are glued to

a stiffer background paper, and the quilt is hung on the wall.

Communication

The ability to communicate effectively is fundamental to internal organizational issues such as problem-solving, leadership, planning, coalition-building, and conflict resolution. It is also a central piece of lobbying and media work.

The fundamentals of communication

Simply put, communication involves two people interacting with one another. Each person brings their own values, beliefs, prejudices, and life experiences to the interaction, and each takes on different communication roles at different moments — as speaker or listener. Each tries to convey meaning to the other, sometimes with words or gestures, sometimes with silence. Given different backgrounds, cultures, and means of expression, any communication between people has the potential for distortion and misunderstanding. When working with organizations and coalitions, that potential is compounded.

The ability to listen carefully and interpret meaning effectively are important skills for any communication. However, most people are not good listeners. Too often, we are thinking about what we are going to say next and not really paying careful attention to the other person's points of view. The *Communication and Listening Techniques* chart on the following page provides questions designed to promote better interpersonal understanding and interaction. It can be used as the basis for an exercise. After reviewing the chart, people can break into pairs and have a conversation applying the questions to their discussion.

Communication & Listening Techniques

The following examples provide a reference for helping people frame questions and responses that promote better communication.

TYPES	PURPOSE	POSSIBLE RESPONSES
Clarifying	- To get at additional facts - To clarify understanding	- Can you clarify that? - Do you mean this...? - Can you give me an example? - Is this the problem as you see it now? - Let me see if I'm understanding...
Paraphrasing / Restatement	-To check meaning - To show you are listening and that you understand what the other has said	- As I understand it then, your suggestion is... - To be clear, this is what I am hearing you say.
Neutral	-To convey that you are interested and listening -To encourage the person to continue talking	- I see. - That's very interesting - I understand.
Reflective	- To show that you understand how the other feels about what s/he is saying - To help the person to evaluate his or her feelings	- You feel that... - It was a disturbing thing, as you saw it. - You felt like you didn't get a fair shake.
Probing	- To help the person explore all sides of the problem	- This is what you have decided to do... and the reasons are? - What other ways are there to look at it? - How do you think other people see it? - What other information might help?
Summarizing	- To bring all the discussion into focus - To serve as a springboard for discussion of new aspects of the problem	- These are the key ideas I have heard you express. - If I understand, you are feeling / thinking...

Adapted from *Training for Transformation*, Volume II, 1995 and Sam Kaner, *Facilitators Guide to Participatory Decision-Making*, New Society Publishers, Philadelphia, 1996

Understanding Power

Drawing the Lines of Power: Factors of Discrimination

What factors determine who has more power and who has less power in society and in the political process? Physical traits and social circumstances that are inherited at birth often determine an individual's opportunities, choices, and even sense of self. This happens not because these characteristics are inborn, but rather because of negative value judgments attributed to them. People then often justify prejudice as "natural" when it is really the *social meaning* we give to biological facts – like being a man or woman, or having a particular skin color – that defines inequality. Although a few people overcome the social barriers of their disadvantage, most do not unless there is a dramatic change in society.

Over the last twenty years, a number of social movements have focused on fighting prejudice and barriers derived from people's identity based on gender, race, age, ethnicity, and religion among others. (See p. 34 for a discussion of *identity politics*.) These factors combine in different ways in different contexts to determine who makes decisions and who has access to resources.

Nature (biology) vs. nurture (socialization) is the subject of much research and debate. But regardless of whether someone's behavior has genetic roots or is primarily a function of socialization, social justice advocates are concerned about inequality. Promoting acceptance of diversity is a fundamental principle of this kind of advocacy. Finding common ground while recognizing difference is critical to healthy, stable societies.

What Is Discrimination?

Discrimination is differentiation between people on the grounds of gender, age, race, class, or other factors. Discrimination can operate institutionally in the public sphere (e.g., racial discrimination in apartheid South Africa and gender discrimination in the Middle East). It can also operate at a less visible level through culture, social beliefs, and ideology which can be measured by relative levels of education, political representation, percentages living in poverty, etc.

Gender

Gender refers to the social descriptions, roles, and responsibilities attached to women and men. Whereas sex is a biological fact and unchanging, gender is a culturally derived, learned behavior that varies over time and is influenced by other socio-economic factors. Common gender stereotypes include: men are strong /women are weak, men are breadwinners/women are nurturers, men are rational/ women are emotional.

Race

Strictly speaking, race refers to people of common origin. But in politics, race usually refers to skin color and facial features. People of color have been discriminated against for hundreds of years. The legacy of this discrimination can be seen in current economic, political, and legal systems, as well as in strong stereotypes.

Ethnicity

Ethnicity refers to a common consciousness about shared origins, traditions, social beliefs, and practices. Ethnicity is a more precise term than race. For example, not all black people share the same ethnicity.

Religion

Religion refers to beliefs and worship of a transcendent or supernatural being(s). Religions usually embody a vision of right and wrong bestowed by the highest moral authority.

Socio-economic status/class

This term has multiple meanings. It generally refers to a person's position in society as determined by a combination of factors, such as education and economic means. Socio-economic status is one of the most important sources of disadvantage or privilege.

Age

A person's age is the number of chronological years one has lived. Age is a common source of discrimination that affects men and women differently, and is weighted differently in different contexts. For example, in Africa and South Asia age affords a woman more status, while in parts of the West older women have less or no status.

Sexual orientation

The term refers to a person's preference for a sexual partner. Whether an individual is heterosexual, homosexual, or bisexual is usually highly politicized. There are, for example, different views as to whether sexual orientation is a matter of socialization or innate behavior, and whether homosexuality is immoral. Many societies are extremely oppressive toward people who do not follow social norms.

Geographic location (place)

The location where one lives can often determine choices, opportunities, and resources. For example, rural residents are usually discriminated against in comparison to urban residents because they have less access to resources, services, and decisionmakers.

Another important geographic cleavage exists between the global north, which controls most of the world's resources, and the global south.

Disability

Disability refers to a physical or mental condition that makes a person different than what is considered normal. Disabilities often make a person operate at a different pace and require some assistance to attain "normal" activity. Societies are often abusive to people with disabilities.

Many strategies aimed at social and political change fail to take into account these variations in experiences of subordination and exclusion. These factors combine in different ways in different contexts to determine who is dominant and who subordinate.

Power Over: Dominance and Subordination

Invisible mechanisms of *power over* can socialize people into accepting an inferior role in society, as is the case with women in many societies. Simultaneously, socialization affirms feelings of entitlement among dominant groups. Socialization thus helps to maintain the unequal relationships that determine whose voices are heard in decisionmaking.

The chart on the next page, developed by PLAN International, examines behaviors associated with *power over* by looking at domination and subordination. The chart focuses principally on behaviors shaped by gender. However, it can also be applied to behaviors shaped by class, race, and other axes of disadvantage and exclusion. The exercise on page 340 can enable people to reflect about the many faces of power.

Dominant & Subordinate Behavior

DOMINANT BEHAVIOR	SUBORDINATE BEHAVIOR
Dominant behavior is accepted:	**Subordinates do not address domination directly:**
- Is given at birth by cultural standards	- Self-iniated action on one's own behalf is avoided
- Defines who subordinates are	- Resort to indirect ways of acting and reacting
- Is hierarchical	- Hidden defiance by subordinates of dominants
- Is patriarchal	**Characteristics of subordinate interactions with dominants:**
Negative labels are used about subordinates:	- Know more about dominants than about themselves
- See subordinates as substandard	- Interest is focused on what the dominant wants or will do
- See subordinates in server roles	- Do not give dominants feedback about how the dominant is perceived
- See subordinates as incapable of "higher" labor, thinking or positions due to immutable factors (i.e., mind, body, race, sex)	**Self-defeating behavior is often present in subordinates:**
Dominant actions and culture encourage subordinates to develop traits of:	- Self-put-downs, inability to see choices, withdrawal, aggression, high control needs of others
- Submissiveness; dependency; passivity; lack of initiative; inability to act, think, do or decide for themselves	- Subordinates have difficulty working with other members of the subordinate group
Dominants build these concepts into society through philosophy, religion, science, morality, media, education, legal systems, cultural laws, rituals, traditions:	- Subordinates often feel more responsible for helping others than helping themselves. This self-denial is used by dominants to keep subordinates in place.
- Acceptance of position: happy with role, supposed to be this way, it is cultural, it is normal, women are naturally this way	- Feel unconscious need to protect the dominant behavior
- Language is used to control behavior of subordinates: negative labels are given to subordinates who stray from the prescribed behaviors	**Subordinates internalize untruths about themselves:**
	- Ambivalence regarding dominant myths vs. internally felt truths
	Despite these traits, subordinates can and do move toward greater freedom of expression and action.

Adapted from Jean Baker Miller, 1976, in PLAN International *Gender and Development Workshop: Participants Workbook.*

Exercise: Dominance and Subordination

Purpose

This exercise helps participants explore how the three levels of power (see page 47) perpetuate imbalances of power and exclusion. It serves to:

- probe assumptions about inequality and what determines dominance or subordination;
- reflect on how people are socialized to accept their status and how people resist their subordinate role;
- assist activists in understanding the psychological and cultural challenges of organizing, citizen participation, and advocacy.

Process

(Time: 2 hours)

1. Divide participants into two small groups: dominant and subordinate.

2. Ask each group to discuss the following questions and write their answers on newsprint:
   - How do people usually behave when their status is dominant or subordinate?
   - What are some of the stereotypes people hold about poor people, old people, women and men, people of different races, etc.?
   - What are the social justifications for different groups being dominant or subordinate?
   - What are the mechanisms that keep this status from changing?

3. After groups have discussed these questions for 20-30 minutes, open the discussion up to plenary. If there is time, ask the groups to present their analysis in the form of a skit. As a summary, hand out copies of the chart on page 339 and ask for further comments.

Adapted from Jean Baker Miller, 1976, in PLAN International *Gender and Development Workshop: Participants Workbook.*

Advocacy Institute and Oxfam America. *Advocacy Learning Initiative* (draft version). Bloomfield, CT: Kumarian Press, 2000.

Africa Community Publishing and Development Trust. *Democratic Governance in Zimbabwe: Citizen Power.* Harare: ACPDT, 1999.

———. *Participation, Development, Power, and Democracy.* Harare: ACPDT, 1997.

Agende. *Advocacy em Direitos Reproductivos e Sexuais.* Brasilia: Starprint Grafica, 1999.

Agende, Flora Tristan and others. *Mujeres al Timon.* Mexico, D.F.: Equidad de Genero, 1998.

Albrecht, Lisa and Rose Brewer, eds. *Bridges of Power: Women's Multicultural Alliances.* Philadelphia: New Society Publishers, 1990.

Alinsky, Saul D. *Rules for Radicals: A Pragmatic Primer for Realistic Radicals.* New York: Vintage Books, 1989.

Alvarez, Sonia E., Evelina Dagnino, and Arturo Escobar, eds. *Cultures of Politics, Politics of Cultures: Re-Visioning Latin American Social Movements.* Boulder, CO: Westview Press, 1998.

Armani, Domingos. *Democratising the Allocation of Public Resources: A Study of the Participatory Budget of Porto Alegre, Brazil.* Study commissions by Christian Aid (UK) as part of the Local Economy Project, 1997.

Arnstein, Sherry R. *A Ladder of Citizen Participation.* The Journal of the American Institute of Planners, vol 35, no 4. July 1969.

———. *Building Alliances with Civil Society.* Synthesis Report. International Forum on Capacity Building. New Delhi: PRIA, 2001.

Ashman, Darcy. *Democracy Awareness Education Program of the Association of Development Agencies of Bangladesh.* Discourse.1(2). pp. 31–47. Dhaka, Bangladesh: Institute for Development Policy Analysis and Advocacy, 1997.

Asia-Pacific Women in Politics Network. *Increasing Women's Political Awareness and Consciousness: A Manual of Exercises.* Center for Legislative Development (The Philippines). Global Women in Politics-The Asia Foundation (USA), 1996.

Association for Women in Development. *Building Feminist Leadership.* Washington DC: Trialogue, Winter 1999.

Ayales, Ivannia and others. *Haciendo Camino al Andar: Guia Metodologica para la Accion Comunitaria.* Washington, DC: OEF International, 1991

Barndt, Deborah, *Naming the Moment: Political Analysis for Action, A Manual for Community Groups.* Toronto: The Jesuit Centre for Social Faith and Justice, 1989.

Batliwala, Srilatha. *Political Representation and the Women's Movement.* Unpublished lecture given in Hyderabad, India, May 1997, under the auspices of the Women and Society Forum of ASMITA.

———. *Women's Empowerment in South Asia: Concepts and Practices.* New Delhi: Food and Agricultural Organization/Asia South Pacific Bureau of Adult Education, 1995.

———. "The Meaning of Women's Empowerment: New Concepts from Action." *Population Policies Reconsidered.* Gita Sen, Adrienne Germain, and Lincoln Chen, eds. Boston: Harvard University Press, 1994.

Benhabib, Seyla, ed. *Democracy and Difference.* Princeton: Princeton University Press, 1996.

Biagi, Bob. *Working Together.* Amherst, MA: Citizen Involvement Training Project, 1978.

Birdsall, Nancy. *Why Inequality Matters: Some Economic Issues*; Carnegie Endowment for Peace, Discussion Paper #5, August 2001.

Boal, Augusto. *Legislative Theatre: Using Performance to Make Politics.* London: Routledge, 1998.

Bobo, K., J. Kendall, and S. Max. *Organizing for Social Change: A Manual for Activists in the 1990s.* Midwest Academy, Seven Locks Press, Santa Ana, CA: 1991.

Bratton, Michael. *Beyond the State: Civil Society and Associational Life in Africa.* Oxford: World Politics, 1989.

———. *The Politics of Government-NGO Relations in Africa.* Oxford: World Development, 1989.

Budlender, Debbie, ed. *The Women's Budget* (Series of 4 books). Johannesburg, South Africa: Community Action for Social Enquiry, Institute for Democracy in South Africa, and the Parliamentary Gender and Economic Policy Group, 1996.

Budlender, Debbie and Karen Hurt, eds. *Money Matters: Women and the Government Budget.* Johannesburg, South Africa: IDASA, 1998.

Budlender, Debbie, Rhonda Sharp with Kerri Allen. *How to do a gender-sensitive budget analysis: Contemporary research and practice.* Commonwealth Secretariat and AusAid, 1998.

Burgess, Heidi and Guy Burgess. *Intractable Conflicts.* Online course on conflict resolution. <http://www.colorado.edu/conflict/peace> Boulder, CO: University of Colorado, 2001.

Burns, James MacGregor. *Leadership.* New York: Harper Torchbooks, 1978.

Butegwa, Florence and Sydia Nduna. *Legal Rights Organizing for Women in Africa.* Harare, Zimbabwe: WILDAF, 1995.

Bystydzienski, Jill and Joti Sekhon eds. *Democratization and Women's Grassroots Movements.* Bloomington: Indiana University Press, 1999.

Canadian Council for International Co-operation and others. *Two Halves Make a Whole: Balancing Gender Relations in Development.* Ottawa: CIDA, 1991.

Carothers, Thomas. *In the Name of Democracy.* Berkeley: University of California Press, 1991.

———. *Aiding Democracy Abroad: The Learning Curve.* Washington, DC: Carnegie Endowment for International Peace, 1999.

Carpenter, Susan and W.J. Kennedy. *Managing Public Disputes.* San Francisco: Jossey-Bass, 1988.

Chapman, Jennifer and Amboka Wameyo. *Monitoring and Evaluation Advocacy: A Scoping Study.* London: ActionAid, 2001.

Chambers, Robert. *Whose Reality Counts?* London: Intermediate Technology Publications, 1997.

Clark, John. *Democratizing Development.* London: Earthscan. 1991.

Clegg, Stewart. *Frameworks of Power.* London: Sage Publications, 1989.

Cloke, Kenneth and Joan Goldsmith. *Resolving Conflicts at Work.* San Francisco: Jossey-Bass, 2000.

Cloward, Richard and Frances Fox Piven. *Poor People's Movements.* New York: Vintage Books, 1979.

Cohen, David. "Reflections on Advocacy." *Advocacy Learning Initiative* (draft). Washington, DC: Advocacy Institute and Oxfam America, 1999.

Cohen, David, Rosa de la Vega, and Gabrielle Watson. *Advocacy for Social Justice: A Global Action and Reflection Guide.* New York: Kumarian Press, 2001.

Commonwealth Foundation and Civicus. *The Way Forward: Citizens, Civil Society and Governance in the new Millennium.* London: Commonwealth Foundation, 1999.

Cornwall, A and J. Gaventa. "Bridging the Gap: Citizenship, Participation, and Accountability," *Deliberative democracy and citizen empowerment.* Oxford: International Institute for Environment and Development, February 2001.

———. *From users and choosers to makers and shapers: Repositioning participation in social policy.* IDS Bulletin 31 (4): pp. 50–62. 2000.

Covey, Jane G. "Accountability and Effectiveness of NGO Policy Alliances," *IDR Reports,* vol. 11, no. 8. Boston, 1994.

———. "A Note on NGOs and Policy Influence," *IDR Reports,* vol. 9, no.2. Boston, 1994.

Curle, Adam. *Making Peace.* London: Tavistock Publications, 1971.

Dale, Duane. *How to Make Citizen Involvement Work: Strategies for Developing Clout.* Amherst, Mass: Citizen Involvement Training Project, U. Mass, 1978.

Dass, Purvi. *Capacity Building of Newly Elected Gram Panchayat Members in Haryana, Madya Pradesh and Rajasthan.* New Delhi: PRIA, 2000.

Dasso, Elizabeth. *Coloreando Mis Derechos.* Cuadernos Legales 2. Lima, Peru: Peru-Mujer, 1986.

de Montis, Malena. *Feminism, Empowerment and Popular Education in Nicaragua.* Doctoral Dissertation, University of Massachusetts, 1994.

———. "Vistazo a Las Experiencias de Campo: El Regadio." in *Conocimiento y Poder Popular* by Orlando Fals Borda. Mexico, D.F.: Siglo Viente-Uno Editores, 1986.

de Montis, Malena and Sofia Montenegro: *Transgresion y Cambio, Imagenes Desde el Liderazgo Femenino.* Cuadernos de Trabajo. Managua, Nicaragua: Cenzontle, 1997.

Doyle, Michael and David Straus. *How to Make Meetings Work.* New York: Berkeley Publishing Group, 1976.

Eade, Deborah. *Capacity-Building: An Approach to People-Centered Development.* Oxford: Oxfam UK and Ireland, 1997.

Edward, Michael and John Gaventa, eds. *Global Citizen Action.* London: Earthscan Publications Ltd., 2001.

Ekins, Paul. *A New World Order: Grassroots Movements for Global Change.* London: Routledge, 1992.

Empowerment Through People, Programs, and Institutions: A Report of the Facets Phase III Workshop. Stanford, CT: Save the Children, 1998.

Engendering Deveopment: Through Gender Equality in Rights, Resources, and Voice. Washington, DC: The World Bank and Oxford University Press, 2001.

Evans, Sarah and Harry Boyte. *Free Spaces: The Sources of Democratic Change in America,* Chicago: University of Chicago Press, 1992.

Farah, Douglas and David B. Ottaway. "Watchdog Groups Rein in Government in Chad Oil Deal." *Washington Post*, January 4, 2001.

Fisher, Julie. *The Road From Rio: Sustainable Development and the Nongovernmental Movement in the Third World.* Westport, CT: Praeger, 1993.

Fisher, Roger. *Getting to Yes.* New York: Penguin Books, 1983.

Fletcher, Joyce. *Disappearing Acts: Gender, Power, and Relational Practice at Work.* Cambridge, MA: Massachusetts Institute of Technology Press, 1999.

Florini, Ann M. *Does the Invisible Hand Need a Transparent Glove? The Politics of Transparency.* Washington, DC: Carnegie Endowment for International Peace, 1999.

Formas de Violencia en el Hogar contra la Mujer. Cuadernos Legales 3. Peru-Mujer, 1988.

Fowler, Alan. *Striking a Balance.* London: Earthscan, 1997.

Fox, Jonathan and L. David Brown. *The Struggle for Accountability.* Cambridge, MA: MIT Press, 1998.

Freire, Paulo. *Education for Critical Consciousness.* Myra B. Ramos, translator. New York: Continuum, 1973.

———. *Pedagogy of Hope.* Robert B. Tarr, translator. New York: Continuum, 1995.

———. *Pedagogy of the Oppressed: 20th Anniversary Edition.* Myra B. Ramos, translator. New York: Continuum, 1993.

———. *The Politics of Education: Culture, Power, and Liberation.* Donaldo P. Macedo, translator. Massachusetts: Bergin & Garvey Publishers, Inc. 1985.

Freire, Paulo and Myles Horton. *We Make the Road by Walking.* Philadelphia: Temple University Press, 1990.

Gaventa, John. "Citizen Knowledge, Citizen Competence, and Democracy Building." *The Good Society,* vol. 5, no. 3, 1997.

———. *Power and Powerlessness.* Urbana: University of Illinois Press, 1980.

Jenkins, Robert and Anne Marie Goetz. "Accounts and Accountability: Theoretical Implications for the Right-to-Information Movement in India." *Third World Quarterly,* vol.20, no.3, 1999.

Goldberger, Nancy and others. *Knowledge, Difference, and Power.* New York: Basic Books, 1996.

Grassroots Policy Project. *Power and Organizing.* Washington DC: GPP, 2000.

Grassroots Policy Project. <http://www.grassrootspolicy.org>, January 2002.

Gubbels, Peter and Catheryn Koss. *From the Roots Up: Strengthening Organizational Capacity Through Guided Self-Assessment.* Oklahoma: World Neighbors, 1999.

Guijt, Irene and Meera Kaul Shah, eds. *Myth of Community: Gender Issues in Participatory Development.* London: Intermediate Technologies Publications, 1998.

Heise, Lori L. "Violence Against Women: Global Organizing for Change." *Future Interventions with Battered Women and their Families.* Jeffrey L. Edleson and Zvi C. Eisikovits, eds. Newberry Park, CA: Sage Publications, 1997.

Hope, A. and S. Timmel. *Training for Transformation,* Volumes 1–3. London: IT Publications, revised version 1995.

Institute for Development Research. *Strategic Thinking: Formulating Organizational Strategy. Facilitator's Guide.* Boston: Institute for Development Research, 1998.

Institute for Development Studies Participation Group. *Strengthening Participation in Local Governance: The Use of Participatory Methods.* Brighton, UK: Institute for Development Studies, 1999.

International Budget Project. *A Taste of Success: Examples of Budget Work by NGOs.* <http://www.internationalbudget.org>. Washington, DC, 2000.

International Human Rights Internship Program (Washington, DC) and Asian Forum for Human Rights and Development. *Circle of Rights: Economic, Social, and Cultural Rights Activism: A Training Resource.* IHRIP/Forum-Asia, 2000.

International Institute for Environment and Development. *Deliberative Democracy and Citizen Empowerment.* Participatory Learning and Action (PLA) Notes. London: February 2001.

International Planned Parenthood Federation, Western Hemisphere Region, IPPF/WHR Regional Council. *Advocacy Guide.* Aruba: International Planned Parenthood Federation, Western Hemisphere Region, September 30–October 1, 1994.

Jordan, Lisa and Peter Van Tuijl. "Political Responsibility in Transnational NGO Advocacy." *World Development* vol. 28, no. 12. 2000.

Kabeer, Naila. *Reversed Realities: Gender Hierarchies in Development Thought.* London: Verso, 1994.

Kaner, Sam and others. *Facilitator's Guide to Participatory Decision-Making.* Philadelphia: New Society's Publishers, 1996.

Kaye, Gillian and Tom Wolff, eds. *From the Ground Up: A Workbook on Coalition Building and Community Development.* Amherst, MA: AHEC/Community Partners. 1995.

Kelsey, Dee and Pam Plumb. *Great Meetings: How to Facilitate Like a Pro.* Portland, ME: Hanson Park Press, 1999.

Klein, Naomi. 'The Vision Thing." *The Nation*, July 10, 2000.

Kling, Joseph and Prudence Posner, eds. *Dilemmas of Activism.* Philadelphia: Temple University Press, 1990.

Kolb, Deborah and Judith Williams. *The Shadow Negotiation: How Women Can Master the Hidden Agendas that Determine Bargaining Success.* New York: Simon and Schuster. 2000.

Kreisberg, Seth. *Transforming Power.* Albany, NY: State University of New York Press, 1992.

Kritek, Phyllis Beck. *Negotiating at an Uneven Table.* San Francisco: Jossey-Bass. 1994.

Lagarde, Marcela. *El Sentido Politico de la Propuesta de las Mujeres en America Latina.* Bogota: REPEM, 1992

Lamas, Mara. "Feminismo y Liderazgo." *Mujeres al Timon.* Mexico, D.F.: Equidad de Genero, 1998.

Lederach, John Paul. "Revolutionaries and Resolutionaries." *Conciliation Quarterly,* vol. 8, no. 3. Akron, PA: Mennonite Conciliation Service, 1989.

Legal Rights Organizing for Women in Africa: A Trainer's Manual. Harare, Zimbabwe: WILDAF, revised edition, 1995.

Lukes, Steven. *Power: A Radical View.* London: Macmillan Press Ltd, 1974.

Making the Most of the Media: Tools for Human Rights Groups Worldwide. New York: Center for Sustainable Human Rights Action, 2001.

Mansbridge, Jane. *Beyond Adversary Democracy.* New York: Basic Books. 1980.

marino, dian. *Wild Garden: Art, Education, and the Culture of Resistance.* Toronto: Between the Lines, 1997.

Marshall, Judith. *Training for Empowerment: Mozambique, Brazil, and Nicaragua.* Toronto: ICAE, 1988.

Marshall, T.H. *Class, Citizenship, and Social Development.* Westport, CT: Greenwood Press: 1973.

Mukhopadhayay, Maitryee and others. *A Guide to Gender-Analysis Frameworks.* Oxford: Oxfam Publishing, 1999.

Mukhopadhayay, Maitryee. "Gender relations, development, and culture." *Women in Culture,* Caroline Sweetman, ed. Oxford: Oxfam UK. 1995.

Mbogori, Ezra and Hope Chigudu. *Harnessing the Creative Energy of Citizens (Regional Synthesis: Africa).* In the New Millenium Project of the Commonwealth Foundation. London: November 1999.

Medel-Anonuevo, Carolyn. *Negotiating and Creating Spaces of Power: Women's Educational Practices Amidst Crisis.* Hamburg: UNESCO, 1997.

Miller, Jean Baker. *Gender and Development Workshop: Participants Workbook.* Washington, DC: PLAN International, 1976.

Miller, Valerie. *Africa Briefing Manual.* Amherst, MA: University of Massachusetts/Africa Forum, 1975.

———. *NGOs and Grassroots Policy Influence: What is Success?* Boston: Institute for Development Research, vol. 11, no. 5, 1994.

———. *Policy Influence by Development NGOs: A Vehicle for Strengthening Society?* (Vol. 11:No. 1). Boston: Institute for Development Research, 1994.

———. *Politics, Power, and People: Lessons from Gender Advocacy, Action, and Analysis.* Paper for Coady International Institute Symposium on Advocacy, Nova Scotia. Boston: Just Associates, 2001.

———. *Understanding Conflict and Negotiation for Social Justice Advocacy and Citizen Participation.* Unpublished paper. Boston: Just Associates. 2001.

Miller, Valerie and others. *Advocacy Sourcebook: Frameworks for Planning, Action, and Reflection.* Boston: Institute for Development Research, 1997.

———. *Children in Crisis: Advocacy Initiative.* Cambridge, MA: Unitarian Universalist Service Committee, 1991.

Molyneux, M. "Mobilization without Emancipation? Women's Interests, the State, and Revolution in Nicaragua." *Feminist Studies*, vol. 11, no. 2, 1985.

———. "Gender, Citizenship, and Democracy: Reflections on Contemporary Debates", a paper for Instituto de la Mujer, Mexico City: 1997.

Moran, Robert and Phillip Harris. 1982. "Managing Cultural Synergy." in *Networking for Policy Change*. The Policy Project. Washington DC: The Policy Project, 1999.

Mouffe, Chantal. "Feminism, citizenship, and radical democratic politics" in *Feminists Theorize the Political*, Judith Butler and Joan W. Scott, eds. London: Routledge, 1992.

Narayan, Deepa with Raj Patel, Kai Schafft, Anne Rademacher, and Sarah Koch-Schulte. *Voices of the Poor: Can Anyone Hear Us?* New York: Published for the World Bank, Oxford University Press, 2000.

Narayan, Deepa, Robert Chambers, Meera Kaul Shah, and Patti Petesch. *Voices of the Poor: Crying Out for Change.* New York: Published for the World Bank, Oxford University Press, 2000.

Nelson, Nici and Susan Wright, eds. *Power and Participatory Development.* London: Intermediate Technology Publications, 1995.

Nussbaum, Martha C. *Women and Human Development: The Capabilities Approach.* Cambridge: Cambridge University Press, 2000.

Networking for Policy Change. Washington, DC: The Policy Project, 1999.

Outhwaite, William and Tom Bottomore, eds. *The Blackwell Dictionary of Twentieth Century Social Thought.* Oxford: Blackwell Publishers, 1993.

Perry, Cynthia. *Organizing for Change: IAF.* Chicago: Industrial Areas Foundation, 1990.

Phillips, Anne. *Engendering Democracy.* University Park, PA: Pennsylvania State University Press, 1991.

Pimbert, Michel and Tom Wakeford. "Overview: deliberative democracy, and citizen empowerment." *PLA Notes* (Notes on Participatory Learning and Action). International Institute for Environment and Development, 2001.

La Planificación Participative para la Incidencia Política: Una guía práctica. Washington, DC: Washington Office on Latin America, 2000.

Pretty, Jules. *Regenerating Agriculture: Policies and Practices for Sustainability and Self-Reliance.* Washington, DC: Joseph Henry Press, 1995.

Pretty, Jules and others. *Participatory Learning and Action.* London: International Institute for Environment and Development, 1995.

Public Policy Advocacy: Women for Social Change in the Yugoslav Successor States. Zagreb: The Star Project, 1998.

Putnam, Robert. *Making Democracy Work.* Princeton, NJ: Princeton University Press, 1992.

———. *Bowling Alone.* New York: Simon Schuster. 2000.

Rawls, Amanda. "Media-Advocacy Relationships: The View from the Other Side." *ChangeExchange,* Part 1, Issue #6 (*Common Threads*). Washington, DC: The Advocacy Institute, October, 1999.

Reyes, Socorro. *Navigating and Mastering the Policy Arena: A Manual.* Quezon City, The Philippines: The Center for Legislative Development, 1999.

Richan, Willard and Laura Carnell. *Lobbying for Social Change.* New York: The Haworth Press, 1994.

Rohmann, Chris. *A World of Ideas: A Dictionary of Important Theories, Concepts, Beliefs, and Thinkers.* New York: The Ballantine Publishing Group, 1999.

Scholtes, Peter. *The Team Handbook: How to Use Teams to Improve Quality.* Madison: Wisc.: Joiner Associates, 1998.

Schuler, Margaret. *Women's Human Rights Step by Step: Advocates' Strategy Workbook* (draft). Washington DC: Women, Law, and Development International, 2001.

Schuler, Margaret, ed. *Empowerment and the Law: Strategies of Third World Women.* Washington, DC: OEF International, 1987.

———. *From Basic Needs to Basic Rights: Women's Claim to Human Rights.* Washington DC: WLDI, 1995.

Schuler, Margaret and Sakuntala Kadirgamar-Rajasingham, eds. *Legal Literacy: A Tool for Women's Empowerment.* Washington, DC: Women, Law, and Development/ OEF International, 1993.

Schuler, Margaret and Lisa VeneKlasen. *Women, Empowerment, and the Law.* Training Manual for Women, Law, and Development in Africa. Washington, DC: OEF International, 1989.

Sen, Amartya. *Development as Freedom.* New York: Knopf, 1999.

Shapiro, Isaac, ed. *A Guide to Budget Work for NGOs.* Washington, DC: International Budget Project, 2000.

Sharma, K. "Grassroots Organizations and Women's Empowerment: Some Issues in the Contemporary Debate," in *Samya Shakti,* vol. 6, pp. 28–43, 1991.

Shields, Katrina. *In the Tiger's Mouth*. Gabriola Island, BC: New Society Publishers, 1994.

Shronk-Shenk, Carolyn. *Mediation and Facilitation Training Manual*. Akron, PA: Mennonite Conciliation Service, 2000.

Slocum, Rachel, Lori Wichhart, Dianne Rocheleau, and Barbara Thomas-Slayter, eds. *Power, Process, and Participation: Tools for Change*. London: Intermediate Technology Publications, 1995

Speeter, Greg. *Power: A Repossession Manual*. Amherst, MA: Citizen Involvement Training Project, University of Massachussets, 1978.

Spencer, Jane. "Raising a Ruckus: Students Take the Bus to D.C.," *The Nation*, April 24, 2000.

Stein, Jane. *Empowerment and Women's Health*. London: Zed, 1997.

Suarez Toro, Maria. *Women's Voices on Fire: Feminist International Radio Endeavor*. Austin, TX: Anomaly Press, 2000.

Susskind, Lawrence and Patrick Field. *Dealing With an Angry Public: the Mutual Gains Approach to Resolving Disputes*. New York: The Free Press, 1996.

Taylor, Viviene. *Marketisation of Governance: Critical Feminist Perspectives from the South*. Cape Town: SADEP/DAWN, 2000.

TB Advocacy: A Practical Guide. Geneva: Global Tuberculosis Programme, World Health Organization (WHO), 1998.

Thomas, Barb and others. *Educating for a Change*. Toronto: Between the Lines and the Doris Marshall Institute, 1991.

Thomas-Slayter, Barbara, Rachel Polestico, Andrea Lee Esser, Octavia Taylor, and Elvina Mutua. *A Manual for Socio-Economic and Gender Analysis: Responding to the Development Challenge*. Worcester, MA: SEGA, Clark University, 1995.

Together For Change: The Botswana Consultation, The Africa-America Institute, Emang Basadi, and the United Nations Development Fund for Women (UNIFEM). New York, 1995.

Vargas, Virginia. "Procesos de Formacion de las Ciudadanias Globales en el Marco de Sociedades Civiles Globales." *Pistas de Analisis*. Lima, Peru, 1999.

VeneKlasen, Lisa. *El Regadio*, unpublished report, 1983.

———. "The Challenge of Democracy-building: Practical Lessons on NGO Advocacy and Political Change." *NGOs, Civil Society, and the State: Building Democracy in Transitional Societies*, Andrew Clayton, ed. Oxford: INTRAC Publications, 1996.

———. "Legal Rights Organizing and Women's Political Participation in Africa," in *Legal Literacy: A Tool for Women's Empowerment*. Margaret Schuler and Sakuntala Kardirgamar-Rajasingham, eds. Washington, DC: Women, Law, and Development International, 1992.

Vitti, Jane. *Legislative Traps . . . and how to stay out of them*. California State Assembly, 1994.

Walters, S., "Her Words on His Lips: Gender and Popular Education in South Africa," in *ASPBAE Courier* vol. 52, no.17, 1991.

Werner, David and Bill Bower. *Helping Health Workers Learn*. The Hesperian Foundation, California: 1982.

Williams, Jody. International Campaign to Ban Landmines. Interview with Lisa VeneKlasen, Washington DC. August 2000.

Williams, Suzanne and others. *The Oxfam Gender Training Manual*. Oxford: Oxfam UK, 1995.

The World Bank Participation Sourcebook. Washington, DC: The International Bank for Reconstruction and Development, 1996.

Yuval-Davis, Nira and Pnina Werbner, eds. *Women, Citizenship, and Difference*. New York: Zed Books, 1999.